Microsoft Sharepoint 2013

Step by Step

Olga M. Londer
Penelope Coventry

Published with the authorization of Microsoft Corporation by:

O'Reilly Media, Inc.
1005 Gravenstein Highway North
Sebastopol, California 95472

ISBN: 978-0-7356-6703-7

1 2 3 4 5 6 7 8 9 LSI 8 7 6 5 4 3

Printed and bound in the United States of America.

Microsoft Press books are available through booksellers and distributors worldwide. If you need support related to this book, email Microsoft Press Book Support at *mspinput@microsoft.com*. Please tell us what you think of this book at *http://www.microsoft.com/learning/booksurvey*.

Acquisitions and Developmental Editor: Kenyon Brown

Production Editor: Kristen Borg

Editorial Production: Zyg Group, LLC

Technical Reviewer: Chris Casingena

Copyeditor: Kim Burton-Weisman

Indexer: BIM Indexing Services

Cover Design: Microsoft Press Brand Team

Cover Composition: Ellie Volckhausen

Illustrator: Rebecca Demarest

To Gregory, Dina, and Michael, with love and gratitude—for everything.

—Olga Londer

I dedicate this book to my godchildren, Jack and Erin, Erin's husband Mark, and their parents Helen and Chris. Thank you for including Peter and I in your family.

—Penelope Coventry

Contents

1   Introducing SharePoint 2013   1

2   Navigating a SharePoint site   21

3   Working with documents and information in lists and libraries   53

7   Getting social   243

8   Working with wikis and blogs   275

9   Searching for information and people   303

10   Managing work tasks   343

11   Working with workflows   369

12 Using SharePoint with Excel and Access 401

13 Working with business intelligence 449

Introduction

A part of Microsoft Office 2013, Microsoft SharePoint 2013 is a server-side product that provides a powerful toolset for organizing websites and content, sharing knowledge, connecting with others, providing robust collaboration environments, managing documents, and finding information and people. *Microsoft SharePoint 2013 Step by Step* offers a comprehensive look at the capabilities and features of SharePoint 2013 that people will use most frequently.

Who this book is for

Microsoft SharePoint 2013 Step by Step and other books in the *Step by Step* series are designed for beginning to intermediate-level computer users. The examples shown in this book teach skills that can be used in organizations of any size. Whether you are new to SharePoint, or you are already comfortable working in SharePoint and want to learn about the new features in SharePoint 2013, this book provides an invaluable hands-on experience so that you can create, modify, and share sites, documents, and other content and capabilities, and collaborate with others with ease.

How this book is organized

This book is divided into 15 chapters. The first four chapters address foundation skills such as navigating a SharePoint site, working with documents and information in lists and libraries, and creating and editing webpages. Chapters 5 and 6 show you how to create and manage SharePoint sites, and how to make lists and libraries work for you. Chapters 7 and 8 focus on SharePoint 2013 social capabilities such as newsfeeds, community sites, blogs, and wikis. Chapter 9 drills into search functionality and discovering information and people. Chapters 10 and 11 show how to use the business process features, such as tasks and workflows. Chapters 12–14 cover using SharePoint with Microsoft Office Excel and Microsoft Office Access, the power of business intelligence, and using SharePoint with Microsoft Office Outlook and Microsoft Lync. Finally, Chapter 15 drills into the content management capabilities of SharePoint 2013.

The first part of Chapter 1 contains introductory information that will primarily be of interest to readers who are new to SharePoint or are upgrading from Microsoft SharePoint 2010 or an earlier version. If you have worked with a more recent version of SharePoint, you might want to skip past that material.

This book is designed to lead you step by step through all the tasks that you'll most likely want to perform with SharePoint 2013. If you start at the beginning and work your way through all the exercises, you will gain enough proficiency to be able to work efficiently with most capabilities in SharePoint 2013. However, each topic is self-contained, so you can jump in anywhere to acquire exactly the skills that you need.

Download the practice files

Before you can complete the exercises in this book, you need to download the book's practice files to your computer. We recommend you copy the practice files to a separate folder, for example, Documents\Microsoft Press\SP2013SBS, or any folder where you can access the practice files easily.

These practice files can be downloaded from the following page:

http://aka.ms/SP2013SbS/files

IMPORTANT The SharePoint 2013 software is not available from this website. You must have access to a SharePoint 2013 installation on the server before performing exercises in this book. Alternatively, you can use Microsoft SharePoint Online for most exercises in this book.

The following table lists the practice files for this book.

Chapter	File
Chapter 1: Introducing SharePoint 2013	No practice files
Chapter 2: Navigating a SharePoint site	Chapter2 Team Site.wsp
	Chapter2 Travel Subsite.wsp
	Chapter2 Facilities Subsite.wsp
	WideWorldTravelGuidelines.docx

Chapter	File
Chapter 3: Working with documents and information in lists and libraries	OakChest.docx
	OakDesk.docx
	OakEndTable.docx
	OakNightStand.docx
	WideWorldInvoice.dcox
	WideWorldPurchaseOrder.docx
Chapter 4: Working with webpages	Wildlife.wmv
	pjcov.jpg
Chapter 5: Creating and managing sites	No practice files
Chapter 6: Making lists and libraries work for you	Global Proposal.docx
Chapter 7: Getting social	Sales.jpg
Chapter 8: Working with wikis and blogs	No practice files
Chapter 9: Searching for information and people	Chapter9 Starter.wsp
	Oak Chest.docx
	Oak Desk.docx
	OakEndTable.docx
	OakNightStand.docx
	Oak chairs are best with Oak tables.docx
	Our Oak furniture range consists of both Oak chairs and Oak tables.docx
Chapter 10: Managing work tasks	No practice files
Chapter 11:Working with workflows	No practice files
Chapter 12: Using SharePoint with Excel and Access	ExpImpoWideWorldImporters.accdb
	Furniture_Price.xlsx
	MoveWideWorldImporters.accdb
	Sales_Figures.xlsx
Chapter 13: Working with business intelligence	SalesData.xlsx
Chapter 14: Using SharePoint with Outlook and Lync	Chapter14 Starter.wsp
Chapter 15: Managing content	Holiday budget planner.docx
	ProductProposalFinancials.xslx
	ProductProposalPresentation.pptx
	ProductSheet.docx

The exercises in this book cover features across the three SharePoint 2013 solutions. Each solution provides a different set of features and functionalities, depending on the client access licenses (CALs) activated in your organization, as follows:

- SharePoint Server 2013 Enterprise CAL
- SharePoint Server 2013 Standard CAL
- SharePoint Foundation 2013

SEE ALSO For SharePoint 2013 feature availability in each of the solutions, refer to Appendix B, "SharePoint 2013 features."

All the exercises in the book will work in SharePoint Server 2013 Enterprise. Any exercises that cover features available in SharePoint Server 2013 Standard can be completed if you are using this solution. However, you will not be able to complete an exercise that covers a feature that is not available in SharePoint Server 2013 Standard. For example, the business intelligence features are only available in the SharePoint Server 2013 Enterprise, and therefore the exercises in Chapter 13, "Working with business intelligence," require SharePoint Server 2013 Enterprise.

Any exercises that cover features available in SharePoint Foundation 2013 will work if you are using this solution. However, you will not be able to complete an exercise that covers a feature that is not available in SharePoint Foundation 2013. For example, promoting search results is an available functionality in SharePoint Server 2013 Standard and Enterprise, but it is not included in SharePoint Foundation 2013; therefore, the exercise on influencing the search results ranking in Chapter 9, "Searching for information and people," requires SharePoint Server 2013.

SEE ALSO For a list of the SharePoint 2013 solutions—Foundation, Standard, or Enterprise—that you can use to complete each exercise, refer to Appendix C, "SharePoint 2013 solutions required to complete the exercises in this book."

Using the practice files

You need to download the practice files to a location on your hard disk before you can use them in the exercises.

IMPORTANT The location for practice files that we use in this book is Documents\Microsoft Press\SP2013SBS. If you install the practice files to another location, you may need to substitute that path within the exercises.

The practice files for this book are stored on your hard disk in chapter-specific subfolders. Each exercise in a chapter includes a paragraph that lists the files needed for that exercise and explains any preparations needed before you start working through the exercise.

Whenever possible, we start each chapter with a standard SharePoint 2013 team site, which occasionally must be a top-level team site. If you follow all the exercises in all the chapters, you may choose to start with a new team site for every chapter.

However, for a few chapters, there are additional settings that are needed for a practice site. This is where the starter .wsp files will come in handy.

If you have sufficient rights, you can create a new practice site (see the following "Using the WSP templates" section) from the chapter's starter .wsp file, which is provided in the practice folder for this chapter. The starter .wsp files contain the lists, libraries, files, and pages that you will require during the exercises. There are three chapters that require the creation of a site based on the .wsp file: Chapter 2, Chapter 9, and Chapter 14. Exercises in Chapter 2 use two subsites in addition to the standard team site, and the practice folder for the chapter contains two .wsp files for the subsites, which are clearly marked.

Using the WSP templates

To create a practice site for a chapter based on a starter .wsp file, perform the following steps.

> **IMPORTANT** Verify that you have sufficient rights to upload to the site template gallery of a site collection. If in doubt, see Appendix A, "SharePoint 2013 user permissions and permission levels."

1. In the browser, open the top level SharePoint site of the site collection where you would like to create the practice site. If prompted, type your user name and password, and click **OK**.

2. On the top right of the screen, click the **Settings** button, and then select **Site settings.** The **Site Settings** page of the top level site is displayed.

3. In the **Web Designer Galleries** section, click **Solutions. The Solution Gallery** is displayed.

4. Click the **Upload Solution** button on the left of the Solutions ribbon. The **Add Document** dialog is displayed.

5   In the **Add Document** dialog, click **Browse**.

6   In the **Choose File to Upload** dialog, go to the practice files folder **ChapterNN** (where NN is the chapter number) and click the .wsp file that you want to use to create the new site, and then click **Open**.

7   In the **Add Document** dialog, click **OK** to upload the file.

8   In the **Solution Gallery - Activate Solution** dialog, click the **Activate** button. The **Solution Gallery** is displayed. Validate that the template has been uploaded and activated.

You can now create a new practice child site based upon the uploaded WSP template.

1   Browse to the SharePoint site that you want to be the parent of the new practice site.

2   Click the **Settings** button, and then click **Site contents**.

3   In the **Site Contents** page, scroll to the bottom of the page and click **new subsite**.

4   In the **New SharePoint Site** page, in the **Title** text box, type a logical name for the new site. You could simply provide the chapter number if you like, for example, **Chapter09**.

5   Optionally, in the **Description** text box, type a description, such as **SharePoint SBS Chapter 9 Practice Site**.

6   In the **URL name** text box, enter the same name that you typed in the **Title** text box.

7   In the **Template Selection** section, click the **Custom** tab and select the **ChapterNN Starter** template, which is now available.

8   Under **Navigation**, select the **No** option for displaying the link to this site on the top link bar of the parent site.

9   You can leave all the other options at their default values and click the **Create** button. The new practice site has been created and its home page is displayed.

❌ CLEAN UP **Close the browser.**

Removing the WSP site templates

To remove the chapter starter WSP template from the Solution Gallery, perform the following steps.

IMPORTANT Verify that you have sufficient rights to delete WSPs from the Solution Gallery of a site collection. If in doubt, see Appendix A.

1 In the browser, open the top level SharePoint site where you previously uploaded the .wsp files. If prompted, type your user name and password, and then click **OK**.

2 On the **Settings** menu, click **Site settings.** The **Site Settings** page is displayed.

3 In the **Web Designer Galleries** section, click **Solutions.** The **Solution Gallery** is displayed.

4 In the **Solution Gallery - Solutions** page, hover the mouse over the template that you want to remove, and then click the arrow that appears on the right to display the context menu. On the context menu, click **Deactivate**.

The **Solutions Gallery - Deactivate Solution** dialog appears.

5 In the **Solutions Gallery - Deactivate Solution** dialog, on the **View** tab, click **Deactivate**.

6 In the **Solution Gallery - Solutions** page, once again, hover over the template that you wish to remove, and then click the arrow that appears on the right to display the context menu. On the context menu, click **Delete**. In the confirmation message box, click **OK** to complete the removal of the site template.

7 The **Solutions Gallery - Solutions** page is redisplayed. Verify that the practice site template has been removed.

8 Repeat steps 4–6 to remove each practice site template that you no longer require.

❌ CLEAN UP **Close the browser.**

Deleting a practice site

If you created a practice site that you no longer require, you can delete it. Perform the following steps to delete a practice site.

> **IMPORTANT** Verify that you have sufficient rights to delete a site. If in doubt, see Appendix A.

1   In the browser, open the SharePoint site that you want to delete. If prompted, type your user name and password, and then click **OK**.

2   On the **Settings** menu, click **Site settings**. The **Site Settings** page is displayed.

3   In the **Site Actions** section, click **Delete this site**. The **Delete This Site** confirmation page is displayed.

4   Click the **Delete** button to delete the site.

5   The site has been deleted.

✖ CLEAN UP **Close the browser.**

Your companion ebook

With the ebook edition of this book, you can do the following:

- Search the full text
- Print
- Copy and paste

To download your ebook, please see the instruction page at the back of the book.

Getting support and giving feedback

The following sections provide information about getting help with SharePoint 2013 or the contents of this book, and contacting us to provide feedback or report errors.

Errata

We've made every effort to ensure the accuracy of this book and its companion content. Any errors that have been reported since this book was published are listed on our Microsoft Press site at oreilly.com:

http://aka.ms/SP2013SbS/errata

If you find an error that is not already listed, you can report it to us through the same page.

If you need additional support, email Microsoft Press Book Support at

mspinput@microsoft.com

Please note that product support for Microsoft software is not offered through the preceding addresses.

We want to hear from you

At Microsoft Press, your satisfaction is our top priority, and your feedback our most valuable asset. Please tell us what you think of this book at:

http://www.microsoft.com/learning/booksurvey

The survey is short, and we read every one of your comments and ideas. Thanks in advance for your input!

Stay in touch

Let's keep the conversation going! We're on Twitter at: *http://twitter.com/MicrosoftPress*.

Chapter at a glance

Log On

Log on to your SharePoint site, page 4

Explore

Explore the Team Site home page, page 5

Focus

Focus on page content, page 6

Use

Use SharePoint Help, page 7

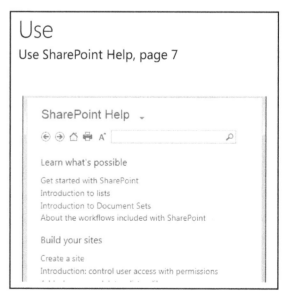

Introducing SharePoint 2013

IN THIS CHAPTER, YOU WILL LEARN

- What SharePoint 2013 is.

- How SharePoint 2013 enables team collaboration and sharing.

- What user permissions are found in SharePoint 2013.

- What SharePoint Online is.

- What differences exist between SharePoint 2013 on-premises solutions and SharePoint Online subscription plans.

- How Office integrates with SharePoint 2013.

- How SharePoint 2013 integrates with Microsoft Dynamics AX to provide a web storefront.

In the modern business environment, with its distributed workforce that assists customers at any time and in any location, team members need to be in closer contact than ever before. Effective collaboration is becoming increasingly important; however, it is often difficult to achieve. Microsoft SharePoint 2013 addresses this problem by incorporating a variety of collaboration and communication technologies into a single web-based environment that is closely integrated with desktop applications such as Microsoft Office.

In this chapter, you will learn what SharePoint 2013 is and how it works with Office applications, providing enhanced productivity environments for users and teams. You will also learn the differences between on-premises SharePoint 2013 solutions and Microsoft SharePoint Online subscription plans, and how to decide which product is right for you, as well as whether an on-premises deployment, a cloud model, or a hybrid environment is better suited to the needs of your organization. You will also understand how SharePoint 2013 integrates with Microsoft Dynamics AX to provide a web storefront and a multichannel retail functionality.

IMPORTANT The exercises in this book involve a fictitious business called Wide World Importers. In the scenarios, Wide World Importers is setting up a SharePoint environment for team collaboration and information sharing. There are four people involved in setting up and providing content for this environment: Olga Kosterina, the owner of Wide World Importers; Todd Rowe, her assistant; Bill Malone, the head buyer; and Peter Connelly, the help desk technician.

PRACTICE FILES You don't need any practice files to complete the exercises in this chapter.

What is SharePoint 2013?

SharePoint 2013 is a technology that enables organizations and business units of all sizes to improve team productivity and to increase the efficiency of business processes. SharePoint 2013 gives you a powerful toolset for organizing content, managing documents, sharing knowledge, providing robust collaboration environments, and finding information and people. The social functionality in SharePoint 2013 allows you and your colleagues to build communities, share thoughts and ideas, and to discover resources and knowledge in your organization.

SEE ALSO For system requirements for installing SharePoint 2013, refer to *technet.microsoft. com/en-us/library/cc262485(v=office.15).aspx.*

SharePoint 2013 helps teams stay connected and productive by providing an infrastructure and capabilities that allow easy access to people, documents, and information that they need. With SharePoint 2013, teams can create websites to share information and foster collaboration with other users. You can access content stored within a SharePoint site from a web browser and through client applications such as Office, running on multiple devices, such as a PC, a tablet, and a mobile phone.

Team collaboration and sharing

SharePoint sites provide places to capture and share ideas, information, communications, and documents. The sites facilitate team participation in communities, document collaboration, tracking tasks and issues, blogging and microblogging, building knowledge bases using wikis, and more. The document collaboration features allow for easy check-in and checkout of documents, document version control, and recovery of previous versions, as well as document-level security.

TIP A *blog*, or web log, is an online diary in which the diarists, called bloggers, post articles, whereupon readers can comment on them. A *wiki* (pronounced *wee-kee*) is a web environment in which a web browser user can quickly and easily add and edit the text and links that appear on the webpage. The term *wiki* originates from the Hawaiian word *wikiwiki*, which means "quick." A wiki site can be used, for example, to build a knowledge base, a community resource, or an online encyclopedia, such as Wikipedia.

SEE ALSO For more information about blogs and wikis, refer to Chapter 8, "Working with wikis and blogs."

A SharePoint site can have many subsites, the hierarchy of which, on web servers, resembles the hierarchy of folders on file systems—it is a tree-like structure. Similar to storing your files in folders on file systems, you can store your files within SharePoint sites. However, SharePoint sites take file storage to a new level, providing communities for team collaboration and making it easy for users to work together on documents, tasks, contacts, events, calendars, wikis, and other items. This team collaboration environment can increase individual and team productivity greatly. For example, you can store your files and documents in SkyDrive Pro, your own professional library, where only you can see them, and at the same time, you can share them with your coworkers, as well as access them on multiple devices, including a PC, a tablet, and a smartphone.

The collaborative tools provided by SharePoint 2013 are intuitive and easy to use, so you can share files and information, and communicate with your coworkers more effectively. You can create and use SharePoint sites for any purpose. For example, you can build a site to serve as the primary website for a team, create a site to facilitate the organization of a meeting, create a wiki site to capture team knowledge, or create a community site to build a community for a particular project or subject area. A typical SharePoint site might include a variety of useful tools and information, such as document libraries, contacts, calendars, task lists, and other information-sharing and visualization tools.

SharePoint site users can find and communicate with key contacts and experts using email, instant messaging, or microblogging. Site content can be searched easily, and users can follow a site or a document and receive newsfeed notifications to tell them when existing documents and information have been changed or when new ones have been added. Custom business processes can be attached to the documents. You can customize site content and layout to present targeted information to specific users on precise topics.

In this exercise, you will locate your SharePoint site and familiarize yourself with its home page.

SET UP Open the browser.

1 In the browser **address bar**, type the Uniform Resource Locator (URL), or location, of your SharePoint site: **http://<yourservername/path>**.

The *yourservername* portion of the URL is the name of the SharePoint server that you will be using for the exercises in this book. The path portion might be empty, or it might include one or more levels in the site hierarchy on your SharePoint server. If you are in doubt about the location of the SharePoint site, check with your SharePoint administrator.

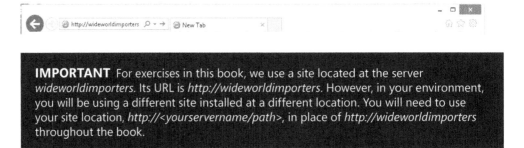

IMPORTANT For exercises in this book, we use a site located at the server *wideworldimporters*. Its URL is *http://wideworldimporters*. However, in your environment, you will be using a different site installed at a different location. You will need to use your site location, *http://<yourservername/path>*, in place of *http://wideworldimporters* throughout the book.

2 If prompted, type your user name and password.

3 Click **OK**.

The home page of your site appears. Although it might look somewhat different from the typical SharePoint team site that Wide World Importers starts with, it is still likely to include links to a variety of information, as well as the information-sharing tools provided by SharePoint 2013.

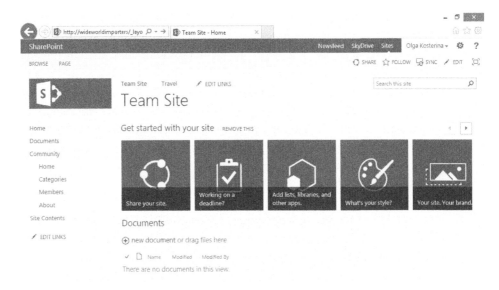

On the left side of the page, you might see links to one or more of the following: **Home**, **Documents**, **Community**, and **Site Contents**. This collection of links to frequently used site resources is called a *Quick Launch*. With **Quick Launch**, as the name suggests, you can go straight to the information and tools that you require.

Below **Quick Launch**, on the left side of the page, you may see an **EDIT LINKS** option that allows you to add and delete links in the **Quick Launch** from within the browser.

> **IMPORTANT** Your screen might not include links to all parts of the site, such as the **EDIT LINKS** for **Quick Launch**, because of the way that security permissions on your server have been set up. SharePoint site users see only the parts and the functionality of the site that they can actually access: if you don't have access to a specific part or a particular functionality of the site, the link to it is not displayed. To obtain additional access, contact your SharePoint administrator.

In addition to **Quick Launch**, there is another navigation area located at the top of the page. This area contains a top link bar that appears at the top of each page, above the page title. It consists of several tabs with links, such as the link to the home page of the current team site. It may also include other tabs with links to the subsites of this website; for example, the second tab on the left says **Travel**. In our scenario, because the Wide World Importers staff travel extensively worldwide, this is a link to a subsite that provides Wide World Importers employees with the necessary information and guidelines for arranging business travel.

Team Site   Travel

To the left of the top link bar, you may see an **EDIT LINKS** option that allows you to add and delete links in the top link bar from within the browser, provided you have the appropriate security permissions set up.

The navigation aids, while important, take a lot of space on the screen. You will now hide them.

4   Locate the button with a rectangle image at the top right of the screen. Hover your mouse over the button to see its name, **Focus on Content**, displayed in the button tip.

5   Click the **Focus on Content** button to hide the left and top panels and display only the content area of the page.

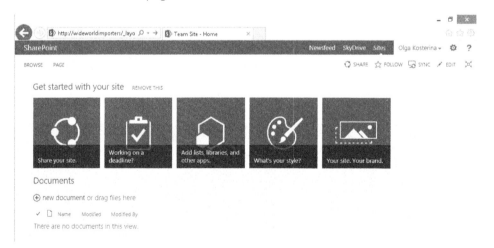

Notice that the image on the **Focus on Content** button has changed to a small rectangle with four arrows pointing outward from its corners.

6   Click the button again to bring back the fullpage view.

7   In the top-right part of the page, click the **Help** button with the question mark. SharePoint 2013 Help opens in a separate window.

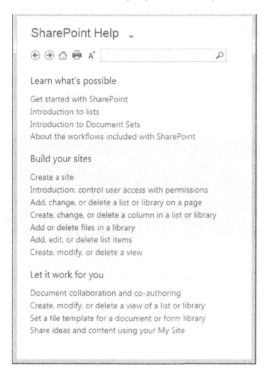

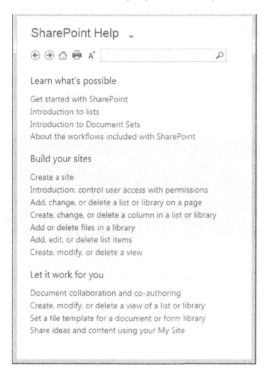 CLEAN UP **Close the browser.**

SEE ALSO For more information on SharePoint site navigation, refer to Chapter 2, "Navigating a SharePoint site."

SharePoint user permissions

In SharePoint 2013, access to sites is controlled through a role-based system that uses permission levels. *Permission levels* specify what permissions users have on a SharePoint site. These permissions determine the specific actions that users can perform on the site; in essence, each permission level is a collection of permissions. SharePoint has a number of default permission levels, including the following examples:

- **Read** This permission level gives you read-only access to the website.

- **Contribute** In addition to all the permissions included in the Read permission level, the Contribute permission level allows you to create, edit, and delete items in existing lists and document libraries.

- **Design** In addition to all the permissions included in the Contribute permission level, the Design permission level allows you to create lists and document libraries, approve items, and edit pages in the website.

- **Full Control** This permission level gives you full control.

- **Limited** The Limited permission level allows access to a shared resource within a site, such as a specific list, document library, folder, list item, or document, without giving access to the entire site.

> **IMPORTANT** You will need Read or Contribute permission levels for most of the exercises in this book. We will instruct you to verify whether you have a sufficient permission level before introducing exercises, particularly those in which a higher level of access, such as Design or Full Control, is needed. If you are not sure what permissions are set on your SharePoint site, check with your SharePoint administrator.

SEE ALSO For more information about permission levels, refer to Chapter 5, "Creating and managing sites." A full list of permissions and their associated permission levels is provided in Appendix A, "SharePoint 2013 user permissions and permission levels."

SharePoint 2013 solutions

There are three SharePoint 2013 solutions that can be deployed on servers in your organizational infrastructure. They provide different sets of features and functionality depending on the client access licenses (CALs), as follows:

- SharePoint Server 2013 Enterprise CAL

- SharePoint Server 2013 Standard CAL

- SharePoint Foundation 2013

All SharePoint 2013 solutions facilitate collaboration both within an organization and with partners and customers. However, each of these products provides a different set of capabilities.

SharePoint Foundation 2013 is a collection of services for Windows Server 2012 that is available as a free download. You can use SharePoint Foundation 2013 to share information and collaborate with other users. It provides a common framework for document management, a common repository for storing documents of all types, and a platform for collaboration applications. You can create sites in multiple languages without requiring separate installations of SharePoint Foundation 2013 by using language packs.

SEE ALSO You can download SharePoint Foundation 2013 and its language packs from the Microsoft Download Center at *www.microsoft.com/en-us/download/details.aspx?id=35488* and *www.microsoft.com/en-us/download/details.aspx?id=35492*, respectively.

Both Microsoft SharePoint Server 2013 solutions—Standard and Enterprise—are built on top of SharePoint Foundation 2013. SharePoint Server 2013 extends SharePoint Foundation by providing social capabilities, flexible organization, and management tools for SharePoint sites, and by making it possible for teams to publish information to the entire organization. Because SharePoint Server 2013 requires SharePoint Foundation, all features of SharePoint Foundation are available in SharePoint Server 2013. However, SharePoint Server 2013 provides significant additional enterprise-level features and functionality, including social capabilities, business intelligence, content management, a powerful search, workflow, and many others.

The two SharePoint Server 2013 solutions have a different feature set. To decide whether you require a SharePoint Server 2013—Enterprise or Standard—or SharePoint Foundation 2013, you need to assess how your requirements are met by the particular features and functionality of these solutions.

A comparison between the feature sets of the different SharePoint Server 2013 solutions is provided in Table 1-1.

Table 1-1 *SharePoint 2013 solutions comparison*

Feature	SharePoint 2013 solution		
	Foundation	Standard CAL	Enterprise CAL
App Catalog & Marketplace	Yes	Yes	Yes
Team Sites	Yes	Yes	Yes
Work Management	No	Yes	Yes
Social	No	Yes	Yes
External Sharing	Yes	Yes	Yes

Feature	SharePoint 2013 solution		
	Foundation	Standard CAL	Enterprise CAL
Basic Search	Yes	Yes	Yes
Standard Search	No	Yes	Yes
Enterprise Search	No	No	Yes
Content Management	No	Yes	Yes
Records Management	No	Yes	Yes
E-discovery, ACM, Compliance	No	No	Yes
Excel Services, PowerPivot, PowerView	No	No	Yes
Scorecards & Dashboards	No	No	Yes
Access Services	No	No	Yes
Visio Services	No	No	Yes
Form-Based Applications	No	No	Yes
SharePoint 2013 Workflow	No	Yes	Yes
Business Connectivity Services	Yes	Yes	Yes

SEE ALSO For a detailed comparison of features in SharePoint 2013 solutions, refer to Appendix B, "SharePoint 2013 features."

It's all in the cloud: SharePoint Online

SharePoint Online is a web-based service that is hosted outside your organization in the cloud, instead of residing on a server in your organization, or on-premises. Being in the cloud means that the IT infrastructure resides off your organization's property, or off-premises, and that the infrastructure is maintained by a third party. Many services on the Internet are cloud services; for example, online photo sharing or web-based email. These services are located online, or in the cloud, and you can access them anywhere—from a PC, tablet, mobile phone, or other device with an Internet connection. SharePoint Online is also a cloud service that you can use to access information and to interact with your team from nearly anywhere, on many types of devices.

Cloud services are subscription-based. Instead of installing SharePoint software in your organization, you can buy a subscription plan to use this software as a service. SharePoint Online is a part of Microsoft Office 365 that also includes Microsoft Exchange Online for the web-hosted mail service, and Microsoft Lync Online for web-based conferencing. There are a number of subscription plans available that provide different sets of features and capabilities, from basic to enterprise level, for a monthly fee. The SharePoint Online service is available as a part of multiple Office 365 subscription plans, or as a standalone subscription plan.

SEE ALSO For more information on Office 365 and available plans and pricing, see *office365.microsoft.com*.

The features of SharePoint Online are engineered to run in the same way as the features of SharePoint 2013 deployed on-premises. However, there are a few exceptions. In particular, the gap exists between the implementation of business intelligence (BI) analytics capabilities, such as scorecards and dashboards, which are not available in SharePoint Online. There are also some differences in the Web Content Management functionality, with on-premises deployments providing a richer feature set.

A comparison between the features in the SharePoint Online standalone subscription plans is provided in Table 1-2.

Table 1-2 *SharePoint Online plans comparison*

Feature	SharePoint Online plan	
	P1	P2
App Catalog & Marketplace	Yes	Yes
Team Sites	Yes	Yes
Work Management	Yes	Yes
Social	Yes	Yes
External Sharing	Yes	Yes
Basic Search	Yes	Yes
Standard Search	Yes	Yes
Enterprise Search	No	Yes

Feature	SharePoint Online plan	
	P1	P2
Content Management	Yes	Yes
Records Management	Yes	Yes
E-discovery, ACM, Compliance	No	Yes
Excel Services, PowerPivot, PowerView	No	Yes
Scorecards & Dashboards	No	No
Access Services	No	Yes
Visio Services	No	Yes
Form-Based Applications	No	Yes
SharePoint 2013 Workflow	Yes	Yes
Business Connectivity Services	No	Yes

SEE ALSO For a detailed comparison of features in SharePoint Online subscription plans, including standalone subscription plans and Office 365 subscription plans, refer to *technet. microsoft.com/en-us/library/jj819267.aspx.*

In your organization, you may use an on-premises SharePoint deployment, or a cloud SharePoint Online solution, or a hybrid environment. The hybrid solution combines an on-premises SharePoint deployment with a SharePoint Online cloud solution and delivers a consistent user experience across a combined environment. For example, the unified search capability allows you to search across both parts of a hybrid solution (on-premises and on-line) using the single search query.

Hybrid environments are helpful when it is not possible for an organization to fully migrate the SharePoint deployment to the cloud due to business, technical, or other reasons. For example, there might be a compliance or a data sovereignty policy in your organization that requires that data is to be hosted in a particular location. Using the hybrid model, your organization can start to achieve the benefits associated with the use of a cloud solution while at the same time continue using an on-premises deployment that provides the data governance and customization flexibility. With the hybrid solution, your organization can achieve a higher degree of flexibility than forcing a choice between either an on-premises or a cloud model. For users, the hybrid model is largely transparent.

Office integration with SharePoint

Microsoft Office 2013 and SharePoint 2013 are designed to create an integrated productivity environment across the server and the client software on multiple devices. They work together to provide you with a set of seamlessly integrated capabilities. In other words, many Office features and functionality as well as commands and menus are integrated closely with SharePoint features and functionality. You can use SharePoint 2013 functionality not only from a browser, but also from within your Office applications.

The Office Backstage feature provides the ability to surface SharePoint 2013 capabilities in the context of Office applications, including access to document libraries, social capabilities, and SharePoint sites. For example, you can create a new SharePoint site and save your files to it without leaving your Office client application. The collaborative content of a SharePoint site—including documents, lists, events, calendars, task assignments, blogs, and membership rosters—can be read and edited within Office applications. You can also share your documents and specify their SharePoint permissions without leaving the Office 2013 application.

In addition, rich BI capabilities provided in SharePoint 2013 integrate with Microsoft Office Excel 2013 to explore and visualize data.

SEE ALSO For more information on BI capabilities provided by SharePoint 2013, refer to Chapter 13, "Working with business intelligence."

SharePoint 2013 provides close integration with Microsoft Office Web Apps, a collective name for the online companions to Microsoft Office applications such as Word, Excel, PowerPoint, and OneNote. With Office Web Apps, the user can view and edit documents using a browser. Office Web Apps services include the Word Service, PowerPoint Service, and Excel Calculation Services, which run within the context of the services provided by SharePoint.

TIP Office Web Apps are available for documents stored on your SkyDrive Pro and are accessible on multiple devices from virtually anywhere.

Office Web Apps give you a browser-based viewing and editing experience by providing a representation of an Office document in the browser. For example, when you click a document stored in a SharePoint document library, the document opens directly in the browser. The document appearance in the browser is similar to how it appears in the Office client application. While an Office Web App provides lighter editing functionality than the associated Office client application, it provides the user an opportunity to open a document for editing in the associated client application (if an application is installed on the client device) by using a button within the Office Web App page. On a SharePoint site where Office Web Apps have been installed and configured, you can view and edit Office documents in the browser from anywhere you have a connection to your SharePoint site, including mobile devices.

SEE ALSO For more information on Office Web Apps, refer to *office.microsoft.com/en-gb/web-apps*.

There are different levels of integration between various versions of Office and SharePoint Foundation. The Office 2013 family of products provides a most powerful, tight, native, rich, built-in integration with SharePoint 2013, followed by Microsoft Office 2010, which is also well integrated with SharePoint 2013. Microsoft Office 2007 provides a contextual interoperability between SharePoint and Office client applications. Earlier versions of Office, such as Microsoft Office 2000 and Microsoft Office XP, provide some integration, but it is considerably simpler and more basic.

Office 2000 provides a file save integration with SharePoint Foundation. For example, you can open and save files stored on SharePoint sites from your Office 2000 applications and receive alerts in Microsoft Outlook 2000. Office XP provides additional data integration, including interactive access to data stored on SharePoint sites. For example, you can export list data from SharePoint sites to Excel 2002 and view properties and metadata for files that are stored on SharePoint sites. However, Office 2000 and Office XP are not integrated with many other features of SharePoint Foundation.

Microsoft Office 2003 adds several more integration features. With Office 2003, you can use SharePoint Foundation to create documents and workspaces, organize team meetings and activities, and access and analyze data from SharePoint sites. You can also use data integration between Office 2003 and SharePoint Foundation, moving data to and from SharePoint sites and creating databases linked to data stored on SharePoint sites.

Starting with Microsoft Office System 2007, integration with SharePoint Foundation is enhanced further. You can interact directly with information stored in SharePoint sites from within Office client applications, without manually downloading the content. For example, starting from Word 2007, you can create and post to a blog on your SharePoint blog site, as well as check documents in and out of a SharePoint library from within Word.

Office 2010 introduces the Backstage feature that provides tighter integration with SharePoint functionality. Office 2010 also includes a SharePoint Workspace 2010 client application, a successor to the Office Groove client, which provides an ability to work offline with SharePoint content and to synchronize the changes when you are reconnected to your network. You can view, add, edit, and delete SharePoint library documents or list items while you are offline. While you are connected to the network, updates to data on your computer and on the network are automatic, providing bidirectional synchronization between your computer and the live SharePoint sites, libraries, and lists. In SharePoint 2013, this functionality is available through synchronizing a SharePoint library to your computer. The synced files in the library on your computer can be viewed by using Windows Explorer, and the updates to the files sync to SharePoint whenever you're online. Both your SkyDrive and a library on a team site can be synced to your computer to allow you to work offline.

While all Office 2013 client applications are well integrated with SharePoint, Outlook provides the closest, most feature-rich integration. Starting from Outlook 2007, you can create and manage sites for sharing documents and organizing meetings, and have a read and write access from Outlook to SharePoint items such as calendars, tasks, contacts, and documents, as well as offline capabilities.

SEE ALSO For more information about integration between SharePoint 2013 and Outlook, refer to Chapter 14, "Using SharePoint with Outlook and Lync."

SharePoint web storefront based on Microsoft Dynamics AX

SharePoint Server 2013 integrates with Microsoft Dynamics AX 2012 for Retail to provide a flexible, configurable, search-based web storefront that is available to users on multiple devices, such as PCs, tablets, and smartphones.

In today's retail environment, there is an explosion in ways to engage the customer, ranging from brick-and-mortar stores to a retailer's website and call center, and to marketplaces and social networks. This multichannel environment represents a tremendous opportunity for modern retailers, but there is also a significant challenge in that the customers expect each point of engagement with a retailer to be connected, transparent, and consistent. Microsoft Dynamics AX 2012 for Retail addresses this challenge by providing a flexible, unified technology offering that reduces complexity for retailers and brings together points of sale, ecommerce, multichannel management, store operations, merchandising, supply chain, and more in an end-to-end solution that delivers full visibility across an entire business operation in a retail enterprise.

In this end-to-end solution, an ecommerce channel is implemented using SharePoint Server 2013. A commerce runtime (CRT) component of Microsoft Dynamics AX 2012 for Retail is required to be installed in the SharePoint environment. The CRT provides shop-front services, as well as an ability to synchronize the data between the central Microsoft Dynamics AX installation in a retail organization and the SharePoint web storefront. Retail master data, including products, prices, promotions, catalogues, categories, loyalty programs, and website-specific configuration details are set up in Microsoft Dynamics AX and propagated to a SharePoint repository. Sales orders and transaction data are uploaded from SharePoint into AX for fulfillment. The brick-and-mortar stores and points of sale operate in a similar way using the CRT to sync with the central Microsoft Dynamics AX installation. This powerful, consistent data replication approach helps ensure critical updates across the organization—including configurable and flexible inventory and financial updates, sales order payments, giftcard usage, and issuance/use of loyalty points—while equipping a retailer with the ability to provide a consistent, streamlined, transparent, and connected experience for shoppers across multiple retail channels. For example, a shopper could order a product from the retailer's website, and then return it in a brick-and-mortar store.

SEE ALSO For more information on Microsoft Dynamics AX for Retail, refer to *www.microsoft.com/en-us/dynamics/erp-retail.aspx*.

Versions of SharePoint

SharePoint Server 2013 and SharePoint Foundation 2013 are the latest versions in the line of SharePoint products and technologies. Previous versions of SharePoint Server 2013 include:

- SharePoint Server 2010
- Search Server 2010
- FAST Search Server for SharePoint
- SharePoint Server 2007
- SharePoint Server 2003
- SharePoint Portal Server 2001

Previous versions of SharePoint Foundation 2013 include:

- SharePoint Foundation 2010
- Windows SharePoint Services 3.0
- Windows SharePoint Services 2.0
- SharePoint Team Services

In comparison with its predecessors, SharePoint 2013 products provide many new, enhanced, and updated features, including many new social features and a new apps model. SharePoint 2013 is built around five major pillars: Share, Organize, Discover, Build, and Manage. The new and enhanced features and functionality in SharePoint pillars include the following:

- Share
  - Social features, such as **Newsfeed** and **Sites**, allow you to view and post updates, use microblogging, and follow documents, sites, and people.
  - A community site allows you to build a rich discussion environment with post ratings, achievements rewards, categorization of content, and built-in search.
  - OneNote integration with team sites provides a OneNote shared notebook as part of the team site. This feature requires Office Web Apps to be installed.
  - Video and rich media enhancements include embedding of video sources external to SharePoint, such as YouTube, and previewing videos directly from a search results page.
- Organize
  - Document libraries enhancements include a new callout feature for managing documents in a library, an ability to drag and drop files from your desktop or other location into a SharePoint library, and an ability to synchronize document libraries with folders in your Windows file system using SkyDrive Pro.
  - Lists enhancements include the ability for inline editing of list items and list columns.
  - The Sites page provides the ability to create new team sites and to follow those SharePoint sites that are important to you.
  - The Tasks list timeline provides visual representation of the tasks.
  - Project sites and site mailboxes allow people in your organization to effectively collaborate on lightweight projects. A project site can also include a site mailbox.

- Discover

  - Search enhancements include navigation enhancements, the ability to search multiple repositories in the same search query, and enhancements to finding people and expertise.

  - Business intelligence enhancements include a new Business Intelligence Center site, enhancements in Excel Services and PerformancePoint Services, and support for viewing business intelligence content on mobile devices such as the Apple iPad and Windows 8 tablets.

- Build

  - Web content authoring enhancements include retaining all text formatting when copying content from Word, and drag-and-drop navigation editing.

  - Cross-site publishing allows you to use one or more authoring site collections to author and store content, and one or more publishing site collections to control the design of the site and to show the content.

  - Site customization enhancements include a new Design Manager, a new theming experience, and an ability to configure your site for mobile devices.

  - Workflows enhancement include new workflow architecture and major improvements to the experience of designing workflows and modeling more complex business logic and processes.

  - External data access enhancements include abilities to analyze external data in Excel and to add external data to published Microsoft Office Visio diagrams.

  - Apps for SharePoint are small-scale, standalone applications that solve a specific end-user need or perform a specific task. SharePoint 2013 provides a new application model that supports the development, installation, management, and use of apps.

- Manage

  - Security, site management, and site upgrade enhancements include an improved site collection upgrade experience, a tightened security for iFrames, and the rights to insert iFrames into pages.

  - eDiscovery and case management capabilities include the eDiscovery Center site template that creates a portal through which you can access cases involving eDiscovery (electronic discovery) requests; for example, a legal case or an audit.

There are a number of features that have been deprecated or removed from SharePoint 2013 in comparison with SharePoint 2010 products, such as Document Workplaces, for example. Deprecated features are included in SharePoint 2013 for compatibility with previous product versions, however, these features will be removed in the next major release of SharePoint.

SEE ALSO A full list of deprecated features in SharePoint 2013 can be found at *technet.microsoft.com/en-us/library/ff607742(v=office.15).aspx.*

1

Key points

- SharePoint 2013 provides a powerful set of tools for information sharing and team collaboration.

- SharePoint websites provide places to capture and share ideas, information, knowledge, documents, and communications.

- You can access content stored within a SharePoint site from both a web browser and through client applications such as Office.

- Access to a SharePoint site is controlled through a role-based system predicated on permission levels. The five default permission levels are Read, Contribute, Design, Full Control, and Limited.

- SharePoint 2013 technology can be deployed as an on-premises SharePoint installation, or as a cloud SharePoint Online solution, or as a hybrid environment that combines on-premises and cloud models. The user experience is consistent across all types of deployment.

- There are varying levels of integration between different versions of Office and SharePoint 2013, with Office 2013 having the closest integration.

Chapter at a glance

Navigate

Navigate the site components, page 23

Understand

Understand the site structure, page 31

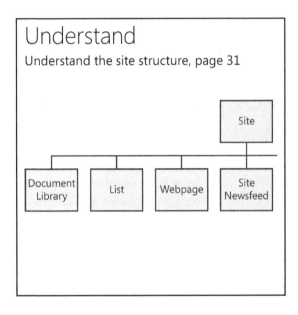

Customize

Customize site navigation, page 34

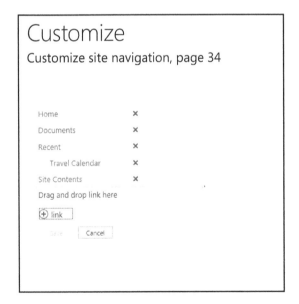

Use

Use the two-stage Recycle Bin, page 47

Navigating a
SharePoint site

2

IN THIS CHAPTER, YOU WILL LEARN HOW TO

- Navigate the home page and the SharePoint site.

- Understand the site structure.

- Navigate the ribbon.

- Customize site navigation.

- Understand Web Part pages.

- Use the Recycle Bin.

A typical Microsoft SharePoint 2013 collaboration website provides you with a structured environment where your team can communicate, share documents and data, and work together. Different types of SharePoint collaboration sites have different structures, such as a team site, a project site, a community site, and a blog site.

In addition to collaboration sites, SharePoint Server 2013 includes templates for enterprise sites that provide set up for content and record management, search, and business intelligence centers.

SEE ALSO For more information about SharePoint sites, refer to Chapter 5, "Creating and managing sites."

The team site may include the following components:

- **Libraries** Document, picture, form, and wiki libraries represent a collection of files that you share and work on with your team members. A typical team site includes a built-in document library called **Documents** that is displayed on the team site home page. You can create your own document, picture, wiki, and form libraries when needed.

- **Lists** With SharePoint lists, you and your team members can work with structured, tabular data on the website. A typical team site includes several list apps that you can add to your site, such as Announcements, Calendar, Links, and Tasks. You can also create custom lists using the Custom list app. In addition, there are other list apps provided by SharePoint that you can add to your site, if required.

- **Newsfeed** A site newsfeed is a site's communication hub. It displays posts and replies among the users of the site. You and your team members can post comments and reply to each others' posts. The site newsfeed, or a site feed, is displayed on the team site home page by default.

- **Surveys** Surveys provide a way of polling team members. SharePoint sites don't have a built-in survey, but you can create your own.

- **Recycle Bin** The Recycle Bin allows you to restore items that have been deleted from the site.

The functionality of a site component is encapsulated in an app. Apps for SharePoint provide self-contained pieces of functionality. For example, a library is implemented as a library app that you can add to your site. Each list is implemented using a list-specific app; for example, a Task list is implemented using a Task app, a newsfeed is implemented via a MicroFeed app, and a survey that you can create on your site is implemented using a Survey app. In addition, you can download apps for SharePoint that extend the SharePoint functionality from your organization's internal App Catalog and from a public SharePoint Store.

SEE ALSO For more information about SharePoint 2013 apps, refer to *msdn.microsoft.com/en-us/library/fp179930.aspx*.

In this chapter, you will learn how to navigate the SharePoint team site structure. You will start with the home page of a typical SharePoint team site and then learn how to browse the site components, as well as your own personal SharePoint social components. You will learn how to customize site navigation and how to navigate the ribbon, as well as understand the concepts of Web Part pages. You will also learn how to use the two-stage Recycle Bin and how to restore files and documents after they have been deleted from your site.

PRACTICE FILES Before you can use the practice site with the two subsites provided for this chapter, you need to download and install the Chapter02 practice files from the book's website, and then create the practice site structure for this chapter. See "Using the practice files" at the beginning of the book for more information.

Navigating the home page and the SharePoint site

2

A *home page* is the main page of a SharePoint website; it provides a navigational structure that links the site components together. Typically, a home page of a SharePoint site has two main navigation areas: the left navigation area, which is a panel at the left of the page, and the top navigation area, which is a strip at the top of the page. Cumulatively, these areas are referred to as the *site navigation*.

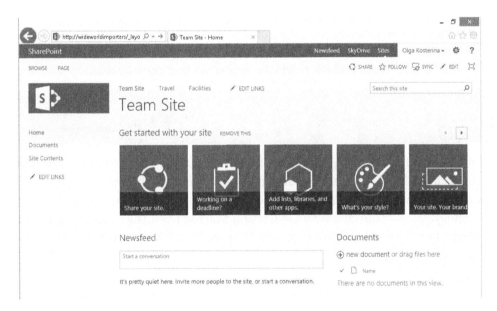

The left navigation panel typically contains a set of *Quick Launch* links. Typically, the **Quick Launch** contains the following links:

- **Home** The **Home** link points to the home page of the current site.

- **Documents** The **Documents** link opens a built-in Documents library.

- **Recent** When a new list or a library is created, its link is displayed in the **Recent** section on the **Quick Launch**. Five of the newest links are shown in this section.

- **Site Contents** The **Site Contents** link opens the **Site Contents** page that lists all of the libraries, lists, newsfeeds, surveys, and other apps on your site. The **Site Contents** page also provides links to the subsites, as well as the site's Recycle Bin.

The **Quick Launch** can also contain links to the subsites of the current site and also the site components created by you and your team members, such as specific document libraries or lists.

The top navigation area contains the *top link bar* located above the page title. It consists of the tabs displayed on all pages within the SharePoint site. The top link bar typically includes the following links:

- **Current Site Title** This is the link to the home page of the current site. It is usually displayed on the first tab on the left.

- **Links To The Subsites** On a well-organized site, the top link bar contains tabs with links to the subsites of the current site, such as the **Travel** link and the **Facilities** link on the second tab and the third tabs, respectively, in our example.

> **IMPORTANT** If a subsite is configured to use the top link bar of the parent site, then the first tab link on the subsite points to the home page of the parent site.

On the top right of the page, to the left of the **Help** button, you can see the **Settings** gear icon. Clicking this button opens the **Settings** menu, which enables you to edit the current page, add a new page or an app, share the site, access the **Site Contents** page, change the settings for your site, and view the **Getting Started** links. The options displayed in the **Settings** menu depend on the permissions that you have on the site: only options applicable to you are displayed.

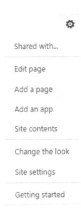

Shared with...

Edit page

Add a page

Add an app

Site contents

Change the look

Site settings

Getting started

The **Site contents** link in the **Settings** menu is identical to the **Site Contents** link on the **Quick Launch**. This link takes you to the **Site Contents** page, which lists all of the libraries, lists, and other apps on your site, as well as the child sites, if there are any. It also has the link to the site's Recycle Bin. The **Site Contents** page contains links to all major parts of the site's structure and is your main navigational aid for the site you are in.

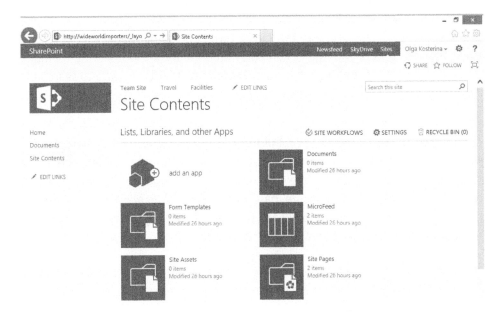

The **Site** settings link on the **Settings** menu opens the **Site Settings** page that enables you to administer and customize your site.

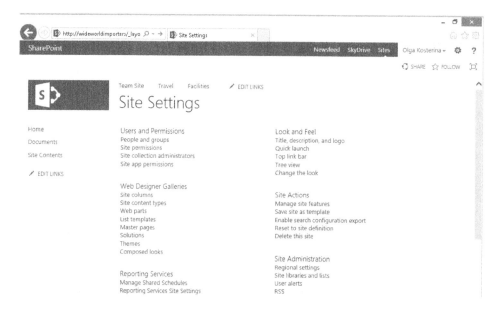

In addition to the site navigation, the home page of a typical SharePoint team site includes the **Getting Started** area with graphical links, the site newsfeed, and also a view of the **Documents** library that is presented within its own page component called a *Web Part*, which allows you to work with the documents in this library without leaving the home page. On the top-right side of the page, there is a **Search** box that allows you to search the current site.

The bar at the very top of the page is referred to as a *global navigation bar*. On its right, it contains links to your personal SharePoint social components, such as **Newsfeed** and **SkyDrive**, as well as **Sites**. While the site components are stored within the site that they are a part of and shared between the site's users, your personal components are dedicated to you and stored centrally in a secure, password-protected location in the cloud or on your organization's SharePoint servers. Links to your **Newsfeed**, **SkyDrive**, and **Sites** accompany you across all SharePoint sites that you have access to.

- **Newsfeed** is your own social hub, where updates from people, posts, documents, and sites that you are following are displayed, as well as the system alerts. Your posts to the site newsfeeds are also displayed, and you can post to a site newsfeed from your own newsfeed.

- **SkyDrive** is your own personal library, where you can store your private work documents. **SkyDrive** allows you to share your private files with your coworkers and give them permission to review or edit the content. You can also sync your work files to your local device to work on the documents offline. In addition, your **SkyDrive** displays the links to the documents that you are following.

- **Sites** is a link that gives you easy access to the sites you are interested in. All the sites that you are following are listed on your **Sites** page.

Underneath the global navigation bar, on the right of the screen, there is a group of buttons that have the following functionality:

- **Share** The **Share** button allows you to share this site with other users and assign them permissions for accessing this site.

- **Follow** The **Follow** button allows you to follow this site and be notified of changes.

- **Sync** The **Sync** button allows you to synchronize the **Documents** library—displayed in the bottom right of the page—with your local device, such as a PC, tablet, or phone, for working offline.

- **Edit** The **Edit** button allows you to edit the current page.

- **Focus on Content** The **Focus on Content** button hides site navigation so that the page content is displayed in full-page view.

In this exercise, you will navigate both your site's components and your own personal components. First, you will go to the **Site Contents** page and explore your site's components. You will then use the global navigation bar to go to your personal components, such as **Newsfeed**, **SkyDrive**, and **Sites**.

 SET UP **Open your SharePoint site (this exercise uses *http://wideworldimporters*, but you can use any site that you wish). If prompted, type your user name and password, and then click OK.**

1   On the **Quick Launch**, click **Site Contents**.

2   Explore the page. Notice that the top link bar and the **Quick Launch** have not changed.

3   Scroll down to the bottom of the page and notice all parts of the site that are listed on the **Site Contents** page, including the apps for libraries and lists, the subsites, and the **Recycle Bin**.

4   Click the **Team Announcements** app to go to the **Team Announcements** list.

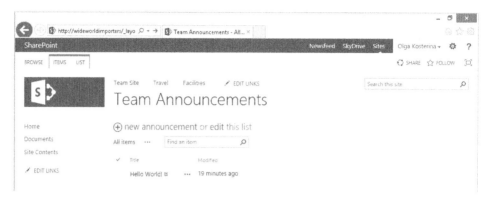

5   On the **Team Announcements** page, on the top link bar, click **Travel** to go to the **Travel** site home page.

6   In the site **Newsfeed** located at the bottom of the page, type **Hi Everyone!**.

7   Click the **Post** button to post to the site newsfeed. Notice that your post has appeared in the site newsfeed, below the text box.

8   In the global navigation bar on the top of the page, click **Newsfeed** to open your own personal newsfeed.

9   Enter your credentials, if prompted.

10   Explore your **Newsfeed** page. In the text box at the top of the page, type **Hello World!**.

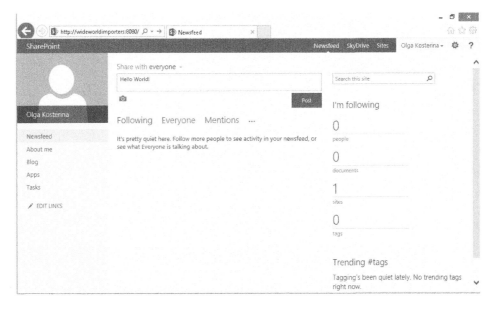

11   Click the **Post** button to post to your newsfeed. Notice that your post has appeared in the newsfeed, below the text box.

12   Click the browser's **Back** button, located in the top-left corner of the browser window, to return to the **Travel** home page.

13   Type the address of your team site in the browser address bar, such as **http://wideworldimporters**, to return to your site home page.

14   On the global navigation bar on the top of the page, click **Newsfeed**. Verify that this is the same page as the **Newsfeed** that you were taken to from the **Travel** site.

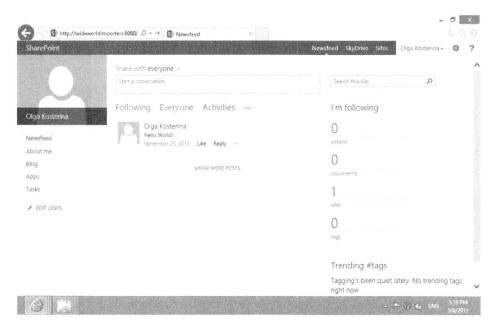

TIP If you don't see your post, click the ellipsis below the text box, and then select **Activities** from the menu that appears.

15 Click the browser's **Back** button to return to the site's home page.

16 On the global navigation bar, click **SkyDrive** to open your own personal library.

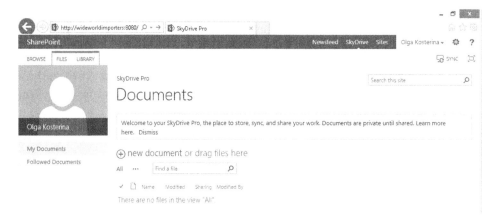

17 Explore your library, and then click the browser's **Back** button to return to the site's home page.

18   On the site home page, click the **Follow** button to follow this site. The confirmation that you follow this site is displayed.

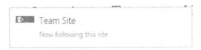

19   On the global navigation bar, click **Sites** to open your **Sites** page.

20   Explore the page. Notice that your team site is now listed as the site you are following. Click the browser's **Back** button to return to your team site's home page.

✖ CLEAN UP **Leave the browser open if you are continuing to the next exercise.**

Understanding the site structure

A typical SharePoint site contains the following components: webpages, document libraries, lists, newsfeed, and other apps. These items are created and maintained by SharePoint and are linked together within the site structure. In a graphical form, this site structure can be represented as a tree-like diagram.

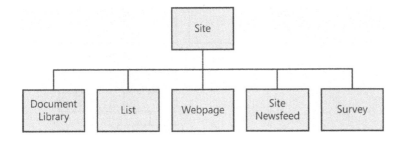

In addition to its own components, such as pages and document libraries, a SharePoint site can have many subsites, the hierarchy of which, on web servers, resembles the hierarchy of folders on file systems. Sites that do not have a parent site are referred to as *top level sites*. Top level sites can have multiple subsites, and these subsites can have multiple subsites, proceeding downward as many levels as you need. The entire hierarchical structure of a top level site and all of its subsites is called a *site collection*.

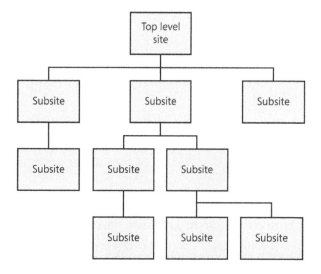

Because the subsites are contained within their parent's site, the overall hierarchical structure of a SharePoint site has the site's own items—such as pages, document libraries, lists, and other apps—as well as the child sites. This overall structure can be represented as a *site contents tree*.

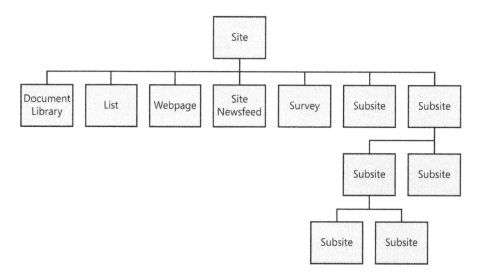

SET UP **Open the SharePoint site in which you'd like to view the subsites (for example, *http://wideworldimporters*), if it is not already open. If prompted, type your user name and password, and then click OK.**

IMPORTANT Verify that you have sufficient permissions to view the subsites. If in doubt, see Appendix A, "SharePoint 2013 user permissions and permission levels."

1. On the **Quick Launch**, click **Site Contents**.
2. On the **Site Contents** page, scroll down to see a list of subsites.

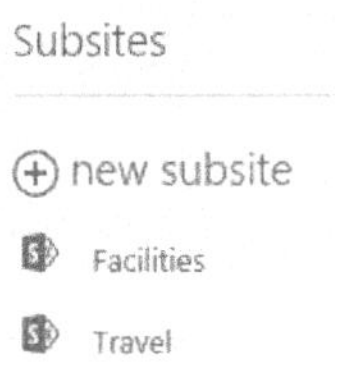

3. Click the link to the **Travel** subsite.
4. On the **Travel** subsite home page, notice that the top link bar is different from the top link bar of the parent site. The first left tab points to this subsite home page. This subsite is independent and there is no link to the parent site.

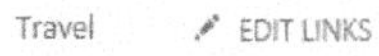

5. Click the browser's **Back** button to return to the parent site home page.
6. On the top link bar of the parent site, click the link to the **Facilities** subsite.
7. On the **Facilities** subsite home page, notice that the top link bar is the same as the top link bar on the parent site. The first left tab points to the parent site home page. This subsite is set up to inherit the top link bar from the parent site.

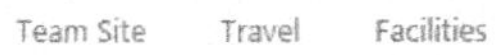

IMPORTANT If the subsite is inheriting the top link bar from the parent site, the top link bar can only be edited in the parent site and not in the subsite.

8. Click the first link on the left, **Team Site**, to return to the parent site home page.

CLEAN UP **Leave the browser open if you are continuing to the next exercise.**

SEE ALSO For more information on setting up navigation between the site and its subsites, refer to Chapter 5, "Creating and managing sites."

Customizing the site navigation

In a SharePoint site, you can customize both the top and left navigation areas. There are many options available for navigation customization. You can add new links, edit and re-position existing links, and delete those links that you no longer require in both the top link bar and the **Quick Launch** by using the in-page editing functionality. You can also drag and drop items from the **Site Contents** page to create new links. In addition, you can group and sort the links and do more advanced customization using the **Site Settings**.

In the following exercise, you will use an in-page editing functionality to customize the top link bar and the **Quick Launch**. You will add a link to the parent SharePoint site to the top link bar, change the position of this link, and then rename a link on the **Quick Launch**.

SET UP **Open your SharePoint site from the address bar of your browser (for example,** *http://wideworldimporters/travel*)**. If prompted, type your user name and password, and then click OK.**

> **IMPORTANT** Verify that you have sufficient permissions to change the site navigation. If in doubt, see Appendix A.

1   On the **Travel** site home page, at the right of the top link bar, click **EDIT LINKS**.

     Notice that the layout of the top link bar area has changed. It now displays additional controls that allow you to add and delete links.

2   Click **link** to add a new link to the top link bar. The **Add a link** dialog appears.

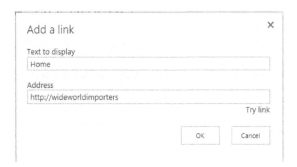

3　In the **Text to display** field, type a display text for the new link, such as **Home**. In the **Address** field, type the URL of the parent site, such as **http://wideworldimporters**.

4　Click **OK** to add the new link to the top link bar. The new link is added to the right of the existing links.

5　Drag the new link to the left, so that it is positioned before the **Travel** link.

6　Click **Save** to save your changes and display the modified top link bar on the **Travel** site home page.

7　You will now rename the **Home** link on the **Quick Launch** that points to the **Travel** site home page so that this link is not confused with the link to the parent site home page in the top link bar that you created in steps 1–6.

8　On the left navigation panel, below the **Quick Launch**, click **EDIT LINKS**. Notice that the layout of the left navigation panel has changed. It now displays additional controls that allow you to add and delete links on the **Quick Launch**.

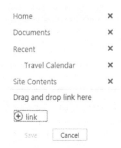

9　Click the **Home** link to select it.

10　To rename this link, type **Travel**. After you've finished typing, click outside the link.

11　Click **Save** to save your changes and display the modified **Quick Launch** on the **Travel** site home page.

✖ CLEAN UP **Leave the browser open if you are continuing to the next exercise.**

In the following exercise, you will drag and drop an app from the **Site Contents** page to the navigation to add a link to it.

➜ SET UP **Open the SharePoint site where you'd like to customize navigation (for example, *http://wideworldimporters/travel*), if not already open. If prompted, type your user name and password, and then click OK.**

IMPORTANT Verify that you have sufficient permissions to edit the site navigation. If in doubt, see Appendix A.

1　On the **Quick Launch**, click **Site Contents**.

2　On the **Site Contents** page, locate the **Travel Calendar**.

3　On the **Quick Launch**, click **EDIT LINKS**.

4　Drag the **Travel Calendar** and drop it on the **Quick Launch**, above the **Documents** link, to create a permanent link to it on the **Quick Launch**.

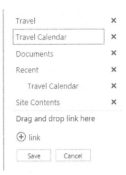

5   You will now remove the temporary link to **Travel Calendar** from the **Recent** section. Click the **x** to the right of the **Travel Calendar** link under the **Recent** section to remove it.

6   Click **Save** to save your changes to the **Quick Launch**.

7   Click **Travel** on the **Quick Launch** to return to the **Travel** site home page.

✖ CLEAN UP **Leave the browser open if you are continuing to the next exercise.**

For more advanced customization of site navigation, the **Site Settings** can be used to modify the top link bar and the **Quick Launch**. In this exercise, you will add a new section to the **Quick Launch** and rearrange the **Quick Launch** links using the **Site Settings**.

➜ SET UP **Open the SharePoint site where you'd like to customize navigation (for example, *http://wideworldimporters/travel*), if not already open. If prompted, type your user name and password, and then click OK.**

> **IMPORTANT** Verify that you have sufficient permissions to edit the site navigation. If in doubt, see Appendix A.

1   On the **Travel** site home page, click **Settings,** and then select **Site settings** from the menu.

2   On the **Site Settings** page, in the **Look and Feel** section, click **Quick launch**. The **Quick Launch** page appears.

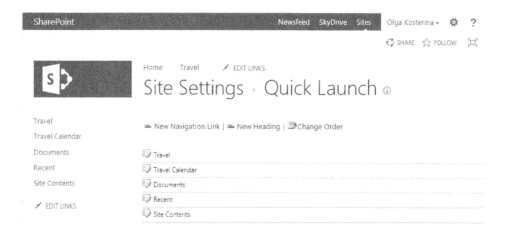

3   On the **Quick Launch** page, click **New Heading**. The **New Heading** page appears.

4   In the **URL** section, in the **Type the Web** text box, type #, and in the **Type the description** text box, type **SharePoint Resources**. Click **OK** to create a section heading on the **Quick Launch**.

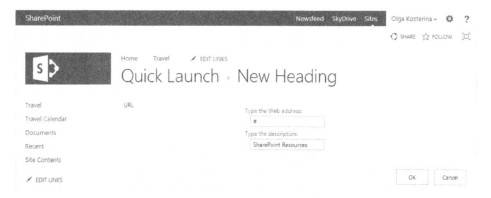

TIP If you'd like to create a heading on the **Quick Launch** that is a link, type its URL in the **Web address** text box.

Back on the **Quick Launch** page, notice that the new section heading has been created. You will now add a link to this section.

5   On the **Quick Launch** page, click **New Navigation Link.**

6   On the **New Navigation Link** page, in the **URL** section, type a web address for the new link, such as **http://sharepoint.microsoft.com**, and then type a description, such as **SharePoint Products**.

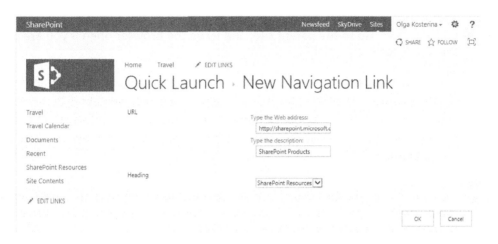

7   In the **Heading** section, select **SharePoint Resources** from the drop-down list.

8   Click **OK** to add the new link to the **SharePoint Resources** section on the **Quick Launch**. Notice that the new link has been added.

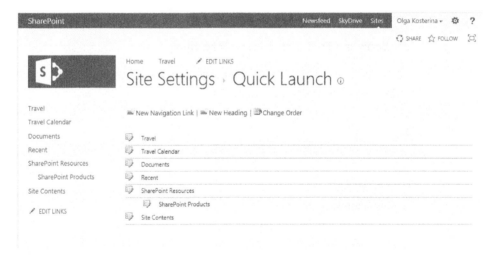

9   Click **Travel** on the **Quick Launch** to return to the **Travel** site home page.

10 To test the new link, click it to open the **SharePoint Products** home page at the Microsoft website. Explore the site, and then return to the **Travel** site home page using the browser **Back** button.

> **IMPORTANT** You need Internet access to view a page at an external website, such as the Microsoft site.

CLEAN UP Go to the parent site, and leave the browser open if you are continuing to the next exercise.

While **Quick Launch** represents the frequently needed links, it is sometimes useful to see the full structure of the site visually, in a graphical representation. In this exercise, you will modify the left navigation panel for the parent site to display the tree view of the site's structure. You will then return to the original configuration and bring back the **Quick Launch**.

SET UP Open the SharePoint site where you'd like to modify the left navigation panel (for example, *http://wideworldimporters/*), if not already open. If prompted, type your user name and password, and then click **OK**.

> **IMPORTANT** Verify that you have sufficient permissions to edit the site navigation. If in doubt, see Appendix A.

1   On the **Settings** menu, select **Site settings**. The **Site Settings** page is displayed.

2   In the **Look and Feel** section, click **Tree view**.

3   On the **Tree View** page, clear the **Enable Quick Launch** check box and select the **Enable Tree View** check box. Click **OK**.

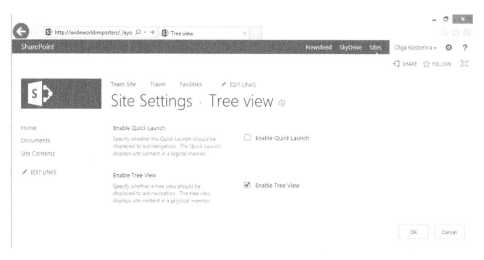

You are taken back to the **Site Settings** page.

4   Return to the current site's home page by clicking its link on the top link bar.

The left navigation panel on the home page has changed. It now displays the **Site Content** panel, which shows the parts of the site, as well as subsites, in a tree view. In the **Site Content** panel, notice the difference in the icons that represent different parts of the site's infrastructure, for example, the **Travel** and **Facilities** subsites, the **Documents** library, and the **Team Announcements** list.

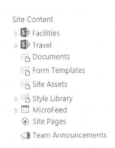

You will now bring the left navigation panel back to its original configuration, in which it displays the **Quick Launch** and does not display the **Site Content**.

5   Using steps 1–4 of this exercise as a guide, on the **Tree view** page, enable the **Quick Launch** and disable the **Tree View**. Return to the site home page and verify that the left navigation panel displays the **Quick Launch**.

❌ CLEAN UP **Leave the browser open if you are continuing to the next exercise.**

Navigating the ribbon

In SharePoint 2013, the ribbon provides a consistent interface for accessing the commands and tools that you require for the tasks that you want to accomplish, much like the ribbon in other Office applications, such as Microsoft Word and Microsoft Excel. In a SharePoint site, the ribbon appears across the top of a webpage and is designed to help you quickly locate the most commonly used commands and tools for performing actions on pages, documents, and lists.

Commands on the ribbon are organized in logical groups, displayed together under tabs that provide titles for each group of commands that form a ribbon. Each ribbon relates to a type of SharePoint site component that you are working with, such as a document library or a webpage. Tabs, groups, and commands on the ribbon are contextual: the ribbon commands available to you change depending on the context of what you are doing and where you are on the SharePoint site. The tabs are displayed at the top of a webpage on your site. To use the ribbon commands, you need to select the tab that corresponds to the kind of task you want to perform. The currently selected tab is highlighted. Each ribbon provides a specific set of commands, depending on the actions that you would like to perform.

The **Browse** tab, as the name suggests, allows you to browse the current page. It is selected when you open a page, providing you with the ability to view the page in the browser. The top link bar is displayed on the **Browse** tab. This tab does not have ribbon-based tools associated with it.

Depending on the page that you are viewing, other tabs become available. For example, the home page of the team site provides a **Page** tab that allows you to modify the page and its settings.

Commands on the ribbon are represented as buttons, drop-down lists, and other controls. To make it easier for you to locate the necessary command, they are grouped together by common functionality into several sections on the ribbon. The names of the groups are shown at the bottom of the ribbon. For example, on the **Page** tab, the **Edit** group contains commands that provide you with the ability to edit the page, whereas the **Manage** group contains commands that allow you to manage the page.

The number and types of commands that are available to you under each tab on the ribbon depend not only on the context of where you are and what you are doing, but also on your permission level and the configuration of your site. Some commands on the ribbon may be unavailable because you do not have sufficient permissions to use them, or because they have not been enabled for your site. In other cases, to enable a command, you may need to select an object. In a document library, for example, you must first select a document in the library to enable the ribbon commands for working with the document.

When the ribbon is displayed, the top links bar is not visible. On all pages with the ribbon, you can use the following navigation aids for moving to other pages within the site and the site collection:

- **Browse** A tab that displays the top link bar.

- **Site contents** A link on the **Settings** menu that takes you to the **Site Contents** page.

- **Sites** A link that takes you to the sites that you are following listed on your personal **Sites** page.

In addition, on the pages with the ribbon where the left navigation panel is available, you can use **Quick Launch**, including the **Site Contents** link.

On a list page, SharePoint provides two ribbons: **Items** and **List**. The Items ribbon provides a set of commands for working with the individual list items. The List ribbon provides the commands for working with the list as a whole. Similarly, a library page provides two ribbons—**Files** and **Library**—for working with individual documents and configuring a library, respectively.

SEE ALSO For more information on working with lists and documents, refer to Chapter 3, "Working with documents and information in lists and libraries." For more information on configuring lists and libraries, refer to Chapter 6, "Making lists and libraries work for you."

In this exercise, you will browse to a **Documents** library, explore its ribbon, use the ribbon control to rename the document in the library, and then return to the home page.

 SET UP **Open your SharePoint site, such as** *http://wideworldimporters*, **if not already open. If prompted, type your user name and password, and then click OK.**

> **IMPORTANT** Verify that you have sufficient permissions to edit the **Documents** library. If in doubt, see Appendix A.

1   On the top link bar, click **Travel** to open the **Travel** subsite.

2   On the **Quick Launch**, click **Documents** to open the **Documents** library.

3   On the top left of the screen, notice the **Browse** tab. To the right of the **Browse** tab, notice two additional tabs: **Files** and **Library**.

4   Click the **Files** tab to display the ribbon that contains the commands for working with documents.

Explore the ribbon and notice the ribbon groups, such as **New**, **Open & Check Out**, **Manage**, **Share & Track**, **Copies**, **Workflow**, and **Tags & Notes**. Notice that only the New group commands are available, while the others are dimmed out.

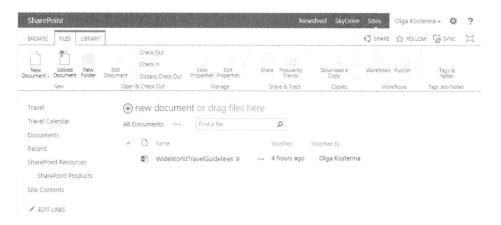

5   Select a document, such as **WideWorldTravelGuidelines**, by hovering your mouse over its name and clicking the tick mark that appears on the left of the name. Notice that the commands on the **Files** ribbon become available and are not dimmed out any longer.

6   To rename the selected document, in the **Manage** group on the ribbon, click the **Edit Properties** button.

7   On the **Edit Properties** page, in the **Name** field, change the name of the document to **TravelGuidelines**.

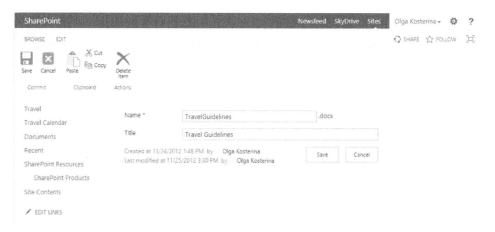

8   Click **Save** to save the changes and to go back to the **Documents** library.

9   Click the **Library** tab. The **Library** tab opens and displays the commands on the ribbon that allow you to configure the library.

Explore the ribbon and notice the ribbon groups, such as **View Format**, **Manage Views**, **Share & Track**, **Tags & Notes**, **Connect & Export**, **Customize Library**, and **Settings**.

10   On the **Quick Launch**, click **Travel** to return to the site home page.

❌ CLEAN UP **Leave the browser open if you are continuing to the next exercise.**

Understanding app parts and Web Parts

A webpage on a SharePoint site can contain—in addition to text, images, and links—one or more Web Parts. A Web Part is an independent component that can be reused, shared, and personalized by all users who have permission to access it. Web Parts are the basic building blocks of a page; each Web Part occupies its own rectangular area within the page.

An app part is a type of Web Part that xposes the content of a SharePoint app, such as a list or a library in a Web Part. For example, the home page of a newly created team site contains a Web Part that displays the content of the Documents library app.

Webpages can contain several Web Parts that can be connected together if necessary. SharePoint provides built-in app parts for all lists and libraries on the current site that you can insert in a webpage. By using Web Parts, you can organize disparate information and consolidate data (such as lists and charts) and web content (such as text, links, and images) into a single webpage.

SEE ALSO For more information on webpages, Web Parts, and app parts, refer to Chapter 4, "Working with webpages."

In this exercise, you will explore the Web Parts on the home page of the team site.

SET UP Open your SharePoint site, such as *http://wideworldimporters/travel*, if not already open. If prompted, type your user name and password, and then click **OK**.

IMPORTANT Verify that you have sufficient permissions to edit the site home page. If in doubt, see Appendix A.

1   On the top left of the screen, click the **Page** tab.

2   In the **Edit** group on the **Page** ribbon, click the **Edit** button. The Web Parts on the page are displayed within rectangular areas that show the position of each Web Part on the page. Click the **Focus on Content** button on the top right of the page to better see the page.

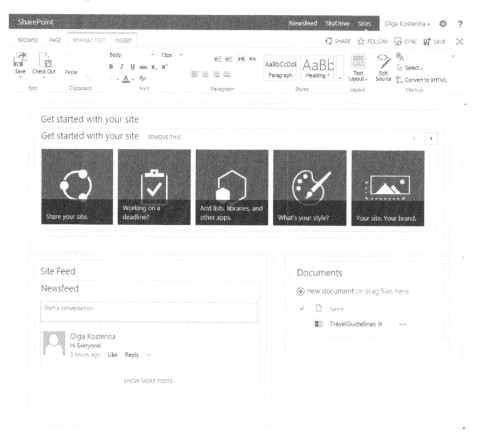

3   Notice that two additional ribbon tabs have appeared to the right of the **Page** tab: the **Format Text** tab, which is selected, and the **Insert** tab. The **Format** ribbon provides controls that allow you to change and format the text on the page, as well as its markup. The **Insert** ribbon provides controls to insert video, audio, graphics, and Web Parts into the page.

4   In the bottom right of the page, click in the **Documents** Web Part to select it. This Web Part provides access to the content of the Documents library directly on the home page. Notice the document that you modified in the previous exercise.

5   Notice that three additional ribbon tabs have appeared: the **Files** and the **Library** tabs that provide the ribbon commands for working with the library and individual documents that are displayed in this Web Part, and the **Web Part** tab that provides commands for working with the Web Part.

6   Click the **Save** button on the top right of the page to close the ribbon.

7   Click the **Focus on Content** button to redisplay the page navigation.

❌ CLEAN UP **Leave the browser open if you are continuing to the next exercise.**

Using the Recycle Bin

The Recycle Bin in SharePoint provides two-stage protection against accidental deletions. When you delete a document or other item from the SharePoint site, it is deleted from the site and moved to the site Recycle Bin, where it can be restored, if needed. If you then delete this item from the site Recycle Bin, it is moved to the Recycle Bin in the site collection. From there, the document can be either restored to its original location or deleted.

IMPORTANT By default, the site Recycle Bin holds items for 30 days. Your SharePoint administrator can modify this setting.

TIP A site owner can restore any content from the site Recycle Bin, whereas a site user will only be able to restore the content that has been deleted by that user.

In this exercise, you will delete and restore a document from the Recycle Bin.

SET UP Open the SharePoint site in which you'd like to delete and restore the document, if not already open. This exercise uses the *http://wideworldimporters/travel* site, but you can open any site you want. If prompted, type your user name and password, and then click **OK**.

> **IMPORTANT** Verify that you have permissions to delete and restore items on this site. If in doubt, see Appendix A.

1. On the **Quick Launch**, click **Documents**.

2. On the **Documents** library page, select a document that you would like to remove by hovering your mouse over its name and selecting the tick mark that appears on the left of the name.

3. Click the **Files** tab to open the ribbon.

4. In the **Manage** group on the ribbon, click **Delete Document**, and then click **OK** in the confirmation message box when it appears.

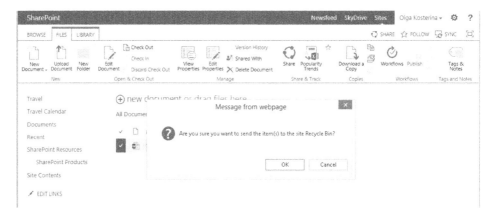

The document has been deleted from the Documents library. You will now restore this document from the site Recycle Bin.

5. On the **Quick Launch**, click **Site Contents**.

6. On the top right of the **Site Contents** page, click **Recycle Bin**.

7. On the **Recycle Bin** page, select the document you have just deleted by clicking the check box to the left of its name. Then, to restore the document to its original location, click the **Restore Selection** option on the top of the page.

8   Click **OK** in the message box to confirm that you would like to restore this document. The document has been restored.

9   Return to the **Documents** library by clicking **Documents** on the **Quick Launch**. Verify that the document has been restored.

⊗ CLEAN UP **Leave the browser open if you are continuing to the next exercise.**

If an item has been deleted accidentally from the site Recycle Bin, it can be restored from the Recycle Bin of the site collection. In this exercise, you will restore the document that has been removed from the site and its Recycle Bin.

➡ SET UP **Open the SharePoint site in which a document to be deleted and restored is residing, if not already open. If prompted, type your user name and password, and then click OK.**

> **IMPORTANT** Verify that you have permissions to manage the top level site. If in doubt, see Appendix A.

1   Using steps 2–7 of the previous exercise as a guide, delete a document from the **Documents** library, and then go to the site **Recycle Bin** page.

2   On the **Recycle Bin** page, select the document by clicking the check box to the left of its name. Then, click **Delete Selection** on the top of the page.

3   Click **OK** in the confirmation message box when it appears. The document has been deleted from the site Recycle Bin.

4   On the top right of the page, click the **Settings** gear icon and select **Site settings**.

5   On the **Site Settings** page, at the bottom left, under the **Site Collection Administration**, click **Go to top level site settings** to display the **Site Settings** page for the top level site.

6   On the **Site Settings** page for the top level site, in the **Site Collection Administration** section, click **Recycle Bin**.

7   On the **Site Settings - Recycle Bin** page, in the left navigation area under **Select a View**, click **Deleted from end user Recycle Bin**.

8   Select the document you have just deleted by clicking the check box to the left of its name, and then clicking **Restore Selection**.

9   Click **OK** in the confirmation message box when it appears. The document has been restored to its original location.

10   Using the top link bar, go to the home page of the **Travel** subsite from which the document was removed, and verify that it has been restored and is displayed in the Documents Web Part.

❌ CLEAN UP **Close the browser.**

Key points

- The structure of a typical SharePoint 2013 team site includes the following components: libraries, lists, newsfeed, and a Recycle Bin. The SharePoint 2013 components are implemented as apps.

- The **Site Contents** page displays all site components, such as libraries, lists, newsfeed, and other apps on your site. It also provides links to the child sites.

- A home page of a SharePoint site has two main navigation areas at the top and left of the page, which are known collectively as the site navigation. The top navigation area contains the top link bar that provides navigation between the sites. The left navigation panel contains the set of **Quick Launch** links that provide navigation within the current site.

- Site navigation can be customized to include the links of your choice. You can add and delete links in the site navigation using the in-page editing. You can also drag and drop items to create new links. More advanced customization can be done using the Site Settings.

- A SharePoint site can have many subsites, the hierarchy of which, on web servers, resembles the hierarchy of folders on file systems. Sites that do not have a parent site are referred to as top level sites. Top level sites can have multiple subsites, and these subsites can have multiple subsites, proceeding downward as many levels as you need.

- The SharePoint ribbon is contextual and is designed to help you quickly locate the commands for performing actions on pages and documents. Commands on the ribbon are organized in logical groups, with each group displayed together under a tab with the ribbon title. Each ribbon relates to a type of SharePoint site component that you are working with, such as a document library or a webpage.

- The home page of a typical SharePoint site contains one or more Web Parts.

- A Recycle Bin provides two-stage protection against accidental deletions.

2

Chapter at a glance

Discover

Discover list and library apps, page 53

Create

Create and edit list items, page 65

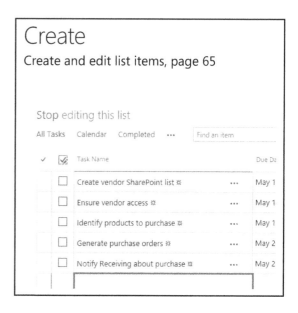

Edit

Edit documents, page 78

Add & Remove

Add and remove list and library columns, page 92

Working with documents and information in lists and libraries

3

IN THIS CHAPTER, YOU WILL LEARN HOW TO

- Discover lists and libraries in a site.

- Create a list.

- Add and edit list items.

- Create a library.

- Create a new document in a library.

- Add and edit documents in a library.

- Check documents in and out from a library.

- Work with version history.

- Create a new folder in a list or a library.

- Add, edit, and remove list and library columns.

- Sort and filter a list and library.

- Delete and restore list items and documents.

- Set up alerts.

- Follow documents.

- Sync a library to your computer.

The information managing capabilities of Microsoft SharePoint come through the lists and the libraries.

You can think of the *lists* found in Microsoft SharePoint 2013 as spreadsheets that you and your coworkers can simultaneously use on the Internet. SharePoint lists represent editable, web-based tables that facilitate concurrent, multiuser interactions against a common, centralized, extensible set of columns and rows. They empower you to provision your own repositories of structured information in which *list items* behave like rows consisting of self-labeled *columns*. All of the webpages needed to create, review, update, delete, and manage a list and its data are automatically and dynamically generated by SharePoint.

One of the most compelling features that SharePoint 2013 provides is libraries. A *library* can be thought of as a list of files. Libraries are a great place to store documents or forms. In the business world, being able to work with documents quickly and effectively is of paramount importance. While lists provide an effective way to work with all types of data, SharePoint libraries function similarly for documents and forms, such as Microsoft Office Word documents. Using SharePoint document libraries, you can filter and group documents, as well as view metadata for documents stored in the library.

In this chapter, you will learn how to work with lists and list items, as well as how to work with libraries and their documents in SharePoint 2013. Depending on a site that you initially create, a **Documents** library may be provisioned when the site is created, and you need only to begin using it. Yet, there will come a time when the library that is autoprovided does not quite meet a need. Therefore, this chapter explores how you can create your own custom lists and libraries. You will also do the following: discover the default lists and libraries that can be provisioned on your site; create new lists and libraries; alter existing lists; create and upload new documents; edit existing documents; organize lists and libraries; delete and restore list items and documents; set up alerts and follow-up documents to get notified when changes occur; and take libraries offline and synchronize them with the live site.

SEE ALSO For more information on how to manage and configure SharePoint lists and libraries, refer to Chapter 6, "Making lists and libraries work for you."

PRACTICE FILES Before you can complete the exercises in this chapter, you need to copy the book's practice files to your computer. The practice files that you'll use in this chapter are in the **Chapter03** practice file folder. A complete list of practice files is provided in "Using the practice files" at the beginning of this book.

IMPORTANT Remember to use your SharePoint site location in place of *http://wideworldimporters* in the exercises.

Discovering default lists and libraries in a site

Many default lists and libraries are included with SharePoint 2013. Each type of list or library has a specific purpose, and some have a different set of features. When you need to create a new list or a library, you can use the default library and list *apps* accessible from the **Your Apps** page to generate a new a list or a library with a specific predefined functionality and a set of columns. Each list and library app has its own tile that visually indicates the type of list or library. Later in this chapter, we'll explore how additional columns can be added and how most default columns can be altered or deleted, even after data has been entered into them.

There are 10 library apps and 20 list apps provided by SharePoint 2013, which are described in Table 3-1.

Table 3-1 Apps for libraries and lists

Library apps

Tile	Library app	Description
	Asset library	Create an asset library to share and manage digital media assets, such as image, audio, and video files. An asset library provides content types with properties and views for managing and browsing media assets, such as thumbnails and metadata keywords.
	Dashboards library	Create a dashboards library to contain PerformancePoint-deployed dashboards.
	Data Connections library	Create a data connection library to simplify the maintenance and management of data connections. A data connection library is a centralized place to store Office Data Connection (ODC) files. Each of these files (.odc) contains information about how to locate, log on, query, and access an external data source.
	Document library	Create a document library when you have a collection of documents or other files that you want to share. Document libraries support features such as folders, versioning, and check out.
	Form library	Create a form library when you have XML-based business forms, such as status reports or purchase orders, that you want to manage. These libraries require an XML editor, such as Microsoft Office InfoPath.

Tile	Library	Description
	Picture library	Create a picture library when you have pictures you want to share. Picture libraries provide special features for managing and displaying pictures, including a slide show.
	Record library	Create a record library to keep a central repository for storing and managing your organization's records or important business documents. You can set policies that determine what records to store, how to route and manage the documents, and how long these records must be retained.
	Report library	Create a report library to simplify the creation, management, and delivery of webpages, documents, and key performance indicators (KPI) of metrics and goals. The report library is a central place where you can create and save reports and dashboards.
	Process Diagram library	Create a process diagram library to store and share diagram process documents, such as those created with Microsoft Office Visio.
	Wiki Page library	Create a wiki page library when you want to have an interconnected collection of wiki pages that enable multiple people to gather information in a format that is easy to create and modify. Wiki page libraries support pictures, tables, hyperlinks, and internal wiki linking.

List apps

Tile	List app	Description
	Announcements	Create an Announcements list when you want a place to share news, status, and other short bits of information.
	Calendar	Create a Calendar list when you want a calendar-based view of upcoming meetings, deadlines, and other important events. You can share information between your Calendar list and Microsoft Office Outlook.
	Circulations	Create a Circulations list when you want a publication to be sent to specific recipients. This list contains many unique capabilities for distributing information to these selected users.
	Contacts	Create a Contacts list when you want to manage information about people with whom your team works, such as customers or partners. You can share information between your Contacts list and Outlook.

	Custom	Create a Custom list when you want to specify your own columns. The list opens as a webpage and you can add or edit items one at a time.
	Custom list in Datasheet view	Create a Custom list in Datasheet view when you want to specify your own columns. The list opens in a spreadsheet-like environment for convenient data entry, editing, and formatting.
	Discussion Board	Create a discussion board when you want to provide a place for newsgroup-style discussion. Discussion boards provide features for managing discussion threads and ensuring that only approved posts appear.
	External list	Create an external list to work with data that is stored outside SharePoint, but that you can read and write within SharePoint. The data source for an external list is called an External content type. Unlike a native SharePoint list, an external list uses Business Connectivity Services to access data directly from an external system.
	Import Spreadsheet	Import a spreadsheet when you want to create a list that has the same columns and contents as an existing spreadsheet. Importing a spreadsheet requires Microsoft Office Excel.
	Issue Tracking	Create an Issue Tracking list when you want to manage a set of issues or problems. You can assign, prioritize, and follow the progress of issues from start to finish.
	KPI List	Create a KPI list to track Key Performance Indicators and to display the status of the indicator on a dashboard page. You can set up KPI lists to track performance by using one of four data sources: manually entered data, data in a SharePoint list, data in Excel workbooks, or data from SSAS (SQL Server Analysis Services).
	Languages and Translators	Create a Languages and Translators list to use with a Translation Management workflow. The workflow uses the list to assign translation tasks to the translator specified in the list for each language.
	Links	Create a Links list when you have links to webpages or other resources that you want to share.

	Microsoft IME Dictionary list	Create the Microsoft IME (Input Method Editor) Dictionary list for when you want to use data in the list as a Microsoft IME dictionary.
	PerformancePoint Content List	Create a PerformancePoint Content list to store dashboard items, such as scorecards, reports, filters, dashboard pages, and other dashboard items that you create by using PerformancePoint Dashboard Designer.
	Project Tasks	Create a Project Tasks list when you want a graphical view (a Gantt chart) of a group of work items that you or your team needs to complete. You can share information between your Project Tasks list and Outlook.
	Promoted Links	Create a Promoted Links list to display a set of link actions in a visual layout.
	Status list	Create a status list to display and track the goals of your project. The list includes a set of colored icons to communicate the degree to which goals are met.
	Survey	Create a survey when you want to poll other website users. Surveys provide features in which you can quickly create questions and define how users specify their answers.
	Tasks	Create a Tasks list when you want to track a group of work items that you or your team must complete.

TIP There are two additional library apps, **Data Feed** library and **PowerPivot Gallery**, which are made available in the **Your Apps** page when you install Microsoft SQL Server 2012 SP1 PowerPivot for SharePoint Server 2013. For more details, refer to Chapter 13, "Working with business intelligence."

In the following exercise, you will browse to the **Your Apps** page to see the list and library apps available on your site.

 SET UP **Open a SharePoint site where you'd like to explore the list and library apps. The exercise will use the *http://wideworldimporters* site, but you can use whatever site you wish. If prompted, type your user name and password, and then click OK.**

1   Click **Settings** on the top right of the screen, and then select **Add an app**.

   TIP Alternatively, you can click **Site Contents** on the **Quick Launch**, and then on the **Site Contents** page, select **Add an app**.

2   The **Your Apps** page is displayed. It shows all apps that are available to you on your site in the **Apps you can add** section. In addition, the **Noteworthy** section on top of the **Your Apps** page shows the apps that are most popular for the sites of the same type as the current site.

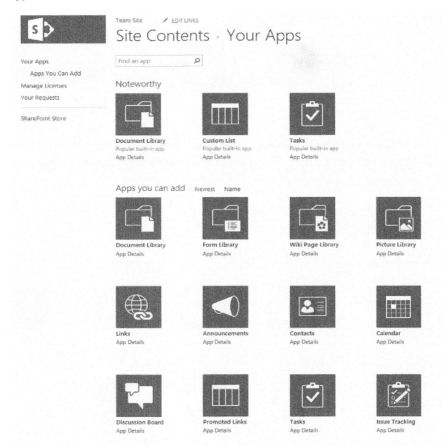

3   On the **Your Apps** page, in the search box on the top of the page, type **list** and press **Enter** on the keyboard. The list apps available on your site are displayed.

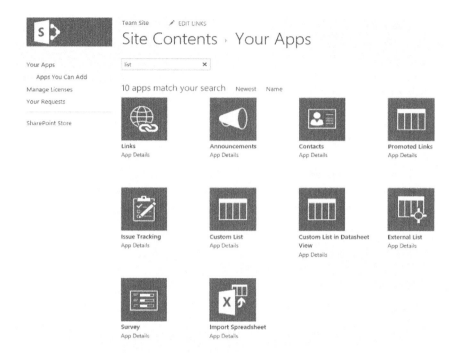

4   In the search box on the top of the page, delete your previous typing, and then type **library** and press **Enter** on the keyboard. The library apps available on your site are displayed.

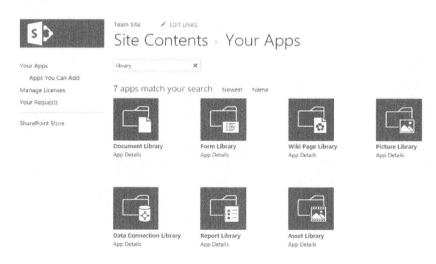

TIP Because the SharePoint pages are security trimmed, you would only see those list and library apps on the **Your Apps** page that you have permission to create.

5   Click the **X** on the right side of the search box to remove the search results and redisplay all available apps.

✖ CLEAN UP Leave the browser open if you are continuing to the next exercise.

Creating a new list

The first step in creating a new list is to ask yourself, "What kind of information do I want to gather/display?" The answer to this question will help you determine which list type to choose. Perhaps you want to start with a list that is close to your end goal, and then add, delete, and alter the default columns to provide the solution you are trying to achieve. For example, if you are planning to collect information such as names and addresses, you can choose the Contacts list app to create your initial list, and then modify it. Perhaps you want to start with a bare-bones list and build it entirely from scratch. In that case, you would likely choose the Custom list app to create your initial list.

TIP If the list items in the list that you want to create always begin with a document, consider using a document library instead of a list.

In the following exercise, you will create a list for the buyers at Wide World Importers to track the status of tasks involved in the buying process. This task list will be based on the **Tasks** app. Once the list is created, you will alter the display name so that it displays **Common Buyer Tasks**.

➔ SET UP Open the SharePoint site where you would like to create the new list. The exercise will use the *http://wideworldimporters* site, but you can use whatever site you wish. If prompted, type your user name and password, and then click OK.

IMPORTANT Verify that you have sufficient permissions to create lists in this site. If in doubt, see Appendix A.

1   Click **Settings** on the top right of the screen, and then select **Add an app** to display the **Your Apps** page, if it is not already displayed.

2   On the **Your Apps** page, scroll down to the **Tasks** tile and click it.

TIP You can also search for the **Tasks** app using the search box on the top of **Your Apps** page.

3   The **Adding Tasks** dialog is displayed. In the **Name** box, type **BuyerTasks** to establish a display name for the new list. This box also supplies the value that SharePoint uses for the new list's URL.

TIP There is no restriction on the number of copies of any list that you can create in a site. You can create as many task lists as you like.

IMPORTANT When you initially create a list in SharePoint, you are establishing two name values: the display name, usually labeled Name or Title, and the URL name, also known as the internal name. The display name that you provide is used to populate both names. However, only the display name can be easily changed after the list is created.

TIP The best practices for naming a list in SharePoint Foundation include the following guidelines: The initial name should be descriptive, intuitive, and easy to remember. The initial name should be concise. The initial name should not contain spaces. The initial name should be consistently used throughout the site. Your organization may also have specific naming conventions that you will want to follow.

SEE ALSO More details about these naming recommendations and the reasons they are needed can be found in the "Naming a URL" sidebar in Chapter 5, "Creating and managing sites."

4   Click the **Create** button to complete the list creation.

5   The **Site Contents** page is displayed, with a new tile for the **BuyerTasks** list and a green **new!** icon to the right of the tile. The new **BuyerTasks** link is also shown on the **Quick Launch** in the **Recent** section.

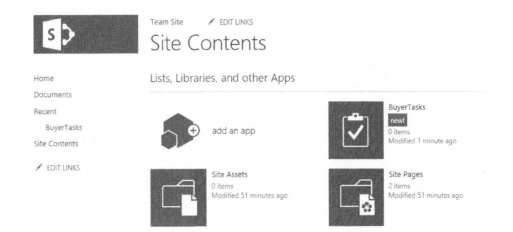

6   Click the **BuyerTasks** tile (or the **BuyerTasks** link on the **Quick Launch**) to go to the
default list view page (AllItems.aspx).

Because this list was named without a space between Buyer and Tasks, it would be
useful to change the display name so that it has a space in it. The remainder of this
exercise demonstrates that revisions to the list name only impact the display name
and not the URL name.

7   On the top left of the page, click the **List** tab to display the ribbon, and then click **List
Settings** in the **Settings** group on the right side of the ribbon.

8   On the **BuyerTasks - Settings** page, in the **General Settings** area, click **List name, description and navigation**.

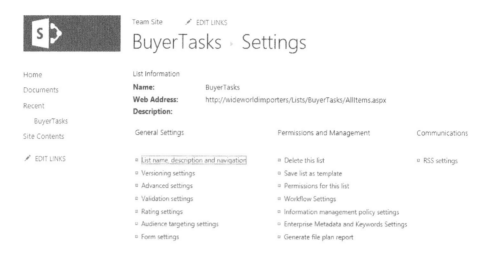

SEE ALSO For more information on configuring the lists, refer to Chapter 6.

9   On the **Settings - General Settings** page, replace the **BuyerTasks** name by typing **Common Buyer Tasks** (with spaces) in the **Name** box.

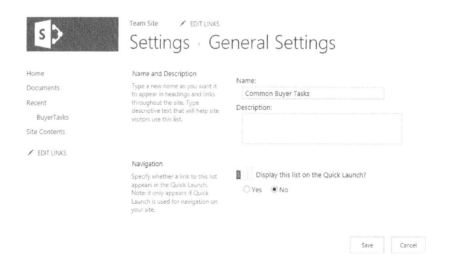

TIP On the **General Settings** page, you can enter the list description and select to permanently display the list link on the **Quick Launch**.

10   Click the **Save** button to save the change and display the list **Settings** page. Notice that the list name on the top of the page and the link on the Quick Launch now reflects the modified display name.

11   On the **Quick Launch**, in the **Recent** section, click the new display name, **Common Buyer Tasks**, to go to the Common Buyer Tasks default list view page.

      The title on the top of this page and all other pages associated with this list shows the modified display name. However, you can see that the browser's address bar still reflects the initial name (internal name) given to this list.

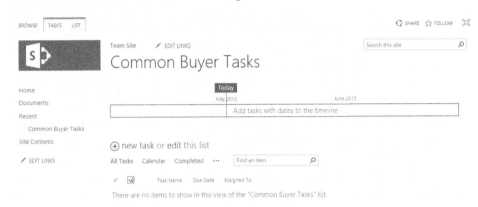

❌ CLEAN UP **Leave the browser open if you are continuing to the next exercise.**

Adding and editing list items

Creating a SharePoint list automatically generates the pages needed to view the list as a whole, to view a list item, to add a new list item, and to edit an existing list item. In addition to adding and editing list items using a form in a separate page, you can create and edit lists within the list page, in a grid that is similar to working in Microsoft Office Excel.

TIP If you need to import data from an Excel spreadsheet into a SharePoint list, use the **Import Spreadsheet** app that can be found in the **Your Apps** page. In the **Import Spreadsheet** app, you can browse to the Excel spreadsheet that you'd like to import the data from, and specify the range of cells that contain this data, and then you can import the data into the newly created SharePoint list. Please refer to Chapter 12, "Using SharePoint with Excel and Access," for more information.

SEE ALSO You can export data from Microsoft Office Access into a SharePoint list. Please refer to Chapter 12 for more information.

While some lists only have a single view when initially created, multiple list views are generated when a new **Tasks** list is created. A *view* defines how the information in a list or library is displayed to the users. The **Common Buyer Tasks** list was created using the **Tasks** list app that has the following six list views: **All Tasks** (default), **Calendar**, **Completed**, **Gantt Chart**, **Late Tasks**, **My Tasks**, and **Upcoming**. Several list views are shown on top of the list, so that you can switch between them at will. You can display your list in more views by clicking the ellipsis to the right of the displayed view links.

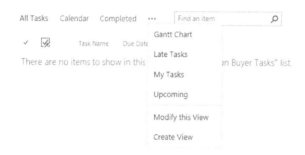

You can go to a list's default list view page from other locations by clicking the list's name on the **Quick Launch**, or by clicking the link at the top of any **List View** Web Part for that list.

In this exercise, you will add several **Tasks** list items for the buyers at Wide World Importers to use in their buying process. You will add the first task using a form, and then add list items using inline editing.

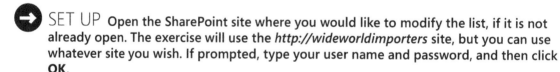 SET UP **Open the SharePoint site where you would like to modify the list, if it is not already open. The exercise will use the *http://wideworldimporters* site, but you can use whatever site you wish. If prompted, type your user name and password, and then click OK.**

> **IMPORTANT** Verify that you have sufficient permissions to modify this list. If in doubt, see Appendix A.

1   On the **Quick Launch**, click the **Common Buyer Tasks** list (created in the last section) to display the **Common Buyer Tasks** default list view page, if it is not already displayed.

2   In the body of the page, click **new task**.

> **TIP** You can also click the **Tasks** tab on the ribbon, and then click **New Item**.

3   On the list item page, in the **Task Name** textbox, type **Create vendor SharePoint list**.

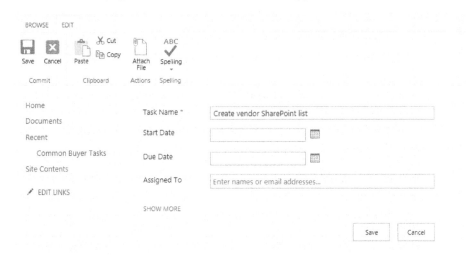

4   In the **Due Date** text box, enter a future date, for example, 10 days from now.

5   Click the **Save** button to save the list item and redisplay the **Common Buyer Tasks** default list view page.

The newly created list item shows in the body of the page. A green icon displays to the right of the Task Name text, indicating that this list item was recently created.

6   You will now create and edit list items within the list page. In the body of the page, on top of the list, click the **edit** link to the right of the **new task** link. The list is redisplayed as a grid in the datasheet view, also known as the Quick Edit view, with a new empty line at the bottom.

7   Position your cursor in the **Task Name** column on the new line and type **Ensure vendor access**.

8   Position your cursor in the **Due Date** column and type any date of your choosing as a due date for the new task, or select a date from the calendar by clicking the **calendar** icon that appears to the left of the field you are working with.

9   Note that a new empty line has been added to the bottom of the table. Using steps 14 and 15 as a guide, create another three list items with the values in the following table.

Task name	Due date
Identify products to purchase	Any date of your choosing.
Generate purchase orders	A date after the previous date.
Notify Receiving about purchase	A date after the previous date.

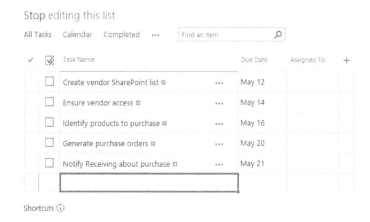

10   After all the new tasks have been added, click **Stop** on the top of the list. The list is redisplayed in its default view, showing all the tasks that you have created.

✖ CLEAN UP **Leave the browser open if you are continuing to the next exercise.**

You will find that you need to edit existing list items in a list at some stage after they have been created. For instance, after the **Common Buyer Tasks** list was created, it transpired that Todd Rowe had already identified products to purchase. In this exercise, you will edit a list item, **Identify products to purchase**, to specify that the task has been completed. You will then display all tasks on the timeline for better visual representation.

➡ SET UP **Open the SharePoint list that you would like to modify, if it is not already open. The exercise will use the Common Buyer Tasks list at** *the http://wideworldimport-ers site*, **but you can use whatever site you wish. If prompted, type your user name and password, and then click OK.**

1   Select the list item that you are going to edit, **Identify products to purchase**, by clicking in its leftmost column.

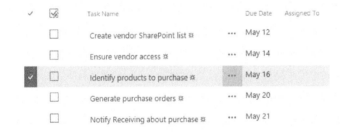

2   Click the **Tasks** tab on the top of the screen to display the ribbon.

3   On the ribbon, click **Edit Item** in the **Manage** group to open the list item page in edit mode.

4   In the **% Complete** field, type **100** to specify that this task is 100% completed, and then click **Save**.

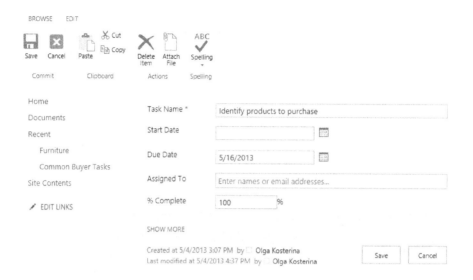

5   The list page is redisplayed. Note that the completed task is now checked and crossed through to show that it has been done already.

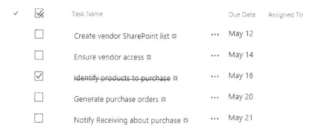

6   You will now display all tasks on the timeline. Select all items in the list by clicking the check mark on top of the leftmost column.

7   Click the **Tasks** tab on the top of the page to display the ribbon, if it is not already displayed.

8   On the ribbon, click **Add to Timeline** in the **Actions** group. All selected tasks are plotted on the timeline. Click the check mark on top of the leftmost column again to deselect all list items.

CLEAN UP **Leave the browser open if you are continuing to the next exercise.**

Occasionally, you might want to attach one or more documents to a list item. By default, all lists in SharePoint allow attachments. In this exercise, you will attach a document to an existing list item in the **Common Buyer Tasks** list.

PRACTICE FILES You will use the WideWorldPurchaseOrder.docx practice file, located in the **Chapter03** folder.

SET UP **Open the SharePoint list that you would like to modify, if it is not already open. The exercise will use the Common Buyer Tasks list at the *http://wideworldimport-ers* site, but you can use whatever site you wish. If prompted, type your user name and password, and then click OK.**

IMPORTANT Verify that you have sufficient permissions to modify items on this list. If in doubt, see Appendix A.

1   Select the **Generate purchase orders** list item by clicking in its leftmost column, and then click the **Tasks** tab on the top of the page to display the ribbon, if not already displayed.

2   On the ribbon, in the **Action** group, click **Attach File** to display the **Attach File** dialog.

3   Click **Browse**. In the **Choose File to Upload** dialog, go to the practice files folder, **Chapter03**, select **WideWorldPurchaseOrder.docx**, and then click **Open**. Once chosen, the location of the selected document is displayed in the **Name** text box in the **Attach File** dialog.

> **IMPORTANT** At this point, the document is only associated with the list item in memory. Closing the browser abandons the attachment. You must click **OK** to save the attachment's association with this task.

4   Click **OK** to attach the document to the list item. The default list view page is displayed.

5   To validate that the document has been successfully attached, click the **Generate purchase order** list item to display its page. Check that the **WideWorldPurchaseOrder.docx** is shown in the **Attachment**s field at the bottom of the list item page.

TIP Multiple attachments are supported on each list item. You can click **Attach File** repeatedly and attach as many documents as you wish. However, the interface only supports attaching a single document at a time.

6   Click **Close** to return to the list page.

❌ CLEAN UP **Close the browser.**

Creating a document library

A library is a location on a site where you can create, collect, update, and manage files with other team members. Each library displays a list of files and key information about the files, which helps people to use the files to work together.

You can use *document libraries* to store your documents on a SharePoint site, rather than on your local computer's hard drive, so that other employees can find and work with these documents more easily. Libraries are used to store files, whereas lists are used to store other types of content. Like lists, libraries contain metadata, so that you can easily filter, sort, and group items in the libraries.

When you create a new SharePoint team site, a generic document library, called **Documents**, is created. Because this library lacks a descriptive name, you should create new libraries for a particular business category or subject instead. You want to make sure that the name of a document library is descriptive and that each library has a specific topic to make it easier to find documents. Storing all documents together in the default **Documents** or any document library defeats the purpose of using SharePoint sites to make information easier to locate.

In the following exercise, you will create a new document library, called **Furniture**, on your SharePoint site.

➡ SET UP **Open the SharePoint site in which you would like to create your document library. The exercise will use the *http://wideworldimporters* site, but you can use whatever site you wish. If prompted, type your user name and password, and then click OK.**

IMPORTANT Verify that you have sufficient permissions to create a library in this site. If in doubt, see Appendix A.

1   Click **Settings** gear icon on the top right of the screen, and then select **Add an app** to display the **Your Apps** page.

2   On the **Your Apps** page, click the **Documents Library** tile.

3   The **Adding Document Library** dialog is displayed. In the **Name** box, type the name that you want to give to the new document library; for example, **Furniture**.

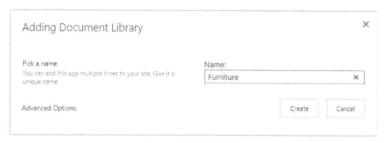

4   Click the **Create** button.

5   The **Site Contents** page is displayed, with a new **Furniture** library tile and a green **new!** icon to the left of the tile. The new **Furniture** link is also shown on the **Quick Launch** in the **Recent** section.

6   Click the **Furniture** tile, or the **Furniture** link on the **Quick Launch**, to go to the default library view page.

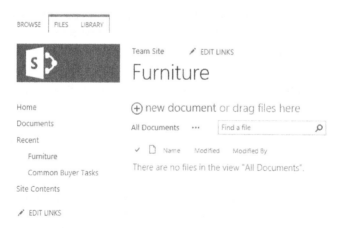

❌ CLEAN UP **Leave the browser open if you are continuing to the next exercise.**

Creating a new document

After a library has been created, you can populate it with documents. In this section, you will create a new document from the SharePoint document library. The new document will use the default template for the library.

SEE ALSO For more information about templates in document libraries, please refer to Chapter 6.

The new document can be created in a Microsoft Word client application, if it is installed on your computer, or in an online Word Web App using the browser.

TIP Microsoft Office Web Apps are a part of Microsoft Office 365 and are available if you are using Microsoft SharePoint Online. If you are using SharePoint 2013 in an on-premises environment, then Office Web Apps should be installed and activated on your server so that users can create and edit documents online using Office Web Apps such as Word, Excel, PowerPoint, or OneNote Web Apps. You can then view and, depending on the license, edit Office documents by using a supported web browser on computers and various mobile devices, such as Windows Phones, and Apple iPhones and iPads. The Office Web Apps can be used on any device in which a browser is available; however, they have less functionality than client applications.

SEE ALSO For more information on using Office Web Apps with SharePoint 2013, refer to *technet.microsoft.com/en-us/library/ff431685.aspx*.

In the following exercise, you will create a new document from the SharePoint document library.

 SET UP **Open the SharePoint site and document library in which you want to create a new document, if it is not already open. If prompted, type your user name and password, and then click OK.**

> **IMPORTANT** Verify that you have sufficient permissions to create a document in this library. If in doubt, see Appendix A.

1   On the **Quick Launch**, click the **Furniture** link.

2   On the top of the page, click the **Files** tab, and then click the **New Document** button at the left of the ribbon.

Depending on your server settings, a new document will open either in a browser or in a Word client application, if it is installed on your computer. If a new document opens in the browser, please move to step 7 in this exercise. Otherwise, please continue to the next step.

3   A new document opens in Word. If a warning about allowing this website to open a program on your computer appears, click **Allow**. The document is based on the default template for this SharePoint library, called template.dotx. If a warning about this template appears, click **Yes** to confirm that you want to proceed with opening a file.

4   If prompted, provide your user name and password. Microsoft Word opens. If a **Read Only** banner appears on the top of the document, click **Edit Document** on the banner. Then, in the new document, type some text; for example, **Oak Mirror**.

5   In **Word**, click the **File** tab, and then click **Save** to save the document back to the **Furniture** document library. In the **Other Web Locations** section, under **Current Folder**, click **Furniture**.

6   The **Save As** dialog opens. Note that the location points to the **Furniture** document library. Enter **OakMirror** as the name of your new document, and then click **Save**.

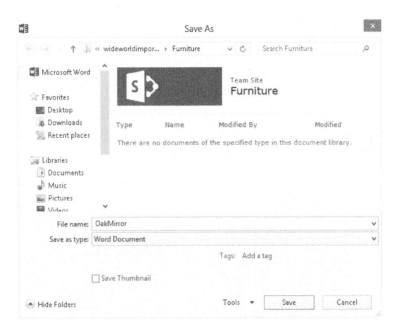

Go back to the browser where the **Furniture** library is displayed.

Move to step 10 in this exercise.

7   The browser opens an empty document based on the library's default template in the Word Web App. If prompted, provide your user name and password. The Word Web App interface is similar to the interface of Microsoft Word, and you can perform many light-editing tasks in Word Web App. Click **Edit Document** on top left of the page, and then select **Edit in Word Web App** from the menu.

8   In the **Word Web App**, in the new document, type some text, for example, **Oak Mirror**.

9   Click the **File** tab, and then click **Save** to save the document back to the **Furniture** document library. The **Furniture** library is displayed.

10   Validate that the **OakMirror** document is listed in the **Furniture** library. There is a green icon next to the document, indicating that this document is a new addition to the library.

TIP If the document is not shown, refresh your browser.

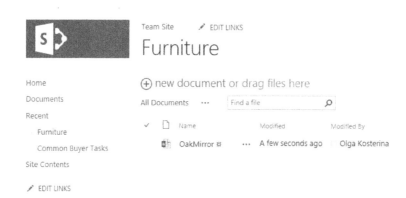

CLEAN UP **Exit Microsoft Word. Leave the browser open if you are continuing to the next exercise.**

Editing documents

Once documents are placed in the library, you can search and filter them to make it easier to find what you are looking for, as well as to collaborate with others to help develop the final version of the document. At times, you will find that you need to edit a document in a SharePoint document library.

SharePoint allows you to edit documents in Office client applications such as Word and Excel, or in the browser using Office Web Apps that provide online companion web applications to Office client applications, such as Word Web App or Excel Web App. For in-browser editing to be available, Office Web Apps must be installed and activated on your on-premises SharePoint 2013 server, or available to you as a part of your SharePoint Online or Office 365 subscription.

In the following exercise, you will edit in Microsoft Word the document called **OakMirror. docx**, which was created in the previous exercise in the **Furniture** library.

SET UP **Open the SharePoint site where you'd like to edit a file in a document library.**

If prompted, type your user name and password, and then click OK.

> **IMPORTANT** Verify that you have sufficient permissions to edit a document in this library. If in doubt, see Appendix A.

1   On the **Quick Launch**, click the **Furniture** document library.

2   To open a document for editing, click the ellipsis to the right of its name, and then select **Edit** from the callout menu.

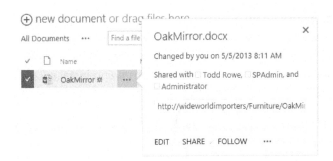

Alternatively, to open a document for editing, you can select the document by clicking its leftmost column, clicking the **Files** tab on top of the page to open the ribbon, and then clicking **Edit Document** on the ribbon.

TIP Depending on your server settings, you might be able to just click the document you would like to edit, such as **OakMirror.docx**, to open it for editing. The document will open in either a Word client application, if it is installed on your computer, or in a Word Web App in a browser. If a new document opens in Word Web App in a browser, on the **Edit Document** menu, select **Edit in Microsoft Word**, and continue to the next step.

3   The document opens in Word. If a warning about opening the program on your computer appears, click **Allow**. If a Microsoft Office warning about opening a file appears, click **Yes** to confirm that you want to open the file. If a **Read Only** banner appears on the top of the document, click **Edit Document** on the banner.

4   In **Word**, make some changes to the document; for example, select the **Oak Mirror** text and make it bold and centered.

5   In **Word**, click **File | Save** to save the document back to the **Furniture** document library.

6　Go back to the browser and validate that the document has been saved to the document library by checking its timestamp.

 CLEAN UP **Exit Word. Leave the browser open if you are continuing to the next exercise.**

When you're on the move, it is often very useful to have the ability to edit your document within a browser, without the need for a client application to be installed on the device you're using.

TIP You can configure whether to open a document within the browser as opposed to having the document open in its native Microsoft Office client application, such as Word. The default option is to open in the browser using an Office Web App such as Word Web App, so that a user can use the browser to view the document online. For on-premise deployments, this capability depends on Office Web Apps being installed and activated on the SharePoint server. For more details, refer to Chapter 6.

In the following exercise, you will modify the **OakMirror.docx** document using in-browser editing in Word Web App.

➡ SET UP **Open the SharePoint site where you'd like to edit a file in a document library, if it is not already open. If prompted, type your user name and password, and then click OK.**

> **IMPORTANT** Verify that you have sufficient permissions to edit a document in this library. If in doubt, see Appendix A.

1　On the **Quick Launch**, click the **Furniture** document library.

2　Click the document you would like to edit, such as **OakMirror.docx**, to open it for editing.

3　The document opens in Word Web App in the browser. Click **Edit Document** on the top left of the page, and then select **Edit in Word Web App** from the menu to open the Word Web App ribbon.

TIP Office Web Apps should be installed and activated to enable in-browser editing. If the **Edit Document** option is not displayed or is dimmed in the Word App, it means that Office Web Apps has not been activated for editing in your environment. You will not be able to complete this exercise.

4   Make some changes to the document; for example, select the **Oak Mirror** text and italicize it.

5   Click the **Save** icon in the top-left corner of the page—or click the **File** tab, and then click the **Save** menu option—to save the document back to the **Furniture** document library.

6   Validate that the newly edited document has been saved to the document library by checking its timestamp.

❌ CLEAN UP **Leave the browser open if you are continuing to the next exercise.**

Uploading documents

Document libraries let keep track of the new versions of a document as the document is modified, and revert to older versions if necessary. First, you need to ensure that your documents are uploaded and available in the SharePoint library.

There are several ways to add documents to a document library, including the following:

- Using the browser to upload documents to the library via the SharePoint interface.
- Using File Explorer to copy or move documents into the library, including dragging between your desktop, or any other location, and SharePoint.
- Using sync to upload the documents stored offline.

In this section, you will use the first two methods: the browser and File Explorer. Later in this chapter, you will use sync to add a document to the library, as well.

You will now add a document to the library using a browser. In the following exercise, you will upload a new furniture description to the **Furniture** library.

PRACTICE FILES You will use the **OakDesk.docx** practice file, located in the **Chapter03** folder.

SET UP **Open the SharePoint site where you'd like to upload a file to a document library. If prompted, type your user name and password, and then click OK.**

1   On the **Quick Launch** pane, click the **Furniture** document library.

2   In the **Furniture** document library, in the body of the page, click the **new document** link. The **Add a Document** dialog appears.

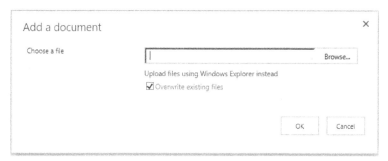

3   Click the **Browse** button.

TIP To upload multiple documents from the same location at the same time, click **Upload files using Windows Explorer instead**. In this exercise, you'll upload a single document.

4   In the **Choose File to Upload** dialog, browse to the file you would like to upload, such as **OakDesk.docx**, in the **Chapter03** folder. Select the file, and then click **Open**.

5   In the **Add a Document** dialog, click **OK** to confirm the upload, and then return to the **Furniture** library.

6   Validate that the **OakDesk** document has been uploaded and is listed in the **Furniture** library.

⊕ new document or drag files here

All Documents ••• | Find a file   🔍 |

✓ ☐ Name   Modified   Modified By

📄 OakDesk ✹   •••   A few seconds ago   ☐ Olga Kosterina

📄 OakMirror ✹   •••   7 hours ago   ☐ Olga Kosterina

✖ CLEAN UP **Leave the browser open if you are continuing to the next exercise.**

You can also drag a document—or a selection of multiple documents—to the library from the desktop or any other location via File Explorer. In the following exercise, you will drag a document to the **Furniture** document library.

PRACTICE FILES You will use the **OakChest.docx** practice file, located in the **Chapter03** folder.

➡ SET UP **Open the SharePoint site where you'd like to upload a file to a document library, if it is not already open. If prompted, type your user name and password, and then click OK.**

> **IMPORTANT** Verify that you have sufficient permissions to add a document to this library. If in doubt, see Appendix A.

1   On the **Quick Launch**, click the **Furniture** document library to open it, if it is not already open.

2   Open **File Explorer** and go to the **Chapter03** practice folder.

3   Position the **File Explorer** window next to the browser window, displaying the **Furniture** library, so that you can drag a file from the **File Explorer** to the browser.

4   In **File Explorer**, select the file OakChest.docx, and drag it to the **Furniture** library where it says **drag files here** in the body of the page in the browser.

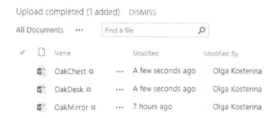

5   Validate that the **OakChest** document has been uploaded and is listed in the
Furniture library. Click **Dismiss** on the top of the documents list to dismiss the confirmation that an upload has been completed and one document has been added to
the library.

Upload completed (1 added)   DISMISS

All Documents   •••   [Find a file   🔍]

✓	📄	Name		Modified	Modified By
	📄	OakChest ✿	•••	A few seconds ago	Olga Kosterina
	📄	OakDesk ✿	•••	A few seconds ago	Olga Kosterina
	📄	OakMirror ✿	•••	7 hours ago	Olga Kosterina

✖ CLEAN UP **Leave the browser and File Explorer open if you are continuing to the
next exercise.**

Another way to add documents to the library is to copy and paste using **File Explorer**. This
way of uploading works well if you need to upload multiple documents. In the following
exercise, you will copy two documents to SharePoint library by using the **Explorer** view of
the **Furniture** document library.

PRACTICE FILES You will use the **OakEndTable.docx** and **OakNightStand.docx** files,
located in the **Chapter03** folder.

SET UP Open the SharePoint site where you'd like to upload files to a document library, if it is not already open. If prompted, type your user name and password, and then click OK.

> **IMPORTANT** Verify that you have sufficient permissions to add a document to this library. If in doubt, see Appendix A.

1 On the **Quick Launch**, click the **Furniture** document library to open its page, if it is not already open.

2 Click the **Library** tab on the top of the page to display the ribbon.

3 In the **Connect and Export** group, click **Open with Explorer**. The library content is displayed in File Explorer.

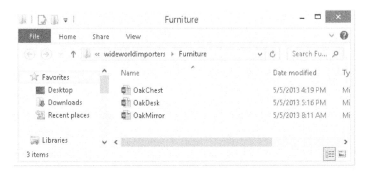

4 Open **File Explorer** and go to the folder where the documents that you wish to copy to the library are stored, such as the **Chapter03** folder, if it is not already open.

5 Select the files titled **OakNightStand.docx** and **OakEndTable.docx** by clicking the first file, and then holding down the **Ctrl** key and clicking the second file.

6 Right-click in **File Explorer** and select **Copy**, or press **Ctrl+C** on the keyboard.

TIP When you cut and paste, you are moving the file. When you copy and paste, or drag between **File Explorer** and the SharePoint library, you are copying the file.

7   Go to the **File Explorer** window with **Furniture** library. Right-click and select **Paste**, or press **Ctrl+V** on the keyboard, to add the files to the library.

8   In the browser where the **Furniture** library is displayed, refresh the page and verify that **OakNightStand.docx** and **OakEndTable.docx** are listed in the library.

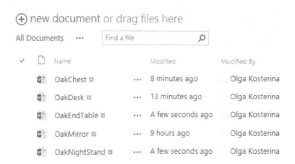

CLEAN UP **Exit the two File Explorer windows. Leave the browser open if you are continuing to the next exercise.**

Checking documents in and out from the document library

One of the features provided by SharePoint Server 2013 is document management. *Checking out* and *checking in* documents lets others know what documents you are working on so that they don't work on them at the same time. When using check-in, you can also enter comments about what you've changed, which others can then view.

When you check out a file, you lock the file for editing to prevent other users from editing the file at the same time. When you have finished editing the file, you check the file back in, allowing other users to edit the file.

In the following exercise, you will check out a document from a document library, and then check it back in and change the comments to reflect that this is the final version of the document.

SET UP **Open the SharePoint site from which you'd like to check in or check out a document, if it is not already open. If prompted, type your user name and password, and then click OK.**

1   On the **Quick Launch**, click **Furniture** to open the **Furniture** document library, if it is not already open.

2   Select a document that you would like to check out, such as **OakChest,** by clicking in its leftmost column.

3   On the top of the screen, click **Files** to display the ribbon, and then click **Check Out** in the **Open & Check Out** group on the ribbon.

     TIP Alternatively, you can check out the document using its callout. Click the ellipsis to the right of the document name to open the callout, click the ellipsis in the bottom right of the callout, and then select **Check Out** from the menu that appears.

4   The document has been checked out. The file icon has changed and shows a green, downward-pointing arrow, indicating that the document is now checked out. No one else can change this document and no one else can see your changes while you have it checked out.

     You will now check in the document.

5   In the browser window, select the **OakChest** document by clicking its leftmost column.

6   On the **Files** ribbon, click **Check In** in the **Open & Check Out** group.

     TIP Alternatively, you can check in the document using its callout. Click the ellipsis to the right of the document name to open the callout, click the ellipsis in the bottom right of the callout, and then select **Check In** from the menu.

7   In the **Check In** dialog that appears, in the **Comments** box, type **This is the final version of the document**.

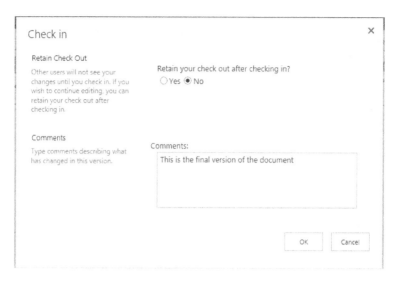

8   Click **OK** to check in the document and to return to the **Furniture** document library. The document has been checked in, and its icon no longer shows a green arrow.

CLEAN UP **Leave the browser open if you are continuing to the next exercise.**

Working with version history

When *versioning* is enabled, SharePoint Foundation 2010 creates a separate copy of the document each time it is edited. Although this takes up extra space on the server, it also makes it easy to revert to an older version of the document if necessary.

You can keep major versions only, or major and minor versions. Major versions are whole numbers such as 1, 2, 3, and so on. Minor versions are decimals such as 1.1, 1.2, 1.3, and so on. A major version number is associated with a version that has been published. A minor version number is associated with a version that is in progress but is not yet published.

SEE ALSO A more in-depth discussion of versioning is covered in Chapter 6.

When you view a document's version history, you see a list of the occasions when this document was edited and saved, as well as the author's comments on those changes.

In the following exercise, you will see the changes that have been made to the **OakChest. docx** document, and then revert to the final copy of the document.

SET UP **Open the SharePoint site where you'd like to see the version history of a document, if it is not already open. If prompted, type your user name and password, and then click OK.**

> **IMPORTANT** Verify that you have sufficient permissions to check out, modify, and check in a document in the document library. If in doubt, see Appendix A.

1 On the **Quick Launch**, click **Furniture** to open the Furniture document library, if it is not already open.

2 Select a document that you would like to see the version history for, such as **OakChest,** by clicking in its leftmost column.

3 On the **Files** ribbon, click **Version History** in the **Manage** group to display the **Version History** dialog that lists the versions saved for the **OakChest.docx** file. Each version of the saved document, the date and time that version was created, and any comments for the version appear.

> **TROUBLESHOOTING** If the **Version History** button on the ribbon is dimmed, it means that the versioning is disabled for this document library. To enable versioning, on the **Library** ribbon, click **Library Settings**, and then on the **Settings** page, under **General Settings**, select **Versioning settings**. On the **Versioning Settings** page, in the **Document Version History,** select **Create major versions**, and then click **OK**. To continue with this exercise, go back to the **Furniture** library, check out the **OakChest** document, and then check it in to create a second version.

> **TIP** Alternatively, you can display the **Version History** dialog for the document using its callout. Click the ellipsis to the right of the document name to open the callout, click the ellipsis in the bottom right of the callout, and then select **Version History** from the menu.

4   You will now restore an earlier version of the document. Move the mouse over the time stamp that identifies the earlier version of the document, and then click the arrow that appears to the right of the timestamp. On the menu that appears, click **Restore**.

5   The dialog box that appears indicates that you are about to replace the current version with the selected version. Click **OK**.

6   Note that there is a new version shown in the **Version History** dialog, which is a copy of an earlier version that you restored. If major versioning is enabled, then this is the latest version that is published on the site. Close the **Version History** dialog to return to the library page.

TIP If minor versioning is enabled, then there is now an additional, unpublished version. SharePoint 2013 actually copies the version that you want to restore and makes it the newest minor version. If you want to publish this version, you need to do so manually using the **Publish** button on the ribbon.

❌ CLEAN UP **Leave the browser open if you are continuing to the next exercise.**

Creating a new folder in a library or a list

Using folders provides a common way to organize documents in an efficient way. With SharePoint 2013, you can create folders in libraries and lists.

TIP SharePoint 2013 provides other mechanisms for the organization of your documents, including views and filters. However, people are often most familiar with folders, and thus find it easier to create a folder structure.

In this exercise, you will create a folder in the **Furniture** library for documents classified as **In Progress** so that they can be differentiated from completed documents.

SET UP Open the SharePoint site that you'd like to use to add a folder to a document library, if it is not already open. If prompted, type your user name and password, and then click **OK**.

> **IMPORTANT** Verify that you have sufficient permissions to create a folder in the document library. If in doubt, see Appendix A.

1   On the **Quick Launch**, click **Furniture** to open the **Furniture** document library, if it is not already open.

2   On the **Files** ribbon, click **New Folder** in the **New** group to display the **Create a new folder** dialog.

> **TIP** You can create a new folder in most lists in the same way by clicking **New Folder** in the **New** group on the **Items** ribbon. The list should be set up to allow the creation of folders. For example, this is a default setting for the **Links** list.

3   In the **Name** box, type the name of the folder you would like to create, such as **In Progress**.

4   Click **Save**. The **In Progress** folder has been created and is shown on the Furniture library page.

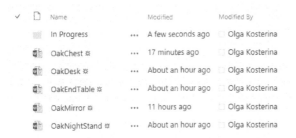

CLEAN UP Close the browser.

Adding, editing, and removing list and library columns

The list and library apps provided by SharePoint 2013 offer an easy way to generate a list or a library with very little effort. However, should you need to customize the lists and libraries views, with SharePoint 2013, you can add, edit, and remove existing list and library columns, as well as create additional columns using the **Settings** page for this list or library. In addition, for a list, you can add columns without leaving the list page.

There are many types of columns that can be added to the list or a library, including a single line of text, currency, the date and time, a **Yes/No** check box, a drop-down list of options, and others. You can remove a column from being displayed in a list or a library view, and most columns in the list or the library can be deleted. However, all lists have at least one column that cannot be deleted. For instance, the **Title** column can be renamed but not deleted. Certain lists also prevent the deletion of columns so that the list can display properly or integrate with Microsoft Office applications properly. For example, the **Assigned To**, **Status**, and **Category** columns of any list based on the Issues list app cannot be deleted, and all of the default columns in any list based on the Calendar list app cannot be deleted.

There are also columns that are automatically created and populated for each list item or document in a library that cannot be changed: **ID**, **Created**, **Created By**, **Modified**, and **Modified By**. The ID column ensures that the list item is unique in the list. It contains a sequential number beginning with 1 and increments by 1 for each new list item. SharePoint automatically captures when the list item was **Created**, who it was **Created By**, when it was last **Modified**, and who it was last **Modified By**. Initially, the **Created** and **Modified** columns are equal, as are the **Created By** and **Modified By** columns.

In the following exercise, you will use inline editing to create a column called **Sequence** of type **Number** in the **Common Buyer Tasks** list, which will be used to order tasks. You will then modify the default list view by adding, removing, and rearranging the existing columns.

 SET UP **Open the SharePoint site where you would like to modify a list, if it is not already open. The exercise will use the** *http://wideworldimporters* **site, but you can use whatever site you wish. If prompted, type your user name and password, and then click OK.**

1 On the **Quick Launch**, click **Common Buyer Tasks** to display the **Common Buyer Tasks** list in its default **All Tasks** view. On top of the list, click **edit** to switch to the datasheet view and display the list in a grid.

2 In the list header row, on top of the rightmost empty column, click the **plus sign** (+), and then select **Number** from the menu of column types that appears.

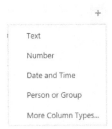

3 The new column has been created. It is named **Number** after its type, and the name is displayed highlighted and boxed, showing that you can rename the column. Position your cursor within the box and type **Sequence** to rename the column.

TIP You can rename a column in datasheet view at any time by clicking its name and selecting **Rename Column** from the menu that appears.

4 Fill in the new **Sequence** column with numbers from 1 to 5 to identify the preferred order of tasks in the list, as shown in the following table:

Title	Sequence
Create SharePoint list	2
Ensure vendor access	3
Identify products to purchase	1
Generate purchase orders	5
Notify Receiving about purchase	4

You may want to alter the tasks' **Due Dates** to any dates of your choosing to reflect the new order of tasks. Note that the new dates are immediately plotted on the timeline.

5   On the top of the list, at the right side of the line that displays links to the views and begins with **All Tasks**, click the ellipsis, and then select **Modify this View** from the menu that appears.

6   On the **Settings - Edit View** page, in the **Columns** section, explore the list of columns that are available for the list. Then, in the **Display** column, clear the check boxes for the **Assigned To** column and the **Due Date** column to remove them from the default list view. Select the **%Complete** column to display it in the default list view.

7   Scroll down to select the **Priority** column, and then change **Position from Left** to **3** so that it is displayed immediately to the left of the **Task Name** column in the list view page.

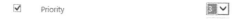

8   Scroll to the top or to the bottom of the page, and then click **OK** to confirm your changes and return to the list page. Validate that the list page in default view is set up in the way that you expected.

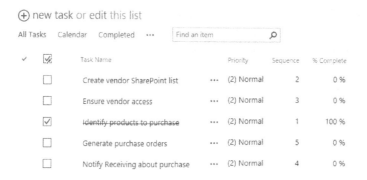

CLEAN UP **Leave the browser open if you are continuing to the next exercise.**

You will now work with the library columns. In the following exercise, you will change the default view for the **Furniture** library. You will add the **Version** column to display the document version and remove the **Modified By** column.

SET UP **Open the SharePoint site where you would like to modify a library view, if it is not already open. The exercise will use the** *http://wideworldimporters* **site, but you can use whatever site you wish. If prompted, type your user name and password, and then click OK.**

1 On the **Quick Launch**, click **Furniture** to display the **Furniture** document library in its default **All Documents** view.

2 On the top of the file list, to the right side of **All Documents**, click the ellipsis and select **Modify this View** from the menu that appears.

3 On the **Settings - Edit View** page, in the **Columns** section, explore the columns that are available for the document library and note that they are different from the columns available for a list that you explored in the previous exercise. Then, in the **Display** column, clear the check box for the **Modified By** column to remove it from the default library view, and then select the **Version** column to display it in the default list view.

Display	Column Name	Position from Left
☑	Type (icon linked to document)	1 ∨
☑	Name (linked to document with edit menu)	2 ∨
☑	Modified	3 ∨
☐	Modified By	4 ∨

4 Scroll to the top or to the bottom of the page, and then click **OK** to confirm your changes and return to the library page. Validate that the list page in default view is set up in the way that you expected.

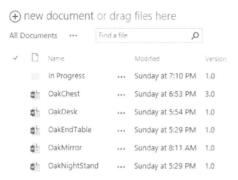

CLEAN UP **Leave the browser open if you are continuing to the next exercise.**

Sorting and filtering a list or a library

As a list or a library grows, it eventually becomes difficult to see the entire list or the entire library on a single page. To this end, SharePoint provides built-in sorting and filtering capabilities. On any standard list and library view page, individual column headers can be used to alphabetically sort the entire list by ascending or descending order.

Filtering the list and library pages works similarly to the way that an Excel AutoFilter works. Filtering is enabled on the top-right corner of every column, and a unique list of the values for each column is generated and presented as a drop-down list above that column. Filters are cumulative but temporal; the next time a list view is chosen, its settings, including filters, will be applied to the list regardless of what was previously chosen for a given column.

TIP In datasheet view, sorting and filtering are available from the drop-down arrow, which is also located in the top-right corner of every column.

SharePoint allows you to save the view that you have created by sorting and filtering a list or a library so that you can keep the sorting orders and filters, and come back to it again.

In this exercise, you will first sort and filter the **Common Buyer Tasks** list, and then sort the documents in the **Furniture** library in ascending order.

SET UP Open the SharePoint site where you would like to sort and filter the list and the library, if it is not already open. The exercise will use *the http://wideworldimport-ers* site, but you can use whatever site you wish. If prompted, type your user name and password, and then click **OK**.

> **IMPORTANT** Verify that you have sufficient permissions to sort and filter lists and libraries. If in doubt, see Appendix A.

1   On the **Quick Launch**, click **Common Buyer Tasks** to display the **Common Buyer Tasks** page.

2   On the list page, click the **Sequence** column heading. The list items are displayed in ascending numerical order sorted by this column, and a thin up arrow icon displays to the right of the column name, indicating that the list is sorted by this column in ascending order. Note the **Save This View** option that appears in the top right of the list.

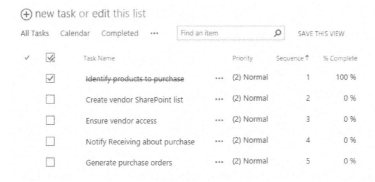

3   Click the **Sequence** column heading again. The list items are displayed in descending order, and a thin down arrow icon displays to the right of the column name.

> **TIP** Clicking another column will abandon the sort on the current column. You must use a datasheet view to sort more than one column.

4   Next, click **edit** on the top of the list to switch to the datasheet view. Change P**riority** to **(1) High** for **Ensure Vendor Access** and **Generate Purchase Order** list items by clicking within the **Priority** column for each list item and selecting **(1) High** from the drop-down list. When you've completed the changes in the Priority column, click **Stop** on the top of the list to return to the default list view.

5　Hover over the **Priority** column heading and click the down arrow that appears on the right to show the sorting and filtering options for this column. On the menu that appears, click **(1) High** for **Priority.**

6　Click **Close**. The page redisplays the filtered list with only those list items that are set to a high priority.

Note the **Filtered** icon (displaying to the right of the **Priority** column) that has an applied AutoFilter.

7　To display a full list, hover over the **Priority** column heading one more time, click the down arrow at the right to display a menu, and then click the **Clear Filters from Priority** option.

8　You will now sort the documents in the Furniture library, first in the ascending order, and then in the descending order. On the **Quick Launch**, click **Furniture** to display the **Furniture** library page.

9　On the library page, click the **Name** column heading. The documents are displayed in ascending alphabetical order, and a thin up arrow icon displays to the right of the column name, indicating that the documents are in ascending order. Click the **Name** column, heading again to sort the documents in descending order. Note that the thin arrow is now pointing downward to identify a descending sort order.

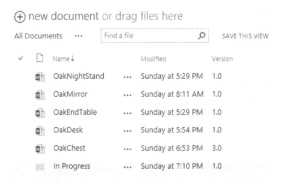

Deleting and restoring list items and documents

When documents, list items, folders, or even entire lists are deleted, they are simply flagged as removed so that they no longer appear in the site from which they were deleted. By default, sites in a SharePoint web application are configured to display the deleted item in the site's **Recycle Bin** for 30 days. The *Recycle Bin* provides a safety net when deleting documents, document sets, list items, lists, folders, and files. If the user hasn't restored the deleted item within that time, it is permanently expunged from the database. If the user empties his Recycle Bin before the 30 days have elapsed, the deleted item is still available to a site collection administrator from the site collection's **Recycle Bin**. However, the total size of the deleted items must remain below a given percentage (50%, by default) of the total size that a site is allowed to consume (the site quota). If a deleted item exceeds the configured size allowed by the SharePoint central administrator for sites in the web application, the items that were deleted first are purged, even if 30 days have not elapsed, to make room for the newly deleted item. In this way, SharePoint administrators can make disaster recovery plans based on the allowable total maximum size of the **Recycle Bin**. Of course, a SharePoint administrator can set the number of days that a Recycle Bin retains deleted items, ranging from the default 30 days to some other specific number of days, as well as to **Never retain deleted items** or to **Never remove deleted items**.

Todd suggests that creating the vendor SharePoint list is only done when a new vendor is established, rather than at each buying cycle. He therefore wants the task removed. He also wants to remove the **OakChest** document from the **Furniture** library. In the next part of the exercise, you will delete the **Create Vendor SharePoint list** task from the **Common Buyer Tasks** list, and the **OakChest** document from the **Furniture** library.

SET UP **If it is not already open, open the SharePoint site where you would like to delete an item from the list and a document from a library. The exercise will use the** *http://widewordimporters* **site, but you can use whatever site you wish. If prompted, type your user name and password, and then click OK.**

> **IMPORTANT** Verify that you have sufficient permissions to delete list items and documents. If in doubt, see Appendix A.

1   On the **Quick Launch**, click **Furniture** to display the **Furniture** library, if it is not already displayed.

2   Click the ellipsis to the right of the document that you'd like to delete, such as **OakChest**, to display the document callout, and then click the ellipsis in the bottom-left corner of the callout to display the menu.

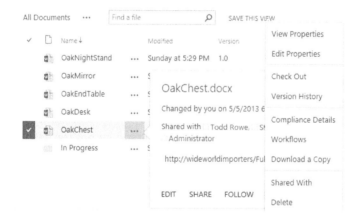

3   Click **Delete** in the callout menu. In the dialog that asks whether you are sure you want to send the item to the site's Recycle Bin, click **OK**. The document is removed from the library and placed into the site Recycle Bin.

4   On the **Quick Launch**, click the **Common Buyer Tasks** list.

5   Click the ellipsis to the right of the list item that you'd like to delete, such as **Create Vendor SharePoint list**, to display the list item callout, and then click the ellipsis in the bottom-left corner of the callout to display the menu.

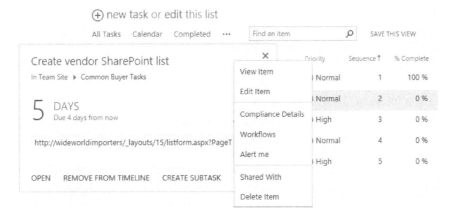

6   Click **Delete** on the callout menu, and then click **OK** to confirm the deletion.

Todd realizes that deleting the **Create Vendor SharePoint List** task and the **OakChest** document was a mistake. He visits the site **Recycle Bin** and restores the data.

7   On the **Quick Lunch**, click **Site Contents**, and then on the top right of the **Site Contents** page, click **Recycle Bin** to display the site **Recycle Bin** page.

8   Select the **Create vendor SharePoint list** item and the **OakChest** document by clicking the check boxes to their left.

9   On the top left of the list of deleted items, click **Restore Selection** to restore the selected items, and then click **OK** to confirm.

10   Using the **Quick Launch**, go to the **Common Buyer Tasks** list, and then go to the **Furniture** library to validate that the list item and the document have been restored to their respective original locations.

✖ CLEAN UP **Leave the browser open if you are continuing to the next exercise.**

Setting up alerts

SharePoint 2013 includes a handy feature that sends an email notification or a text message whenever changes are made to the content in a site, including changes made to list items in a list. The setup for this notification is called an *alert*. You can set up an alert for a list, a library, a folder, a file, or a list item. No alerts are set up automatically, so you must sign up for the alerts that you want. Alerts can be set up for different types of changes, so that you can learn about the changes that you are most interested in.

Alerts are quite easy to set up. Every list and library in a SharePoint 2013 site displays an **Alert Me** button in the **Share & Track** group on the ribbon. By clicking this option on a **List** or a **Library** ribbon, you can subscribe to an alert on a list or a library level. When you select an item in the list or a document in a library, the **Alert Me** button on the **Items** or **Files** ribbons, respectively, allows you to subscribe to the item-level or document-level alert. Alternatively, for a list item, you can select an **Alert Me** option in the callout.

TIP For email alerts to be available, the SharePoint central administrator must configure the outgoing email settings for your server. Similarly, for the text alerts to be available, the SharePoint Farm administrator must configure the SMS/MMS service settings. Both settings can be configured in SharePoint Central Administration. If these settings are not configured, the **Alert Me** button on the ribbon and the **Alert Me** option in the callout menu will not be available.

Alerts specify to whom the alert will be sent, the kind of changes for which the alert will be sent, and the frequency. By default, the alert is sent to the email address of the user setting up the alert. If no email address has been established for the authenticated user, an email prompt is generated in the **Send Alerts To** area. Once provided, the address will be remembered for subsequent subscriptions.

When setting up alerts, you have a choice as to the type of change for which you want an alert to be initiated. For example, list-level alerts offer subscriptions when **All Changes to Any List Item** are made or, alternatively, when **New Items Are Added Only**, **Existing Items Are Modified Only**, or **Items Are Deleted Only**. If you wish to see added and changed items, but not deleted items, you need to set up two alerts. List item–level alerts, on the other hand, are only fired when that item changes, because you can only set up this alert once the list item already exists, and a deletion is considered a change to the list item.

You must specify when to send alerts; the default is when anything changes. Different lists and libraries have different options available. For example, a document library has the following options:

- Anything changes
- Someone else changes a document
- Someone else changes a document created by me
- Someone else changes a document last modified by me

You must also specify the alert frequency. The following three choices exist for any type of alert:

- Send email immediately
- Send a daily summary
- Send a weekly summary

Choosing to receive an alert immediately actually queues the notice to be sent as soon as the next job runs once the alert is triggered. By default, the alert job runs every 5 minutes, but it could be configured by your administrator to wait as long as 59 minutes. The daily and weekly summaries store all changes made to the list or list item, and send a summary at the end of the period chosen. By default, daily summary alerts are generated at midnight each night, and weekly summary alerts are generated at midnight every Sunday night.

In this exercise, you will set up an alert for an item in the **Common Buyer Tasks** list.

IMPORTANT Your server has to be configured to send email messages; otherwise, you will not be able complete the steps in this exercise.

SET UP Open the SharePoint site where you would like to set up an alert, if it is not already open. The exercise will use the *http://wideworldimporters* site, but you can use whatever site you wish. If prompted, type your user name and password, and then click **OK**.

> **IMPORTANT** Verify that you have sufficient permissions to set up alerts. If in doubt, see Appendix A.

1   On the **Quick Launch**, click **Common Buyer Tasks** to display the **Common Buyer Tasks** list page, if it is not already displayed.

2   Select the **Generate purchase orders** task by clicking its leftmost column. Then click **Tasks** to display the ribbon, click the **Alert Me** button in the **Share & Track** group, and then select **Set alert on this item** from the drop-down list.

   Alternatively, click the ellipsis to the right of the list item you'd like to set an alert for, then click the ellipsis in the bottom-left corner of the callout that appears, and then select the **Alert Me** option from the callout menu.

3   In the **New Alert** dialog, scroll down to explore the options available. Leave the default options unchanged, and then click **OK**.

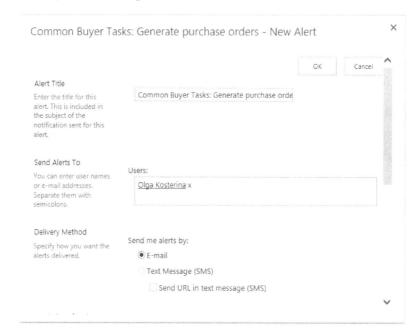

The email alert has been set. You will now modify the list item to trigger an alert.

4   On the top of the list, click **edit** to switch to the datasheet view, and then change the **Priority** for the **Generate purchase orders** task to **(2) Normal**. Then, on the top of the list, click **Stop editing** to switch back to the list default view.

5   Open your email application, such as Outlook 2013, and verify that you have received an email alert notifying you of a change in priority in this list item.

❌ CLEAN UP **Exit your email application. Leave the browser open if you are continuing to the next exercise.**

Following documents

SharePoint 2013 includes the ability to follow documents to track their updates in your newsfeed. Whereas *setting* an alert for document changes keeps you notified of specific changes on a predefined frequency via email or SMS, *following* a document adds a link to this document in your newsfeed and provides notifications of all document changes via your newsfeed. In addition, people who are following you will get a newsfeed notification that you're following this document, provided that they have appropriate permissions to access it. All documents that you follow are shown in one place in your newsfeed, in the list of followed documents.

In the following exercise, you will set a follow-up for the **OakDesk** document.

➡ SET UP **Open the SharePoint site where you would like to follow up a document. The exercise will use the *http://wideworldimporters* site, but you can use whatever site you wish. If prompted, type your user name and password, and then click OK.**

> **IMPORTANT** Verify that you have sufficient permissions to view the document that you'd like to follow. If in doubt, see Appendix A.

1   On the **Quick Launch**, click **Furniture** to display the **Furniture** library page.

2   Click the ellipsis to the right of the document, and then click **Follow** in the callout.

3   On the top right of the page, click **Newsfeed**.

4   On the right side of the **Newsfeed** page, under **I'm following**, click the number of documents to open your list of followed documents. Verify that the **OakDesk** document is listed under **Docs I'm following**.

TIP If the document is not shown, you may need to wait a few moments, and then refresh the page.

❌ CLEAN UP **Close the browser.**

Working offline

For mobile users, it's not always possible or convenient to connect to SharePoint every time they want to read or modify documents. SharePoint 2013 provides the ability to work with your documents offline. You can synchronize, or *sync*, a SharePoint library to your computer. This process creates a copy of the library on your computer in the SharePoint Libraries folder, under the name that combines the name of the source SharePoint site with the name of the source library, with a hyphen in between; for example, Team Site-Documents. You can modify the location to one of your choosing. You can then work with files in the library by using File Explorer. When working offline, you can view and modify the content in the same way that you do when working in SharePoint. Updates to the files synchronize back to SharePoint when you are back online. For example, if you create a new document in a library folder on your computer, it will be synced back into the source library when you are online.

TIP There are limits on the number and the size of files that you can sync. You can sync up to 5,000 items in a SharePoint library, including folders and files. You can download files up to 2 GB.

IMPORTANT To use sync, you must have Microsoft Office 2013 installed on your computer, or an Office 365 subscription that includes Office applications.

In the following exercise, you will sync a **Furniture** library to your computer.

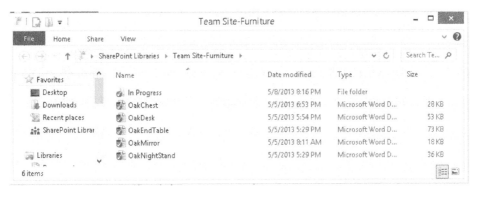

SET UP Open the SharePoint site from where you would like to sync a library to your computer. The exercise will use the *http://wideworldimporters* site, but you can use whatever site you wish. If prompted, type your user name and password, and then click **OK**.

> **IMPORTANT** Verify that you have sufficient permissions to sync the library. If in doubt, see Appendix A.

1   On the **Quick Launch**, click **Furniture** to display the **Furniture** library page.

2   Click **SYNC** in the top-right corner of the page.

3   In the dialog that appears, note that you can change the default location for the copy of the library on your computer. Leave it as default and click **Sync Now** to start synchronizing the library.

4   In the confirmation dialog, click **Show my files** to open your synced library folder in Files Explorer. The synced library folder is located in the **SharePoint Libraries** folder and is named **Team Site-Furniture**.

CLEAN UP Close the browser.

Key points

- Lists are like editable, web-based tables.

- Libraries provide a central location to store and share documents, forms, and pictures.

- List and library apps can be used to generate a new list or a new library with a specific set of features. SharePoint 2013 provides 20 list apps and 10 library apps.

- There are many ways to add existing documents to a document library, including via the browser or File Explorer, or using sync. You can drag files from your computer into the SharePoint library.

- Remember to check out a document before you edit it.

- You can use versioning to manage the history of your documents in SharePoint.

- You can create folders to organize content in list and libraries.

- With SharePoint 2013, you can add, edit, and delete the columns in any list or library.

- Column headings can be used to sort and filter lists and libraries.

- Deleted documents and list items can be restored from the site **Recycle Bin** to their original locations.

- You can set up an alert for a list, a library, a folder, a file, or a list item for notification via email or SMS about any changes. You can follow documents via your newsfeed.

- You can take documents in a SharePoint library offline by using sync.

Chapter at a glance

Edit
Edit a page, page 113

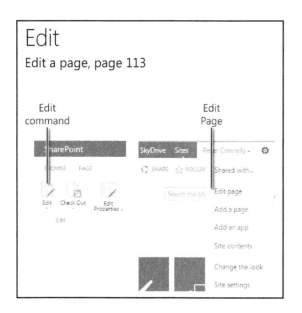

Change
Change the layout of a page, page 118

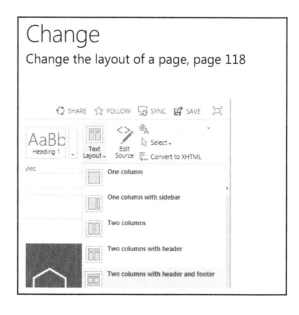

Create
Create a new page, page 119

Add
Add a Web Part from the Web Part pane, page 128

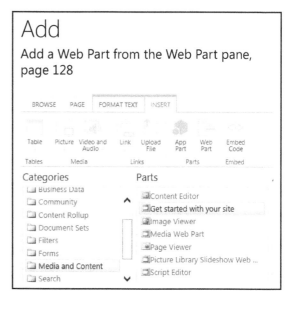

Working with webpages

4

IN THIS CHAPTER, YOU WILL LEARN HOW TO

- Edit and change the layout of wiki and publishing pages.

- Add links and use alerts.

- Create new wiki and publishing pages.

- Work with page history and versions.

- Add, move, and remove Web Parts and SharePoint app parts.

- Customize Web Parts and app parts by using the Web Part tool pane.

- Edit Web Part pages.

A website is a collection of webpages. The types of pages that you can create depend on the site that you have created. Most users will be familiar with Team sites within a Microsoft SharePoint 2013 installation or a Microsoft SharePoint Online environment. When you create a new Team site, SharePoint creates a wiki page library, named Site Pages, where the webpages are stored and new pages can be created. You will find it easy to add content to these pages and to modify the layout of the page using the browser. Wiki pages should be used when you wish to share content that does not require an approval mechanism and the site contains many content authors.

Web Content Management (WCM) sites are used for public-facing sites or for company portals, where content needs to go through a formal approval process. WCM pages, known as *publishing pages*, are created from publishing templates, known as *page layouts*. Once a publishing page is created, you can switch the layout of the page by choosing a different page layout.

SEE ALSO More information on WCM can be found in Chapter 15, "Working with content management."

Pages that display the contents of lists or libraries use *Web Part pages*. Such pages can be changed using the browser, but many users do not find the mechanism of changing such pages easy. Using the browser, these pages can only contain *app parts* and *Web Parts*. The addition of static text and images is possible only by adding Web Parts, such as the Content Editor Web Part (CEWP) or the Image Web Part. Web Part pages are still a popular choice for creating interactive dashboards or pages that aggregate information from several resources.

Both *wiki pages* and Web Part pages can contain app parts and Web Parts. Publishing pages may be able to contain Web Parts and SharePoint app parts; however, it depends on the page layout that you have chosen for the publishing page. These three types of pages are flexible and highly customizable using three types of tools:

- A browser

- A SharePoint Foundation–compatible webpage editing tool, such as Microsoft Share-Point Designer 2010 or Microsoft SharePoint Designer 2013

- A professional development tool such as Microsoft Visual Studio 2012

No one tool can do everything, and therefore it is likely that in any deployment of SharePoint, all three tools will be used at some point.

There is a fourth type of page, known as *application pages* or *system pages*. Examples of these pages include the List Settings and the Site Settings pages. Application pages cannot be changed using the browser or SharePoint Designer.

This chapter introduces the basic concepts of wiki pages, publishing pages, Web Part pages, app parts, and Web Parts. Using the browser, you will learn how to view wiki pages and Web Part pages in different ways, as well as how to change the appearance of these pages by adding and removing static text and images, and adding and removing app parts and Web Parts.

PRACTICE FILES Before you can complete the exercises in this chapter, you need to copy the book's practice files to your computer. The practice files you'll use in this chapter are in the **Chapter04** practice file folder. A complete list of practice files is provided in "Using the practice files" at the beginning of this book.

IMPORTANT Remember to use your SharePoint site location in place of *http://widewworldimporters* in the following exercises.

Editing a page

The first page you see on a SharePoint site is known as the *home page*, because as with any website, this is the page where all site visitors start. In your organization, the home page may be known as the welcome page, the default page, or the landing page. Home pages tend to aggregate information from elsewhere, and as you click links, you are directed to other pages that display content; for example, on a Team site, when you click **Documents** on the **Quick Launch**, you are taken to the default view of the Documents library. This is, by default, a Web Part page that dynamically changes as you upload, modify, and delete files in the Documents library.

On a Team site, Site Pages (the wiki library) inherits its permissions from the site. Therefore, anyone who is mapped to the Contribute permission level at the site level—that is, anyone who is a member of the site's Members SharePoint group—is allowed to change any wiki page or create new pages, which is known as *open editing*. If a page is found to be incomplete or poorly organized, any member of the site can edit it as he or she sees fit. Therefore, the content evolves as users share their information, knowledge, experience, ideas, and views. Site members can work together to change or update information without the need to send emails or attend meetings or conference calls. All users are allowed to control and check the content, because open editing relies on the assumption that most members of a collaboration site have good intentions.

When the content of a page is to be visited by most of the employees of your organization, and the content needs to be approved before an employee sees that content, then using a publishing site and publishing pages may be a better choice than a Team site and wiki pages. On publishing sites, most visitors to the site will not have Contribute permission level at the site level, and will not be able to edit pages.

TIP Publishing pages are stored in a library named Pages.

Many of your pages may contain static text and images that describe, for example, the company's expenses policy, and contain links to other pages with related information. The approach of thinking of your site as a number of pages is natural and in line with websites not based on SharePoint, where each site is a collection of webpages, and those webpages are interconnected.

You can edit a wiki page using one of the following three methods:

- On the **Page** tab, in the **Edit** group, click **Edit**.

- Click the **Settings** gear icon in the top-right corner, and then click **Edit Page**. When you use this method to open a wiki page in edit mode, the ribbon will not automatically display. To display the ribbon, you need to click the **Page** tab.

- To the far right of the tabs, click **Edit**. When the page is in edit mode, the word Edit is replaced with the word Save.

On Web Part and publishing pages, there is only one method for editing a page, which is the **Edit Page** command on the **Settings** menu.

TIP To the far right of the tabs is the **Focus On Content** icon (to the right of **Sync** and **Edit**). Use this icon to make the **Quick Launch** disappear when reading or editing a page.

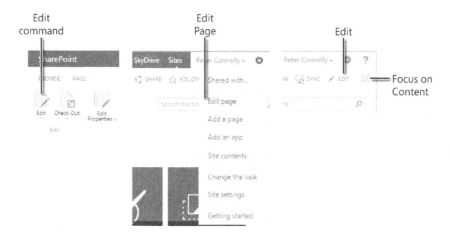

Below the ribbon are the status bar and the notification area, which provide you with contextual information. The status bar displays persistent information and uses four predefined background colors to identify the level of importance of the information. Very important information has a red background, important information has a yellow background, successful information has a green background, and all other information has a blue background. For example, when you check out a page, a notification message briefly appears below the ribbon and to the right, displaying the text "Page Checked Out." A yellow status bar also appears below the ribbon, stating that the page is checked out and editable. On the ribbon, the **Check Out** command in the **Edit** group is replaced with the **Check In** command.

TIP When you edit a page, you should always check it out before you modify the content. This is to prevent other users on your team from editing the page at the same time. On wiki pages and Web Part pages, you will need to use either the **Page** tab or the **Format Text** tab to check out the page. However, when you edit a publishing page, the page will automatically be checked out to you.

When you edit the default home page of a Team site, you're able to see that it consists of three content areas, where each content area contains a Web Part or an app part:

- **Get Started With Your Site** This Web Part displays a set of tiles with common Share-Point actions that you might like to complete on a new Team site. As you move your mouse over each title, a description of the task is displayed. You can remove this Web Part by clicking **Remove This**.

- **Site Feed** This Web Part displays a Facebook-like newsfeed on your site, also known as *microblogging conversations*. These conversations are stored in the MicroFeed list app.

- **Documents** This app part displays the contents of the **Documents** library app.

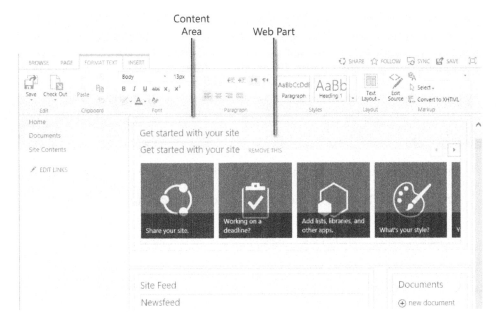

You might like to add static text to the content areas on the home page, stating the site's purpose and any assumptions that apply to the site's pages, as well as content that is stored in the site's list and libraries. When you edit an existing wiki page, you need not necessarily add new content to the top or the bottom of the page. You should emphasize the flow of ideas, be concise, write factual information, and stay on topic for the page. You should also check for spelling and grammatical errors that can detract from the content.

Publishing pages allow you to check spelling by clicking **Spelling** in the **Spelling** group on the **Format Text** tab. When you edit a wiki page, the **Format Text** tab does not contain this command; however, if you check out the page, when you check it back in, any misspellings are identified, with misspelled words underlined with a red squiggly line. You can then right-click the misspelled word to display suggested words, similar to the experience in Office programs. If you merely save the page, any misspelled words will not be identified.

Alternatively, you could enter the text in Microsoft Office Word first, check it for spelling and grammar using the **Spelling & Grammar** feature of Word, and then paste it into the Wiki Content area. When pasting contents from programs such as Word, by default, the content is added to the page as unformatted, semantically correct HTML markup. This is new in SharePoint 2013 and is known as *Paste Clean*. When you paste content from websites, the formatting from the copy or cut source is maintained.

In this exercise, you will edit the home page of a Team site.

➡ SET UP **Open the SharePoint Team site where you would like to edit the home page. If prompted, type your user name and password, and then click OK. This exercise uses the image file, pjcov.jpg, in the Chapter04 practice folder; you could use any image file.**

IMPORTANT Verify that you have sufficient rights to edit the home page of this site. If in doubt, see Appendix A, "SharePoint 2013 user permissions and permission levels."

1   On the **Page** tab, in the **Edit** group, click **Edit** to place the page in edit mode.

2   On the **Format Text** tab, in the **Edit** group, click **Check Out**.

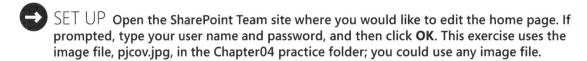

3   Place the cursor below the **Get started with our site** Web Part and type **Welcome to the Financial Team site**.

4   Press **Enter** to move the cursor to a new line, type **This website is used by members of the Wide World Importers Financial team and allows us to share content**, and then press **Enter** again.

5   Click to place the cursor to the left of **Welcome** and press **Shift+End** to select the whole line.

TIP You can use keyboard shortcuts, similar to the ones you can use in Office programs. You can find the keyboard shortcuts that map to the command on the ribbon by placing the cursor above the commands.

6   On the **Format Text** tab, in the **Styles** group, click **Heading 1** to format the line.

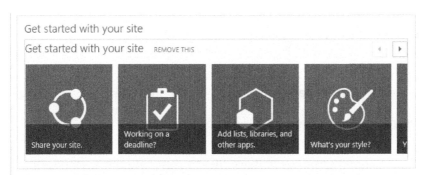

7   Place the cursor on the new line below **This website** and click the **Insert** tab.

8   Click **Picture** in the **Media** group, and then click **From Computer** to open the **Upload Image** dialog box.

9   Click **Browse** to go to the **Chapter04** practice file folder. Click **pjcov.jpg**, and then click **Open**.

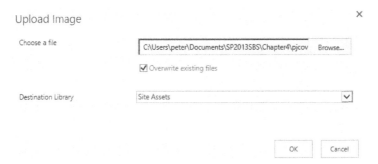

10 In the **Destination Library** drop-down list, keep the default, **Site Assets**, as the location where the image will be uploaded, and then click **OK**.

11 On the **Format Text** tab, in the **Edit** group, click **Check In**.

12 In the **Check In** dialog box, in the **Comments** box, type **Welcome message added to the page**, and then click **Continue** to save the page.

 CLEAN UP **Leave the browser open if you are continuing to the next exercise.**

Changing the layout of a page

The home page of a Team site contains three content areas. You can change the number of content areas that a wiki page contains using the **Format Text** tab.

In this exercise, you will change the layout of your page.

➡ SET UP **You don't need any practice files to complete this exercise. Open the Share-Point site that you used in the previous exercise, if it is not already open.**

> **IMPORTANT** Verify that you have sufficient rights to edit the home page of this site. If in doubt, see Appendix A.

1 Click the **Settings** gear icon, and then click **Edit page**.

2 On the **Format Text** tab, in the **Layout** group, click **Text Layout**, and then click **Two columns with header and footer**.

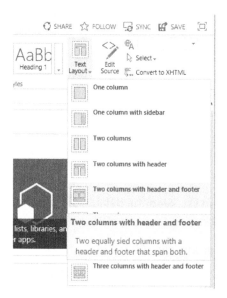

The page redisplays and now contains four content areas.

3   Select **Welcome to the Financial Team site**, the text you entered in the previous exercise. On the **Format Text** tab, in the **Clipboard** group, click **Cut**. If an Internet Explorer window appears, click **Allow access**.

4   Place the cursor in the bottom content area. On the **Format Text** tab, click the down arrow on the **Paste** command, and then click **Paste Plaintext**. If an Internet Explorer window appears, click **Allow access**.

5   On the **Format Text** tab, in the **Edit** group, click **Save**.

✖ CLEAN UP **Leave the browser open if you are continuing to the next exercise.**

Creating a new page

Typically, you add content to pages so that there are no more than two or three screens of information. This enables the information on the page to be in an easily accessible and modifiable format. There are four methods that you can use to create a new page in a wiki page library:

- Create a forward link, also known as a wiki link, denoted by a dotted underline, and then click the link. This is the recommended method because it is easier for people to find a page when another page is linked to it. To create a wiki link, type the name of the page within two sets of double square brackets.

- The **Add A Page** command on the **Settings** gear icon menu.

- The **New Wiki Page** link on the default view of the **Site Pages** library.

- The **New Document** command on the **Files** tab of the **Site Pages** library.

TIP When you add content to a wiki page and suggest a topic that other contributors to the Team site may know the answer to, try to enter text on the page in the form of a forward link; that is, place text between double square brackets. Other contributors to the page can enter information by clicking the forward link and creating new pages.

In this exercise, you will create wiki pages using these four methods.

➜ SET UP **You don't need any practice files to complete this exercise. Open the Share-Point site that you used in the previous exercise, if it is not already open.**

1   Click **Edit**, which is displayed to the far right of the **Browse** tab. In the bottom content area, create a new line under **Welcome**, and then type **WideWorldImporters are specialist importers of unique furniture (**[[to display a list of pages that exist in the Site Pages wiki library.

2   Type **B** to display a message stating that the Item does not exist (that is, there is no page in the Site Pages library with a name starting with the letter B).

3   Type **edRoom]], [[OfficeFurniture]] and [[GardenFurniture]]**) to create three wiki links, and then press **Enter**.

4   Click **Save**.

TIP The naming convention for wiki pages, known as *WikiWords* or *WikiNames*, is to concatenate two or more words. Each word is composed of two or more letters, with no spaces between words. The first letter of each word is capitalized and the remaining letters are lowercase. This formatting is known as *camel case*. The wiki page name is used to form part of the Uniform Resource Locator (URL).

5   Click **BedRoom**.

> Add a page   ×
>
> The page 'BedRoom' does not exist. Do you want to create it?
> Find it at http://intranet.wideworldimporters.com/sites/IT/SitePages/BedRoom.aspx
>
>   Create   Cancel

6   On the **Add a page** dialog box, click **Create** to display the BedRoom page.

7   Click the **Settings** gear icon, and then click **Add a page**.

8   In the **New page name** box, type **KitchenFurniture**, and then click **Create**.

9   On the **Page** tab, in the **Page Library** group, click **View All Pages** to display the **Site Pages** library.

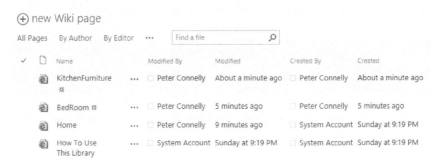

10 Click **new Wiki page** to display the **New Item** page. In the **Name page name** box, type **Seating**. Click **Create**.

11 Repeat step 9 to go to the Site Pages library. On the **Files** tab, click the **New Document** down arrow, and then click **Wiki Page**.

12 In the **New page name** text box, type **FloorCoverings**, and then click **Create**.

❌ CLEAN UP   **Leave the browser open if you are continuing to the next exercise.**

Adding links

In the previous section, you created a forward link to a page yet to be created by enclosing the name of the page in double square brackets. You can use a similar method to create a link to a page and have the link display text that is different from the page name.

TIP On a page that is not a wiki page, forward links to nonexistent pages are also known as *broken links*.

In this exercise, you will add a forward link, and then you will use the Incoming Links feature to identify those pages that link to a wiki page before you delete the page.

 SET UP **You don't need any practice files to complete this exercise. Open the Share-Point site that you used in the previous exercise, if it is not already open. Be sure to complete the previous exercises in this chapter before beginning this exercise.**

IMPORTANT Verify that you have sufficient rights to edit the home page in this site. If in doubt, see Appendix A.

1   On the **Quick Launch**, click **Site Contents**, and then click **Site Pages.** In the **Name** column, click **Home**.

2   Click **Edit**, which is displayed to the far right of the **Browse** tab.

3   Place the cursor on a new line below **WideWorldImporters**. Type [[s. Press **Tab** to select **Seating**, and then type | **Seating Furniture]]**.

   TIP To display double open or closed square brackets without making a link, type a backslash before the two brackets, such as \[[or \]].

4   Click **Save** to create a forward link pointing to the existing **Seating** page that you created in the previous exercise.

5   To display the **Seating** page, click **Seating Furniture**.

6   On the **Page** tab, in the **Page Actions** group, click **Incoming Links** to display pages that link to the **Seating** page.

Seating › Incoming Links

The following pages link to this page:
Home

7   Click **Home**, and then click **Edit**.

8   In the content area, select **[[Seating|Seating Furniture]]**, press **Delete**, and then click **Save**.

9   On the **Page** tab, click **View All Pages**, and then click to the left of **Seating**.

10 On the **Files** tab, in the **Manage** group, click **Delete Document**.

11 Click **OK** to send the page to the Recycle Bin.

IMPORTANT If you do not delete the forward links to a page before you delete the page, the forward links are displayed with a dashed underline, identifying them as forward links to a nonexistent page; that is, a page that has yet to be created.

❌ CLEAN UP **Leave the browser open if you are continuing to the next exercise.**

Working with page history and versions

A wiki library has all the features of a document library, such as history and version management. Therefore, no amendments are lost. Major versioning is turned on by default when you create a wiki page library. You can also use content approval and workflow, as well as restrict the rights as to who can publish and edit pages.

You can manage page versions using the **Page History** page, which displays the static contents and images of the page, where deletions have a strikethrough font. In the left navigation pane of the **Page History** page, each version of the page is listed with the date and time that the version was created. You can use this list to compare one version of the page with another version of the page. You can also use the **Page History** page to delete a version, restore a version, or to go to the **Version History** page, which displays the static content and images for all versions.

TIP The content of Web Parts or app parts are not displayed on the Page History or Version History pages.

When you restore a previous version of a page, a yellow status bar appears, stating that the current page has been customized from its template. This message can also appear when using a program such as SharePoint Designer 2013. If you have only restored the page to a previous version, you should click **Revert To Template**; otherwise, you should contact the person who may have used SharePoint Designer to edit the page.

SEE ALSO To learn more about customized pages, see Chapter 9, "Creating and formatting content pages," in *Microsoft SharePoint 2013 Inside Out* by Darvish Shadravan, Penelope Coventry, Thomas Resing, and Christina Wheeler (Microsoft Press, 2013).

In the following exercise, you will view the history of a page, observe the changes to the page, and then revert to the previous copy of the page.

 SET UP **Open the SharePoint site that you used in the previous exercise, if it is not already open. Be sure to complete the previous exercises in this chapter before beginning this exercise.**

IMPORTANT Verify that you have sufficient rights to manage pages in this site. If in doubt, see Appendix A.

1   On the **Page** tab, in the **Manage** group, click **Page History**.

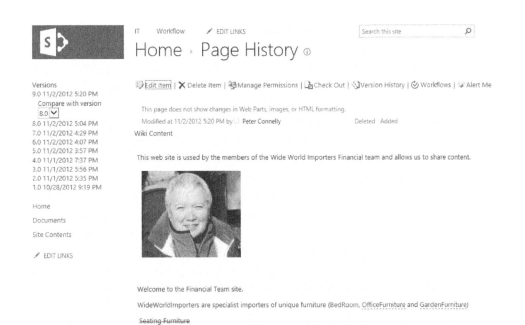

2 In the left navigation pane, in the **Compare with version** drop-down list, select **4.0** to compare the current version of the page with the 4.0 version.

3 In the left navigation pane, under **Versions**, click **4.0** to display the fourth version of the page, and then click **Restore this version**.

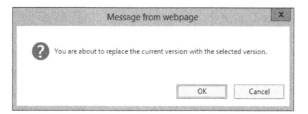

4 Click **OK** to replace the current version of the wiki page with the selected version.

5 On the status bar, click **Revert to template**.

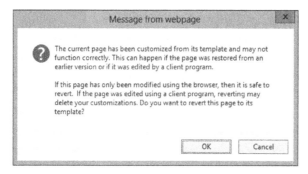

6 Click **OK** to revert the page to its template.

✕ CLEAN UP Leave the browser open if you are continuing to the next exercise.

Using alerts

One of the most difficult obstacles encountered in the business world is knowing when information changes. SharePoint can help with this problem by enabling you to subscribe to an alert. When a webpage to which you subscribe undergoes changes, you receive an email message stating that the page has changed.

In the following exercise, you will set up an alert for a page, and then receive an alert that it has been changed. You will then remove the alert.

SET UP **Open the SharePoint site that you used in the previous exercise, if it is not already open.**

> **IMPORTANT** Verify that you have sufficient rights to create alerts and edit the home page in this site. If in doubt, see Appendix A.

1　On the **Page** tab, in the **Share & Track** group, click **Alert Me**, and then in the drop-down list, click **Set an alert on this page** to display the **New Alert** dialog box.

2　Retain the default values for this exercise and click **OK**.

> **TROUBLESHOOTING** If your server is not configured to send an email message, an Error page will appear. If this page appears, you cannot complete the rest of the steps in this section. Check with your server administrator before you proceed.

3　Click **Edit**, which is displayed to the far right of the **Browse** tab.

4　Place the cursor in the content area to the left of the **Welcome** pane, press **Ctrl+A** to select all the content in the top area, and then press **Delete**.

> **TIP** Other keyboard shortcuts can be found by placing the cursor over the ribbon commands on the **Format Text** tab.

5　Click **Save**.

6　Check your email for two new email messages. One message indicates that an alert was successfully created, and another message indicates that home.aspx has been modified.

7　On the **Page** tab, in the **Share & Track** group, click **Alert Me**, and then in the drop-down list, click **Manage My Alerts** to display the **My Alerts on this Site** page.

My Alerts on this Site ⓘ

📧 Add Alert | ✖ Delete Selected Alerts

Alert Title

Frequency: Immediate   Delivery Method(s)

☐　Site Pages: Home.aspx   E-mail

8   Select the check box to the left of **Site Pages:Home.aspx**, and then click **Delete Selected Alerts**.

9   Click **OK** to confirm the deletion of the selected alerts.

❌ CLEAN UP **Leave the browser open if you are continuing to the next exercise.**

Adding app parts and Web Parts to your page

As you customize your site, you might decide to add information other than static text and images. This information may be stored in lists or libraries, or in some other data source. You can do this by adding components such as video, audio, app parts, and Web Parts. You can insert these components on multiple pages, as well as insert them multiple times on the same webpage.

App parts display the contents of list and library apps; each time that data in the list or library apps changes, the changes are reflected in the app part. App parts can also be used to display information from SharePoint apps, which are similar to the apps that you might use with Facebook or LinkedIn, or on your Android phone or iPhone. You can add SharePoint apps to your site from either your organization's app catalog or from the Microsoft SharePoint Store. For example, you may want to show on your home page the weather forecast for your office location. You could search the SharePoint Store for a weather app, which you would add to your site. You could then add to your page the app part that came with the weather app, and configure it to show the weather at your office location.

SEE ALSO Information on how to add an app to your site can be found in Chapter 3, "Working with documents and information in lists and libraries."

Web Parts are used to expose built-in SharePoint functionality, such as displaying in the browser, content from a Microsoft Office Excel workbook, or Microsoft PerformancePoint reports and scorecards.

TIP In addition to built-in list and library app parts and Web Parts, app parts and Web Parts can be created by using tools such as Visual Studio 2012. You can also import custom Web Parts.

SharePoint provides built-in app parts and Web Parts for each website created. Adding an app part is similar to adding a Web Part to the page. You will commonly add app parts and Web Parts via the browser, although you can also add them using a tool, such as SharePoint Designer.

The app parts and Web Parts that you can add to your page are listed in a **Parts** pane. When you want to add a Web Part to a page, the **Parts** pane displays the Web Parts in categories so that you can quickly find the Web Part that you want. The Web Parts listed in the **Parts** pane act like templates, and once a Web Part is placed on a page, it can be uniquely customized; but the template from which the Web Part is created remains in the category displayed in the **Web Parts** pane.

TIP You can add the Media Web Part to a page by using the **Video And Audio** command on the **Insert** tab in the **Media** group. This is quicker than using the **Parts** pane. By using the ribbon command, you can add the Media Web Part to the page, upload the media file, and configure the Web Part properties in one action.

The built-in categories and the Web Parts available in each category are summarized in Table 4-1. Not all app parts and Web Parts are available on all pages or sites.

Table 4-1 Web Part categories

Category	Description
Apps	This category displays app parts. The number of app parts in this category depends on the number of apps installed on your site. You will have one app part for each list or library that is created. Other app parts may be available that have been added from your organization's app catalog or from the SharePoint Store.
Blog	This category contains three Web Parts—Blog Archives, Blog Notifications, and Blog Tools—that you can use to help display and manage your blog posts.
Business Data	This category contains six Business Data Connectivity (BCS)–related Web Parts, as well as the Excel Web Access, Indicator Details, Status List, and Visio Web Access Web Parts. These Web Parts are primarily used to display content that is not stored within SharePoint lists and libraries. These Web Parts are only available with the Enterprise edition of Microsoft SharePoint Server.
Community	This is a new category with SharePoint 2013 and contains Web Parts that work with the Community Features, such as those used on the Community Site. More information on Community Site can be found in Chapter 5, "Creating and managing sites," and Chapter 7, "Getting social." The Web Parts in this category are About This Community, Join, My Membership, Tools, and What's Happening. SharePoint Foundation does not contain the Community Features, and therefore does not contain this Web Part category.

Category	Description
Content Rollup	Use these Web Parts to aggregate or summarize data stored both within the current site and from other sites. The Web Parts in this category include Categories, Content Query, Content Search, Project Summary, Relevant Documents, RSS Viewer, Site Aggregator, Sites In Category, Summary Links, Table Of Contents, Term Property, Timeline, WSRP Viewer, and XML Viewer. In SharePoint Foundation, only the Relevant Documents, Timeline, and XML Viewer Web Parts are available in this category.
Document Sets	Use these Web Parts—Document Set Contents and Document Set Properties—to display the contents or properties of a Document Set. The Web Parts in this category are only available in SharePoint Server.
Filter	Use these Web Parts to filter the contents of other Web Parts on the page. The Web Parts in this category include Apply Filters Button, Choice Filter, Current User Filter, Date Filter, Page Field Filter, Query String (URL) Filter, SharePoint List Filter, SQL Server Analysis Services Filter, and Text Filter. The Web Parts in this category are only available in SharePoint Server.
Forms	Use these Web Parts to display HTML or InfoPath forms. You can also use the HTML Form Web Part if you want to send data to another Web Part via a Web Part connection. The content displayed in the other Web Part depends on the data that it receives. The HTML Form Web Part is the only Web Part available in this category if you are using SharePoint Foundation.
Media and Content	Use these Web Parts to add content to a Web Part page. This category includes the Content Editor Web Part (CEWP), which is useful on Web Part pages to add formatted text, tables, and images. Other Web Parts in this category include Get Started With Your Site, Image Viewer, Page Viewer, Picture Library Slideshow Web Part, Script Editor, and the Silverlight Web Part. For example, the Media Web Part allows you to embed media clips (video and audio) in a webpage.
PerformancePoint	Use these Web Parts with PerformancePoint Services. These Web Parts are only available with the Enterprise edition of SharePoint Server and consist of the Web Parts, PerformancePoint Filter, PerformancePoint Report, PerformancePoint Scorecard, and PerformancePoint Stack Selector.
Search	Use these Web Parts with the Search service. The Web Parts in this category include Refinement, Search Box, Search Navigation, and Search Results. If you are using SharePoint Server, the Taxonomy Refinement Panel Web Part is also available.

Category	Description
Search-Driven Content	Use the Web Parts in this category to return content as the results of a search query. The Web Parts in this category include Catalog-Item Reuse, Items Matching A Tag, Pages, Pictures, Popular Items, Recently Changed Items, Recommended Items, Video, Web Pages, and Wiki Pages. For example, if you place the Wiki Page Web Part on a page, it will show any files from the current site derived from the Wiki Page content type. All wiki pages that you create are derived from this content type. You can change the search criteria of the Web Part to show wiki pages from another site or list. These Web Parts are only available with SharePoint Server.
Social Collaboration	Use these Web parts to display social content. The Web Parts in this category include Contact Details, Note Board, Organization Browser, Site Feed, Site Users, Tag Cloud, and User Tasks. The Site Users Web Part, for example, displays a list of the site users and their online status, and the User Tasks Web Part displays tasks that are assigned to the current user. In SharePoint Foundation, this category contains the Site Users and User Tasks Web Parts.
SQL Server Reporting	Use this Web Part to view Microsoft SQL Server Reporting Services reports.

TROUBLESHOOTING The Web Analytics Web Part that was available in SharePoint 2010 is not supported in SharePoint 2013. If your site has been upgraded to SharePoint 2013 from SharePoint 2010, then no instances of the Web Analytics Web Part will function. You will be able to see the page that includes an Analytics Web Part in the browser; however, a message appears stating that the Web Part is no longer supported. The next section details how to remove a Web Part from a page.

In this exercise, you will customize the home page of a SharePoint site. You will add an app part and two Web Parts.

 SET UP **Open a SharePoint site that contains a list with data. This exercise uses a media file, wildlife.wmv, in the Chapter04 practice folder; you could use any media file. Also, this exercise uses the Site Assets library; you could use any list or library.**

IMPORTANT Verify that you have sufficient rights to edit the home page in this site. If in doubt, see Appendix A.

1   Click **Edit**. Click to place the cursor in the upper content area, if it is not already there, and then click the **Insert** tab. In the **Parts** group, click **App Part** to display the **Parts** pane.

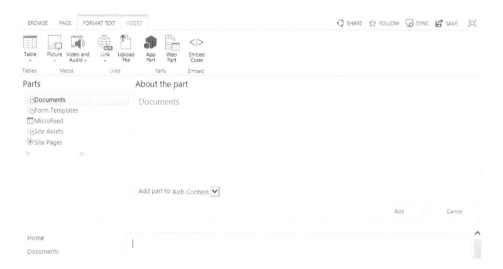

2. In the **Parts** pane, click the list or library app that contains data, such as the **Site Assets** library app, and then click **Add** to add the app part to your page.

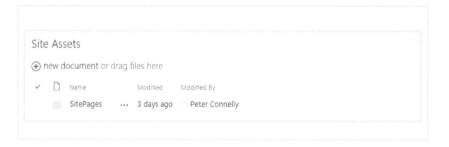

3. Place the cursor in the upper content area, if it is not already there. On the **Insert** tab, click **Web Part** to display the **Web Parts** pane.

4. Under **Categories**, click **Media and Content**, and then under **Parts**, click **Get started with your site**.

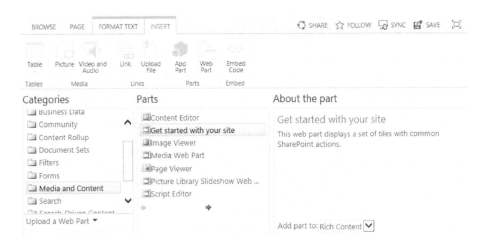

5   Click **Add** to add the Web Part to the page.

6   On the **Insert** tab, in the **Media** group, click **Video and Audio**. Click **From Computer**.

7   In the **Upload Media** dialog box, click **Browse** to go to the **Chapter04** practice file folder. Click **Wildlife.wmv**, and then click **Open**.

8   In the **Destination Library** list, keep the default, **Site Assets**, as the location where the image will be uploaded, and then click **OK**.

> **TIP** On a wiki page, you can use embedded HTML code to play audio and video that is not stored in SharePoint. The **Insert** tab contains two commands: the **Embed** command on the **Video and Audio** split button and **Embed Code**. These commands allow you to embed external sources like Bing Maps, Vimeo videos, YouTube videos, and other resources. A site collection administrator can prevent users from using these commands. On a Web Part page, you would need to use the HTML Form Web Part to embed the HTML code to play audio and video that is not stored in SharePoint.

9   Click **Save**.

✖ CLEAN UP **Leave the browser open if you are continuing to the next exercise.**

Removing a Web Part

When created, SharePoint sites can contain a number of apps, and one or more webpages that can contain one or more app parts or Web Parts. As you customize your site, you might decide that you do not need all the app parts or Web Parts on your pages, and you might want to remove them.

You can delete an app part or Web Part to permanently remove it from the page. Some app parts or Web Parts allow you to close them. You can liken closing an app part or Web Part to sending them to a Recycle Bin.

Closed app parts or Web Parts can be found in the **Parts** pane in the **Closed Parts** category, which is displayed only when your page contains closed Web Parts. Unlike Web Parts in other categories, Web Parts in the **Closed Parts** categories cannot be likened to templates, but are Web Parts that have previously been added to a page and whose properties you may have modified. When you add a Web Part to a page from the **Closed Parts** category, the Web Part is removed from the **Closed Parts** category. Having closed Web Parts on a page can cause the browser to take some time to display the page, which can be very annoying to users who frequently visit the page.

App parts and Web Parts can be badly written. If they are not tested thoroughly, you might find that when using a browser, a webpage does not display when you add an app part or Web Part to it. In such situations, append *?Contents=1* to the URL of the Web Part page, such as *http://wideworldimporters/SitePages/home.aspx?Contents=1*. The Web Part Page Maintenance page is displayed, which can be used to delete the offending Web Part.

Home › Web Part Page Maintenance ⓘ

Close | Reset | Delete | Go Back to Web Part Page | Switch to personal view

☐ Select All

Web Part Title	Type	Open on Page?
☐ Site Feed	SiteFeedWebPart	Yes
☐ Documents	XsltListViewWebPart	Yes
☐ Picture Library Slideshow Web Part	PictureLibrarySlideshowWebPart	Yes
☐ Site Assets	XsltListViewWebPart	No

Caution: You are modifying this Web Part Page for all users.

If you do not wish to delete the offending Web Part that is causing the webpage not to render in the browser, but you just want to change one of its properties, then you need to use a tool similar to SharePoint Designer to amend the Web Part property. The Web Part Page Maintenance page can be very useful in determining whether a page has any closed Web Parts, and it can be used to delete any closed Web Parts quickly.

In this exercise, you will delete a Web Part to remove it from a website's home page.

 SET UP **Open a SharePoint Team site.**

> **IMPORTANT** Verify that you have sufficient rights to edit the home page in this site. If in doubt, see Appendix A.

1   Click **Edit**. In the middle-left content area, hover the mouse over the title of the **Site Feed** app part and select the **Select or deselect Site Feed Web Part** check box that appears.

2   On the **Web Part** tab, in the **State** group, click **Delete**.

3   Click **OK** to confirm that you wish to delete the Web Part permanently, and then click **Save**.

⊗ CLEAN UP **Leave the browser open if you are continuing to the next exercise.**

Customizing app parts and Web Parts

Once you add an app part or a Web Part to a page, you might find that you have to customize it to display the content that you want visitors to your website to see. You might also have to tailor the properties for it to take on the design that you want.

In the following exercise, you will customize the Media Web Part and an app part.

➔ SET UP **Open the SharePoint site that you used in the previous exercise, if it is not already open. Be sure to complete the previous exercise in this chapter before beginning this exercise.**

IMPORTANT Verify that you have sufficient rights to edit the home page in this site. If in doubt, see Appendix A.

1   On the **Page** tab, click **Edit**, and then click the title bar of the **Media Web Part** to display the **Media** tab.

2   In the **Properties** group, select the **Start media automatically** check box.

3   In the **Player Styles** group, click **Styles**, and then click **Light**.

4   On the **Web Part** tab, in the **Properties** group, click **Web Part Properties**.

5   In the **Media Web Part** tool pane, in the **Chrome Type** drop-down list, click **Title and Border**, and then scroll to the bottom of the **Web Part** tool pane and click **OK**.

TIP The **Web Part** tool pane is always displayed immediately under the ribbon to the right of the page. You may need to scroll up the page and scroll to the right to see it.

6   Place the cursor over the title bar of the **Site Assets** Web Part, click the down arrow that appears, and click **Edit Web Part** to display the **Site Assets** Web Part tool pane.

7   In the **Site Assets** tool pane, below the Selected View list, click **Edit the current view**.

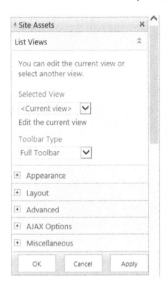

8   Click **OK** to save the page.

9   On the **Edit View** page, in the **Columns** area, clear the **Modified** and **Modified By** check boxes.

10 At the bottom of the page, click **OK** to save your settings and to return to the home page.

11 Click **Edit**. Click the title bar of the **Site Assets** Web Part, and then click the **Web Part** tab.

12 Click **Web Part Properties** to display the **Site Assets** tool page.

13 Click the **expand (+)** icon to the left of Appearance, and then type **Image and Video files** in the **Title** text box.

14 Click the **expand (+)** icon to the left of Advanced, and then clear the **Allow Minimize** check box.

15 At the bottom of the **Site Assets** tool pane, click **OK**.

16 Click the title bar of the **Image and Video files** Web Part, and then click the **Web Part** tab. Notice that the Minimize command is inactive.

✖ CLEAN UP **Save the page, but leave the browser open if you are continuing to the next exercise.**

Editing Web Part pages

When you go to a list or library, the default view is displayed. You can create other views of the information stored in lists and libraries. The type of pages used for views are Web Part pages, as well as the default pages on other sites, such as a blog site. Web Part pages consist of only Web Part zones. They do not contain wiki page content areas, and therefore can contain only Web Parts. To add static text or images to a Web Part page, you must first add either the Content Editor Web Part, or the Image Web Part, and then use the **Web Part** tool pane properties to add text or images.

TIP Using a tool such as SharePoint Designer, you can add Web Parts outside of Web Part zones on a Web Part page.

There are two versions of a Web Part page:

- **Shared version** This version is the Web Part page that every user with the appropriate permissions on a site can view. To edit the Shared version of a Web Part page, place the page in edit mode by using the **Settings** gear icon, and then click **Edit Page**.

- **Personal version** This version of a Web Part page is available only to you and not to others. To edit the Personal version of a Web Part page, click the down arrow to the right of your name in the top corner of the page, and then click **Personalize This Page**. When you have a personal view of a Web Part page, it will be displayed by default when you first visit the page. When you edit the Personal version of a page, a yellow status bar appears, stating that this is the Personal version of the page and that any changes that you make to the Web Part page affect only your view of this webpage.

TIP When a Web Part page is not in edit mode, there is no visible indication as to whether the page shows the Shared version or the Personal version. If the **Show Personal View** option is displayed on the *your name* drop-down list, you are viewing the Shared version of the page. If the **Show Shared View** option appears, you are viewing the Personal version of the page. You can remove the Personal version of the page by clicking **Reset Page Content** on the *your name* drop-down list. The Shared version of the page is your default version. As an administrator or web designer, you cannot customize the personal views of specific users; you can customize only the shared view and your own personal view.

To customize the Shared version of any Web Part page for a list or library, you must have the following rights, all of which are included in the Design and Full Control permission levels by default:

- Manage Lists
- Add And Customize Pages
- Apply Themes And Borders
- Apply Style Sheets

A member of a website's Site Owners group has Full Control permissions, and therefore is able to customize the Shared version of Web Part pages.

To customize the Personal View of any Web Part page, the Web Part page must be designed to be personalized. You must have the following rights, all of which are included in the Contribute, Design, and Full Control permission levels by default:

- Manage Personal Views
- Add/Remove Personal Web Parts
- Update Personal Web Parts

A member of a website's Members group has Contribute permissions, and therefore is able to customize the Personal version of Web Part pages, if they are designed to be personalized.

TIP When a Web Part page is designed to be personalized, editors of the page can disable the personalization of Web Parts on an individual basis by configuring the Web Part properties in the **Web Part** tool pane.

Web Parts within Web Part zones can be connected to one another to provide interactive dashboards displaying related data from a number of data sources. A ribbon command in SharePoint makes it easy to create a Web Part connection when two lists have a related column. For example, on a blog site, the Posts list has a lookup column to the Comments list. On a page where the Blog Posts Web Part is displayed, click the title of the Blog Posts Web Part. On the Web Part tab, click **Insert Related List**, and then click **Comments**. This will add the Comments XLV Web Part to the page and connect the two Web Parts. When a user clicks a blog post in the Posts Web Part, the comments related to that post will be shown in the Comments Web Part. Using a tool such as SharePoint Designer, you can also connect Web Parts on one page with Web Parts on another page.

SEE ALSO For more information on connecting Web Parts, see Chapter 10, "Adding, editing, connecting, and maintaining web parts," in *Microsoft SharePoint 2013 Inside Out*.

In the following exercise, you will familiarize yourself with editing a Web Part page.

 SET UP **Open the SharePoint site that you used in the previous exercise, if it is not already open.**

IMPORTANT Verify that you have sufficient rights to edit views in the Shared Documents library. If in doubt, see Appendix A.

1   On the **Quick Launch**, click **Documents**. Click the **Settings** gear icon, and then click **Edit page** to show the page in edit mode.

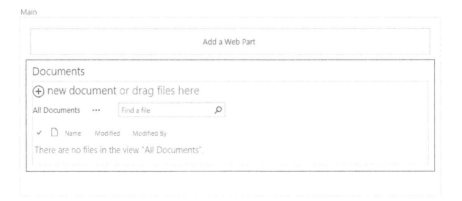

TIP Web Part pages might contain more than one Web Part zone, depending on the Web Part page template used when creating the page. You can also add or remove zones from a Web Part page by using a tool such as SharePoint Designer. Ribbon tabs are sometimes specific to a Web Part; for example, if you insert a Web Part on your page that displays the contents of a list, the Items and List tabs may not be displayed until you click the title of the list Web Part.

2   On the **Page** tab, click **Stop Editing**.

3   In the top-right corner of the page, click the arrow next to your name, and then click **Personalize this Page**.

4   On the **Page** tab, click **Stop Editing**.

 CLEAN UP **Close the browser.**

Moving Web Parts

As you customize your webpage by adding and removing Web Parts, you might find that the Web Parts are not located where you would like them to be. In this situation, you can move the Web Parts around on the page to obtain the layout that you want.

In this exercise, you will move Web Parts on the home page of a SharePoint site.

➡ SET UP **Open the SharePoint site that you used in the previous exercise, if it is not already open.**

> **IMPORTANT** Verify that you have sufficient rights to edit views in the Shared Documents library. If in doubt, see Appendix A.

1 Click **Edit** to display the home page of your site in edit mode.

2 Pause the mouse over the title bar of the **Media Web Part** so that the pointer changes to a hand. While holding down the mouse button, drag the Web Part to the content area to the left of **Getting Started**.

3 Click **Save**.

 CLEAN UP **Close the browser.**

Key points

- A website is a collection of webpages.

- There are four types of webpages—publishing pages, wiki pages, Web Part pages, and application pages. On a Team site, blank site, or document workspace, the default webpages are wiki pages that are stored in a wiki library named Site Pages.

- Both wiki pages and Web Part pages can contain Web Parts. A publishing page may contain Web Parts; however, it depends on the page layout that is used for the publishing page.

- A page can contain static and dynamic content, which is typically limited to no more than two or three screens of information.

- On a wiki page, create forward links to pages by using the double square brackets around a WikiWord. For example, type **[[BedRoom]]** to create a link to the page named **BedRoom**. The page does not have to exist when the forward link is created.

- The easiest way to create a new wiki page is to create a forward link to a nonexistent page.

- Major versioning is enabled on wiki page libraries, and therefore no amendments are lost.

- Parts (app parts and Web Parts) are reusable components that can contain any type of web-based content. They can display the contents of list and library apps, as well as other content, such as the results of database queries, websites, webpages, files, and folders.

- Parts are organized by categories.

- The Apps category contains an app part for each list or library app created in the site, plus any app parts that were installed when you added a SharePoint app from your organization's app store or from the SharePoint Store.

- The Closed Web Parts category is a temporary storage space for Web Parts that have been removed from a webpage by using the **Close** option.

- A Web Part page can have two versions: a Shared version and a Personal version. All users can see changes made to the Shared version. Changes made to the Personal version are visible only to the user who altered her Personal version of the Web Part page. A user can reset the Personal View to the Shared View setting, if desired.

4

Chapter at a glance

Create

Create a SharePoint site, page 146

Share

Share your site, page 156

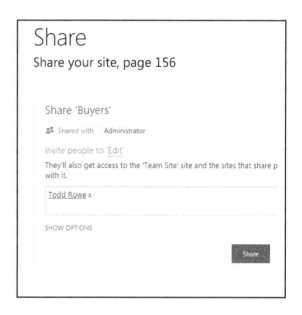

Change

Change a site theme, page 172

Save

Save your site as a template, page 174

Creating and managing sites

5

IN THIS CHAPTER, YOU WILL LEARN HOW TO

- Create a site.

- Share a site.

- Manage site users and permissions.

- Create a personal site.

- Change a site theme.

- Save and use a site template.

- Manage site features.

- Manage site content syndication.

- Delete a site.

Microsoft SharePoint *sites* are containers for the webpages and the apps, such as lists and libraries, as well as features and settings that provide the site's functionality. You can use a site as a single container for your data, or you can create as many child sites as you need to make your data easier to find and manage. As a container, sites can be used to secure their contents. You will frequently find yourself creating sites to secure a place for a given group of people to collaborate on its contents. For example, you might create a site to manage a new team or to collaborate on a project.

As we discussed in Chapter 2, "Navigating a SharePoint site," sites are organized hierarchically within a *site collection.* There is always one top level site and there can be one or more child sites as well. Typically, top level sites are created for an entire team, and therefore have many visitors (that is, people who only read), a few members (that is, people who can create and update content), and one or two owners. But as child sites and grandchild sites are created, the total number of users typically decreases while the number of people designated as members increases.

Site templates are used in SharePoint as a blueprint to jump-start a new site's usefulness by autogenerating webpages and apps that likely will be most useful in a given situation.

In this chapter, you will learn how to create a site using default site templates, as well as how to use the self-service site creation to create a personal site. You will also learn to manage site users and permissions. You may want to differentiate a site by the way it is presented to the user, so you will learn how to apply a *theme* to your site. In addition, you will learn how to create and use a custom site template, how to manage the site functionality using the site features, and how to delete a site.

PRACTICE FILES You don't need any practice files to complete the exercises in this chapter.

IMPORTANT Remember to use your SharePoint site location in place of *http://wideworldimporters* in the exercises.

Creating a site

The catalyst for organizing your data into different site containers will often be the same catalyst as for creating multiple subdirectories on the file system. You may have too much information to use a single container and still locate your information easily. If all your files were kept in the root of the hard drive along with the operating system files and other pro-gram files, the list of files would be difficult to sort through, work with, and manage. Just as you would create subdirectories to organize your file system data, you likely will create child sites to help organize your SharePoint data in logical ways.

The initial site created in a SharePoint site collection is called the *top level site*. Top level sites are created from within *SharePoint Central Administration* because they don't have a parent site. Although the top level site functionally is not different from its child sites, it includes administrative links on its Site Settings page to manage the site collection.

To create a child site, you must go to the **New SharePoint Site** page of the would-be parent site by clicking the new subsite link from the **Site Contents** page.

Subsites

⊕ new subsite

TIP Alternatively, you can go to the **New SharePoint Site** page directly from the browser address bar. See the following "Layouts directory" sidebar for details on how to gain direct access to the destination directly from the browser address bar.

5

Layouts directory

The administrative pages of a Microsoft SharePoint 2013 site are kept in a common folder named _layouts/15. By using the website address in the address bar of your browser, you can quickly go to administrative pages that are buried relatively deep within a site's administrative links.

The following table displays examples that are typically found on the home page of a SharePoint site.

Website address (URL)	Administrative page
http://[site]/_layouts/15/viewlsts.aspx	Site Contents
http://[site]/_layouts/15/settings.aspx	Site Settings
http://[site]/_layouts/15/newsbweb.aspx	New SharePoint Site

The following table displays the same examples for a child site.

Website address (URL)	Administrative page
http://[site]/[childsite]/_layouts/15/viewlsts.aspx	Site Contents
http://[site]/[childsite]/_layouts/15/settings.aspx	Site Settings
http://[site]/[childsite]/_layouts/15/newsbweb.aspx	New SharePoint Site

Note that the suffix for each website address is the same no matter how deeply you delve into the site hierarchy.

When you initially create objects like sites, lists, and libraries in SharePoint, you are establishing two name values: the display name, usually labeled **Title** or **Name**, and the **Uniform Resource Locator (URL)** name. Typically, as is the case with sites, there is an option to provide the URL name separately, after the site has been created. The best practices for specifying the URL name are outlined in the sidebar called "Naming a URL."

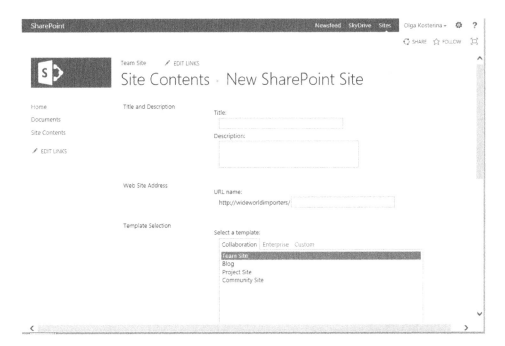

Naming a URL

Follow these best practices when initially establishing a URL for objects in SharePoint. For example, providing a URL name of "Todd Rowe" for a new child site would result in the following website address in the browser address bar: *http://wideworldimporters/Todd%20Rowe*. Subsequently, providing a URL name of "My Cool Docs" for a new document library within that site would result in the following website address in the address bar: *http://wideworldimporters/Todd%20Rowe/My%20Cool%20Docs*. Notice that replacing the spaces with underscores improves the appearance of the website address: *http://wideworldimporters/Todd_Rowe/My_Cool_Docs*.

The best practices for naming URLs include the following:

- The URL name should be descriptive, intuitive, and easy to remember.

- The URL name should be concise. There is a limit on the number of total characters available for the entire website address, so you will eventually encounter problems if you consistently use long URL names.

- The URL name should not contain spaces. Spaces in the address bar are replaced with *%20* and take up three characters each. Spaces also make the website address difficult to use in an email and difficult for others to read. To reduce frustration and improve readability, an underscore can be used in place of a space.

- The URL name should be used consistently. By default, tasks are found in a list called Tasks, contacts in a list called Contacts, and so on. Similarly, if you frequently create a document library to house proposals, consistently using a name such as Proposals will help others to locate that content. Of course, you cannot have two lists with the same name in a site. Therefore, you may need to differentiate them by putting a prefix on the name, such as Customer_Proposals and Product_Proposals.

It is wise to establish naming conventions as early as possible. This should help prevent unintuitive, verbose, space-laden, and inconsistent objects from being created.

5

After you've provided the title, the optional description and the URL for your new site, you need to choose how to initially provision your site using one of the SharePoint 2013 built-in site templates. Each site template provisions a site structure for a specific purpose, with relevant apps, as well as webpages prepopulated with Web Parts that use the navigation best suited for the purpose of the site template.

The built-in site templates in SharePoint 2013 are grouped together into three categories: Collaboration, Enterprise, and Publishing. Table 5-1 lists the SharePoint 2013 built-in site templates by category.

TABLE 5-1 *SharePoint 2013 site templates*

Name	Description
Collaboration sites	
Team site	A collaboration environment for a group of people to work together.
Blog	A site for a person or team to post ideas, observations, and expertise that site visitors can comment on.
Developer site	A site for developers to build, test, and publish Microsoft Office apps.
Project site	A site for managing and collaborating on a project. This site template brings all status, communication, and artifacts relevant to the project into one place.
Community site	A place where community members discuss topics of common interest. Members can browse and discover relevant content by exploring categories, sorting discussions by popularity, or by viewing only posts that have a best reply. Members gain reputation points by participating in the community, such as starting discussions and replying to them, liking posts, and specifying best replies.
Enterprise sites	
Document Center	A site to centrally manage documents in an enterprise.
E-discovery Center	A site to manage the preservation, search, and export of content for legal matters and investigations.
Records Center	A template that creates a site designed for records management. Records managers can configure the routing table to direct incoming files to specific locations. The site also lets you manage whether records can be deleted or modified after they are added to the repository.
Business Intelligence Center	A central site for presenting business intelligence content in an enterprise.

Name	Description
Enterprise Search Center	A site that provides an enterprise-wide search. It includes a welcome page with a search box that connects users to four search results pages: general searches, people searches, conversation searches, and video searches. You can add and customize new results pages to focus on other types of search queries.
My Site Host	A site used for hosting personal sites (My Sites) and the public People Profile page. This template is provisioned by a SharePoint administrator only once per User Profile Service Application.
Community Portal	A central site for communities in an enterprise.
Basic Search Center	A site that provides a basic search experience. It includes a welcome page with a search box that connects users to a search results page and an advanced search page.
Visio Process Repository	A site for viewing, sharing, and storing Microsoft Visio process diagrams. It includes a versioned document library and templates for Basic Flowcharts, Cross-functional Flowcharts, and BPMN diagrams.
Publishing sites	
Publishing Portal	A starter site hierarchy for an Internet-facing site or a large intranet portal. It includes a home page, a sample press releases subsite, a Search Center, and a login page. Typically, this site has many more readers than contributors, and it is used to publish webpages with approval workflows.
Enterprise Wiki	A site for publishing knowledge that you capture and want to share across the enterprise. It provides a content editing experience in a single location for coauthoring content, discussions, and project management.
Product Catalog	A site for managing product catalog data that can be published to an Internet-facing site through search. The product catalog can be configured to support product variants and multilingual product properties. The site includes administration pages for managing faceted navigation for products.

All collaboration site templates provision a **Quick Launch** navigation that contains links to the parts of the site. However, the apps and the pages are provisioned differently, depending on the site purpose.

The *Team Site* template provisions a Documents library that is made more visible by placing a Web Part for it on the site's default home page for easier collaboration. The *Blog* site template provides a way to publish a type of journal known as a web log, or a blog. The blog owner creates posts on which other users can comment. Each post is a separate content page, and a rollup summary of these pages is typically presented in reverse chronological order (with newest entries listed first) on the home page of the blog site. Blogs are commonly used as news sites, journals, and diaries. A blog focuses on one or more core competencies of the author and is sometimes used as a soapbox for the blog owner to state an opinion. Blogs can also be used as a one-way communication tool for keeping project stakeholders and team members informed.

SEE ALSO For more details on blogs, refer to Chapter 8, "Working with wikis and blogs."

TIP Blog site content can be syndicated using a Really Simple Syndication (RSS) feed. RSS feed-aggregating software allows people to subscribe to the content that they are interested in and to have new and updated posts delivered to them. Using such a tool, you can aggregate the content from many blogs into one common reader, where posts from selected authors can be sorted, filtered, and grouped. Microsoft Outlook 2013 and Microsoft Outlook 2010 can aggregate RSS feeds; there are also many vendors that give away or sell RSS feed-aggregating software.

The *Developer Site* template provides a site for developers to create and publish Microsoft Office apps. The *Project Site* template provisions a site for collaborating on a project, with all information and artifacts relevant to the project available in one place.

SEE ALSO For more details on working with a Project site, refer to Chapter 10, "Managing work tasks."

The *Community Site* template provisions an environment for community members to discuss the topics of common interest.

SEE ALSO For more details on working with a Community site, refer to Chapter 7, "Getting social."

The type of top level site in the site collection where your new site would be located defines the list of built-in templates that are available for your new site. For example, the Publishing templates are not available for site creation in the site collection where the top level site is a Team Site.

TIP The built-in templates are actually *configurations* of the underlying site definitions. Additional configurations, and even alternate site definitions, can be created by the administrators of your SharePoint servers. Built-in configurations can also be removed or altered.

You will likely focus, at least initially, on using the built-in site templates. However, it is also possible to save the websites you create as custom site templates that you and others can then choose as a foundation for a new site from the list of Custom site templates on the **New SharePoint Site** page. When you save the website as a template, a custom *web template* is created by SharePoint and saved as a file with a .wsp extension. This is done by using the **Save site as template** link in the **Site Action** section of the **Site Settings** page of any site. Custom web templates saved in this way are initially available only in the same site collection in which they are saved. The "Saving and Using a Site Template" section, which appears later in this chapter, explains how to copy a saved web template into another site collection. All alterations, except security-related settings, are retained on those sites provisioned by using saved custom web templates.

After you've selected a site template, you need to choose from the two options for site permissions that are listed on the **New SharePoint Site** page.

5

Permissions

You can give permission to access your new site to the same users who have access to this parent site, or you can give permission to a unique set of users.

Note: If you select **Use same permissions as parent site**, one set of user permissions is shared by both sites. Consequently, you cannot change user permissions on your new site unless you are an administrator of this parent site.

User Permissions:
- ● Use same permissions as parent site
- ○ Use unique permissions

The default option, **Use same permissions as parent site**, checks the parent site's permission every time the user visits the child site to determine what the user is allowed to do on that site. As the permissions on the parent site change over time, the permissions on the child site also reflect those changes. The other option is **Use unique permissions**. When you click this option as the site's creator, you break the permission inheritance and you are initially the only user with access to the site, associated with the Administrator permission level.

> **IMPORTANT** If you choose **Use same permissions as parent site**, it is possible to have the right to create a new site but not have the right to delete it. However, if you choose **Use unique permissions**, you are the site's administrator and, as such, will always have the right to delete the new site.

You also have two other options for assigning permissions to a new site that are less obvious. If you initially choose **Use unique permissions**, you are the only user with access to the site and can make any changes you wish. You can then switch to **Use same permissions** as parent site, whereby everyone who has access to the parent site (including you) will subsequently have access to the child site using the permissions assigned on the parent site. If you initially choose **Use same permissions** as parent site, the parent site's permissions will be used. Yet, if you subsequently switch to **Use unique permissions**, all the permissions of the parent site are copied to the child site. This can save a great deal of time if most of the people who have access to the parent site also need access to the child site.

Having assigned user permissions to your new site, you need to set up navigation options.

Three navigation options can be specified when creating a new site. The first two deal with the visibility of the child site being created within the navigation of the parent site. You can choose to show the child site on either the **Quick Launch** or the top link bar of the parent site. The former defaults to No, and the latter defaults to Yes. In addition, you can specify whether the top link bar of the parent site should display on the top link bar of the created child site. This setting is referred to as *navigation inheritance*. The default is No.

In the following exercise, you will create a child site that the buyers at Wide World Importers will use for collaboration. As a team, the buyers need a centralized place to collaborate and share. You will use the Team Site template to provision the new child site.

SET UP **Open the top level, would-be parent site from which you'd like to create the new site. The exercise will use the *http://wideworldimporters* site, but you can use whatever site you wish. If prompted, type your user name and password, and click OK.**

IMPORTANT Verify that you have sufficient permissions to create a site. If in doubt, see Appendix A, "SharePoint 2013 user permissions and permission levels."

1 Go to the **Site Contents** page by clicking the **Settings** gear icon on the top right of the page, and then selecting **Site contents**.

2 Scroll down to the bottom of the **Site Contents** page and click the **new subsite** link.

3 On the **New SharePoint Site** page, in the **Title** text box, type **Buyers** to establish a display name for the new site.

Title and Description

Title:

> Buyers

Description:

> Site for general buyer collaboration

Web Site Address

URL name:

http://wideworldimporters/ buyers

4 In the **Description** text box, type a description, such as **Site for general buyer collaboration,** to help users understand the purpose of the new site.

5 In the **Web Site Address** section, in the **URL name** text box, type **buyers**.

This determines the value in the browser address bar, which users will see when they visit the site. Refer to the sidebar titled "Naming a URL," earlier in this chapter, for best practices regarding naming conventions.

6 In the **Template Selection** section, click the **Collaboration** tab, and then select **Team Site** from the list of available templates, if not already selected.

TIP If you have installed the practice sites for other chapters from the book's companion website, you will see these templates under the Custom tab.

7 Click the option button that defines the type of permissions that you want to use on the site initially. For the **Buyers** site, use the default permission **Use same permissions as parent site**.

8 In the **Navigation** section, define whether the links to this site will appear on the **Quick Launch** and the top link bar of the parent site. Keep the default options for the link to this child site so that it will appear on the top link bar of the parent site.

9 In the **Navigation Inheritance** section, define whether this site will use the top link bar from the parent site or have its own. For the **Buyers** site, keep the default **No** option for this site to have its own top link bar.

10   Scroll down to the bottom of the page and click **Create**.

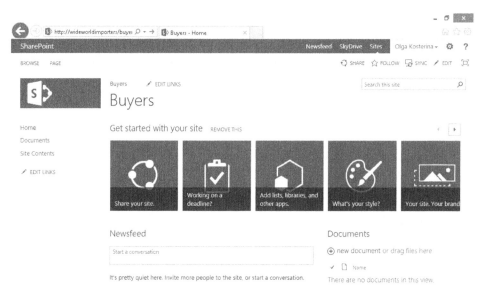

The new Team site has been created and is displayed in the browser.

IMPORTANT Clicking Cancel returns you to the Site Contents page of the would-be parent site, and will not create the new site.

❌ CLEAN UP **Leave the browser open if you are continuing to the next exercise.**

Sharing a site

After you've created a site, you can give access to this site to other people in your organization using a Share command. If email has been enabled for your SharePoint installation, you also have an option of sending a message to let people know that they have access to your site.

Sharing a site means granting access permissions to the people you want to use your site. You can assign different levels of access to different people. For example, when you share the site with Edit permission level, users are able to create and modify the site content, including lists and libraries.

If your site inherits permissions from its parent site, when you add users to your new site, they will also have access to the parent site and the sites that share permissions with it. Because of this, you will need to be an administrator of the parent site to be able to share the new child site with other people. If you are not the site administrator, you can still use the Share command to invite people to the site, but your request will be then sent to the site administrator for approval.

TIP In SharePoint Online, you may also be able to use the Share command to share your site with external users outside of your organization who do not have licenses for your subscription.

In the following exercise, you will share the **Buyers** site created in the previous exercise with Todd Rowe, the Wide World Importers owner's assistant.

 SET UP **Open the Buyers child site, *http://wideworldimporters/buyers* (created in the first exercise), from the address bar of your browser, if it is not already open. If prompted, type your user name and password, and click OK.**

> **IMPORTANT** Verify that you have sufficient permissions to manage site permissions. If in doubt, see Appendix A.

1   On the top right of the screen, click **Share**.

      ○ SHARE

2   In the **Share** dialog that is displayed, type the beginning of the user name, such as **Todd Rowe**, in the text box. SharePoint will then map your typing to the Active Directory users and display the matching names below the text box. Select the user name you'd like to share your site with, such as **Todd Rowe**.

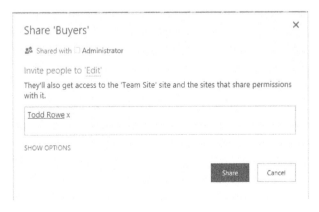

TIP On the top of the **Share** dialog, notice the list of users that the site is already shared with. This list may include, for example, the SharePoint administrators who manage your SharePoint environment.

3   Click the **Share** button. The confirmation message stating that the site has been shared appears at the top right of the screen.

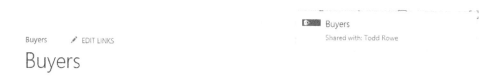

CLEAN UP **Leave the browser open if you are continuing to the next exercise.**

Managing site users and permissions

Information in SharePoint is secured at one of four levels, as follows: site level, list or document library level, folder level, and list item or document level. By default, all lists and libraries inherit the permissions of the site that contains them; all folders inherit the permissions of the list or library that contains them; and all list items or documents inherit the permissions of the folder that contains them.

SEE ALSO For deeper discussion about list, library, folder, and list item security, refer to Chapter 6, "Making lists and libraries work for you."

Selecting the default option, **Use same permissions as parent site**, provides permissions inheritance from the parent site to a newly created child site. SharePoint checks the parent site's permission every time the user visits the child site. This is the option you selected when you created the **Buyers** site earlier in this chapter. If you select the **Use unique permissions** option when creating a new site, SharePoint initially categorizes users of a new site into three SharePoint groups, as follows:

- **Visitors** People or groups who only need to be able to read content on a site

- **Members** People or groups who need to be able to create and edit content, but not create subsites or manage site membership

- **Owners** People who are responsible for all aspects of managing and maintaining a site

Selecting the **Use unique permissions** option breaks the permission inheritance and sets you, as the site's creator, with sole access to the new site as its owner. After you click **Create** in the **New SharePoint Site** page, you are presented with the **Set Up Groups for this Site** page to add users to the three groups, to provide them with access to the newly created site.

People and Groups › Set Up Groups for this Site ⓘ

Visitors to this Site

Visitors can **read** content in the Web site. Create a group of visitors or re-use an existing SharePoint group.

◉ Create a new group   ○ Use an existing group

Team Site Visitors

Members of this Site

Members can **contribute** content to the Web site. Create a group of site members or re-use an existing SharePoint group.

◉ Create a new group   ○ Use an existing group

Team Site Members

Olga Kosterina

Owners of this Site

Owners have **full control** over the Web site. Create a group of owners or re-use an existing SharePoint group.

◉ Create a new group   ○ Use an existing group

Team Site Owners

Olga Kosterina

OK

A site can be toggled between inherited permissions and unique permissions using its **Permissions** page, which you can go to by clicking **Site Permissions** on the **Site Settings** page. Once on the **Permissions** page, choosing **Delete unique permissions** for a site using unique permissions allows you to toggle the site to have inherited permissions. Choosing **Stop inheriting permissions** for a site inheriting permissions allows you to toggle the site to have unique permissions. A warning message will display, asking you to confirm your action.

TIP Changing from unique permissions for a site to inheriting permissions from a parent site leads to all custom permissions for the site being lost.

A site using unique permissions has no tie to the parent site, so you are allowed to add and remove users from the site regardless of whether they have permissions on any other site. When users are added to a site, they must be added to a *SharePoint group* or associated with at least one *permission level*.

SharePoint groups are maintained at the site collection level and represent a collection of users or groups with a defined set of one or more permission levels and a few governing attributes. When a new user or group is added to a SharePoint group, they are granted the permissions of that group in all sites that the group has access to.

> **IMPORTANT** Editing a SharePoint group affects the membership of all sites, lists, folders, and items that are using that SharePoint group.

Think of permission levels as a named collection of permissions that can be assigned to SharePoint groups or individual users. There are a number of default permission levels in SharePoint 2013, as follows:

- **Read** The user can only view site content.
- **Contribute** The user can view, add, update, and delete site content.
- **Edit** The user can add, edit, and delete lists, and can view, add, update, and delete list items and documents.
- **Design** The user can view, add, update, delete, approve, and customize site content.
- **Moderate** The user can view, add, update, delete, and moderate list items and documents.
- **Approve** The user can edit and approve pages, list items, and documents.
- **Manage Hierarchy** The user can create sites and edit pages, list items, and documents.
- **Restricted Read** The user can view pages and documents, but not historical versions or user permissions.
- **Full Control** The user has full control over site content.

- **Limited Access** The user has no permissions to the site in its entirety, but only to specific lists, document libraries, folders, list items, or documents when given explicit permission.

- **View Only** The user can view pages, list items, and documents. Document types with server-side file handlers can be viewed in the browser but not downloaded.

Table 5-2 provides the list of individual permissions and shows the permissions levels that they are included into by default. The individual permissions are grouped into three categories: site permissions for site access, list permissions for lists and libraries access, and personal permissions for personal Web Parts and pages.

SEE ALSO For more details on the individual permissions and permission levels, refer to Appendix A.

When you create a new site based on a site template, SharePoint automatically assigns a predefined set of default SharePoint groups with specific permission levels to the site. For example, default SharePoint groups in a Team site have the following permission levels:

- The Visitors group has the permission level of Read.

- The Members group has the permission level of Edit.

- The Owners group has the permission level of Full Control.

In addition to Visitors, Members, and Owners groups, a Community Site includes the Moderators group with the permission level of Moderate, whereas a Publishing Portal includes the Approvers group with the permission level of Approve, the Designers group with the permission level of Design, and the Hierarchy Managers group with the permission level of Manage Hierarchy.

Not only can you associate existing SharePoint groups and individual users with permission levels, but you can also associate *Windows groups* (including *Active Directory groups* and *Local Machine groups*) with permission levels. This is a very practical approach to providing tight security with minimal maintenance. However, you may not have control over the Windows groups defined in your organization.

Although you can create your own permission levels and even alter all permission levels except for Full Control and Limited, you will likely find the built-in levels to be adequate for most business scenarios. You may also want to provide all users with some level of access to the data on your site; for example, using permission levels of either a Restricted Read or a View Only.

TABLE 5-2 *SharePoint 2013 permissions*

Permission	Full Control	Design	Edit	Contribute	Read	Limited Access	Moderate	Approve	Manage Hierarchy	Restricted Read	View Only
Site permissions											
Manage Permissions	X								X		
View Web Analytics Data	X								X		
Create Subsites	X								X		
Manage Web Site	X								X		
Add and Customize Pages	X	X							X		
Apply Themes and Borders	X	X									
Apply Style Sheets	X	X									
Create Groups	X										
Browse Directories	X	X	X	X			X	X	X		
Use Self-Service Site Creation	X	X	X	X	X		X	X	X		X
View Pages	X	X	X	X	X		X	X	X	X	X
Enumerate Permissions	X										
Browse User Information	X	X	X	X	X	X	X	X	X		X
Manage Alerts	X										
Use Remote Interfaces	X	X	X	X	X	X	X	X	X		X
Use Client Integration Features	X	X	X	X	X	X	X	X	X		X
Open	X	X	X	X	X	X	X	X	X	X	X
Edit Personal User Information	X	X	X	X			X	X	X	X	X

Permission	Full Control	Design	Edit	Contribute	Read	Limited Access	Moderate	Approve	Manage Hierarchy	Restricted Read	View Only
List permissions											
Manage Lists	X	X	X				X		X		
Override List Behaviors	X	X					X	X	X		
Add Items	X	X	X	X			X	X	X		
Edit Items	X	X	X	X			X	X	X		
Delete Items	X	X	X	X			X	X	X		
View Items	X	X	X	X	X		X	X	X	X	X
Approve Items	X	X						X			
Open Items	X	X	X	X	X		X	X	X	X	
View Versions	X	X	X	X	X		X	X	X		
Delete Versions	X	X	X	X			X	X	X		
Create Alerts	X	X	X	X	X		X	X	X		X
View Application Pages	X	X	X	X	X	X	X	X	X		X
Personal permissions											
Manage Personal Views	X	X	X	X			X	X	X		
Add/Remove Private Web Parts	X	X	X	X			X	X	X		
Update Personal Web Parts	X	X	X	X			X	X	X		

TIP If anonymous access has been enabled for web application in SharePoint Central Administration and has not been denied via the Anonymous User Policy, anonymous users can be granted some access, either to the entire site or to individual lists on a case-by-case basis. This provides the central administrator with the option to decide whether to grant anonymous access for each web application before its site administrators can begin to turn on this option.

When you share your site using the Share command, you add a user to the SharePoint group that has a permission level that you are assigning to the user. For example, in the previous exercise, the user Todd Rowe was added to the Members group that has an Edit permission level.

TIP You can provide all authenticated users with site access on each site's **Permissions** page using the Grant Permissions command and the Everyone group.

After all users and groups are assigned to various permission levels, it is possible—even likely—that someone will be associated with more than one permission level. Rather than enforcing the most restrictive permission level, all associated rights are aggregated and the cumulative list of unique rights apply. This can be overridden only by policies created in SharePoint Central Administration.

TIP It is wise to associate every user in the various child sites in a site collection with at least the Read permission level in the top level site. Users might be unable to use custom site templates and list templates imported into a site collection unless they are associated with one of the built-in permission levels in the top level site.

In the following exercise, you will break the permission inheritance from a parent site to a child site by changing the permissions for the child site from inheriting permissions from its parent site to using unique permissions. You will then create new SharePoint groups for the child site access, assign a new owner to the site, and grant a Windows group representing Wide World Importers buyers the Edit permission level. You will also remove the child site access from the parent site's groups, as well as assign the Design permission level to an individual user.

 SET UP **Open the Buyers child site, *http://wideworldimporters/buyers* (created in the first exercise) from the address bar of your browser, if it is not already open. If prompted, type your user name and password, and click OK.**

1　Click **Settings** on the top right of the screen and select **Site settings**.

2　On the **Site Settings** page, in the **Users and Permissions** section, click **Site Permissions**.

3　The **Permissions** page is displayed, showing permission levels that have been assigned to the users and groups associated with this site. There is a yellow box across the top of the page stating that this website inherits permissions from its parent. Because this child site is inheriting permissions, you see the SharePoint groups from the parent site listed.

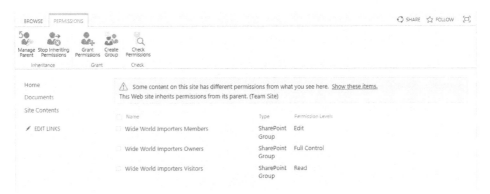

You might also see a warning in the yellow box regarding some content having different permissions. This warning usually refers to the access to the site's feed folder that might have different permissions than the rest of the site.

Click the **Members** group, such as **Wide World Importers Members**. The list of group members is displayed, including the user who you shared the site with in the previous exercise, such as Todd Rowe in our scenario. User Todd Rowe was assigned the Edit permission level, and therefore SharePoint added this user to the Members group that has the Edit permission level by default.

People and Groups ▸ Wide World Importers Members ⓘ

New ▾   Actions ▾   Settings ▾   View: Detail View ▾

		Name	About me	Title	Department
☐		Todd Rowe			

4 Click the browser's **Back** button in the top-left corner to return to the **Permissions** page.

5 On the ribbon, click **Stop Inheriting Permissions** to establish unique permissions for this site.

6 Click **OK** in the message box that appears to confirm the change.

The **Set Up Groups for this Site** page is displayed. You will now create a SharePoint group for the members of the **Buyers** site.

7 In the middle section, **Members of this Site**, click **Create a new group**. The section expands and displays two text boxes. The first text box is prepopulated with the default name for a new group, Buyers Members. The second text box lists the members of this new group, with the names separated by semicolons. Only the owner name type is listed initially. It defaults to you; this example uses Olga Kosterina.

8 For the **Buyers** site, everyone in a Windows group called Buyers needs to be added to the Buyers Members group that is associated with the Edit permission level. In the group Members text box, type the name of the Windows group, such as **Buyers**, after the name of the owner. Make sure that the names are separated by the semicolon, and click the **Check Names** icon at the bottom-right corner of the text box to validate the Windows group name.

You can also browse for the users and groups using the **Browse** icon.

9   Bill Malone, who is Wide World Importers' head buyer, needs to become the owner of the **Buyers** site with the Full Control permission level. You will now grant Bill the Full Control permission level by creating a new site owners group and adding Bill to it. In the **Owners of this Site** section, click **Create a new group**.

10   Keep the default name for the new group, Buyers Owners, and add another user, such as **Bill Malone**, to the list of members, after the name of the initial owner, separated by the semicolon.

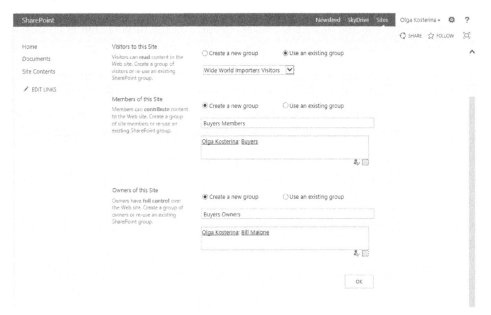

11   Click **OK** to create new SharePoint groups and to add users and groups to them, as follows: the Buyers Windows group is added to the Buyers Members SharePoint group, and the user Bill Malone is added to the Buyers Owners SharePoint group.

12   The home page of the **Buyers** site is displayed. On the **Settings** menu, click **Site settings**, and then in the **Site Settings** page, click **Site Permissions**. Notice how the site permissions page has changed. Next to each group, there are now check boxes to select the groups. There are also additional commands on the ribbon that allow you to modify the permissions and the group's membership. The yellow bar across the top of the page now states that this website has unique permissions.

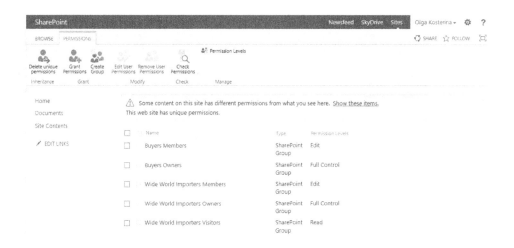

Verify that the **Buyers Members** group and the **Buyers Owners** group are listed on the permissions page with **Edit** and **Full Control** permission levels, respectively.

13 No other SharePoint group needs permissions on the **Buyers** site. You will now remove all other groups. Select the remaining parent's site SharePoint groups (for example, **Wide World Importers Members**, **Wide World Importers Owners**, **Wide World Visitors**) by clicking the check boxes to the left of their names.

14 On the ribbon, click **Remove User Permissions**.

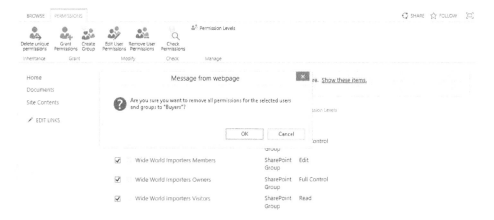

15 In the confirmation message box, click **OK**. The groups have been removed. Only the Buyers Members and the Buyers Owners groups have permissions on the site.

16 Bill Malone, the new **Buyers** site owner, has decided to assign Todd Rowe the Design permission level on the **Buyers** site. Note that when the parent site's groups were removed, the user Todd Rowe lost his Edit permissions on the **Buyers** site as he was granted these permissions via membership of the parent site's members group. To grant permissions, click the **Grant Permissions** button on the ribbon.

17 In the **Share** dialog, type the user name, such as **Todd Rowe**. Select Todd Rowe from the list of users and groups that appears below the text box when you start typing.

18 At the bottom of the dialog, click **Show Options** and select the **Design** permission level from the list of groups and permission levels. Click **Share**.

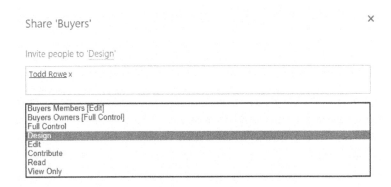

19 On the **Permissions** page, verify that the specified user, for example Todd Rowe, has been assigned the **Design** permission level for the **Buyers** site.

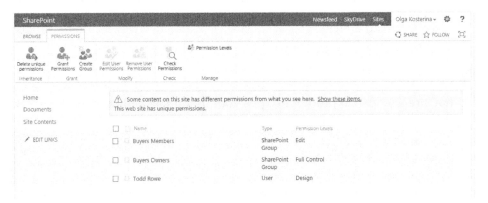

❌ CLEAN UP **Leave the browser open if you are continuing to the next exercise.**

Creating a personal site

In SharePoint Server 2013, you can create a personal site to save and share your work, and to work with other people. Your new site will be based on a Team Site template but it will not inherit either the navigation or the permission settings of any other site. You will be assigned the site owner permission level, and you will be able to manage site access and share your site with other people.

The site will be created in the location that your administrator has set up for Self Service Site Creation (SSSC). Depending on how SSSC is set up in SharePoint Central Administration, there may be more than one SSSC location available that you can choose from when you create a new site. Your site may be a top level site in a site collection, or a subsite.

SEE ALSO For more information on configuring Self Service Site Creation in SharePoint 2013, refer to *technet.microsoft.com/en-us/library/ee624362.aspx*.

You can create a personal site using the new site link on your Sites page that is accessible to you via the global navigation from any location within your SharePoint environment. After the site has been created, it is added to the list of sites that you're following, which is displayed on your Sites page, and you can access this site from any location. You can share the site with other users, add content to it, and generally use its capabilities as you would with any other Team site that you own.

TIP The new site link is only visible in the **Sites** page when the SSSC is enabled in SharePoint Central Administration and you are granted permission to use SSSC.

In the following exercise, you will create a site for a new project, called Vendors, using your **Sites** page. You will then share your new site with the Buyers group.

 SET UP **Open a page on your SharePoint site, such as** *http://wideworldimporters*, **if it is not already open. If prompted, type your user name and password, and click OK.**

> **IMPORTANT** Verify that you have sufficient permissions to use self-service site creation. If in doubt, see Appendix A.

1   On the top right of the screen, in the global navigation bar, click **Sites**.

2   On your **Sites** page, click **new site**.

⊕ new site

3   In the **Start a new site** dialog, type a name for your new site, such as **Vendors**. Notice
that the full URL for your new site is displayed beneath the text box. In our example,
it is *http://wideworldimporters:8080/sites/vendors*.

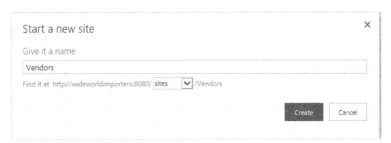

TIP Your site name will be used as a title for your new site, as well as a suffix of your
site's URL. When specifying the site name, remember to follow the best practices
outlined in the "Naming a URL" sidebar.

4   Click **Create**. Your new **Team Site** has been created and you are taken to its home
page.

5   On the top right of the screen, click **Share**.

6   In the **Share** dialog that is displayed, notice the site is only shared with you.

7   In the text box, type the user or group name that you'd like to invite to your site with
Edit permission level, such as **Buyers**. Select the **Buyers** group from the list of users
and groups that appears below the text box when you start typing.

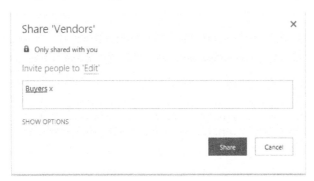

8 Click **Share**. The Buyers group that has been assigned the Edit permission level to access your site, and in the top right of the screen, a confirmation displays that the Vendors site is shared with Buyers.

9 On the top right of the screen, click **Sites** and verify that your new site has been added to the list of sites that you are following.

Sites I'm following
_____

Vendors
http://wideworldimporters:8080/sites/Vendors
Stop following

⊗ CLEAN UP **Leave the browser open if you are continuing to the next exercise.**

Changing a site's theme

The appearance of the default blue SharePoint sites is all right initially, but eventually the sites blur together and start to look too similar. Thankfully, SharePoint provides us with the ability to apply themes to our sites. Themes can radically affect display items such as colors, text, background images, banners, and borders. There are many built-in themes available from which to choose. Each SharePoint site can have its own theme, or you can set several sites so that they all have a common theme and that they are related visually.

TIP Because of many changes in the user interface in SharePoint 2010 and SharePoint 2013, the themes created in SharePoint 2007 and Windows SharePoint Services 3.0 are not compatible with SharePoint 2013. You can create new themes in SharePoint 2013 and apply them to your existing sites.

Perhaps the buyers at Wide World Importers want to create a theme for their site so that it stands out from other sites. In this exercise, you will go to the **Buyers** site and apply a theme.

➡ SET UP **Open the Buyers site,** *http://wideworldimporters/buyers*, **from the address bar of your browser, if it is not already open. If prompted, type your user name and password, and click OK.**

1   Click the **Settings** gear icon on the top right of the screen and select **Site settings** to go to the **Site Settings** page.

2   In the **Look and Feel** section, click **Change the look**.

3   In the **Change the look** page, explore the themes thumbnails, and then click the one you like most, for example, Sea Monster.

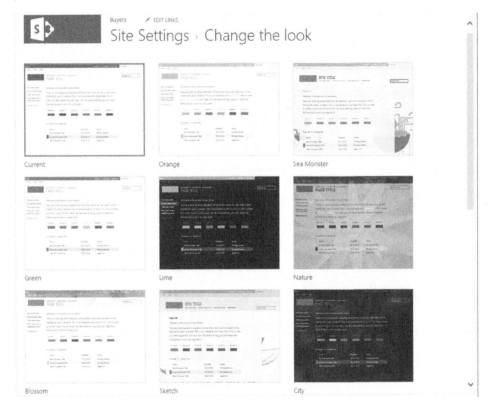

4   The selected theme page is displayed. On the left of the screen, note the options for changing the background graphics, the color scheme, the site layout, and the fonts. When you choose an option, the theme preview changes to reflect your selection. Browse through the available choices and select the ones that you like most.

Buyers   ✎ EDIT LINKS

Site Settings › Change the look

⊛ Start over   Try it out ⊛

TIP Notice that the Seattle site layout displays the **Quick Launch**, whereas the Oslo site layout does not.

5   On the top right of the screen, above the theme preview, click **Try it out**. The changes have been processed, and the preview of the **Buyers** site in the new theme is displayed.

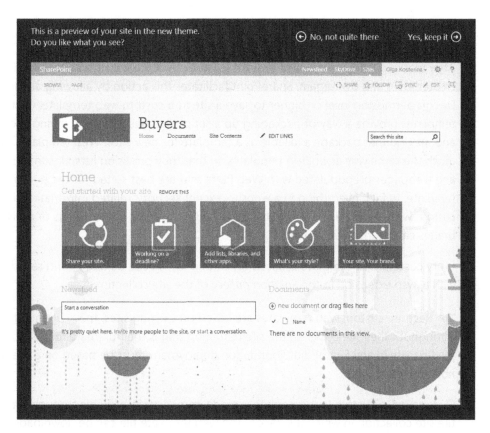

6   If you like what you see, click **Yes, keep it** on the top right, above the preview screen. The **Site Settings** page is displayed.

7   If you prefer to change your choice, click **No, not quite there**, to return to the theme page (step 4). Change the options to your liking, or click **Start over** on the top left to return to the theme thumbnails page to select another theme (step 3). Repeat steps 3–6 until you like what you see in the Buyers preview page.

8   On the **Site Settings** page, notice that the new theme has been applied, and then go to the home page of the **Buyers** site using the top link bar.

❌ CLEAN UP **Leave the browser open if you are continuing to the next exercise.**

Saving and using a site template

After working with a site, you may want to save it just the way it is so that it can be re-created over and over again. SharePoint facilitates this action by allowing anyone with a Design permission level or higher to save a site as a custom web template. Custom web templates provide a way of packaging up a set of changes to an underlying site definition and making that package available as a template for new sites. Web templates behave in much the same way as built-in templates, in that they provision lists, document libraries, and webpages prepopulated with Web Parts that are best suited for the purpose of the template. In fact, everything in a website, except security-related information, is saved in a custom web template, including its theme and navigation. The contents of all lists and libraries can be included as well.

Every custom web template is based on an underlying site definition and saved as a file with a .wsp extension in the *Solution gallery* of the site collection.

TIP Because custom web templates are based on existing sites, they continue to depend, throughout their life cycle, on the site definition that is their ultimate foundation. Therefore, the first site in any SharePoint Foundation deployment must be based on a site definition, not a web template.

Once saved, a custom web template is made immediately available throughout the entire site collection in which it is saved. The web template file can be downloaded from the Solution gallery of the current site collection and redeployed to other site collections. When creating a new child site, a user with sufficient permissions to create a child site can select the custom web template from the **Custom** tab in the **Template Selection** section in the **New SharePoint Site** page.

TIP The .wsp files on this book's companion website that are used to create the practice sites for exercises are actually custom web templates saved to a file.

Let's assume that the unique look that the buyers of Wide World Importers created for their Team site has caught on, and they want to be able to use it repeatedly. In the following exercise, you will save the **Buyers** site as a web template, and then use it to create another site.

 SET UP **Open the Buyers site,** *http://wideworldimporters/buyers,* **from the address bar of your browser, if it is not already open. If prompted, type your user name and password, and click OK.**

1   On the **Settings** menu, click **Site Settings**.

2   On the **Site Settings** page, in the **Site Actions** section, click **Save site as template** to display the **Save as Template** page.

3   In the **File name** text box, type **Buyers** to establish a name for the .wsp file.

4   In the **Template name** text box, type **Buyers Site**.

5   In the **Template description** text box, type a description, such as **Sea Monster themed site created by buyers**, to help site creators understand the intended purpose of this custom web template.

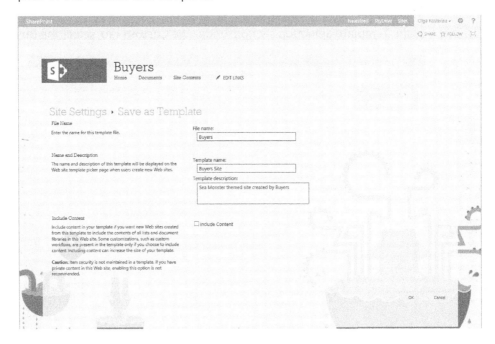

6   Click **OK** to create the custom web template file, save it in the Solution gallery, and activate the template within the site collection. When the **Operation Completed Successfully** page is displayed, click **OK**.

TIP If you want to see where the custom web template is placed, you can click the **Solution gallery** link on the **Operation Completed Successfully** page.

7   You will now create a new site for the finance department that will be based on the custom template that you've just created. The new site will be a sibling site for the **Buyers** site. To go to the Buyers' parent site, type its URL in the browser address bar, such as **http://wideworldimporters**.

8   On the **Quick Launch**, click **Site Contents**.

9   On the **Site Contents** page, scroll down and click the **new subsite** link.

10   On the **New SharePoint Site** page, in the **Title** text box, type **Finance** to establish a display name for the new site.

11   In the **Description** text box, type a description, such as **Site for Finance Department**, to help users understand the purpose of the new site.

12   In the **URL name** text box, type **finance** as the website address. (Remember the naming conventions listed in the "Naming a URL," sidebar from earlier in this chapter.)

13   In the **Template Selection** section, under the **Custom** tab, select the **Buyers Site**.

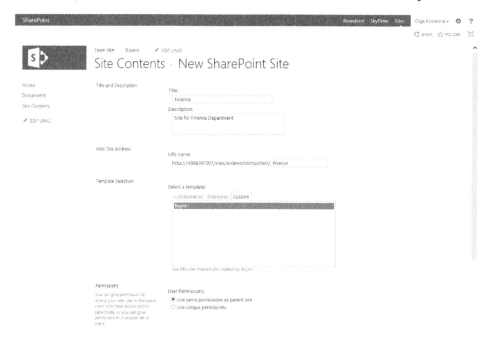

14   Keep the default permissions that are set on **Use same permissions as parent site**. Keep the default navigation and the navigation inheritance options.

15   Click **Create** to create the new site.

     The new **Finance** site is displayed. Note that it is identical to the original **Buyers** site.

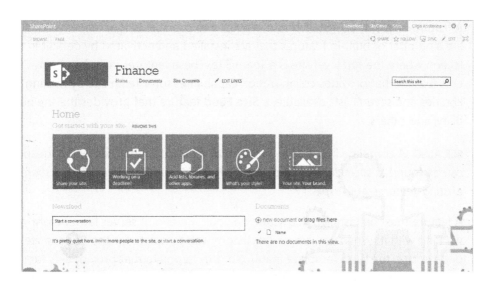

CLEAN UP **Leave the browser open if you are continuing to the next exercise.**

Managing site features

SharePoint features provide site capabilities by grouping together chunks of functionality that developers and administrators can activate to make this combined functionality available at one of four scopes, as follows:

- **Farm level** These features are activated for all sites in the entire SharePoint Foundation farm and are managed by the farm central administrators.

- **Web Application level** These features are activated for all sites where the web address is the same. For instance, all sites that start with *http://wideworldimporters* would be managed under the same web application. These features are also managed by farm central administrators.

- **Site Collection level** These features are activated only for sites within a given site collection. Management of these features is accomplished from the top level site of the site collection and is typically distributed to department-level administrators.

- **Site level** These features are activated only for the site in which the activation is performed. Management of these features may be done by anyone with administrative privileges on the site.

A feature needs to be installed and activated to provide its functionality. For example, there are a number of built-in features that are installed and activated by default in the site collection where the top level site is a Team Site. These features include a Team Collaboration Lists feature that provides collaboration capabilities for a Team site by making document libraries and several lists available, a **Site Feed** feature that provides the site newsfeed capability, and others.

SEE ALSO A complete list of built-in SharePoint 2013 site features with corresponding GUIDs can be found at *social.technet.microsoft.com/wiki/contents/articles/14423.sharepoint-2013-existing-features-guid.aspx.*

A feature must be installed in a scope on your SharePoint server farm before you can begin working with it. When you created a custom web template for the **Buyers** site in the previous exercise, the Web Template feature for this template that provided its functionality was created and activated in the site collection. For example, it is this feature that provides the display of the new template under the **Custom** tab in the **Template Selection** section of the **New SharePoint Site** page.

TIP A custom web template includes a list of activated features from the originating site. If these features are not available at the would-be parent site when the creation of a new site is attempted, SharePoint 2013 will not create a site, but instead will generate an error message that includes a GUID of a missing feature.

In the following exercise, you will work with the **Site Feed** feature that provides the newsfeed functionality. You will first deactivate this feature on the **Finance** site and verify that the **Newsfeed** functionality is no longer available on the site. You will then activate this feature to restore the **Newsfeed** functionality.

 SET UP **Open the Finance site, *http://wideworldimporters/finance*, from the address bar of your browser, if not already open. If prompted, type your user name and password, and click OK.**

> **IMPORTANT** Verify that you have sufficient permissions to manage Features. If in doubt, see Appendix A.

1   On the site home page, verify the site feed functionality by positioning your cursor in the newsfeed text box, typing **Hello World!**, and then clicking the **Post** button.

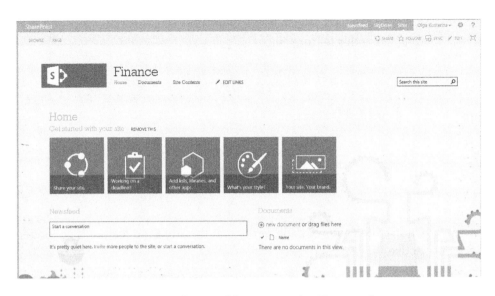

2   You will now deactivate the **Site Feed** feature on the **Finance** site.

3   On the **Settings** menu, click **Site Settings**.

4   On the **Site Settings** page, in the **Site Actions** section, click **Manage site features.**

5   On the **Site Features** page, explore the list of features that are arranged in alphabetical order. Scroll down to the **Site Feed** feature and notice that its status is shown as **Active**.

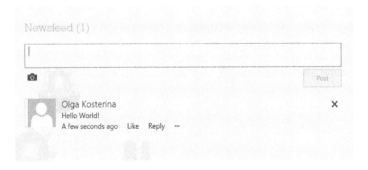

6   To the right of the **Site Feed** feature, click **Deactivate**.

7   A warning page is shown, letting you know that user data might be lost. Click the **Deactivate this feature** link.

8   On the **Site Features** page, verify that the **Site Feed** feature is no longer shown as **Active**.

9   Because the feature has been deactivated, its functionality is no longer available on the site. You will now validate that the site newsfeed has been disabled.

10 Scroll to the top of the **Site Features** page and click **Home** on the top link bar to go to the site home page.

11 On the site home page, notice that the **Newsfeed** text box and the **Post** button are no longer available. Your post has been removed as well.

12 Optionally, you can now activate the **Site Feed** feature to restore the newsfeed functionality on the Finance site.

13 On the **Settings** menu, click **Site Settings**, and then on the **Site Settings** page, in the **Site Actions** section, click **Manage site features**.

14 To the right of the **Site Feed** feature, click **Activate** to enable the newsfeed functionality.

15 Scroll to the top of the page and click **Home** to return to the site home page.

16   Validate that the **Newsfeed** text box is displayed and that the site feed functionality has been restored.

Newsfeed

Start a conversation

It's pretty quiet here. Invite more people to the site, or start a conversation.

❌ CLEAN UP **Leave the browser open if you are continuing to the next exercise.**

Managing site content syndication

Really Simple Syndication (RSS) is a standard way to make new or modified content available to readers of a SharePoint list or document library. Once you subscribe to an RSS feed (the XML emitted from a web request), you can use an RSS aggregator running on your desktop to check for new or modified content as often as you choose.

SEE ALSO Outlook 2013 and Outlook 2010 can be used as an RSS aggregator. This topic is discussed in Chapter 14, "Using SharePoint with Outlook and Lync."

The aggregator gathers all updates into a common pool of data that can be searched, sorted, filtered, and grouped by the aggregator as directed. RSS content is sometimes described as being "pulled" by the subscribers, for they can easily unsubscribe from a feed at any time. This can be a fabulous way to roll up data entered into a SharePoint list. By default, every web application in SharePoint is configured to allow an RSS feed for all the site collections that they contain.

Site collection administrators can specify whether RSS feeds are allowed on lists in the sites within the site collection; they are allowed by default. Each site can then subsequently specify whether RSS feeds are allowed on lists in the site; they are also allowed by default. If sites do allow feeds, several attributes can be defined that will be included in every feed. In the following exercise, you will verify that RSS is allowed on both the site collection and the top level site, and specify the optional attributes.

➡ SET UP **Open a top level site from the address bar of your browser, such as** *http://wideworldimporters*. **If prompted, type your user name and password, and click OK.**

> **IMPORTANT** Verify that you have sufficient permissions to manage a site. If in doubt, see Appendix A.

1   On the **Settings** menu, click **Site settings** to display the **Site Settings** page of a top level site.

2   On the **Site Settings** page, in the **Site Administration** section, click **RSS** to display the **RSS** page.

   If you are on the top level site of the site collection, as in this example, and you are a site collection administrator, you see the **Allow RSS Feeds In This Site Collection** check box in the **Site Collection RSS** area.

   All sites have the **Allow RSS Feeds In This Site** check box in the **Enable RSS** area. If this check box is cleared, no lists in this site are allowed to provide their data in the form of an RSS feed.

   Leave both check boxes selected for this exercise.

3   In the **Copyright** text box, enter **2013**.

4   In the **Managing Editor** text box, enter **Bill Malone**.

5   In the **Webmaster** text box, enter **Todd Rowe**.

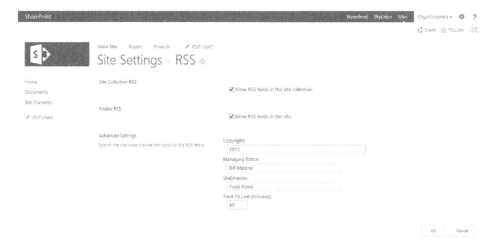

6   Leave the **Time to Live** text box at **60** minutes. This instructs the aggregator to wait at least this long before checking for updates. A shorter period will increase the frequency that a site could receive requests from aggregators, while a longer duration can help to reduce the number of aggregator requests.

7   Click **OK** to commit the changes.

✖ CLEAN UP Leave the browser open if you are continuing to the next exercise.

Deleting a site

There will be times when you want to remove a site that you either created in error or no longer need. SharePoint automatically generates all the necessary user interface elements to create, review, update, manage, and delete your sites.

The creator of the **Finance** site at Wide World Importers had a change in priorities and no longer needs the site. In this exercise, you will delete the Finance site.

➜ SET UP Open the Finance site, *http://wideworldimporters/finance*, from the address bar of your browser. If prompted, type your user name and password, and click OK.

> **IMPORTANT** Verify that you have sufficient permissions to delete a site. If in doubt, see Appendix A.

1   On the **Settings** menu, click **Site Settings**.

2   On the **Site Settings** page, in the **Site Actions** section, click **Delete this site**.

3   On the **Delete This Site** page, click **Delete** to confirm the deletion request.

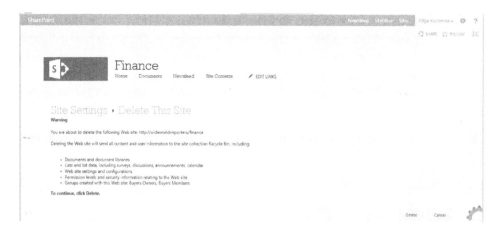

4   Click **OK** in the message box that appears to confirm the site removal. The site has been deleted.

> **IMPORTANT** SharePoint will prevent you from deleting a parent site that still contains child sites.

5   On the confirmation page, click **GO BACK TO SITE** to return to the parent site home page.

Delete Web

Your Web site has been deleted.

GO BACK TO SITE

6   On the parent site home page, verify that the Finance child site is no longer displayed in the top link bar and the **Site Contents** page.

TIP You can restore the deleted site from the site collection Recycle Bin. By default, the deleted sites are kept in the site collection Recycle Bin for 30 days.

❌ CLEAN UP **Close the browser.**

Key points

- Sites are containers for apps such as lists and document libraries, site features and settings, and webpages prepopulated with Web Parts.

- SharePoint 2013 provides a number of built-in site templates that are grouped together into three categories: Collaboration sites, Enterprise sites, and Publishing sites.

- The top level site is the initial site created in a SharePoint site collection.

- You can create a child site using the new subsite link in the **Site Contents** page. The new child site will be located in the same site collection as its parent site.

- You can create a personal site using the new site link in your **Sites** page. The location for your personal site is preconfigured by your SharePoint administrator.

- After a new site has been created, you can share it with other people by granting them access with a permission level on your site. Permission levels are a named collection of permissions. All associated permissions are aggregated, and the cumulative list of unique permissions applies.

- You can change the design of your site by applying a theme to it. Each site can have its own theme.

- Sites can be saved as custom templates and be used immediately to create their clone sites in a site collection.

- Features provide SharePoint functionality and can be installed and activated at farm, web application, site collection, or site level, depending on their scope.

- SharePoint will prevent you from deleting a site that contains subsites. A deleted site can be restored from the site collection Recycle Bin for 30 days.

5

Chapter at a glance

Configure

Configure a SharePoint list, page 190

Set Up

Set up ratings, page 217

Create

Create and manage content types, page 219

Manage

Manage users and permissions, page 228

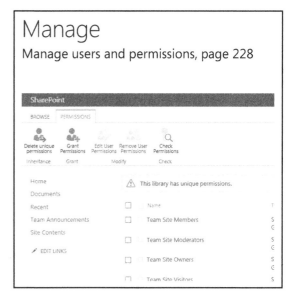

Making lists and libraries work for you

6

IN THIS CHAPTER, YOU WILL LEARN HOW TO

- Set the list or library name, description, and navigation.

- Configure content approval and versioning for a list.

- Configure versioning and required checkout for a library.

- Work with advanced list settings.

- Work with advanced library settings.

- Use validation settings.

- Set up ratings.

- Work with content types.

- Create a view.

- Manage users and permissions.

- Share a document or a folder.

- Grant item level permissions.

- Delete and restore a list or a library.

In this chapter, you focus on the list and library settings. Chapter 3, "Working with documents and information in lists and libraries," discussed how to create and use Microsoft SharePoint lists and libraries, how to add and remove content, how to work with the documents, how to add columns, and how to sort and filter lists and libraries. Now that you have a good grasp of SharePoint lists and libraries, this chapter will explore the settings available to manage and configure the features and functionality of Microsoft SharePoint 2013 lists and libraries to make them work for you.

Because a library is a list of files, the list settings and the library settings are very similar. With list and library settings, you can configure the options for the list or the library, including name, navigation, content types, versioning, and validation, as well as permissions for the users who may require access to the list or the library. There are also configuration settings that apply only to the lists or only to the libraries. For the lists, these settings include, for example, the list item level access, and enabling attachments to list. For the libraries, these settings include, for example, the default behavior for opening documents, managing library templates, and configuring the **Site Assets** library.

In this chapter, we will discuss the configuration options to manage the lists and the libraries on your site. These options are available on the **Settings** page for a list or a library. You can access the settings for a list from the list page by clicking the **List Settings** button in the **Settings** group on the right side of the **List** ribbon.

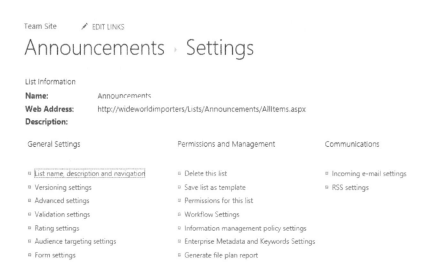

You can access the settings for a library from the library page by using the **Library Settings** button in the **Settings** group on the right side of the **Library** ribbon.

Documents › Settings

List Information

Name: Documents

Web Address: http://wideworldimporters/Shared Documents/Forms/AllItems.aspx

Description:

General Settings	Permissions and Management	Communications
▫ List name, description and navigation	▫ Delete this document library	▫ Incoming e-mail settings
▫ Versioning settings	▫ Save document library as template	▫ RSS settings
▫ Advanced settings	▫ Permissions for this document library	
▫ Validation settings	▫ Manage files which have no checked in version	
▫ Column default value settings	▫ Workflow Settings	
▫ Rating settings	▫ Information management policy settings	
▫ Audience targeting settings	▫ Enterprise Metadata and Keywords Settings	
▫ Form settings	▫ Generate file plan report	

The **Settings** page groups configuration settings in six sections, as follows: **General Settings**, **Permissions and Management**, **Communications**, **Content Types**, **Columns**, and **Views**. The **General Settings** section, for example, provides the ability to change the name of a list or a library, its description and navigation, and the settings for versioning, validation, ratings, audience targeting, as well as the advanced and form settings. For a document library, this section also includes the ability to set up the default values for columns. In this chapter, we will discuss how to use these settings to effectively configure your SharePoint lists and libraries.

6

PRACTICE FILES Before you can complete the exercises in this chapter, you need to copy the book's practice files to your computer. The practice files you'll use in this chapter are in the **Chapter06** practice file folder. A complete list of practice files is provided in "Using the practice files" at the beginning of this book.

IMPORTANT Remember to use your SharePoint site location in place of *http://wideworldimporters* in the exercises.

Setting the name, description, and navigation

It is important to give the name, description, and navigation settings some thought when you create a list or a library. With regards to the list and library names, the default app names are descriptive, but could be made more descriptive within an organization. Consider a Contacts list as an example; if it only contains employees, then *Employees* or *Staff* may be a better name for it. With regards to the list and library navigation, you may need to display your new list on the **Quick Launch**. However, if you have added a list or a library as a Web Part on the page of your site, you may find it unnecessary to also have a link to it on the **Quick Launch**. Under the **Name**, **Description**, and **Navigation** options, you can turn the **Quick Launch** link on or off for the list in question.

TIP To make navigation to a list or a library easier, avoid using spaces within the list name when the list is created. A space in the name shows as **%20** within the URL. For more information, refer to the "Naming a URL" sidebar in Chapter 5, "Creating and managing sites." You can also rename a list and a library after setting up its URL when it is created. For more information, refer to the exercise in the "Creating a new list" section in Chapter 3.

In this exercise, you will create an Announcement list, and then put a permanent link to it on the **Quick Launch**.

TIP You can also create a permanent **Quick Launch** link for a list or a library by dragging its tile onto the **Quick Launch** in edit mode. For more information, refer to the exercise in the "Customizing the site navigation" section in Chapter 2, "Navigating a SharePoint site."

 SET UP **Open the SharePoint site where you would like to create an Announcement list and display its link on the Quick Launch. The exercise will use the *http://wide-worldimporters* site, but you can use whatever site you wish. If prompted, type your user name and password, and then click OK.**

> **IMPORTANT** Verify that you have sufficient rights to create a list. If in doubt, see Appendix A, "SharePoint 2013 user permissions and permission levels."

1 Click the **Settings** gear icon at the top right of the screen, and then select **Add an app** to display the **Your Apps** page.

2 On the **Your Apps** page, scroll down to the **Announcements** tile and click it.

TIP You can also search for the **Announcements** app using the search box on the top of the **Your Apps** page.

3   The **Adding Announcements** dialog is displayed. In the **Name** box, type **Team Announcements** and click **Create** to create a list.

4   On the **Site Contents** page that is displayed, click the new **Team Announcements** tile to go to the newly created list page.

Note that the **Team Announcements** link is displayed under the **Recent** section on the **Quick Launch**. However, this link is temporary because the **Recent** section only displays links to the five newest apps. After another five lists and libraries have been created on the site, the link to Team Announcements will no longer be shown in the **Recent** section on the **Quick Launch**. You will now create a permanent **Quick Launch** link for this list.

5   On the **Team Announcements** list page, click the **List** tab on the top left of the page, and then click **List Settings** in the **Settings** group on the right side of the ribbon to display the **Settings** page for this list.

6   On the **Settings** page, in the **General Settings** section, click **List name, description and navigation**.

7   In the **Navigation** section, click **Yes** to **Display this list on the Quick Launch**, and then click **Save**.

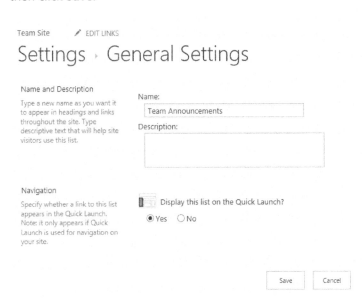

8   Back on the **Settings** page, click the **Team Announcements** list link on the **Quick Launch** to open the list page.

Note that the **Team Announcements** list is displayed on the **Quick Launch** in the main section. The temporary link to this list is no longer displayed under the **Recent** section because there is now a permanent link in the main section of the **Quick Launch**.

9   You will now create a new announcement in this list. On the **Team Announcements** page, click **new announcement**, and then in the new announcement form, in the **Title** field, type **Hello World!**.

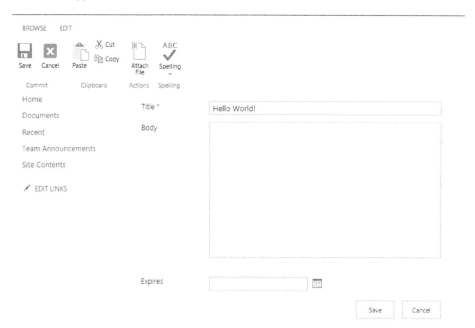

10   Click **Save** to add a new announcement and to display the list page.

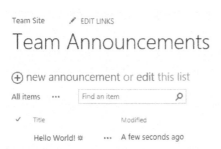

Team Site ✏ EDIT LINKS

Team Announcements

⊕ new announcement or edit this list

All items ⋯ | Find an item 🔍 |

| ✓ | Title | Modified |
| | Hello World! ✦ ⋯ | A few seconds ago |

❌ CLEAN UP **Leave the browser open if you are continuing to the next exercise.**

Configuring content approval and versioning for a list

The **Versioning** settings option under **General Settings** for a list provides **Content Approval**, **Item Version History**, and **Draft Item Security** options. By turning on **Content Approval**, list items can be created as draft items that are not displayed to other users unless the item has been approved. This means that you can work on the item in draft mode, and then submit the item for approval when you are ready to do so. An approver (user with Approve permission) can then approve the item, which allows the list item to show for all users with Read permission. The same options are available for a library.

Content Approval

Specify whether new items or changes to existing items should remain in a draft state until they have been approved. Learn about requiring approval.

Require content approval for submitted items?

◯ Yes   ⦿ No

TIP When a list item is submitted for approval, there is no notification that is automatically sent to the approver. The approver should visit the list periodically to see if list items are waiting for approval. Alternatively, you could use an Approval Workflow or consider configuring alerts for this list. For more information, refer to Chapter 11, "Working with workflows."

Item Version History settings provide you with the benefit of being able to track the editing history of a list item. If versioning is enabled, a new version of the list item will be stored upon each edited version of the list item. With this you can view the history, as well as restore a previous version to become the latest version of the list item. You may specify the number of versions and the number of approved versions to keep in the history. The version history is only available if versioning is enabled. By default, the list versioning is disabled.

Item Version History

Specify whether a version is created
each time you edit an item in this list.
Learn about versions.

Create a version each time you edit an item in this list?
○ Yes   ◉ No
Optionally limit the number of versions to retain:
☐ Keep the following number of versions:

☐ Keep drafts for the following number of approved versions:

TIP SharePoint lists allow you to use major versions only, whereas libraries allow you to use major and minor versions. More information on major and minor versioning settings for a library can be found later in this chapter.

Draft Item Security is an option that is specific to draft items. It provides additional user permissions to the **Permission** settings on list items. Using the **Draft Item Security** settings, you can choose who is allowed to view the item when it is in draft. The default is any user who can read items, but you can also choose **Only users who can edit items** or **Only users who can approve items**. Users with Contribute permissions or higher will see the draft version, while users with less than Contribute permissions will see the last approved item and not the more recent draft item. Therefore, users with different permissions are likely to see different list items and different versions of those list items. The same settings are available for a library and define the permissions for viewing the draft documents in the library.

Draft Item Security

Drafts are minor versions or items
which have not been approved. Specify
which users should be able to view
drafts in this list.   Learn about
specifying who can view and edit drafts.

Who should see draft items in this list?
◉ Any user who can read items
○ Only users who can edit items
○ Only users who can approve items (and the author of the item)

In this exercise, you will configure the versioning settings, and then set up the content approval for the **Team Announcements** list.

 SET UP **Open the SharePoint site where you would like to configure a list, if it is not already open. The exercise will use the** *http://wideworldimporters* **site, but you can use whatever site you wish. If prompted, type your user name and password, and then click OK.**

1   Open the **Settings** page for the **Team Announcements** list by clicking **List Settings** on the **List** ribbon.

2   Under **General Settings**, click **Versioning Settings** to display the **Versioning Settings** page for this list.

3   You will now set up content approval. In the **Content Approval** section, under **Require Content Approval for Submitted Items**, click **Yes**.

Notice in the **Draft Item Security** section, under **Who can see draft items in this list**, the selected option has changed from its default setting to **Only Users Who Can Approve Items (and the Author of the Item)**.

4   You will now configure versioning for this list. In the **Item Version History** section, click **Yes** to **Create a version every time you edit an item in this list**.

5   Click **OK** to save the changes and to go back to the **Settings** page for the list.

6   Click **Team Announcements** on the **Quick Launch** to open the list page.

The **Approval Status** column has been created within the list, and any existing announcement items are set to **Approved**.

7   Click **new announcement** to display the new item form, and then in the **Title** field, type **New Product Announcement**. Notice the warning that the items on this list require approval. Click **Save** to save the new announcement.

> ⓘ Items on this list require content approval. Your submission will not appear in public views until approved by someone with proper rights. More information on content approval.

> Title *   New Product Announcement

8   A new announcement has been created. It has an **Approval Status** of **Pending**. Click the ellipsis to the right of the new announcement title, and then click **Approve/Reject** from the menu that appears to display the **Approve/Reject** dialog.

6

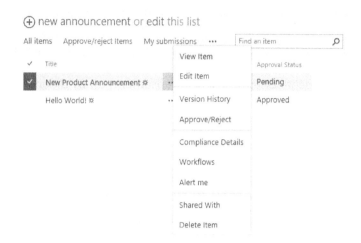

TIP You can also use the **Approve/Reject** button on the **Item** ribbon to approve or reject list items. In addition, the **Approve/reject items** list view shows the full list of documents with their approved status.

9   In the **Approve/Reject** dialog, in the **Approval Status** section, select **Approved**. In the **Comment** section, type a comment such as **Product details correct**, and then click **OK**.

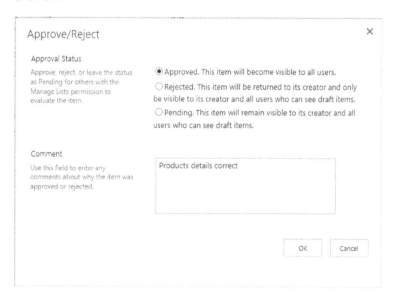

The **Team Announcements** list is displayed, and the **Approval Status** for this list item is now **Approved**.

10 You will now view the version history of a list item. Click the ellipsis to the right of the **New Product Announcement** item, and then click **Version History** from the menu to display the **Version History** dialog.

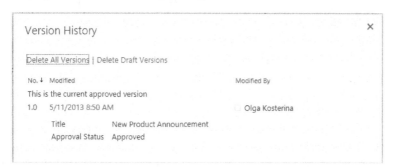

11 Close the **Version History** dialog to return to the **Team Announcements** list page.

12 Using steps 1–3 as a guide, change the setting for content approval for the **Team Announcement** list to **No**.

13 Click **OK** in the confirmation box if it appears, then save your changes by clicking **OK** in the **Versioning Settings** page.

14 Return to the list page by clicking its link on the **Quick Launch** to validate your changes. The **Approval Status** column is no longer displayed.

CLEAN UP **Leave the browser open if you are continuing to the next exercise.**

Configuring versioning and required checkout for a library

The **Versioning** settings for a library include options to configure the **Content Approval** and **Draft Item Security** that are identical to the list versioning settings. However, there are additional options available for libraries under the **Versioning** settings. The library versioning supports major and minor versions, and there is an additional configuration setting for libraries to enforce the document checkout.

Similar to the list items, you can turn on or turn off the versioning for the documents stored in the library via **Versioning** settings. By default, the library versioning is turned off. When the library versioning is turned on, SharePoint saves a copy of the edited version of a document each time the document is changed. This provides you with multiple versions of the same document so that you can easily see what the document contained before the modifications, and revert to any previous version if necessary.

When library versioning is turned on, you can select from two types of versioning: major versions only or major and minor versions. Major versions store a full-text copy of each document version. The latest version is always published, meaning that those with access to the document library can view the most recent version of the document.

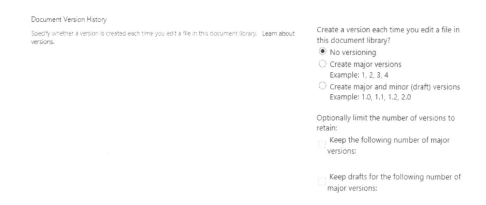

Major and minor versioning allows you to publish major versions of a document while creating modified, minor versions of the same document that only a subset of users with access to the library can view and edit. You can control who views a minor version by using the **Draft Item Security** configuration setting. Using major and minor versions is useful when performing multiple modifications of a document prior to submitting it for approval. When major and minor versioning is selected, you can control the number of versions of each document that are retained in the document library. You can think of this as "version pruning." As mentioned previously, only SharePoint libraries provide the ability to use both major and minor document versions. SharePoint lists also have versioning settings; however, you cannot use major and minor versions as you can use with libraries.

The **Versioning** settings for a library also provide the ability to configure mandatory check-out. Checking out documents from a library is invaluable when several people could be making changes to the same document at the same time. In Chapter 3, you learned how to check out a document, and then how to check it in the library. You can also enforce the checkout of a document before a user can edit it by setting up the **Require Check Out** option. The default for this option is set to **No**, meaning that users are not required to check out a document before it can be edited. In many organizations, the policy requires that all documents always be checked out for editing. To meet this requirement, a SharePoint library can be configured to require checkout before its documents can be edited.

Require Check Out

Specify whether users must check out documents before making changes in this document library.
Learn about requiring check out.

Require documents to be checked out before they can be edited?
○ Yes   ◉ No

In this exercise, you will configure a **Documents** library versioning to use both major and minor versions, and require checkout for all documents. You will then create a new document in the **Documents** library and explore how these settings are working.

6

SET UP **Open the SharePoint site where you would like to configure a library, if it is not already open. The exercise will use the** *http://wideworldimporters* **site, but you can use whatever site you wish. If prompted, type your user name and password, and then click OK.**

> **IMPORTANT** Verify that you have sufficient rights to manage this library. If in doubt, see Appendix A.

1   On the **Quick Launch**, click **Documents** to open the **Documents** library page. Open the **Settings** page for the library by clicking **Library Settings** on the **Library** ribbon. Under **General Settings**, click **Versioning Settings** to display the **Versioning Settings** page for this library. In the **Document Version History** section, select **Create major and minor (draft) versions**.

2   Select the **Keep drafts for the following number of major versions** check box, and then type **10** in the text box.

3   In the **Require Check Out** section, select **Yes**, and then click **OK** at the bottom of the page.

4   You will now create a document in the **Documents** library to validate the settings you have set up. On the **Quick Launch**, click **Documents** to open the **Documents** library page.

5   On the **Documents** library page, click **New Document** on the left of the **Documents** ribbon.

Depending on your server settings, a new document will open either in the browser or in the Microsoft Office Word client application, if it is installed on your computer. If a new document opens in the browser, please move to step 9 in this exercise. Otherwise, please continue to the next step.

6   A new document opens in Word. If a warning about allowing this website to open a program on your computer appears, click **Allow**. If a warning about opening a file appears, click **Yes** to confirm that you want to proceed. If prompted, provide your user name and password. Word opens.

7   Make any edits that you want in the new document. For example, you might want to type =**rand()** followed by pressing the **Enter** key to insert text.

8   In Word, click the **Close** button in the top-right corner of the Word window to close the window. In the Word message box that appears, click **Save** to confirm that you would like to save the document, and then in the **Save As** dialog, enter **Proposal** as the name of your new document. Click **Save** to save the document back to the **Documents** library. If a Word message box appears, asking you to check in the document, click **No**.

Go back to the browser where the **Documents** library is displayed.

Move to step 11 in this exercise.

9   The browser opens an empty document based on the library's default template in the Microsoft Office Word Web App. If prompted, provide your user name and password. Click **Edit Document** on top left of the page, and then select **Edit in Word Web App** from the menu.

10 In the Word Web App, in the new document, type some text, and then click the **Save** icon in the top-left corner of the screen to save the document back to the **Documents** library. In the **Save As** dialog, enter **Proposal** as the name of your new document, and then click **Save** to save the document back to the **Documents** library.

11 On the **Documents** library page, refresh the page to show the new **Proposal** document. Note the green down arrow on the **Proposal document icon**, which shows that the document is checked out, because this library is configured with the setting to require checkout for all documents. To check in the document, click the ellipsis to the left of the document to display its callout, and then in the bottom right of the callout, click the ellipsis to display the document menu and select **Check In** from the menu.

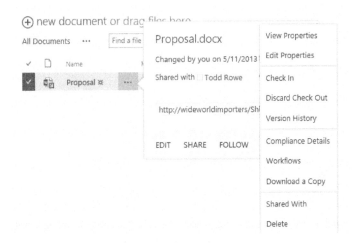

TIP You can also check in the document by using the **Check In** button on the **Documents** ribbon.

12 In the **Check in** dialog box that opens, in the **Version** section, leave the selected option, **0.1 Minor version (draft)**. In the **Version Comments** box, type **Wide World Changes**, and then click **OK** to return to the **Documents** library.

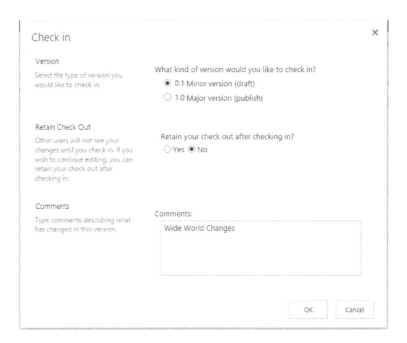

TIP If you have appropriate permissions, the checked out documents that do not have a published version can be managed from the library **Settings** page using the **Manage files that do not have the checked in version** option, located in the **Permissions and Management** group, even though the files might have been checked out by somebody else.

13 You will now view the version history for the **Proposal** document. In the **Documents** library, click the ellipsis to the left of the document to display its callout. In the bottom right of the callout, click the ellipsis to display the document menu and select **Version History** from the menu to open the **Version History** dialog. Note that the document minor version is 0.1, and then close the **Version History** dialog.

14   You will now publish a major version for the **Proposal** document. In the **Documents** library, click the ellipsis to the left of the document to display its callout, if it is not already displayed. In the bottom right of the callout, click the ellipsis to display the document menu, and then select **Publish a Major Version** from the menu to open the **Publish Major Version** dialog.

15   In the **Publish Major Version** dialog, in the **Comments** field, delete the existing text and type **Ready to send to the customer**, and then click **OK**.

16   After the major version of the document has been published, you will view the version history for the **Proposal** document again. In the **Documents** library, click the ellipsis to the left of the document to display its callout, and then in the bottom right of the callout, click the ellipsis to display the document menu and select **Version History** from the menu to open the **Version History** dialog. Note that the current document major version is 1.0.

No. ↓	Modified	Modified By	Size	Comments
This is the current published major version				
1.0	5/11/2013 12:16 PM	☐ Olga Kosterina	18.1 KB	Ready to send to the customer

Delete All Versions | Delete Minor Versions

17   Close the **Version History** dialog, and then close the document callout to return to the **Documents** library page.

✖ CLEAN UP **Leave the browser open if you are continuing to the next exercise.**

Working with advanced settings for a list

Advanced settings for a list include options for content types, item level permissions, list attachments, folders, search, list reindexing, offline client availability, and dialogs. **Item Level Permissions** options and **Attachment** options are only applicable to lists. All other options are equally applicable to libraries. In this section, we will look into all the list configuration options that are available in the list **Settings** page under **Advanced Settings**, with the exception of **Content Types** options, which is covered later in this chapter, in the section "Working with content types."

The **Item Level Permissions** option allows you to refine the default permissions levels, such as **Read**, **Contribute**, **Design**, or **Full Control** for a list item. For example, you can use this option to set up what the creator of the list item is allowed to do. This option allows you to set whether people with Read access may read all items or only those that they created. The default is **Read all items**. You may also set whether users with **Create** and **Edit** access can edit all items or just those that they created, or they can be prevented from creating and editing any list item by clicking the **None** option. The default is **Create and edit all items**. By clicking the **None** option, you are effectively making any user with Contribute permissions a reader for this list. However, users with rights to manage this list are able to read and edit all items.

Item-level Permissions

Specify which items users can read and edit.

Note: Users with the Cancel Checkout permission can read and edit all items. Learn about managing permission settings.

Read access: Specify which items users are allowed to read
- ● Read all items
- ○ Read items that were created by the user

Create and Edit access: Specify which items users are allowed to create and edit
- ● Create and edit all items
- ○ Create items and edit items that were created by the user
- ○ None

Using the **Attachments** option, you can allow or disallow attachments to list items. By default, the attachments to list items are enabled.

SEE ALSO Please refer to the exercise on attaching documents to list items in the "Adding and editing list items" section in Chapter 3.

Attachments

Specify whether users can attach files to items in this list.

Attachments to list items are:
- ⦿ Enabled
- ○ Disabled

TIP You may wish to disable list attachments if you prefer that users store documents within document libraries.

The **Folders** option lets you disable the **New Folder** command in the list. This command is enabled by default. The same setting is available for the libraries.

An alternative to using folders is using the custom columns. Ever since the introduction of SharePoint, users have been taking advantage of custom columns to organize their content. This means that through the use of custom columns, you can organize content into views using filters rather than using folders. If you prefer this method to using folders within lists, you can turn off the use of folders so that users do not become confused as to which approach they should use. If you do use folders, you should consider carefully training your users on how to use folders effectively.

Folders

Specify whether the "New Folder" command is available. Changing this setting does not affect existing folders.

Make "New Folder" command available?
- ○ Yes ⦿ No

TIP In SharePoint, the recommended number of items within a view or folder is limited to 5,000. This limitation is related to the time it takes to display the number of items in a view or a folder. Therefore, if you have 6,000 list items in the list, it would be better to create views or folders to display 5,000 or fewer list items, allowing for future growth.

SEE ALSO More information on managing lists and libraries with a large number of items, as well as the recommended limits for lists and libraries, can be found at *office.microsoft.com/ en-us/sharepoint-server-help/manage-lists-and-libraries-with-many-items-HA102771361. aspx*.

Using the **Search** option, you can exclude the list from the search results. Searching content in SharePoint will return search results from any list or library by default. All of the items that the current user has permission to view will display within the results, and no user will see content that they do not have permission to view. You may exclude an entire list from displaying within search results by clicking the **No** option for **Allow items from this list to appear in search results?**. The same setting is available for the libraries.

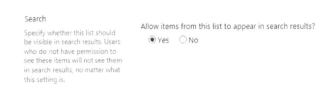

Search

Specify whether this list should
be visible in search results. Users
who do not have permission to
see these items will not see them
in search results, no matter what
this setting is.

Allow items from this list to appear in search results?

◉ Yes ○ No

SEE ALSO For more information on search, please refer to Chapter 9, "Searching for information and people."

With the **Reindex List** button, you can mark the list for full reindexing when the next scheduled content crawl occurs. If the list is not marked for full reindexing, then the content will be indexed incrementally by default. A similar setting, **Reindex Library**, is available for the libraries.

Reindex List

Click the Reindex List button to
reindex all of the content in this
document library during the next
scheduled crawl.

[Reindex List]

The **Offline Client Availability** setting defines whether the list is available for offline viewing in the client applications that allow you to synchronize data for offline use, so that you have access to the SharePoint content while in a disconnected environment. Microsoft Office Outlook can be used for offline access to a list content. The default setting is to allow items to be downloaded to the offline clients. If the list contains sensitive information, you can ensure that it is only available in an online environment and switch off the offline availability.

The same setting is available for the libraries. Turning it off will prevent the library content from being synchronized to users' computers for offline use.

Offline Client Availability

Specify whether this list should
be available for offline clients.

Allow items from this list to be downloaded to offline clients?

◉ Yes ○ No

SEE ALSO For more information on taking lists offline, see Chapter 14 "Using SharePoint with Outlook and Lync."

The **Quick Edit** setting defines whether editing the list within the page using datasheets is allowed. It is enabled by default. The **Quick Edit** view of a list provides a spreadsheet-type view of the list content, allowing you to enter data more quickly and use operations such as fill down. The updates are provided in bulk, which is convenient for making modifications quickly. However, using such operations can result in accidently overwriting content, and the disadvantage is that it is difficult to undo a mistake that has been made in bulk. Therefore, you can decide to not allow the editing of the list using **Quick Edit**, and then the **inline edit** option will not be displayed and the **Quick Edit** button on the ribbon in the **List** tab will be disabled.

The same option is available for the libraries. Turning off **Quick Edit** for a library will disable the **Quick Edit** button on the **Library** tab, which is enabled by default.

Quick Edit

Specify whether Quick Edit can be used on this list to bulk edit data.

Allow items in this list to be edited using Quick Edit?

◉ Yes ○ No

TIP Some lists and libraries, such as **External Lists** and **Picture Libraries**, do not allow the use of **Quick Edit**.

With the **Dialogs** option, you can switch between dialogs and full pages for displaying list forms, including new, edit, and display forms. SharePoint provides the forms within a dialog when accessing a list item. The dialog is displayed within the webpage and the rest of the webpage is dimmed. The dialogs are implemented using Silverlight. If your work environment has desktops that do not have Silverlight installed, you may consider either installing Silverlight or not enabling this option. The default is **No**. The same option is available for the libraries.

Dialogs

If dialogs are available, specify whether to launch the new, edit, and display forms in a dialog. Selecting "No" will cause these actions to navigate to the full page.

Note: Dialogs may not be available on all forms.

Launch forms in a dialog?

○ Yes ◉ No

In this exercise, you will disable the **Attachments** option for the **Team Announcements** list. Formatted content can appear within the attachment's body field, and therefore it would be better to type the content than link to an attachment.

SET UP **Open the SharePoint site that you used in the previous exercise, if it is not already open.**

1   On the **Quick Launch**, click **Team Announcement** to open the list page.

2   Open the **Settings** page for the **Team Announcements** list by clicking the **List Settings** on the **List** ribbon.

3   Under **General Settings**, click **Advanced Settings** to display the **Advanced Settings** page for this list.

4   In the **Attachments** section, set **Attachments to this list are** to **Disabled**.

5   Click **OK**. If a confirmation message appears, notifying you that disabling attachments will remove all existing attachments within the list, click **OK**.

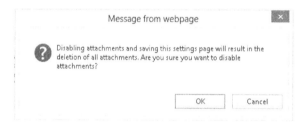

You have disabled attachments in the Team Announcements list.

CLEAN UP **Leave the browser open if you are continuing to the next exercise.**

Working with advanced settings for a library

The advanced settings for a library include options to configure content types, folders, search, library reindexing, offline client availability, and dialogs that are the same as the respective list settings. However, there are also additional options available for libraries under the **Advanced** settings. These additional settings include options for setting up a document template, configuring whether the documents open in the client or the browser, setting up a custom **Send To** destination, and making this library a **Site Assets** library.

The **Document Template** option provides the ability to set up a template for new documents created in this library. When a document library is created, you can choose the document template for this library. Then, when you click the **New Document** command on the **Documents** tab, the document template determines which Office client program, or which Office Web App, is opened. The document template is then used as a basis for the new documents. For example, the Documents library on a Team site, by default, uses a blank Word document as its document template. Using the **Document Template** option, you can change the template for a library. For example, you may prefer a blank Microsoft Office Excel workbook, or a Word template that perhaps contains headers such as your corporate logo. By default, the template document resides in a hidden folder, called **Forms**, within the library. You can edit the existing template, or you can type another URL for an alternative template.

Document Template

Type the address of a template to use as the basis for all new files created in this document library. When multiple content types are enabled, this setting is managed on a per content type basis. Learn how to set up a template for a library.

Template URL:

Shared Documents/Forms/template.dotx

(Edit Template)

6

The **Opening Documents in the Browser** option provides the ability to define the default open behavior for documents in this library, and to choose whether to open a document within the browser, as opposed to having it displayed in its native Microsoft Office client application, such as Word. The default option is to open in the browser using Office Web Apps, such as Word Web App, so that a user can use the browser to view documents online. For on-premises deployments, this feature depends on Office Web Apps being installed and activated on the SharePoint server. The benefit of opening Word, Excel, Microsoft Office PowerPoint, and Microsoft Office OneNote documents in the browser is that you can view and edit the documents using Office Web Apps from any computer or other device that has a browser. While the online functionality of Word Web App, for example, is lighter in comparison to the Microsoft Word client application, there are many everyday editing tasks that Word Web App supports, and this is very handy for making changes to documents when you are on the go. You can configure the default open behavior for a document to always open documents in the client application, to always open documents in the browser, or to go by the server default, which is to open in the browser.

Default open behavior for browser-enabled documents:

○ Open in the client application

○ Open in the browser

● Use the server default (Open in the browser)

The **Custom Send To Destination** option allows you to enter a name and a URL for a document library other than the Official File Repository that your administrators might have set at the SharePoint Server farm level, to which users can automatically send their documents once they are finished and ready for a wider audience's consumption. This is a handy feature if you want to ensure that all documents under development are written in one document library, while those available for public consumption are hosted in a different document library (with different permissions) in the same site. Or you can set up, for example, an archive location that allows you to send the documents from this library to the archive. After you've set up a name and a URL for the custom **Send To** destination, this name will be listed in the drop-down list when the user clicks the **Send To** button in the **Copies** group on the **Files** ribbon on the library page.

Destination name: (For example, Team Library)

URL:

With the **Sites Assets** option, you can specify a library that you would like to use to store site assets, such as images. When you create a team site, the **Site Assets** library is created by default. Site assets are usually images and other files that are uploaded for use within a wiki page. When you upload a file to a site via the **Insert** tab when editing a wiki page, instead of being prompted for a location to save your files, the **Site Assets** library can be used as the default location. This makes it easier to find site assets for wiki pages. However, you do not have to use the **Site Assets** library as the default location. This option allows you to change the default **Site Assets** library to the current one. You can choose any document library as the default location for your site's assets.

Site Assets Library

Specify whether this library
should be presented as the
default location for storing
images or other files that users
upload to their wiki pages.

Should this document library be a site assets library?

○ Yes ● No

In this exercise, you will configure the **Documents** library so that its documents always open in the Microsoft Office client application. You will then modify the default template for the **Documents** library, and then create a new document based on the modified template.

 SET UP **Open the SharePoint site that contains the library that you wish to configure. The exercise will use the** *http://wideworldimporters* **site, but you can use whatever site you wish. If prompted, type your user name and password, and then click OK.**

IMPORTANT Verify that you have sufficient rights to manage this library. If in doubt, see Appendix A.

1   On the **Quick Launch**, click **Documents** to open the library page.

2   Open the **Settings** page for the **Documents** library by clicking **Library Settings** on the **Library** ribbon.

3   Under **General Settings**, click **Advanced Settings** to open the **Advanced Settings** page for this library.

4   In the **Opening Documents in the Browser** section, click **Open in the client application** option, and then click **OK**. From now on, all documents from this document library will always open in the client application.

5   Open the **Advanced Settings** again. In the **Content Types** section, validate that the **Allow Management of content types** option is set to **No** so that the **Template URL** field in the **Document Template** section is enabled.

6   In the **Document Template** section, click **Edit Template** below the **Template URL** box.

7   A template opens in Word. If a warning about allowing this website to open a program on your computer appears, click **Allow**. If a warning about this template appears, click **Yes** to confirm that you want to proceed with opening a file. If prompted, provide your user name and password. Word opens.

6

8   Double-click the top of the blank Word document to enter the Header section. Type
     Wide World Imports, set the text to bold, and increase the font size.

9   Click **File | Close** to close the document. When the **Microsoft Word** confirmation dia-
     log opens, click **Save** to save the modified template to the Documents library.

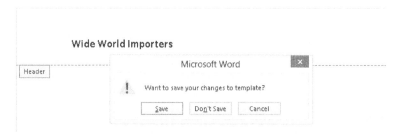

10   You will now create a new document based on this template. In the browser, click **OK**
     in the **Advanced Settings** page, and then go back to the document library by clicking
     Documents on the **Quick Launch**.

11   Click the **Files** tab on the top left of the library page, and then click **New Document**
     on the left side of the ribbon.

12   If a warning about allowing this website to open a program on your computer ap-
     pears, click **Allow**. If a warning about opening a file appears, click **Yes** to confirm that
     you want to proceed. If prompted, provide your user name and password. Word
     opens a new document that is based on the template that you've just created.

13   In the new document, type **Report**. Add any other text that you'd like.

14   In Word, click the **Close** button in the top-right corner of the Word window to close
     the window. In the confirmation dialog box that appears, click **Save** to confirm that
     you would like to save the document, and then in the **Save As** dialog, enter **Report**
     as the name of your new document and click **Save** to save the document back to the
     Documents library.

15   In the Word dialog that appears, click **Yes** to confirm that you would like to check in
     the document.

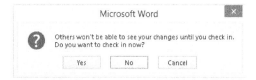

16   In the **Check In** dialog, select **1.0 Major version (publish)** and click **OK**.

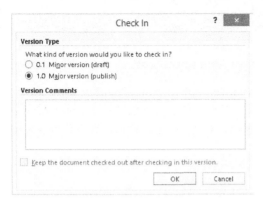

17   In the browser, refresh the **Documents** library page to see the **Reports** document listed in the library.

❌ CLEAN UP **Leave the browser open if you are continuing to the next exercise.**

Using validation settings

The list and library validation settings provide you with the ability to validate user entries into each column in a list or a library. When a user enters a value that does not meet the requirements that you have defined, a custom message is displayed, allowing the user to correct the value.

TIP Validation of user entry can be configured in two places. You can configure validation using validation settings on a list level, and you can configure validation at the column level when creating or modifying the column properties. The difference is that using the column properties does not provide the ability to compare two columns in the same list, whereas the list settings validation option does. The column properties validation settings are useful when comparing a columns value with a static value.

In this exercise, you will add validation to the **Team Announcements** list to ensure that only future dates are added to the **Expires** column.

➡ SET UP **Open the SharePoint site that you used in the previous exercise, if it is not already open.**

1   On the **Quick Launch**, click **Team Announcements** to open the list page.

2   You will now create a new announcement with an expiration date set in the past. Click **new announcement**. In the **Title** field, type **Past Announcement** and in the **Expires** field, click the calendar icon to open a calendar, and then select a date in the past (prior to today).

3   Click **Save**.

    You will now create a validation rule to check that the expiration date of any new announcement is always set in the future.

4   On the **List** tab, click **List Settings** in the **Settings** group, and then on the **Settings** page, under **General Settings**, click **Validation Settings** to display the **Validation Settings** page.

5   In the **Formula** section, in the **Formula** box, type =[Expires]>=[Created].

6   In the **User Message** section, in the **User Message** box, type an error message that will be displayed to the user in case of incorrect entry, such as **Expiration date must be in the future**.

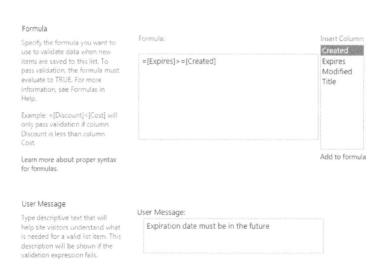

7   Click **Save**.

8 You will now verify the validation rule. On the **Quick Launch**, click **Team Announcements** to go to the list.

9 Click **new announcement**. In the **Title** field, type **Validated Announcement**, and then once again select a past date using the calendar control in the **Expires** field.

10 Click **Save**. The error message that you have set up is displayed at the bottom of the page, indicating that the date is invalid.

11 In the **Expires** field, set a date in the future. Click **Save**. The new **Validated Announcement** item has been created and is shown in the **Team Announcements** list.

12 Using steps 4–7 as a guide, remove the validation settings by deleting the formula for validating the expiration date that you created.

6

❌ CLEAN UP **Leave the browser open if you are continuing to the next exercise.**

Setting up ratings

The **Rating** settings provide the ability to add a rating control to a list or a library, so that users can rate the content in this list or library. You can configure the user experience in terms of whether the content is rated using the **Likes** (**Like** or **Don't Like**) or the **Star Ratings** (from no stars to five stars). The default setting is that rating is not enabled.

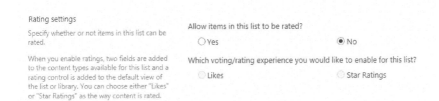

In the following exercise, you will set the **Likes** ratings for the **Team Announcements** list and the **Star Ratings** for the **Documents** library.

 SET UP **Open the SharePoint site that you used in the previous exercise, if it is not already open.**

> **IMPORTANT** Verify that you have sufficient rights to manage a list. If in doubt, see Appendix A.

1   On the **Quick Launch**, click **Team Announcements** to open the list page, if it is not already open.

2   Open the **Settings** page for the list by clicking **List Settings** on the **List** ribbon.

3   On the **Settings** page, under **General Settings**, click **Ratings Settings**.

4   Select **Yes** under **Allow items in the list to be rated**, and then select **Likes** as a voting/rating experience. Click **OK**.

5   On the **Quick Launch**, click **Team Announcements** to open the list page. Notice that the new **Number of Likes** column has been created, with the **Like** links that you can click to rate the list items. Click the **Like** links for those items that you'd like to vote for.

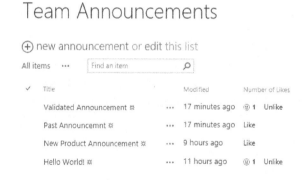

Notice that your Likes are counted. In addition, the **Unlike** link appears, which allows you to withdraw your vote for a list item that you have already voted for.

6   You will now set up the star ratings for the **Documents** library. On the **Quick Launch**, click **Documents** to open the library page.

7 Open the **Settings** page for the library by clicking **Library Settings** on the **Library** ribbon, and then on the **Settings** page, under **General Settings**, click **Ratings Settings**.

8 Select **Yes** under **Allow items in the list to be rated**, and select **Star Ratings** as a voting/rating experience. Click **OK**.

9 On the **Quick Launch**, click **Documents** to open the library page. Notice that the new **Rating (0–5)** column has been created. It displays the five stars that the users can select to rate the list items. The column also counts how many users have voted, and shows the number of voters to the right of the star rating, which displays the average number of stars among all votes. Rate the documents that you'd like to vote for.

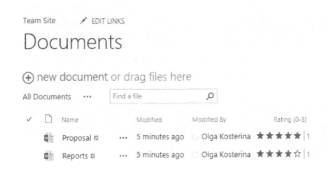

Notice that the star rating is more nuanced because it provides the opportunity to rate the items from zero to five stars, while the Likes ratings are binary.

✖ CLEAN UP Leave the browser open if you are continuing to the next exercise.

Working with content types

Often, we need to redesign a list or a library and to add a new column. For example, in Chapter 3, you added new columns to a list. You would add a new column to a list or a library if you needed to collect more information from the user than what is there by default within the list or library template. For example, consider a Sales Team site in which salespeople can create quotations, proposals, and invoices.

You may want to create a new column to store the type of document, providing choices such as Quotation, Proposal, Invoice, and Report. Collecting the type of document is useful when creating a view and filtering by type, as well as if you decide to roll up the documents using an aggregation Web Part. You would then want to ensure that all document libraries have the option of using this new column, but it would be tedious to add that new column to every library. You could get around the tediousness of creating a library or a list with an additional column by using a custom template. However, what would happen if the choices for the type of document changed? You may want to add another column to the type of document to provide additional information, such as the value of a proposal, for example. This is where site columns and content types are useful. A *site column* could also be described as a shared column. You create a site column once, and it resides in a gallery at the level of a site or a site collection. It is inherited by all sites in the collection that are beneath the site in which it was created. A *content type* is made up of the site columns and other configurations, such as workflows. This enables you to reuse a group of the site columns and perhaps have a workflow associated with the content type, which you would then add to an existing list or library. Each content type has a predefined specific set of columns, workflows, and metadata. Lists and libraries can use more than one content type. In the example Sales Team site, the three document types—Quotation, Proposal, and Invoice—could be created within the same document library, with each one containing its own template.

By default, the content types for a list or a library are turned off. You can enable the management of content types for the list or the library by using the **Content Types** options under the **Advanced Settings** section on the **Settings** page for this list or library.

Content Types

Specify whether to allow the management of content types on this document library. Each content type will appear on the new button and can have a unique set of columns, workflows and other behaviors.

Allow management of content types?

○ Yes ◉ No

In this exercise, you will create a custom content type for proposal documents, called **Global Proposal**, and then create a new document based on this content type. The **Global Proposal** content type will consist of a new document template along with custom metadata to display the **Customer Name** and the **Value** of the proposal.

 SET UP **Open the SharePoint site in which you would like to create a content type.**

IMPORTANT Verify that you have sufficient rights to create content types. If in doubt, see Appendix A.

1   Click the **Settings** gear icon in the top-right corner of the screen, and then select **Site settings** from the menu.

On the **Site Settings** page, under **Web Designer Galleries**, click **Site content types** to display the **Site Content Types** page.

2   Click **Create** on the top of the page, above the list of site content types, to display the **New Site Content Type** page.

3   In the **Name** box, type **Global Proposal**, and in the **Description** box, type **Wide World Importers Customer Proposal**.

4   In the **Parent Content Type** section, in the **Select parent content type from** list, click **Document Content Types** in the list of available options, and in the **Parent Content Type** list, click **Document**.

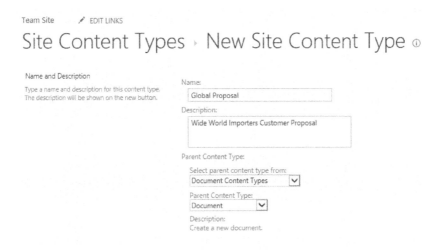

5   Leave the other fields at their defaults and click **OK**. The new **Global Proposal** content type page is displayed.

Site Content Types ▸ Site Content Type

Site Content Type Information

Name: Global Proposal
Description: Wide World Importers Customer Proposal
Parent: Document
Group: Custom Content Types

Settings

▫ Name, description, and group
▫ Advanced settings
▫ Workflow settings
▫ Information management policy settings
▫ Document Information Panel settings
▫ Delete this site content type

6   Under **Settings**, click **Advanced Settings** to display the **Advanced Settings** page.

In the **Document Template** section, click **Upload a new document template**, and then click **Browse.**

7   In the **Choose File to Upload** dialog, go to the **Chapter06** folder and click **GlobalProposal.docx**. Click **Open** to upload the file and to close the **Choose File to Upload** dialog.

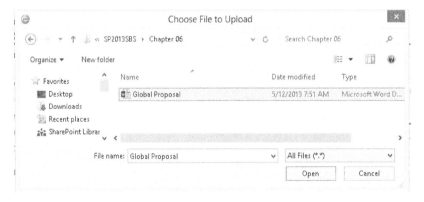

8   On the **Advanced Settings** page, accept the defaults and click **OK**. The **Global Proposal** content type page is displayed.

9   In the **Columns** section, click **Add from new site column** to create the custom column for this content type. The **New Site Column** page is displayed.

10 In the **Column name** box, type the name of your column, such as **Customer Name**, and ensure that **Single Line of Text** is selected. Accept the defaults and click **OK**.

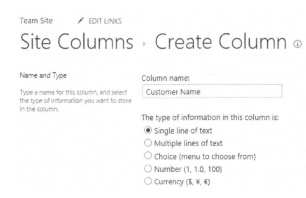

11 The **Global Proposal** site content type page is displayed. In the **Columns** section, click **Add from new site column** again to create another custom column for the proposal value. In the **Name and Type** section, enter the name **Value**, and then select **Currency** as the column type.

12 In the **Additional Column Settings** section, specify a **minimum** value of **50** and a **maximum** value of **10000**. Click **OK** to add this column to the Global Proposal site content type.

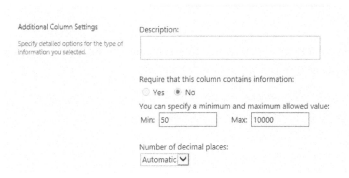

You will now enable the management of content types for the Documents library and add the **Global Proposal** content type to this library.

13 On the **Quick Launch**, click **Documents**. Click the **Library** tab, and then click **Library Settings** on the ribbon to display the **Settings** page for this library.

14   Click **Advanced Settings** from the **General Settings** section. In the **Content Types** section, under **Allow management of content types,** select **Yes**, and then click **OK**.

15   The **Settings** page for the Documents library is displayed. In the **Content Types** section, click **Add from existing site content types** to display the **Add Content Types** page.

16   In the **Select site content types from** list, select **Custom Content Types**. In the **Available Site Content Types** list, select **Global Proposal**, and then click **Add.** Click **OK** to confirm adding the content type to this library.

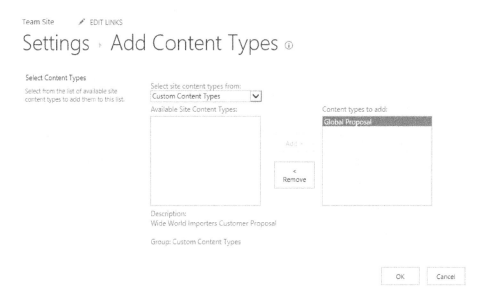

17   You will now create a new document that is based on this content type. Go back to the **Documents** library using the **Quick Launch**.

18   Click the **Files** tab to open the ribbon, and then click the down arrow on the **New Document** button. Select **Global Proposal**.

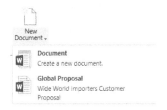

19 A template opens in Word. If a warning about allowing this website to open a program on your computer appears, click **Allow**. If a warning about this template appears, click **Yes** to confirm that you want to proceed with opening a file. If prompted, provide your user name and password.

20 In Word, in the document information panel, in the **Title** field, type **My Company Proposal**. In the **Customer Name** field, type **My Company**. In the **Value** field, type **1000**. If an **Auto Complete** dialog appears, click **No**.

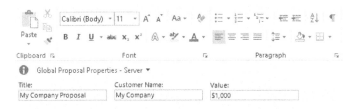

21 Click **File | Save As**. Under **Current Locations**, select the library. In the **Save As** dialog, type the name **My Proposal**, and then click **Save** to save the document back to the library.

22 In the browser, refresh the **Documents** library page to display the new document. Notice that the **My Proposal** document is checked out to you because this library requires mandatory checkout. To check in the document, click the ellipsis to the left of the document to display its callout. Then, in the bottom right of the callout, click the ellipsis to display the document menu and select **Check In** from the menu to open the **Check In** dialog. Select the **1.0 Major version (publish)** option, and then click **OK**.

23 You will now view the properties of the new document to see the values that you set. Click the ellipsis to the left of the document to display its callout. Then, in the bottom right of the callout, click the ellipsis to display the document menu and select **View Properties** to display the document properties dialog.

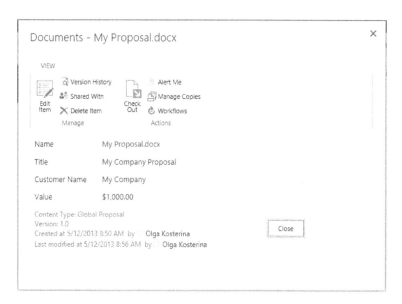

24   Close the document properties dialog, and then close the document callout to return to the library page.

> **TIP** The properties that you set do not display in the default view because you have used a content type. If you had created custom columns directly in the library, the option to display them in the default view would be available. In the next exercise, you will create a custom view to display these columns.

✖ CLEAN UP **Leave the browser open if you are continuing to the next exercise.**

Creating a view

Creating a view in a library is a beneficial way of organizing content within a library. A view can be created with filters based on the columns, providing an easy way to find documents. If a library contains custom metadata, you may want your view to be created with a filter on that custom column. Custom views work very well with the content types that were described in the previous exercise. For example, if you would like to display all proposal documents in their own view to keep them separate from invoices, you could create a filter on each view based upon the content type column.

In this exercise, you will create a new custom view within a document library to display all of the proposal documents that are created with the new Global Proposal template. The custom columns, **Customer Name** and **Value**, will become the columns within the new view.

SET UP **Open the SharePoint site and display the document library where you would like to create a new view, if it is not already displayed.**

> **IMPORTANT** Verify that you have sufficient rights to create views in this library. If in doubt, see Appendix A.

1 Click the ellipsis to the right of the **All Documents** view at the top of the documents list, and then select **Create View** from the menu that appears.

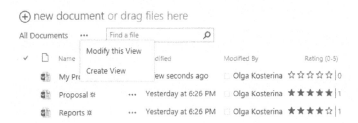

2 On the **View Type** page, click **Standard View** to display the **Create View** page.

3 On the **Create View** page, in the **Name** section, in the **View name** box, type a view name, such as **Global Proposals**.

4 In the **Columns** section, check the **Customer Name** column and change its **Position from left** to 5. Check the **Value** column and change its **Position from left** to 6.

5   In the **Sort** section, in the **First sort by the column** list, select **Customer Name**.

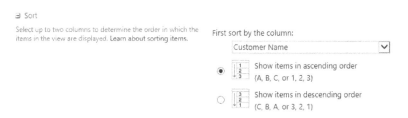

6   In the **Filter** section, click the **Show items only when the following is true** option, and set the filter to **Content Type is equal to Global Proposal**.

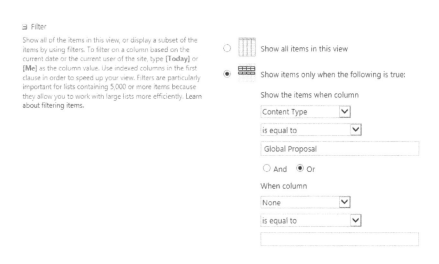

7   Expand the **Totals** section, and then for the Proposal **Value** column, set the **Total** drop-down list to **Average**.

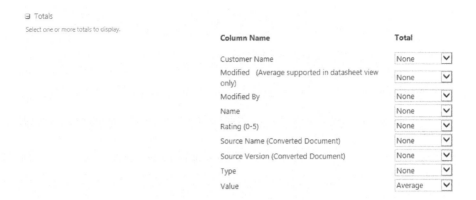

Totals

Select one or more totals to display.

Column Name	Total
Customer Name	None
Modified (Average supported in datasheet view only)	None
Modified By	None
Name	None
Rating (0-5)	None
Source Name (Converted Document)	None
Source Version (Converted Document)	None
Type	None
Value	Average

8   Click **OK** to create the new view.

The library page is displayed in the newly created view. It shows only those documents that were created based on the Global Proposal content type, and displays the two custom columns that you created, along with an average proposal value.

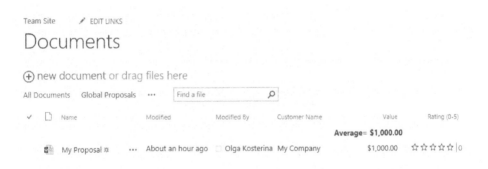

9   Click **All Documents** on the top of the file list to change to the default library view. You can also use the **Manage Views** section on the ribbon to switch between the views.

✖ CLEAN UP **Leave the browser open if you are continuing to the next exercise.**

Managing users and permissions

Within an organization, you are going to find that there are many different roles, and therefore different levels of permissions are going to be required on list and libraries, and their content.

A list or a library can inherit its permissions from the site where the list or library is located, or it can have its own unique permissions. If permissions are inherited, they will be managed either by the site in which the list or the library resides, or a parent of the site. Permission inheritance within a list or a library can also be disabled, and unique permissions can be managed for a folder or a document within a library, or a list item in a list.

SharePoint includes 12 list and library permissions that determine the specific actions that users can perform in the list or the library, as described in Table 6-1.

Table 6-1 *List and library permissions*

Permission	Description
Manage Lists	Create and delete lists and libraries, add or remove columns in a list or a library, and add or remove public views of a list or a library.
Override Check Out	Discard or check in a document that is checked out to another user.
Add Items	Add items to lists and add documents to document libraries.
Edit Items	Edit items in lists, edit documents in document libraries, and customize Web Part pages in document libraries.
Delete Items	Delete items from a list and documents from a document library.
View Items	View items in lists and documents in document libraries.
Approve Items	Approve a minor version of a list item or document.
Open Items	View the source of documents with server-side file handlers.
View Versions	View past versions of a list item or document.
Delete Versions	Delete past versions of a list item or document.
Create Alerts	Create alerts.
View Application Pages	View forms, views, and application pages. Enumerate lists.

The list and library permissions can be assigned to permission levels. Each permission level is a named collection of permissions that can be assigned to SharePoint users and groups. There are a number of default permission levels, including **Read**, **Contribute**, **Design**, **Full Control**, and **Limited Access**. You can use the default permissions levels, or create your own.

SEE ALSO For more information about permissions and permission levels, see Appendix A.

When lists and libraries are created, they automatically inherit their permissions from the site in which they reside. This means, for example, that users who are assigned Contribute permissions to the site will also have Contribute permissions to the list. After creating a list or a library, you might want to grant more privileges to certain people, or restrict their privileges. More often than not, you might want to give some people more access rights to a particular library. For example, Olga Kosterina might have given Edit permission to the overall site to Todd Rowe when it was created. However, she might decide later that she wants him to manage the **Documents** library. Todd currently has only **Edit** access to this library because that is his overall permissions level on the site. Olga Kosterina can assign Todd a permission level of **Full Control** for the **Documents** library so that Todd can manage this library.

In this exercise, you will configure the permissions for the **Documents** library so that a user such as Todd Rowe has a permission level of **Full Control** in this document library. You can follow the same procedure for a list.

 SET UP **Open the SharePoint site that you used in the previous exercise, if it is not already open.**

6

IMPORTANT Verify that you have sufficient rights to manage permissions for this library. If in doubt, see Appendix A.

1   On the **Quick Launch**, click **Documents** to open the **Documents** library, if it is not already open.

2   On the **Library** ribbon, click **Library Settings** to display the **Settings** page for this library.

3   In the **Permissions and Management** section, click **Permissions for this document library** to display the **Permissions** page for this library.

4   On the **Permissions** page, notice the yellow status bar below the ribbon that says that this library inherits its permissions from its parent. You will now check what permission level the user, such as Todd Rowe, has in this library. On the **Permissions** tab, click **Check Permissions**.

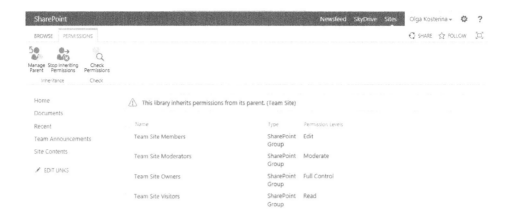

TIP Within your environment, it is likely that you see other groups and permission levels.

5   In the **Check Permissions** dialog, type the user name, such as **Todd Rowe**, and then click **Check Now**. The permissions level for the user in this library is displayed at the bottom of the box, such as the **Edit** permission level for user Todd Rowe, which is given through this user's membership in the **Members** group for the site where the library resides.

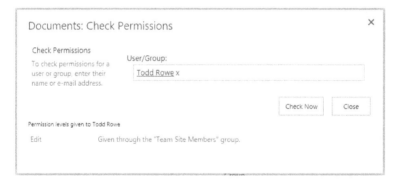

6   Click **Close** to close the **Check Permissions** dialog.

7   You will now grant the user, such as Todd Rowe, a Full Control permission level. On the **Permissions** tab, click **Stop Inheriting Permissions**.

8   A dialog box appears, warning you that you are about to create unique permissions for this document library and that changes made to the parent site permissions will no longer affect this document library. Click **OK**.

Message from webpage   ×

? You are about to create unique permissions for this document library.
  Changes made to the parent site permissions will no longer affect this
  document library.

                              OK   Cancel

9   Notice that the yellow status bar below the ribbon states that this library has unique
    permissions, and that there are now additional commands on the ribbon available to
    you. On the **Permissions** tab, click **Grant Permissions**.

10 In the **Share** dialog that appears, in the **Invite people** box, type the user name or the
    email address of the user to whom you would like to grant permissions, such as **Todd
    Rowe**, and then click **Show Options**.

11 Clear the **Send e-mail invitation** check box, and then in the **Select permission level**
    list, select **Full Control**.

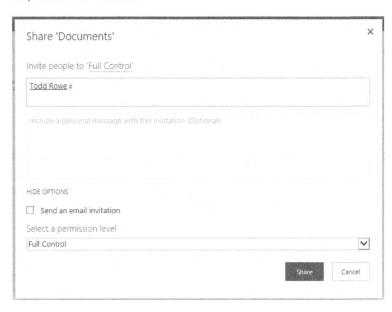

Share 'Documents'   ×

Invite people to 'Full Control'

Todd Rowe x

Include a personal message with this invitation (Optional).

HIDE OPTIONS

☐ Send an email invitation

Select a permission level

Full Control   ▾

                              Share   Cancel

12   Click **Share**. The user, such as Todd Rowe, is now added to the list of users and groups who have access to the document library with the Full Control permissions level.

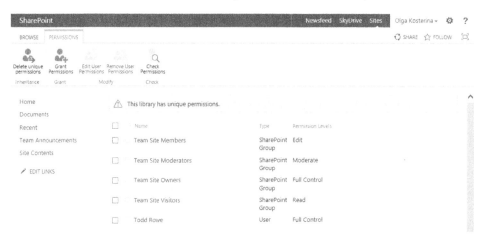

⊗ CLEAN UP **Leave the browser open if you are continuing to the next exercise.**

Sharing a document or a folder

Often, you need to share a document in a library on your site for review and collaboration with other people inside or outside your organization who do not have access to the library or any other content on your internal site. You can give access to the document to other people in your organization using a **Share** command on the document menu. You can also share a folder in the library in the same way.

When you share the document, you can assign different types of access to this document to different people. There are two options: view and edit. When you share the document with the view option, users will be able to open the document but not modify it. The edit option gives users the ability to modify the document. The permission level assigned to those users is Contribute. If email has been enabled for your SharePoint installation, you also have the option of sending a message to let people know that they have access to the document.

TIP If you share documents outside your organization using anonymous guest links, then it is possible for the invitation recipients to share those guest links with others, who could use them to view content. If you want to limit access to the document to invitation recipients only, consider requiring external users to always sign in.

In the following exercise, you will share a document with a user who does not have any access to the library where a document is located, or the site where a library resides. In our example, Olga Kosterina wants to give Bill Malone an **Edit** access to the **My Proposal** document in the **Documents** library.

→ SET UP **Open the SharePoint site where you would like to share a document, if it is not already open.**

IMPORTANT Verify that you have sufficient rights to manage permissions for this library. If in doubt, see Appendix A.

1   On the **Quick Launch**, click **Documents** to open the **Documents** library, if it is not already open.

2   In the **Documents** library, click the ellipsis to the right of the **My Proposal** document to open the document callout.

3   In the document callout, click **Share**.

4   In the **Share** dialog, in the **Invite people** box, type a name or an email address of a user that you would like to share a document with, for example, **Bill Malone**.

5   In the drop-down list to the right of the **Invite people** box, select the level of access you want to give to the user; for example, **can edit**.

6   At the bottom of the dialog, click **Show Options**, and then clear the **Send an email invitation** check box.

6

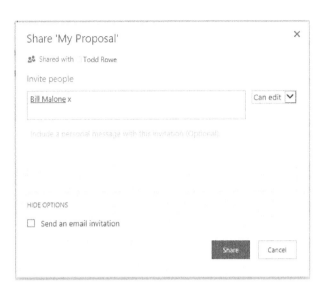

7   Click **Share** to share the document. The confirmation message stating that the document has been shared appears on the top right of the screen.

⊗ CLEAN UP **Leave the browser open if you are continuing to the next exercise.**

Granting list item permissions

Similar to a document or a folder within a library, unique permissions may be granted to a list item or a folder contained within a list. List items and folders in the root of the list inherit permissions from the list itself. In other words, the same inheritance rules that apply to lists also apply to the list items. A list item or a subfolder that is stored within a folder inherits permissions from the parent folder. Permission inheritance can be stopped for any list item or folder at any level.

In the following exercise, you will modify the permissions of a list item, **New Product Announcement**, within the **Team Announcements** list so that a user, such as Bill Malone, has a permission level of **Full Control** for this item.

SET UP Open the SharePoint site that you would like to assign list item permissions, if it is not already open.

1   On the **Quick Launch,** click **Team Announcement** to open the list.

2   Click the ellipsis to the right of the list item that you'd like to grant unique permissions to, such as **New Product Announcement**, and then select **Shared With** from the list item menu that appears.

3   In the **Shared With** dialog, explore the list of users that have access to this list item, and then click **Advanced** to open the Permissions page for this item.

   TIP Alternatively, to open the **Permissions** page for a list item, select the list item by clicking its leftmost column, and then clicking the **Item Permissions** button on the **Items** ribbon.

4   The **Permissions** page for this list item is displayed, with the yellow status line that shows that this list item inherits permissions from its parent. You will now create unique permissions for this list item. On the **Permissions** tab, click the **Stop Inheriting Permissions**, and then click **OK** to the warning message. The permission inheritance for this item has been broken. The yellow status line shows that this item has unique permissions.

5   Click **Grant Permissions** on the ribbon.

6   In the **Share** dialog that appears, in the **Invite people** box, type the user name or the email address of the user to whom you would like to grant permissions, such as **Bill Malone**, and then click **Show Options**.

7   Clear the **Send e-mail invitation** check box, and then in the **Select permission level** list, select **Full Control**.

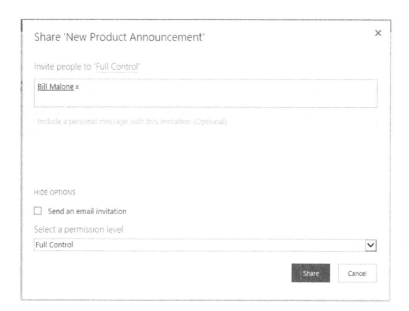

Share 'New Product Announcement'   ×

Invite people to 'Full Control'

Bill Malone x

Include a personal message with this invitation (Optional).

HIDE OPTIONS

☐ Send an email invitation

Select a permission level

Full Control   ⌄

                                                   Share   Cancel

8   Click **Share**. The user, such as Bill Malone, is now added to the list of users and groups who have access to this list item with the Full Control permissions level.

9   You will now validate that the list item has been shared with the user, such as Bill Malone. Go to the list page by clicking its link on the **Quick Launch**, and then click the ellipsis to the right of the list item that you've changed permission to, such as **New Product Announcement**, to display the list item menu. Select the **Shared With** option. Validate that the user, such as Bill Malone, is listed in the **Shared With** dialog, and then close the dialog to return to the list page.

⊗ CLEAN UP **Leave the browser open if you are continuing to the next exercise.**

Deleting and restoring a list or a library

When a SharePoint list or a library is no longer required or was perhaps created by mistake, you may wish to delete this list or library. Deleting the list will also delete all of the list items (content) within that list, and deleting the library will delete all files within the library as well, so deleting should be used with caution. For reassurance, note that sufficient permissions are required to delete the list or the library. For example, a user with a Contribute permission level for a site (or a list or a library) will not be able to delete the list or the library. If a list or a library is accidentally deleted, as with list items and documents, it will be placed within the site **Recycle Bin** for 30 days (by default) and can be restored.

In this exercise, you will delete and restore a SharePoint list.

IMPORTANT For this exercise, do not use a list that contains data that you wish to keep. If you get through half of the exercise and come back to it after 30 days, your list will not be available for restoring.

➡ SET UP **Open the SharePoint site where you would like to delete the list. The exercise will use the** *http://wideworldimporters* **site, but you can use whatever site you wish. If prompted, type your user name and password, and then click OK.**

IMPORTANT Verify that you have sufficient rights to delete and restore this list. If in doubt, see Appendix A.

1   If it is not already open, go to the **Team Announcements** list by clicking its link on the **Quick Launch**.

2   Click the **List** tab, and then click **List Settings** on the ribbon.

3   On the **Settings** page, in the **Permissions and Management** section, click **Delete this list**.

4   Click **OK** in the message that appears, confirming that you want to send the list to the **Recycle Bin**.

5   The list has been deleted and the **Team Announcements** link no longer appears on the **Quick Launch.** You will now restore the list.

6   On the **Quick Launch**, click **Site Contents**, and then on the top right of the **Site Contents** page, click **Recycle Bin**.

7   On the **Recycle Bin** page, select the **Team Announcements** list by clicking the check box to the left of its name, and then click **Restore Selection**.

6

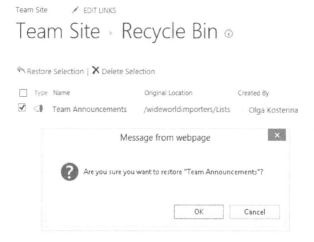

8   In the confirmation message, click **OK** to restore the **Team Announcements** list to its original location.

9   On the **Quick Launch**, click **Site Contents**, and then on the **Site Contents** page, click the **Team Announcements** tile to open the list page. Verify that the list has been successfully restored.

TIP When a list or a library is restored, the navigation link to its original location on the **Quick Launch** is not restored automatically. You need to re-create this link manually.

CLEAN UP **Close the browser.**

Key points

- List and library configuration settings are accessed via the **Settings** page. There are six groups of settings: **General Settings**, **Permissions and Management**, **Communications**, **Content Types**, **Columns**, and **Views**.

- You can think about a library as a list of files, and many library settings are similar to the list settings. However, there are also settings that are specific for libraries, including default open behavior, library template, required checkout, major and minor versioning, and others.

- With versioning, you can view the history of a document in the library, and of list items in a list, and restore previous versions if required. Libraries support major and minor versions, whereas lists only support major versions.

- Adding validation to list and library columns helps to create more consistent and accurate content.

- You can configure **Likes** or **Star Ratings** to allow users to vote for content in lists and libraries.

- Content types provide the ability to group custom columns, workflows, and other metadata and to make it available to any list or library within the current site or a child site. You can use multiple content types within a list or a library, and create different views to display them.

- Lists and libraries inherit permissions from the site that contains them. However, you can stop that inheritance and configure unique permissions for lists, list items, libraries, and the documents that they contain by granting access to individual users or groups. You can share a document for viewing and editing with users who may have no access to its containing library.

- If a list or a library is deleted by accident, it can be restored from the site's **Recycle Bin** within 30 days.

6

Chapter at a glance

Use
Use the Newsfeed hub, page 245

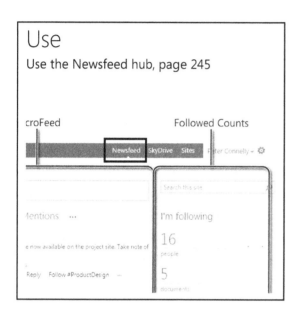

Start
Start a conversation, page 251

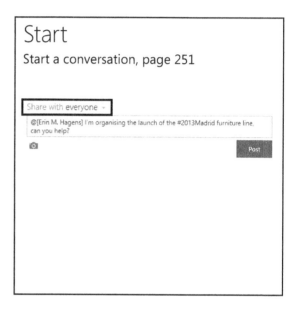

Use
Use Yammer, page 256

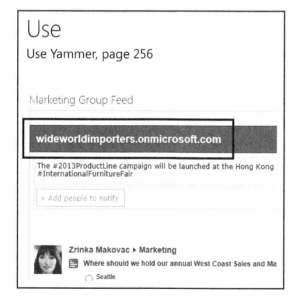

Manage
Manage a Community site, page 264

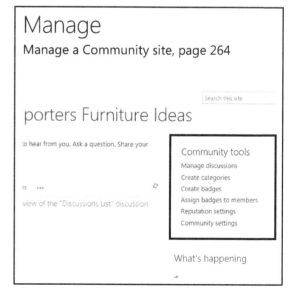

Getting social

7

IN THIS CHAPTER, YOU WILL LEARN HOW TO

- Use the Newsfeed hub and start a conversation.

- Use Yammer.

- Work with tags and notes.

- Create and manage Community sites.

Prior to Microsoft SharePoint Server 2013, you collaborated with others through emails, wikis, blogs, and documents. SharePoint Server now incorporates functions like those you may have seen on Twitter and Facebook, such as writing short messages known as *microblogging* or *status updates*. However, to differentiate between those activities that you may use on other social networks, the features within SharePoint are targeted toward *Enterprise Social Networking*; that is, it focuses on the networks and relations you have with others who share your business interests.

TIP To investigate the areas that are important in Enterprise Social Networking, Microsoft hired Harris Interactive to conduct a study concerning Enterprise Social Networking usage and adoption. The survey found that 59 percent of respondents consider it "absolutely essential" or "extremely important" for Enterprise Social Networking software to be integrated with their companies' existing infrastructure. Regarding the types of communication that Enterprise Social Networking software should facilitate, 67 percent of respondents said instant messaging; followed by email (64 percent); video conferencing (62 percent); being able to "follow" people, documents, or sites (51 percent); audio conferencing (47 percent); activity streams (34 percent); video sharing (33 percent); being able to "like" content or people (28 percent); and microblogging (26 percent). You can find an executive summary of the report at *download.microsoft.com/download/B/D/D/ BDDDA21D-2B10-4426-BC89-944E5AC56112/Harris_Interactive-Executive_Summary.docx.*

With newsfeeds on a site, you can create posts or start "conversations" by using the new *microblogging* feature, which is available on your personal site, known as your **My Site**, and collaboration sites, such as Team sites, Project sites, and Community sites, but not publishing sites.

Community sites are new with SharePoint Server 2013, created from the site template, Community Site. My Sites and Team sites are centered on people, feeds, and following, whereas Community sites offer a forum experience to categorize discussions around subject areas and to connect users who have the expertise or seek information about subject areas.

SEE ALSO For information on Project sites, refer to Chapter 10, "Managing work tasks."

If your organization uses Microsoft Lync Server 2013 or the *Outlook Social Connector* 2013, real-time features such as instance messaging, web conferencing with voice, and video may be available to you.

SEE ALSO For information on SharePoint integration with Outlook and Lync, refer to Chapter 14, "Using SharePoint with Outlook and Lync."

In this chapter, you will learn how to use newsfeeds, how to follow sites and people, and how to use Community sites. In the middle of 2013, Microsoft acquired Yammer, an office social network site that is a tool for making companies and organizations more productive through the exchange of short, frequent answers to one simple question.

Your organization may have customized (or it may not have set up) the social features described in this chapter, and therefore you may not be able to complete all the tasks in this chapter. Your organization may have replaced the SharePoint newsfeed with Yammer, particularly if you are using Microsoft Office 365. Yammer will be briefly discussed in this chapter.

PRACTICE FILES Before you can complete the exercises in this chapter, you need to copy the book's practice files to your computer. The practice files you'll use in this chapter are in the **Chapter07** practice file folder. A complete list of practice files is provided in "Using the practice files" at the beginning of this book.

IMPORTANT Remember to use your SharePoint site location in place of *http://wideworldimporters* in the following exercises.

Using the Newsfeed hub

Your SharePoint Server 2013 personal assets are organized into three distinct hubs:

- **Newsfeed** This is the primary landing page for social activities in SharePoint 2013; thus, it is also referred to as the *social hub*. Newsfeed is hosted in your **My Site**, and it provides quick access to the lists of people, documents, sites, and tags that you are following. In the **Newsfeed** hub, you can create posts or start "conversations" by using the microblog feature. **My Site**, also known as your personal site, is discussed in Chapter 5, "Creating and managing sites."

- **SkyDrive** The SkyDrive hub is the **Documents** library (**My Documents**) on your **My Site**. Because the link to your document library is on the global navigation, you can access your personal library from anywhere.

- **Sites** The Sites hub displays promoted sites, the sites that you are following, and suggested sites.

You can find links to the three hubs on the global navigation bar; therefore, you do not need to specifically visit your **My Site** to find these three hubs.

Below the global navigation bar, on the **Sharing** menu, the following links are available:

- **Share** Use this link to quickly share a site. Permissions are discussed in Chapter 5.

- **Follow** Use this link to follow people, content, documents, sites, and tags. On the **Newsfeed** hub, you can find an aggregation of the content that you follow. Also, if you follow, for example, a document, but someone else is modifying and saving that document, you will receive a notification that the user has changed the document. You do not have to follow sites that you create, because this occurs automatically and will appear on the **Sites** hub.

- **Sync** Use this link to create a synchronized copy of a document library in a folder on your computer. The technology used to synchronize the SharePoint library with the computer folder is SkyDrive Pro, which replaces SharePoint Workspace. SkyDrive Pro is part of Microsoft Office 2013 (Standard or Professional edition) or an Office 365 subscription that includes Office applications. The use of SkyDrive Pro is discussed in Chapter 6, "Making lists and libraries work for you."

When you click **Newsfeed** on the global navigation bar, the **Newsfeed** hub appears.

Profile Photo
and Name   MicroFeed   Followed Counts

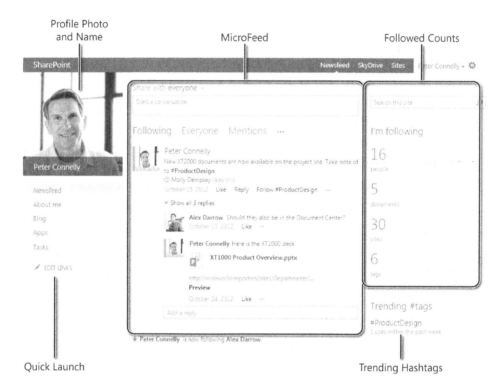

Quick Launch   Trending Hashtags

TIP A SharePoint Newsfeed app for Windows Phone and iOS mobile devices can be found at *office.microsoft.com/en-us/office365-sharepoint-online-enterprise-help/try-the-sharepoint-newsfeed-preview-app-HA103683516.aspx.*

The **Newsfeed** hub contains the following areas:

- **Your profile photo and name** By clicking the photo, you change your photo. By clicking on your name, which is the same as clicking **About Me** on the **Quick Launch**, your profile appears. You can also display your profile from any SharePoint site by clicking the down arrow to the right of your name in the global navigation bar, and then clicking **About Me**.

- **Quick Launch** Here you will find links to the following:

  - **About Me** This page displays your profile, including a bio and personal information such as your name, job title, work address, and phone number. The content on your profile page is used to display information about you so that other users can read about your skills, the projects that you have worked on, ways to contact you, and what you are doing within SharePoint.

- **Blog site** This is your personal blog site, which is created the first time you click **Blog** on the **Quick Launch**. More information on blog sites can be found in Chapter 8, "Working with wikis and blogs."

- **Apps** This link displays the **Site Contents** page, where you can add apps or subsites to your **My Site**. See Chapter 3, "Working with documents and information in lists and libraries," for more information on adding apps to a site. The **Site Contents** page of your **My Site** also contains links to the **MicroFeed** list and the **Social** list, which contains the two views used on the **Sites** hub and the **SkyDrive** hub.

- **Tasks** This link displays your **My Tasks** page, where you can view all the tasks that you need to complete. See Chapter 10 for more information on how to work with tasks on your personal site.

- **MicroFeed** This area consists of two parts: the microblogging text box, labeled **Share with everyone**, which allows you to post a brief message, and a unified overview of content, which you can filter. The brief messages and updates are displayed in modified time sort-order, so that the most recent content appears at the top of the list. The filters available are as follows:

  - Content that you are following.

  - Content available to everyone in your organization.

  - Content in which you are mentioned.

  - Social activities that you have completed, such as links to sites or people that you have followed, documents that you have rated or tagged, any microblogs that you have created, or replies to other users' microblogs.

  - Content where you have clicked **Like**.

The last two filters may not be immediately visible within the **MicroFeed** Web Part. Click the ellipsis to the right of **Mentions** to display the **Additional Options** menu.

The **MicroFeed** area also includes the MicroFeed Web Part, which provides a link to any user who has posted content, including a thumbnail image of his photo, if it is available in his profile. If you click the name of the user or his thumbnail, his profile page appears.

- **Followed Counts** This Web Part displays the counts of followed users, content, and tags for the current user. By clicking one of the numbers, you can see the details on the content that you are following, such as documents, as well as suggested documents that you might like to follow.

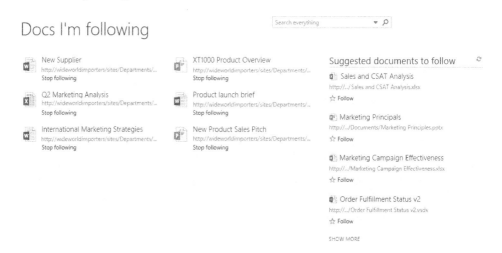

TIP You automatically follow the users who are part of your organizational structure.

- **Trending Hashtags** To monitor a topic that interests you, you may follow a tag for that topic. A tag is a keyword preceded by a hashtag symbol (#). For example, if you want to get the latest information on your organization's marketing campaigns, you might follow #MarketingCampaign. In the **Trending Hashtags** area, you will see the *hashtags* that are currently popular in public newsfeed posts.

Because the **Newsfeed** hub is part of your **My Site**, you may find that when you first click **Newsfeed** in the global navigation bar, you have to wait for your **My Site** to be created before the **Newsfeed** hub appears. The **We're almost ready!** page appears, as well as the **Let's get social!** dialog, also known as the **My Site privacy notification** dialog.

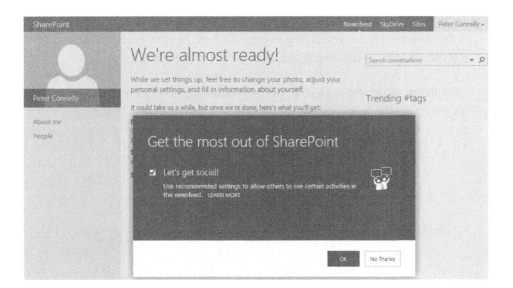

By accepting the default, **Let's get social!**, the newsfeed settings are automatically updated to let other users see and respond to site activities. You can modify the newsfeed settings; for example, you can decide whether to receive emails that notify you of events, such as when you have started following another user. You can allow others to see the list of people that you are following or your list of followers, and choose the activities that you want to share with other users. You can also configure your settings to allow just you (**Only Me**) or other users (**Everyone**) to see the hashtags that you follow.

In this exercise, you will explore the **Newsfeed Settings** page.

 SET UP **Open any SharePoint site.**

> **IMPORTANT** Verify that your organization has set up social features and that your My Site is created. If your organization has customized the social features, then you may not be able to complete the exercise.

1   On the global navigation bar, click **Newsfeed** to display the **Newsfeed** hub.

     TIP You can also go to the **Newsfeed Settings** page from the **Advance Options** menu on your profile page.

TROUBLESHOOTING There may be a delay in displaying data on the **Newsfeed** page. If the newsfeed is not displaying as expected, go to your **About Me** page for an alternative view of the feeds, and then go to the **Newsfeed** hub.

2   Click the number above **tags**, under **I'm following**, to display the tags that you are following on the **Newfeed Settings** page.

3   Review the options that you can modify, and then click **Cancel and go back**.

❌ CLEAN UP **Leave the browser open if you are continuing to the next exercise.**

Starting a conversation

On Team sites or on the **Newsfeed** hub, you will find a MicroFeed Web Part, where you can leave a message, usually one hundred words or less, which can be likened to the messages you might leave on a sticky note. This is known as *microblogging*. On a user's **About Me** profile page, you will see a similar Web Part where you will see only the posts generated by the user.

Like many other microblogging systems, SharePoint limits the number of characters that you can use. In SharePoint 2013, the limit is 512 characters, which is more than what is allowed on Twitter. Before posting, you should look at the way other users are using the 512 characters. To get started, search for other users who are influential in your field of interest, and follow them. You can find more information about searching for people in Chapter 9, "Searching for information and people." By following users, you will see all of their posts on your **Newsfeed** hub. Take note of what the leaders in your niche regularly post about. You will soon recognize that the posts that you like most are from those users who provide great content, great ideas, great links, and breaking news. It is good practice to click the **Like** link that appears below such posts. The posts that you find interesting also appear in the newsfeeds of the people who follow you. You can view your "likes" later and find these posts again.

Next, you should try to add content that supplements and emulates these posts, and you will start to get a following from users with similar interests. With microblogging, you can

- Start a conversation that is shared with everyone in your organization.
- Share a post to a newsfeed on a site that you are following.

7

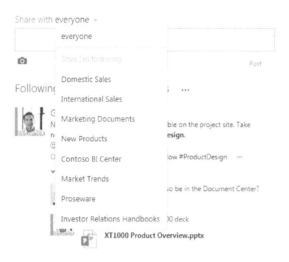

When you share a post on the sites that you are following, the **Newsfeed** hub displays the post with the site name to the right of your name. This site name is a link to the site, so that you can quickly go to it. When you visit the site, the conversation you posted on the **Newsfeed** hub will also appear on the newsfeed for the site.

When you microblog, others who read it may reply, and therefore, by microblogging, you have started a conversation. On a collaboration site, anyone who is a contributor to the site can start a conversation. When you start a conversation on your **My Site**, you can also decide whether to share it with everyone (**Public**) or on sites that you are following.

TIP When you upgrade from Microsoft SharePoint Server 2010, your **Team sites** will not display the **MicroFeed** Web Part that allows you to start a conversation. If you want to include this functionality on those sites, you must first activate the **Site Feed** feature on the **Site Features** page, as discussed in Chapter 5. This feature creates a list, named **MicroFeed**, where conversations are persisted. It provides you with the **MicroFeed** Web Part that you can place on your site's home page. Details on how to add Web Parts to pages can be found in Chapter 4, "Working with webpages." **Site Feeds** will appear on the **Sites** hub when both the **Site Feeds** and the **Following Content** site features are activated.

As you microblog, you may want to ensure that another user sees the post, in which case you would include her name by adding her name prefixed with an at sign (@). This is often referred to as *@mention*. Enter the @, followed by sufficient characters to suggest this person in the **AutoComplete** box.

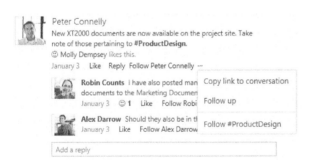

Initially, the **AutoComplete** box displays the users that you are following, but as you type more of the characters in a user's name and fewer users are found, the search is expanded to **Everyone**. The user's name becomes a link in the post, which other users can click to view her **About Me** page. A user is notified when she is mentioned in a post.

When you include the user's *@name* on a popular microblog, this user will likely track who is referencing him and come to see who you are! In this way, microblogging encourages the development of conversations with other users.

As you review other users' microblogs, you will probably have questions for them. If you click the ellipsis to the far right of **Like**, on the **More Options** menu, you can click **Follow up**. This adds a task item to your personal task list. You can also share entire conversations by copying a link to the conversation. Any hashtags that appear in the microblog will also appear on the menu, so that you can quickly follow them.

Alternatively, you can reply to a microblog and ask the user to elaborate; or you can create a new conversation (that is not targeted to a particular user) about a specific topic that you want everyone to see, in the hope that someone will know the answer. In this situation, it is best to include a hashtag symbol (#) before the name of the topic of the question. Keywords that are tagged are dynamically pulled from or added to the Managed Metadata Service (MMS) metadata store.

SEE ALSO For more information on MMS, please refer to Chapter 9.

Similar to @mentions, an **AutoComplete** box displays MMS tags. You can quickly view all conversations that reference that tag by clicking the tag, which displays the **About #<tag>** page. This page also allows you to add a description, edit the tag, and add related tags. When you place the cursor over a post, a callout appears, which contains more information about the conversation.

In your conversations, you can include links to list and library apps, as well as list items and documents. You can also add web URLs and modify the URLs to display as text. You can include pictures and videos in your conversation by clicking the camera icon under the conversation text input box.

In this exercise, you will start a conversation on the **Newsfeed** hub, mention a user, and include a hashtag. You will modify the properties of the hashtag, and then delete the conversation.

 SET UP **You don't need any practice files to complete this exercise. Go to your Newsfeed hub, if it is not already open.**

> **IMPORTANT** Verify that you have a My Site.

1   In the **Start a conversation** text box, type @, followed by the first two characters in the name of a user known to you; for example, **@er**.

2   In the suggest list, click the name of the user, and then type **I'm organizing the launch of the #2013Madrid furniture line, can you help?.**

3   Press **Enter** to save the conversation.

4   Click **#2013Madrid** to be directed to the **About #2013Madrid** page.

5   Under **Related tags**, click **Add**, and then in the text box that appears, type # and select an existing hashtag from the suggestions list, if one exists. If no suggestions are displayed, go to step 7.

Related tags

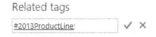

6   Click the check mark to the right of the text box to save the new related tag, if you selected one.

7   Click **Newsfeed** in the global navigation bar to return to the Newsfeed hub.

8   Click the ellipsis to the right of **Mentions**, and then click **Activities** to display your recent activity.

9   Hover over the conversation that you entered in step 3, and then click the **X** that appears in the top-right corner.

10   In the **Get rid of this conversation?** dialog, click **Delete it** to confirm the deletion of the conversation.

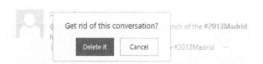

✖ CLEAN UP **Close the browser.**

Using Yammer

Yammer can be used for stand-alone social computing, and as an aggregator of all the social communications that a user might have in an organization. With the Microsoft acquisition of Yammer, there is a kind of a convergence of social computing between SharePoint 2013 and Yammer; however, at the time of this book's writing, full integration between the two products is not there. However, it looks as if Yammer and SharePoint are going to remain separate products; Yammer will be cloud-based and aimed at organizations, where each organization has its own home Yammer network using its own email address.

In Office 365 you can switch your Enterprise Social Collaboration setting to Yammer, and make Yammer your primary experience. The **Newsfeed** link on the global navigation bar is replaced with a link to Yammer. A Yammer app is planned for the SharePoint Store, so that you can easily embed a Yammer group feed into a SharePoint site. At that time, guidance will be provided on how organizations who install their own SharePoint environments replace the **Newsfeed** link. Further Yammer connection updates are expected later in 2013. In the meantime, your organization may view the Yammer newsfeed by displaying Yammer. com in the browser or by using the Yammer Web Part.

Both products have similar social offerings—for example, both SharePoint Server 2013 and Yammer let you create a conversation, and both let you follow objects, such as documents; therefore, the basics described earlier in this chapter are similar in both products.

SEE ALSO Information on picking your social network: Yammer or Newsfeed, can be found at: *office.microsoft.com/en-us/office365-sharepoint-online-enterprise-help/pick-your-enterprise-social-network-yammer-or-newsfeed-HA104037368.aspx*.

In this exercise, you will create a conversation using the Yammer Web Part.

 SET UP **You don't need any practice files to complete this exercise. Go to a page where the Yammer Web Part has been added and is associated with a Yammer network. If Log In With Yammer appears, click it, and then log on to the appropriate Yammer network.**

> **IMPORTANT** Verify that you are able to contribute to the Yammer network associated with the Web Part.

1   In the **Share something with this group** text box, type **The #2013productline campaign will be launched at the Hong Kong Furniture Fair. More information to follow. #Internationalfurniturefair.**

Marketing Group Feed

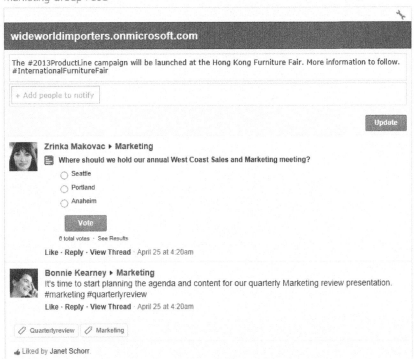

2 Click **Update** to update the feed, and the hashtags become links to Yammer "topics."

Marketing Group Feed

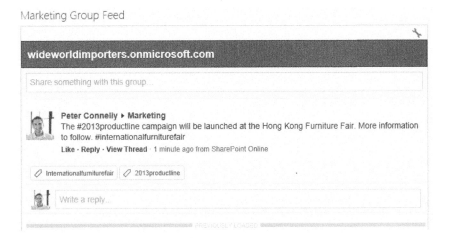

3 Right-click the name of a person in the Yammer feed, and then click **Open link in new tab**. Switch to the new tab to see the person's personal page, which can be likened to a user's profile page in SharePoint.

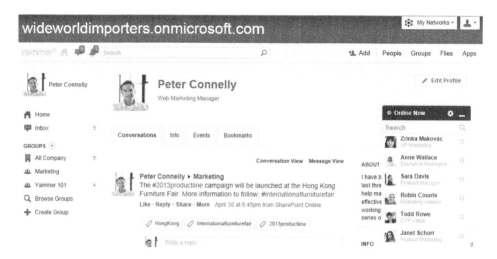

4   Hover over the **2013productline** Yammer topic, and then click the **Edit Topics** link that appears.

5   In the **Add topic** text box, type **HongKong**.

6   Click **Add**, and then click **Done**.

✖ CLEAN UP **Close the browser.**

Working with tags and notes

In SharePoint 2010, you can tag content on a site or leave a note in a document by using the **Tags & Notes** command on the **Browse** tab. In SharePoint 2013, this command is no longer on the **Browse** tab; however, you can still tag and leave notes on pages, lists, libraries, list items, blogs, wikis, images, and tag profiles. Tagging content helps other users quickly find content using search. When a user searches for a term, content that is tagged with that term will appear higher on the search results page than content that is not tagged with that term.

SEE ALSO More information on search can be found in Chapter 9.

You can also use the Tag Cloud Web Part to display a visual depiction of the tags used in your site, where the font size of the words that make up the tag name become larger as the frequency of that tag increases. Click a tag in the **Tags And Notes** dialog or a tag in the tag cloud to display the tag profile page that displays all items that have been tagged with that term and other information. By default, it will only display items that have been tagged in the past 60 days. To search for all items that have been tagged, click **All** to the right of **View**. When you create notes, they appear on the tag profile pages and on your thoughts page. You can go to your thoughts page from a tag profile page or by typing *http://my.wideworldimporters/personal/_layouts/15/thoughts.aspx*, in which *http://my.wideworldimporters* is the web address where your **My Site** is hosted in your organization.

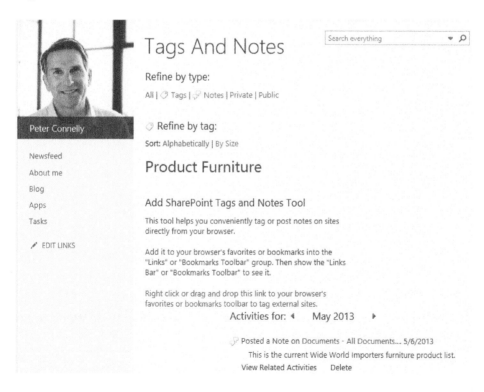

Tags And Notes

Search everything

Refine by type:

All | Tags | Notes | Private | Public

Refine by tag:

Sort: Alphabetically | By Size

Product Furniture

Add SharePoint Tags and Notes Tool

This tool helps you conveniently tag or post notes on sites directly from your browser.

Add it to your browser's favorites or bookmarks into the "Links" or "Bookmarks Toolbar" group. Then show the "Links Bar" or "Bookmarks Toolbar" to see it.

Right click or drag and drop this link to your browser's favorites or bookmarks toolbar to tag external sites.

Activities for: ◀ May 2013 ▶

Posted a Note on Documents - All Documents.... 5/6/2013
This is the current Wide World Importers furniture product list.
View Related Activities   Delete

Peter Connelly

Newsfeed

About me

Blog

Apps

Tasks

✎ EDIT LINKS

TIP In SharePoint 2010, the Note Board Web Part allowed users to quickly add notes to a page. You can still use this Web Part, however, if the **Site Feed** site feature is activated on your site, then microblogging should generally be used.

In the following exercise, you will use tags and notes on a document.

 SET UP **Go to the document library, which contains the document that you would like to tag and make notes in.**

IMPORTANT Verify that you have sufficient rights to modify the document.

1   Click to the left of the document, and then on the **Files** tab, click **Tags & Notes** to display the **Tags and Note Board** dialog.

2   In the **My Tags** text box, slowly type **Product Furniture**, and you may notice that some suggested tags are provided for you.

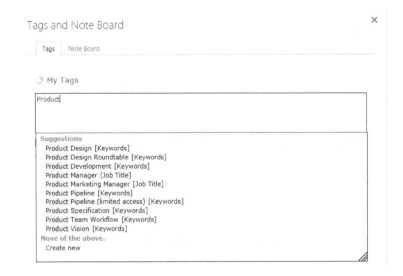

3   Click **Save**.

4   Click the **Note Board** tab, and then type **This is the current Wide World Importers furniture product list**. Click **Post**.

Tags and Note Board   ✕

Tags   Note Board

Post

‹ Previous | Next ›

Peter Connelly 5/23/2013 8:10 AM   Edit   Delete
This is the current Wide World Importers furniture product list.

5   Click the **X** in the top-right corner to close the dialog.

❌ CLEAN UP **Close the browser.**

Creating Community sites

In SharePoint Server 2013, you can create a Community site where like-minded users can collaborate on a common interest. Such groups were probably in existence in your organization and communicating prior to the creation of the Community sites within SharePoint. They may have previously used discussion lists or forums to facilitate communication and exchange information. Members of a community can ask questions on the Community site, knowing that other members of the community are interested in the topic area and may be able to help these answer questions. Such communities are usually based on job types that span the entire organization, such as nurses, lead firefighters, or project managers.

Community sites consist of members and moderators. Users can view the discussions and become members of the community if they want to contribute to those discussions. Moderators manage the community, for example, by setting rules, reviewing and addressing inappropriate posts, and marking interesting content as featured discussions.

Because Community sites are a means for fostering collaboration among large groups of employees in your organization, you should ensure that you have the appropriate backing within your organization. Depending on your organization, this may mean identifying and obtaining the approval of an official sponsor. You also need the commitment of at least two or three moderators. The moderators should welcome new members, be active in the community, and where appropriate, identify replies to posts as a **best reply**. In your organization, there may be other guidelines that your moderators and members need to be made aware of. In large communities, you may also consider engaging the help of users to look after discussions that are associated with specific categories.

TIP Only one post can be marked as a **best reply**. Site owners and the user who created the discussion can remove a reply marked as a **best reply**.

Categories are created in the **Categories** list and consist of a name, description, and picture. The list keeps track of the amount of discussions and replies, so that you can quickly review active discussions.

SEE ALSO More information on planning communities can be found at *technet.microsoft. com/en-us/library/jj219489.aspx*.

In addition to the Community Site template in SharePoint Server 2013, there is a new enterprise site template, Community Portal, where Community sites throughout an organization are listed and where you can visit to search for Community sites that you might want to join. Depending on the way that SharePoint Server is installed in your organization, you may be able to access the Community Portal from the **Sites** hub.

TIP There can only be one Community Portal for an organization, which can only be created as a top level site of a site collection.

Unlike Community sites, once created, a Community Portal requires very little configuration or maintenance by the site owner. The portal is continually updated through tight integration with search, which finds new communities and tracks community statistics such as creation date, number of members, number of discussions, and so forth. The order of Community sites listed on the Community Portal is determined by the number of posts, the number of replies, and the number of members. Posts have a higher weight than replies and members. This means that a community with a smaller number of very active users is considered more popular than a larger, less active community. On the Community Portal home page, you can click the ellipsis to the right of a Community site to display a callout that contains more information.

Communities

Search... 🔍

Welcome to the Community Portal. Check out popular communities, discover topics that interest you, find answers to your questions and connect with others.

Popular Communities

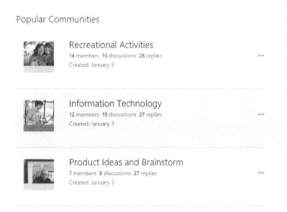

Recreational Activities
14 members 10 discussions 28 replies
Created: January 3
...

Information Technology
12 members 10 discussions 27 replies
Created: January 3
...

Product Ideas and Brainstorm
7 members 9 discussions 27 replies
Created: January 3
...

Information Technology ✕
Community Site

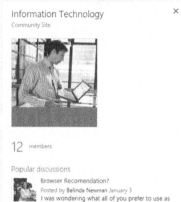

12 members

Popular discussions

Browser Recomendation?
Posted by Belinda Newman January 3
I was wondering what all of you prefer to use as
your default browser when at work or home. I use

TIP You can activate the **Community Site** feature on any site, thereby allowing you to include community functionality on your site; however, the Community Portal uses a Content Search Web Part, which by default is configured to display only those sites that where created using the Community Site template. Sites that were not created from the Community Site template, but have activated the **Community Site** feature, will not appear on the community portal. Of course, the Content Search Web Part on the Community Portal home page could be configured differently. Search is discussed in Chapter 9.

In the following exercise, you will create a community subsite.

 SET UP **Open a SharePoint site where you'd like to create, as a subsite, the new Community site.**

> **IMPORTANT** Verify that you have sufficient rights to create a site. If in doubt, see Appendix A, "SharePoint 2013 user permissions and permission levels."

1 Click the **Settings** gear icon, and then click **Site contents**.

2 Scroll to the bottom of the **Site Contents** page, and then under **Subsites**, click **new subsite**.

3 In the **Title** text box, type **Wide World Importers Furniture Ideas**, and in the **URL name** text box, type **FurnitureIdeas**.

4   Click the **Collaboration** tab, if it is not already active, and then click **Community Site**.

5   At the bottom of the page, click **Create**.

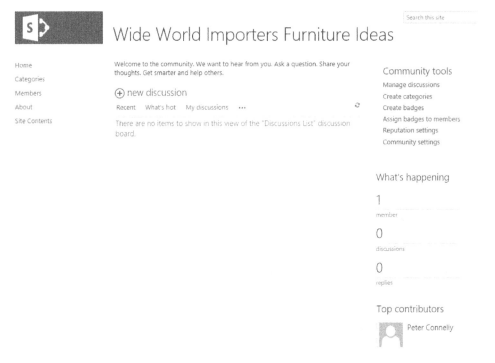

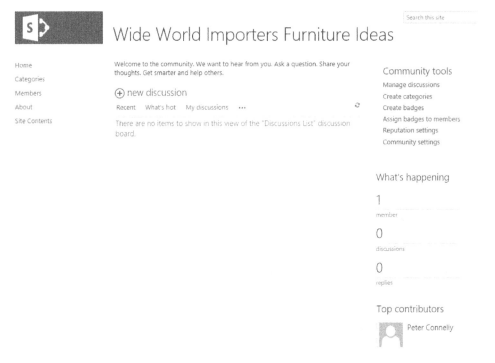 CLEAN UP **Leave the browser open if you are continuing to the next exercise.**

Managing a Community site

Once you create your Community site, you can manage discussions, categories, members, reputation settings, and other community settings. The Community Site template is based on the Team Site template and uses wiki pages stored in the **Site Pages** library. It contains the **Discussions**, **Categories**, **Badges**, and **Community Members** lists.

When you create a Community site with unique permissions, an additional SharePoint Group, named Moderators, is created. It is mapped to the Moderate permission level, which allows moderators to view, add, update, delete, and moderate list items. Members can view, add, update, and delete list items and documents; however, they can only read the Categories and Members list items and site pages.

The **Community Members** list is used to maintain those users who are members of the **Community site**, as well as their reputation settings. The **Members** page displays the **Members** list, which can be sorted by **Top contributors**, **New members**, **A–Z**, or **Z–A**.

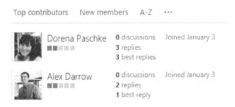

The more that a community member contributes, the higher his reputation. A community owner controls the points for each activity, and can configure point thresholds that are required for the five achievement levels. These achievement levels can be displayed on the **Members** page as either text or an image.

Community owners can also assign gifted badges to members in recognition of their contributions to the community or their expertise. A member can only be assigned one gifted badge; and when it is assigned to a member, the achievement level for that user is not visible on the **Members** page, only the badge.

TIP You can remove yourself from a community by going to the **Members** page, and in the right pane at the bottom of the **My Membership** area, click **Leave This Community**.

You can also use the **Community Settings** page to allow members to report abusive content. Site owners and moderators can review the reported material, and then either remove it or reinstate it.

Site Settings › Community Settings

Established Date

Set the date which represents when your community was established. This date is displayed on the About page of the community. You may want to change this date, for example, if your community existed in some form before this site was created.

4/30/2013

Reporting of offensive content

Select this feature to allow community members to report abusive content. Administrators and Moderators can review reported material and then either remove it or reinstate it.

☐ Enable reporting of offensive content

The **Community site** home page consists of the following areas:

- **Quick Launch** This area provides links to the **Categories**, **Members**, **About**, and **Site Content** pages.

- **Welcome** In this area, you can describe the purpose of the community and any rules that members should abide by.

- **Conversation** This area includes links to create new discussions. Users can sort the discussions by most recent, the most active, and **My Discussions**. By clicking the ellipsis to the right of **My Discussions**, you can use the **Additional Options** menu to find unanswered questions, answered questions, and featured discussions.

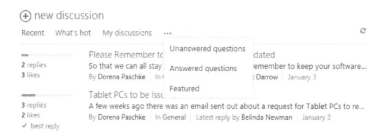

When categories are associated with an image, the conversation area includes a Tile view of all the categories, which, when you hover over them, provide information on the number of discussions and replies.

- **Join this community** This link does not appear on the page for users who are already community members.

- **Community Tools** This area provides administrators with links to manage discussions, create categories and badges, assign badges to members, and configure reputation settings and community settings. These tools are also listed on the **Site Settings** page.

- **What's happening** This area provides a top level summary of the community activi-ties. It is also displayed on the **About** page. The area displays the following informa-tion:
  - The total number of members.
  - The total number of topics, across all categories, where a topic is the root level discussion.
  - The total number of replies to all topics across all categories.
- **Top Contributors** This area lists the top contributors.

In the following exercise, you will upload an image into the **Site Assets** library that will be used for a category. You will create a category, add a discussion for that category, and then modify the reputation settings for the site.

 SET UP **Open the community SharePoint site that you created in the previous exer-cise, if it is not already open. This exercise uses the image file, Sales.jpg, in the Chap-ter07 practice folder, but you could use any image file.**

> **IMPORTANT** Verify that you have sufficient rights to manage the Community site. If in doubt, see Appendix A.

1   On the **Quick Launch**, click **Site Contents**, and then under **Lists, Libraries and other Apps**, click **Site Assets**.

2   Open Windows Explorer and go to the **Chapter07** folder. Drag the image file, **Sales. jpg**, into the **Site Assets** library.

3   Click the ellipsis (to the right of the image file) to display the hover card, and then right-click the URL and click **Copy**.

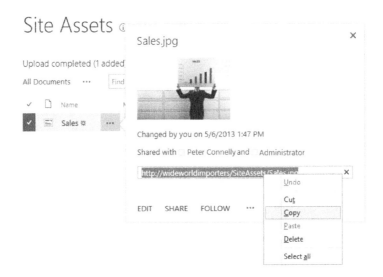

4   On the **Quick Launch**, click **Home**, and then under **Community tools**, click **Create categories**.

5   Click **new item**. In the **Category Name** text box, type **Sales**, and in the **Description** text box, type **Sales questions**.

6   Right-click the text box under **Type the Web address**, and then click **Paste**.

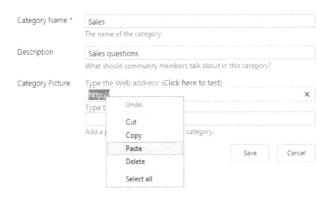

7   Click **Save**.

Categories ⓘ

⊕ new item or edit this list

Category Tiles   Admin View   ⋯   [Find an item   🔍]

✓	Category Name		Description	Discussions	Replies	Last Post By	Last Post Date	Category Picture
	General	⋯	If you don't know where to post, start here.	0	0			
	Sales ✿	⋯	Sales questions	0	0			http://wideworldimporters/SiteAssets/Sales.jpg

8   On the **Quick Launch**, click **Home**, and then click **new discussion**.

9   In the **Subject** box, type **Pricing Guidelines**, and in the **Body** box, type **When will the pricing guidelines be available for the Madrid 2013 furniture line?.**

10   Select the **Question** check box, and then in the **Category** list, select **Sales**.

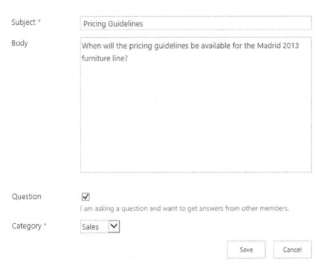

Subject *	Pricing Guidelines
Body	When will the pricing guidelines be available for the Madrid 2013 furniture line?
Question	☑ I am asking a question and want to get answers from other members.
Category *	Sales ▾

Save   Cancel

11   Click **Save**.

12   Click **Pricing Guidelines**. Click the ellipsis for the post, and then click **Mark as featured**.

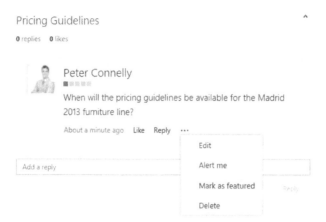

13 In the **Community tools** area, click **Reputation settings** to display the **Community Reputation Settings** page.

14 In the **Member achievements point system** area, in the **Creating a new post** text box, type **5**.

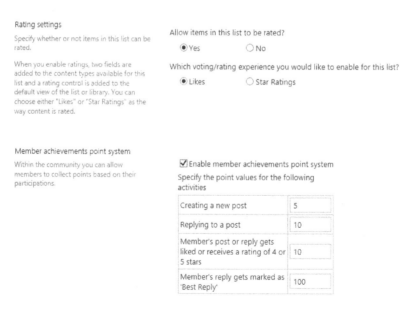

15 In the **Achievement level representation** area, click **Display achievement level as text**. Set **Level 1** to **Beginner**.

Achievement level points

As members accumulate points, they can reach specific levels as milestones of achievement. Specify the number of points required for members to reach each achievement level.

Specify achievement levels

Level 1	More than	0
Level 2	More than	100
Level 3	More than	500
Level 4	More than	2500
Level 5	More than	10000

Achievement level representation

Specify whether achievement levels are represented as a series of boxes or as a textual title. You can customize the title for each level.

○ Display achievement level as image ■■■■■
● Display achievement level as text

Specify a title for each level

Level 1	Beginner
Level 2	Level 2
Level 3	Level 3
Level 4	Level 4
Level 5	Level 5

16   Click **OK.** On the **Quick Launch**, click **Categories** and hover over the **Sales** tile. The number of discussions is 1.

Categories

Pick a category and get into the conversation.

A-Z   Z-A   What's hot   •••

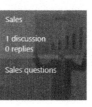

General

Sales
1 discussion
0 replies
Sales questions

✖ CLEAN UP **Close the browser.**

Key points

- The social and collaboration features in SharePoint Server 2013 help you to connect and communicate with other users, and to find, track, and share important content and information.

- The social features within SharePoint are targeted toward Enterprise Social Networking; that is, they focus on the networks and relations you have with others who share business interests.

- Yammer is a cloud-based social network aimed at organizations, where each organization has its own home Yammer network using its own email address. In Office 365, the **Newsfeed** link on the global navigation bar may be replaced with a link to Yammer.

- **My Sites** and **Team sites** are centered on people, feeds, and following.

- You can tag and leave notes on pages, lists, libraries, list items, blogs, wikis, images, and tag profiles.

- Tagging content helps other users quickly find content using search.

- Community sites offer a forum experience to categorize discussions around subject areas, to connect with users who have subject expertise, and to seek information about subject areas.

Chapter at a glance

Categorize

Categorize wiki pages, page 279

Create

Create an Enterprise Wiki site, page 283

Create

Create a blog post, page 296

Add

Add a blog comment, page 299

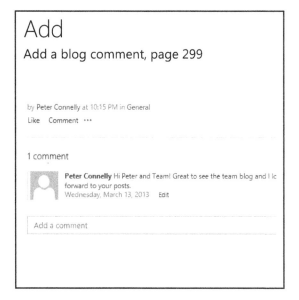

Working with wikis and blogs

8

IN THIS CHAPTER, YOU WILL LEARN HOW TO

- Create a wiki page library.

- Categorize wiki pages.

- Create and use an Enterprise Wiki site.

- Create and manage a blog site.

- Create a blog post.

- Add a blog comment.

Wikis and blogs are methods that enable anyone, including nontechnical users, to write webpages and publish them on Internet, extranet, and intranet websites for other users to see. Both provide users the freedom to publish content for broad consumption. Blogs are personal journals or observations, whereas anyone can contribute to the content on a wiki. When making changes, wiki users are responsible for ensuring accuracy and relevance.

Wiki pages are stored in a wiki library, and when you create a new Team site, Microsoft SharePoint creates a wiki page library, named Site Pages; therefore, your webpages on a Team site are wiki pages. You can create a wiki on any site by creating a wiki library; however, if you want the content on wiki pages to go through a formal approval process, you can create an Enterprise Wiki site. Pages in an Enterprise Wiki site use the same concepts as publishing pages. To create a blog, you must create a blog site.

SEE ALSO For information on wiki pages and publishing pages, please refer to Chapter 4, "Working with webpages," and Chapter 15, "Working with content management."

Most wikis and blogs can use Really Simple Syndication (RSS) feeds to notify users when site content changes. In this chapter, you will learn how to use wikis and blogs, as well as how to enable an RSS feed on a blog.

PRACTICE FILES You don't need any practice files to complete the exercises in this chapter. For more information about practice file requirements, see "Using the practice files" at the beginning of this book.

IMPORTANT Remember to use your SharePoint site location in place of *http:// wideworldmporters* in the following exercises.

Creating a wiki

In organizations, a wiki provides a low-maintenance way to record knowledge. Information that is usually stored in email, discussed around the water cooler, or written on paper can be recorded as knowledge in a wiki, together with similar knowledge. Other example uses of wikis include creating an instruction guide, gathering data from the field, tracking help desk or call center knowledge, brainstorming ideas, and building an encyclopedia of knowledge. For example, wikis are a great way to collate, document, and agree on the practices or ways of working, as well as a way to record work-specific terminology, such as accounting or legal terms. It is a knowledge repository.

If the knowledge is specific to a particular team or project, then a wiki should be created within a site that is used by that team or project. If the knowledge domain will be useful to a number of teams, then you need to create the wiki in a site that all teams can access. Such wikis would store their wiki pages in a wiki library; however, when the knowledge domain is of use for all users in an organization, and the business requires that the content be approved before all users can see it, you should consider using an Enterprise Wiki site.

TIP If your team wants to brainstorm on a project, collect reference material, take notes, or share meeting minutes, then you should consider using a Microsoft Office OneNote notebook for the team. This team notebook should be stored in a document library, and you could provide a link to the team notebook on the **Quick Launch**. Team members need their own copies of OneNote or your organization needs to have installed Microsoft Office Web Apps Companion (WAC) servers, which allow users to view and, depending on the license, edit Office documents, including OneNote notebooks using supported browsers on computers and on mobile devices. If your organization has configured Office Web Apps along with your SharePoint 2013 deployment, then when you create a Team site, a OneNote shared notebook is automatically created as part of the site, and a link to it is provided on the **Quick Launch**. For Team sites that have been upgraded from SharePoint 2010, activating the OneNote site feature will create the shared notebook and link for you. WAC servers are also known as Web Application Open Platform Interface (WOPI) application servers.

By default, all Team sites contain a wiki library where you can store all of your wiki pages, which contain team information, as well as the content that refers to a specific knowledge domain; however, it is best to separate the different types of knowledge into their own wiki page libraries. You can then apply different permission settings on the two wiki libraries; that is, those who create the team pages may not be the users, who should be granted access to contribute, edit, or update the content in a wiki for a specific knowledge domain.

Unlike other libraries, when you click the name of a wiki library, you will be taken to the home page. With other libraries, you are directed to the default view of the library. On the home page of your wiki library, you should specify the purpose of the wiki and any assumptions that apply to the wiki.

For example, if the wiki is to be used for brainstorming, the home page should contain an overview of the brainstorming challenge; you can then provide a list of your thoughts and ideas, which can become links to pages where you and the rest of the team elaborate on them. Other team members can add to your list of thoughts and ideas, which may, in turn, stimulate other brilliant ideas. You may need to monitor the content that others add—not to remove ideas, because in a brainstorming activity, there are no wrong ideas or thoughts; however, if someone has written a judgmental comment, you may need to remove it. Also, as the list of ideas and thoughts grow, you should look for duplicate ideas that you can amalgamate or group together, or for ideas that are not practicable. As the brainstorming wiki progresses, some structure to the content appears. You can first identify the major contender ideas, with supporting comments that other wiki contributors can add to, and then make a decision before sharing the final recommendation to the interested users who were not part of the brainstorming exercise.

8

Therefore, a wiki helps you collect, organize, and share information. Wikis often become the repositories for your unstated knowledge, which otherwise might not be stored anywhere. Wikis can encourage informal learning and sharing tips with other users, which can reduce the need for formal training or continuous IT support.

You might also consider including on the wiki home page a reminder to users to check out wiki pages before editing them. If checkout is not used, information can be lost when more than one person edits a wiki page at the same time; the first person's edits are overwritten when the second user saves the page. You might also have information on how you want contributors to work with your wiki page, which you can include on the home page; for example, when you have recently released a new wiki, you might suggest that contributors limit the time they edit a single page to 10–15 minutes, so that other contributors can add their knowledge.

In this exercise, you will create a wiki page library.

 SET UP **Open the SharePoint site in which you would like to create a wiki page library.**

> **IMPORTANT** Verify that you have sufficient rights to create a library in your site. If in doubt, see Appendix A, "SharePoint 2013 user permissions and permission levels."

1   Click the **Settings** gear icon, and then click **Add an app** to display the **Your Apps** page.

2   Under **Apps you can add**, click **Wiki Page Library** to display the **Adding Wiki Page Library** dialog.

3   In the **Name** text box, type **Company History**, and then click **Create**.

4   On the **Quick Launch**, under **Recent**, click **Company History**. The home page appears with the title, **Welcome to your wiki library**.

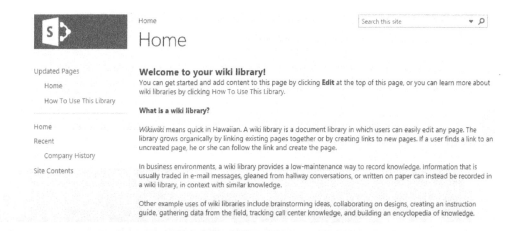

Welcome to your wiki library!

You can get started and add content to this page by clicking **Edit** at the top of this page, or you can learn more about wiki libraries by clicking How To Use This Library.

What is a wiki library?

Wikiwiki means quick in Hawaiian. A wiki library is a document library in which users can easily edit any page. The library grows organically by linking existing pages together or by creating links to new pages. If a user finds a link to an uncreated page, he or she can follow the link and create the page.

In business environments, a wiki library provides a low-maintenance way to record knowledge. Information that is usually traded in e-mail messages, gleaned from hallway conversations, or written on paper can instead be recorded in a wiki library, in context with similar knowledge.

Other example uses of wiki libraries include brainstorming ideas, collaborating on designs, creating an instruction guide, gathering data from the field, tracking call center knowledge, and building an encyclopedia of knowledge.

> **IMPORTANT** The **Name** box is used for both the title and the web address of the wiki page library. A wiki page name should not exceed 128 characters, so you should choose a terse but meaningful name.

✖ CLEAN UP Leave the browser open if you are continuing to the next exercise.

SEE ALSO For more information on using wiki pages, please refer to Chapter 4.

Categorizing wiki pages

If your wiki page library contains many pages, you might want to group pages into categories, and then display those categories on the home page of the wiki library so that visitors to your wiki can easily find information on a specific category. By default, the wiki page library does not provide a method to categorize your pages; however, by adding one or more columns to the wiki page library, and then using a list app on your home page, you can provide an easy category solution for visitors to your wiki.

Before creating a category column in your wiki page library, you need to decide which column type you need to use. You could use a choice column if the categories you wish to use are not specified elsewhere. If the categories are created as items in another list, or as terms in a Term Store, then you could use a Lookup or Managed Metadata column type. When the category choices are used in many lists or libraries, the category column may already be created in your site or site collection as a site column.

SEE ALSO Information on column types can be found in Chapter 3, "Working with documents and information in lists and libraries."

In the following exercise, you will create a category column, categorize a page, and then add a list app to the home page to display the pages grouped by category.

 SET UP **Open the home page of the wiki page library that you created in the previous exercise, if it is not already open.**

IMPORTANT Verify that you have sufficient rights to edit the library settings of the wiki page library. If in doubt, see Appendix A.

1   On the **Page** tab, click **Library Settings**, and then on the **Settings** page in the **Columns** section, click **Create Column**.

2   In the **Column name** text box, type **Category**, and under **The type of information in this column is**, select **Choice**.

3   In the **Type each choice on a separate line** box, enter three choices: **1950s-1980s**, **The 1990s and present**, and **Markets**. Be sure to delete the three predefined generic choices first.

4   Click **OK**, and then on the breadcrumb, click the name of your wiki page library (for example, **Company History**), and then click **Home**.

5   On the **Page** tab, in the **Manage** group, click **Edit Properties**, and then in the **Categories** box, select **The 1990s and present**.

6   Click **Save** to return to the home page, and then on the **Page** tab, click **Edit**.

7   Place the cursor in the wiki content area, to the left of Welcome. Press **Ctrl+A** to select all content, and then press **Delete**.

8   In the wiki content area, type **The History of Wide World Importers**, and then press **Enter** to move the cursor to a new line.

9   On the **Insert** tab, in the **Parts** group, click **App Part**. In the **Parts** pane, under **Parts**, click your wiki page library (for example, **Company History**), and then click **Add**.

10 On the home page, click **Company History**, and then on the **Web Part** tab, click **Web Part Properties** to display the **Company History** Web Part tool pane. You may need to scroll to the right to see the tool pane.

11 Under the **Selected View** box, click **Edit the current view**. If a **Message from webpage** dialog box is displayed, click **OK**.

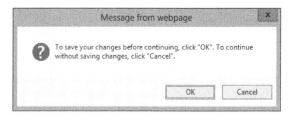

12 On the **Edit View** page, in the **Columns** section, clear the **Modified By**, **Modified**, **Created By**, and **Created** check boxes.

13 In the **Sort** section, in the **First sort by the column** box, select **Name (for use in forms)**.

14 Scroll down and click the **plus sign** (+) to the left of **Group By**. In the **First group by the column** box, select **Category**, and then under **By default, show groupings**, select **Expanded**.

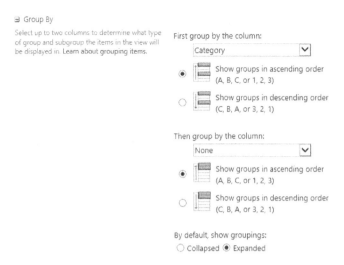

15 At the bottom of the page, click **OK**.

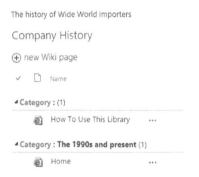

CLEAN UP **Close the browser.**

TIP When a wiki page contributor adds a column to a wiki page library, it may not be obvious that the properties of the page also need to be amended. If you add columns to a wiki page library, you must tell wiki contributors that they need to click **Edit Properties** on the **Page** tab to categorize the page.

Creating an Enterprise Wiki site

An *Enterprise Wiki* is similar to a wiki based on a wiki page library in that it is a knowledge repository; however, it is a publishing site that should be used for sharing and updating large volumes of information across an enterprise. If your organization needs a large, centralized knowledge repository that is designed to both store and share information on an enterprise scale with many authors, consider using an Enterprise Wiki.

Enterprise Wikis can be created as a top level site of a site collection or as a subsite using the Enterprise Wiki site template, which is built on the Microsoft SharePoint Server 2013 publishing infrastructure. This infrastructure provides various ways to control content; for example, you can assign permissions or use a workflow to establish an approval process.

If you believe that the pages of an Enterprise Wiki site will be frequently referenced by a large number of users, and that your wiki will become a valuable business-critical asset to your company, you should consider creating the Enterprise Wiki site as the top level of a site collection. Depending on the implementation of SharePoint in your organization, you may not be able to do this; you may need to contact your IT department. Even if you can create a site collection, you should still contact your IT department because they may wish to implement other infrastructure configurations, such as storing the site collection in a single, dedicated Microsoft SQL Server database so that they correctly prioritize the recovery of the wiki, should a hardware failure occur, or in a disaster recovery scenario.

8

> **IMPORTANT** To create an Enterprise Wiki subsite, the SharePoint Server Publishing Infrastructure site collection feature must be activated. This feature is activated if the top level site of a site collection was created using a publishing site template. Normally, this site collection feature is not activated on site collections where the top level site was created using a Team site; therefore, you usually cannot create an Enterprise Wiki site as a subsite of a Team site.

In the following exercise, you will create an Enterprise Wiki subsite.

SET UP **Open a SharePoint site where you'd like to create a new Enterprise Wiki subsite.**

1   Click the **Settings** gear icon, and then click **Site contents**.

2   Scroll to the bottom of the **Site Contents** page, and then under **Subsites**, click **new subsite**.

Tasks
3 items
Modified 2 weeks ago

Subsites

⊕ new subsite

3   In the **Title** text box, type **SharePoint Governance**, and in the **Description** text box, type **This site contains information on how Wide World Importers are implementing SharePoint, guidance on how to use SharePoint, a knowledge base where answers to questions can be found and who to contact, plus their roles and responsibilities.**

4   In the **URL name** text box, type **WideWorldImporters_Governance**.

5   Click the **Publishing** tab if it is not already active, and then click **Enterprise Wiki**.

TROUBLESHOOTING If the Publishing tab is not displayed, make sure that the SharePoint Server Publishing Infrastructure site collection feature is activated.

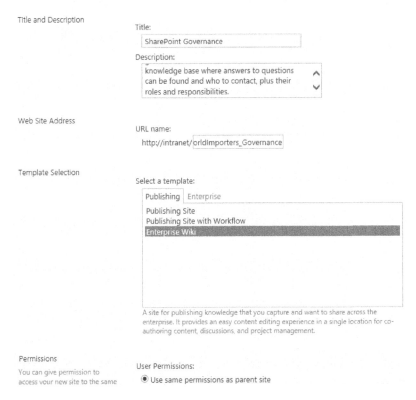

Site Contents › New SharePoint Site

Title and Description

Title:

SharePoint Governance

Description:

knowledge base where answers to questions
can be found and who to contact, plus their
roles and responsibilities.

Web Site Address

URL name:

http://intranet/orldImporters_Governance

Template Selection

Select a template:

| Publishing | Enterprise |

Publishing Site
Publishing Site with Workflow
Enterprise Wiki

A site for publishing knowledge that you capture and want to share across the
enterprise. It provides an easy content editing experience in a single location for coauthoring content, discussions, and project management.

Permissions

You can give permission to
access your new site to the same

User Permissions:

● Use same permissions as parent site

8

6   Keep the default settings for the options in the **Permissions** and **Navigation Inheritance** sections, and then click **Create**.

✖ CLEAN UP **Leave the browser open if you are continuing to the next exercise.**

SEE ALSO Information on sites can be found in Chapter 5, "Creating and managing sites."

Using an Enterprise Wiki site

When an Enterprise Wiki site is first created, the home page of the site describes what an Enterprise Wiki site is and why you might want to use one. The Enterprise Wiki site provides additional capabilities that you do not see when you are using a wiki page library to store your wiki pages, such as assigning a category or rating to the page. Also, wiki pages on an Enterprise Wiki site are stored in a document library named Pages.

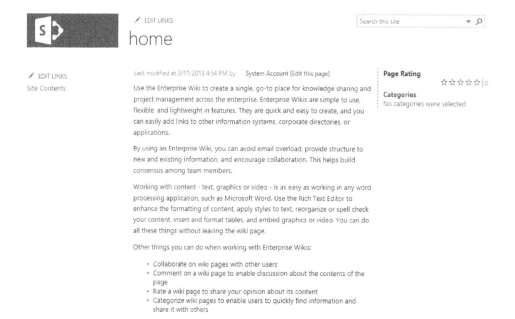

A wiki page on an Enterprise Wiki site behaves similarly to a wiki page in a wiki page library:

- It can contain static and dynamic content, including Parts (app parts and Web Parts).

- You can create forward links to pages by using the double square brackets around a WikiWord. For example, type [[Site-Collection-Administration]] to create a link to the page named Site-Collection-Administration. The page does not have to exist when the forward link is created.

- Major versioning is enabled on the Pages library; therefore, no amendments are lost and you can restore a page to a previous version.

- You use the ribbon tabs, such as **Page**, **Format Text**, and **Insert** to add content to a page and manage pages.

SEE ALSO For more information on editing and managing pages, refer to Chapter 6, "Making lists and libraries work for you."

However, there are some differences:

- The top of the page shows the date the page was last modified and the person who modified it.

- You can edit the page by clicking **Edit This Page**, which appears at the top of the page to the right of the name of the person who last modified the page.

- When you upload an image or a file, the default location is the Images library. By default, the Enterprise Wiki site does not have a Site Assets library. The Documents, Site Collection Documents, and Site Collection Images libraries are other libraries where you might consider storing uploaded files.

- When an Enterprise Wiki site is first created, you cannot change the layout of the page. You are limited to one column of content. Additional page layouts can be created using the Design Manager, which can be accessed from the **Settings** gear icon.

  TIP You cannot convert or migrate Enterprise Wiki pages to wiki pages in a wiki page library without using custom code. You could create a new wiki page in a wiki page library, and then copy and paste the content; however, any content, such as the insertion of apps or Web Parts may need to be deleted and re-created. Also if you included images on a page, when you copy the image from one page to another, the location where the image is stored remains the same; for example, it will still be stored in the Images library. You may consider deleting the image from the page, uploading the image in the Site Assets library on the Team site, and then placing the image on the wiki page.

Because a page on the Enterprise Wiki site is a publishing page, you can complete the following tasks:

- With the page in edit mode, you can check the spelling of text on the page by clicking **Spelling** on the **Format Text** tab. You can also check spelling in another language from the **Spelling** split button command.

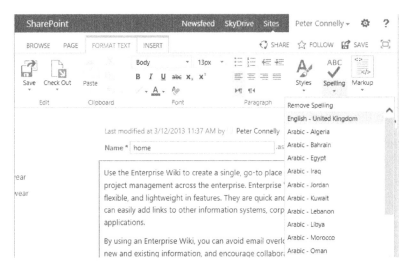

As in Microsoft Office programs such as Word or Excel, misspelled words are under-lined with a jagged red line. When you right-click the misspelled word, a drop-down list provides recommended suggestions, or you can choose to ignore the misspelled word or all misspelled words that were found.

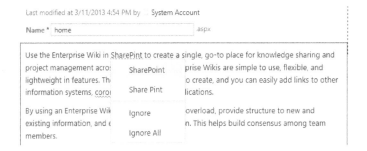

- You can check for unpublished items on your page. This is useful, for example, if you upload images into a library that has been configured for content approval, or you have enabled minor and major versioning, and you include those images on your page; however, if you have not approved the image or you have not published it as a major version, a user who comes to your page and only has Read permission will not be able to see the image. The user may see a red **X** where the image should be; this is known as a broken link. To identify such images or files, you can use the Unpublished Items Report, which is generated by clicking **Draft Check** on the **Page** tab, in the **Page Actions** group.

- On the **Insert** tab, you can add predefined content, such as the company name, a copyright, or a hyperlink. This is known as *reusable content*, which can consist of blocks of text and HTML elements. This allows the wiki owner to create content once, and then the wiki contributors reuse these pieces of content rather than copying and managing duplicate copies of content manually on different pages.

The Pages library on the Enterprise Wiki site is less restrictive than other publishing pages that you may be used to. Scheduling and the Publishing Approval workflow are not enabled in the library.

SEE ALSO Information on publishing pages can be found in Chapter 15.

Adding categories to Enterprise Wiki pages

Pages in an Enterprise Wiki site can be categorized to help readers browse or find related pages. A category can be a word or a phrase. When you first create an Enterprise Wiki site, the category box appears to the left of the wiki content, but it is dimmed and does not allow you to categorize the page. The categorization of Enterprise Wiki pages relies on the *Managed Metadata Service* (*MMS*) and *Term Store*, which allow you to centrally define categories, and then reuse them throughout the organization in multiple site collections.

Categories, also known as terms, are collected together as *term sets*. Term sets are put into groups, which can be managed by one or more designated users. Term sets can be created in the Term Store by the designated users using the browser, or imported from a .csv file. A designated user can go to the Term Store from the Site Settings page by clicking **Term Store Management**, under Site Administration. Before you can categorize pages, you must select a term set for the **Pages** library column: Wiki Categories.

TROUBLESHOOTING The MMS and Term Store are only available in SharePoint Server. The MMS service application and Term Store must be created by your SharePoint server administrator. If the server administrator has not created the MMS service application and Term Store, you will not be able to categorize your Enterprise Wiki pages using the Categories box to the right of the wiki content.

In the following exercise, you will select a term set for the Wiki Category column, and then categorize a wiki page.

 SET UP **Open the Enterprise Wiki site that you created in the previous exercise, if it is not already open.**

IMPORTANT Verify that you have sufficient rights to edit the library settings of the Pages library of the Enterprise Wiki site. If in doubt, see Appendix A.

1   On the **Page** tab, click **Library Settings**.

2   Scroll down the **Settings** page, and then in the **Column** section, click **Wiki Categories**.

3   On the **Edit Column** page, in the **Term Set Settings** section, click the arrow to the left of your Managed Metadata Service to display the term set groups.

4   Click the arrow to the left of a term set group, and then click a term set.

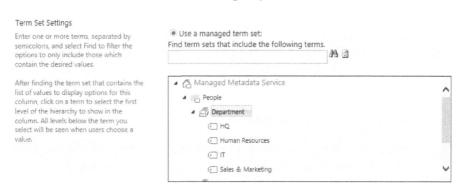

Term Set Settings

Enter one or more terms, separated by
semicolons, and select Find to filter the
options to only include those which
contain the desired values.

After finding the term set that contains the
list of values to display options for this
column, click on a term to select the first
level of the hierarchy to show in the
column. All levels below the term you
select will be seen when users choose a
value.

5   In the **Default Value** section, to the right of the **Default Value** text box, click **Browse for a valid choice** to display the **Select Default** dialog.

6   Click one of the terms, and then click **Select**.

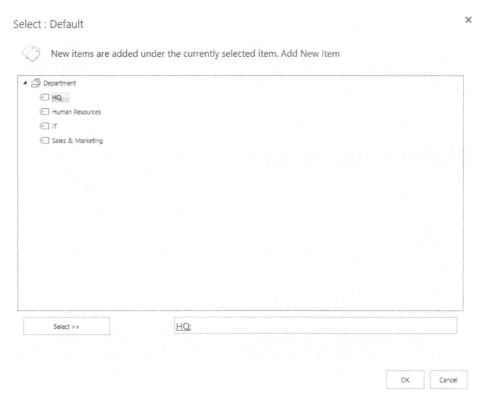

7   Click **OK** to close the **Select Default** dialog.

Default Value
Enter the default value for the column

Default value:

HQ;

Delete   OK   Cancel

8   Click **OK** to close the **Edit Column** page.

9   On the breadcrumb, click **Pages** to display the contents of the Pages library, and then click the page that you would like to categorize, such as **home**.

10 On the line that contains **Last Modified**, click **Edit this page**.

11 To the right of the **Categories** text box, click **Browse for a valid choice** to display the **Select Wiki Categories** dialog.

12 Click one of the terms, and then click **Select**. Click **OK** to close the **Select Wiki Categories** dialog.

13 On the **Page** tab, click **Save**.

❌ CLEAN UP **Close the browser.**

TIP Once you have categorized a page, the term you have used for the category becomes a hyperlink. If you click the term, you will see that all pages have been categorized with that term.

Creating a blog site

A web log, known as a blog, is a personal journal or commentary shared on a website. *Blogging* refers to publishing thoughts, in formal essays or more informal formats, on a blog website. A person who does this is called a *blogger*. The thoughts shared on the blog website are called *posts* or articles. Each post or article is displayed in reverse chronological order, with the most recent additions featured most prominently, and older items grouped in archives organized by the month in which they were created.

Blog posts can be categorized to help users find past conversations. Also, blogs are indexed so that a visitor can search through old blogs and learn from past conversations. Bloggers write blogs frequently, often on a daily basis. Some bloggers allow visitors to comment on the blog to provide feedback and to ask questions.

TIP When using SharePoint, the logical location for a user's blog site is his personal site, or My Site, where a link exists to create a blog.

A blog can also be used by a group of people, such as a team or an organization. The Microsoft SharePoint and the Microsoft Office team blogs, for example, are found at *blogs. office.com* and *blogs.office.com/b/sharepoint*, respectively.

Instead of sending out email or newsletters to the team or organization, you should consider using a blog as a platform where information and opinions can be traded among team members or employees. An organization blog that is published on the Internet is a powerful marketing tool and can influence purchasing decisions by showing visitors to the blog that the organization is an expert in its field.

If you are going to create a team or business blog, then you should spend time thinking of what you want to achieve and the areas of expertise you want to share. You should carefully choose who should join you in posting blogs, ensuring that they commit to blogging, let's say, at least once a month. Choose authors who are smart and passionate about the topics you wish the blog to cover. Also, at least one of you must manage the blog.

In this exercise, you will create a blog site, and then establish categories for your blog posts.

 SET UP **Open a SharePoint site where you'd like to create, as a subsite, the new blog site.**

IMPORTANT Verify that you have sufficient rights to create a site. If in doubt, see Appendix A.

1   On the **Quick Launch**, click **Site Contents**, and then under **Subsites**, click **new subsite**.

2   In the **Title** box, type **IT Blog**, and then, in the **URL name** box, type **IT_Blog**.

3   Under **Select a template** on the **Collaboration** tab, click **Blog**.

4   Click **Create**.

CLEAN UP **Leave the browser open if you are continuing to the next exercise.**

Managing your blog

The home page of a Blog site consists of three areas:

- **Quick Launch** This area contains the following:

  - **Categories** This section provides links to words or phrases that you can use to categorize your posts. When a blog site is created, three sample categories are created: **Events**, **Ideas**, and **Opinions**. The names of the categories are saved in a list named **Categories**.

  - **Archives** This section provides links to old blog posts and displays only those posts that are approved.

- **Left** This area displays blog posts in published date order, 10 blog posts at a time. Posts are stored in a list named **Posts**. Each post states the time that the post was published, and at the bottom of the post are the name of the person who published it and the category. Clicking the category link on this line displays a page where all similarly categorized posts are listed. This behavior is the same as clicking a selection under **Categories** on the **Quick Launch**.

- **Right** This area contains the following:

  - **Blog Tools** This section provides blog owners and administrators links to create and manage posts, to manage comments and categories, and to launch a blogging app. It also allows you to change the layout of the main part of the page. You have three options: **Basic**, **Boxed**, and **Inline**.

  - **About This Blog** This is a Content Editor Web Part (CEWP), which, when you first create a blog site, contains an image and some static text. The CEWP is configured to hide the title of the Web Part, and therefore you will only see the title, About This Blog, when the page is in edit mode.

  - **Blog Notifications** This Web Part allows visitors to your blog site to register for blog post notifications using RSS Feeds or Alerts. The Web Part title—**Quick Links**—is hidden, and is therefore only visible when the page is in edit mode.

In this exercise, you will create categories for your blog posts and remove the categories and blog post that were created when the blog site was created.

➡ SET UP **Open the blog site that you created in the previous exercise, if it is not already open.**

> **IMPORTANT** Verify that you have sufficient rights to edit the home page of the blog site and the rights to amend the Category and Posts lists. If in doubt, see Appendix A.

1 On the **Quick Launch**, under **Categories**, click **ADD CATEGORY**, and then in the **Title** text box, type **Mobile**.

2 Click **Save**.

3 On the home page, under **Blog tools**, click **Manage categories**.

4   Select the **Ideas**, **Opinions**, and **Events** categories, and then on the **Items** tab, click **Delete Item** in the **Manage** group.

5   Click **OK** to confirm that you wish to send the items to the site Recycle Bin.

6   Under **Categories**, click **new item**. In the **Title** text box, type **General**, and then click **Save**.

7   On the **Browse** tab, click **Home** to display the home page of the blog site.

8   Under **Blog tools**, click **Manage posts** to display the **Posts** list.

9   Click the ellipsis to the right of **Welcome to my blog**, and then click **Delete Item** from the list item menu.

10 Click **OK** to send the blog post to the site Recycle Bin.

 CLEAN UP **Close the browser.**

Creating a blog post

A blog post is the method by which you share your opinions and knowledge. You must remember that, as a blogger, you are responsible for the commentary that you post and you can be held personally liable if your posting is considered defamatory, obscene, proprietary, or libelous. Similar to posting information on a wiki, you should practice good manners and understatement.

You can create a blog post by using many tools, including Word 2007, Word 2010, and Word 2013; OneNote 2007, OneNote 2010, and OneNote 2013; Microsoft Live Writer; and the browser. On the blog website, under **Blog Tools**, there is a link that allows you to start a blogging app, such as Word, to quickly create a blog post. The **New SharePoint Blog Account** dialog box appears. The web address of the blog site is listed in the **Blog URL** text box.

A Word dialog box then opens, warning that when Word sends information to the blog service provider, it may be possible for other people to see that information, including your user name and password. If you choose to continue, another Word dialog box opens, stating that the account registration was successful.

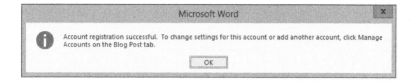

Once a blog post is opened in Word, the **Blog Post** tab is active. The Blog group provides easy access to the home page of your blog site, so that you can insert a category to the blog post, open an existing blog, manage accounts, and publish the blog. Any pictures that you insert into the post using Word are automatically copied to the Photos picture library when the blog post is either published or published as a draft.

In the following exercise, you will create and modify a blog post by using the browser.

SET UP **Open the blog SharePoint site that you created previously in this chapter.**

> **IMPORTANT** Verify that you have sufficient rights to create a post. If in doubt, see Appendix A.

1   On the blog site's home page, under **Blog Tools**, click **Create a post**.

2   In the **Title** box, type **Welcome**, and in the **Body** box, type **Welcome to the IT team blog! My name is Peter Connelly and I'm the IT team leader and I have the honor to create the first entry for the team blog, which will be used by all those working in the IT team. Please use comments to provide feedback to posts.**

3   In the **Category** list, select **General**, and then click **Add**.

TIP Similar to other Microsoft programs, it is possible to add multiple categories in webpages by holding down the Shift key while selecting the categories between the first click and the second click. Holding down the Ctrl key selects or clears categories.

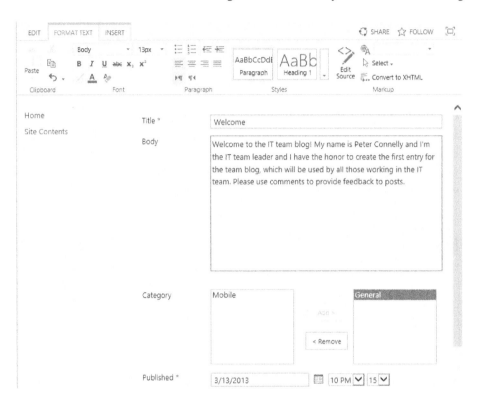

4   On the **Edit** tab, click **Publish**.

TIP If you include pictures on any of your posts, upload them into the Photos picture library on your blog website.

5   At the bottom of the post, click the ellipsis, and then click **Edit**.

6   In the **Title** section, to the right of Welcome, type **to the IT team blog**.

7   Click **Publish**.

✖ CLEAN UP **Leave the browser open if you are continuing to the next exercise.**

Adding a blog comment

To interact with a blogger, you can leave comments on a blog post. As a blogger, you must review the comments on your posts, not only to respond to comments but also to delete comments that are either off-topic or are used to advertise websites or broadcast spam. If the aim of a blog post is to start a discussion but you receive virtually no responses, you could use a comment to post a question to your own blog post.

In this exercise, you will add a blog and delete a comment on a blog post.

➡ SET UP **Open the blog SharePoint site that you used in the previous exercise, if it is not already open.**

> **IMPORTANT** Verify that you have sufficient rights to create comments in the Comments list. If in doubt, see Appendix A.

1   On the blog site's home page, below a post, click **0 comments**.

2   In the **Add a comment** text box that appears, type **Hi Peter and Team! Great to see the team blog and I look forward to your posts.**

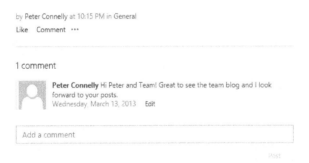

Categories
General
Mobile
ADD CATEGORY

Archives
March
OLDER POSTS

Welcome to the IT team blog
Wednesday, March 13, 2013

Welcome to the IT team blog! My name is Peter Connelly and I'm the IT team leader and I have the honor to create the first entry for the team blog, which will be used by all those working in the IT team. Please use comments to provide feedback to posts.

by Peter Connelly at 10:15 PM in General
Like   Comment   •••

0 comments
There are no comments for this post.

Hi Peter and Team! Great to see the team blog and I look forward to your posts.

Post

3   Click **Post**.

used by all those working in the IT team. Please use comments to provide feedback to posts.

by Peter Connelly at 10:15 PM in General
Like   Comment   •••

1 comment

Peter Connelly Hi Peter and Team! Great to see the team blog and I look forward to your posts.
Wednesday, March 13, 2013   Edit

Add a comment

Post

4   To the right of the date of the comment, click **Edit**.

5   On the **Edit Comment** page, on the **Edit** tab, click **Delete Item**.

6   Click **OK** to send the comment item to the Recycle Bin.

❌ CLEAN UP **Close the browser.**

Key points

- Use a wiki when you need a knowledge repository and you want to encourage informal contributions.

- A wiki helps you create webpages quickly, and it helps users to freely create and edit webpage content by using a web browser.

- Use a wiki page library if you need to set up a project or team area of knowledge.

- An Enterprise Wiki is a good solution for sharing and updating large volumes of information across an enterprise.

- Enterprise Wiki pages can be rated and categorized with enterprise keywords.

- A page on the Enterprise Wiki site is a publishing page, and therefore you can complete other tasks that you cannot complete on a wiki page in a wiki page library, such as spell check, draft check, and reusable content.

- Blogs are personal journals or observations that are usually maintained by one person.

- Blog posts can be categorized to help users find past conversations.

- To interact with a blogger, you can post comments on the blog.

- Bloggers should moderate posted comments for objectionable or inappropriate content.

- The Blog Posts list is enabled for RSS support, thereby allowing users to syndicate content.

8

Chapter at a glance

Search

Search a SharePoint site, page 304

Use

Use Advanced Search, page 316

Add

Add promoted results, page 320

Customize

Customize search results pages, page 328

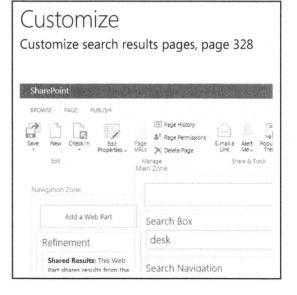

Searching for information and people

9

IN THIS CHAPTER, YOU WILL LEARN HOW TO

- Search your SharePoint site.

- Use a search query.

- Configure search behavior for your site.

- Use Advanced Search.

- Set up search alerts.

- Influence relevance rankings.

- Customize the search results page.

- Search for people.

- Define your site visibility.

In today's workplace, huge volumes of increasingly different types of content are produced. Information workers need to quickly find people and content to get answers to their questions and to get their everyday tasks completed. That's where the new Microsoft SharePoint 2013 search capabilities can help you surface the information that you need, when you need it.

TIP Search capabilities in SharePoint 2013 are powered by a new search engine that brings together the simplicity of SharePoint Search and the flexibility of FAST Search, which were separate products in SharePoint 2010.

Searching is the process of entering one or more search words in the search box to form a search query that is executed against the index built on the SharePoint server farm. The search application that runs on the server farm processes your *query* and returns a set of *search results* that match your query. These search results contain links to the webpages, documents, list items, lists, libraries, or sites that you want to find.

At the heart of the SharePoint search engine is its ability to get the search results that users are looking for. However, the results you are looking for can differ based on who you are, your context, and your previous searches. The SharePoint Search uses relevancy algorithms combined with an analysis engine to provide a search experience that is flexible, intuitive, and tailored to user needs.

In this chapter, you will learn how to search your SharePoint site, use search queries, modify the search behavior on your site, connect to the Search Center, use advanced search and search verticals, set up search alerts, influence relevance rank to promote the search results, customize search results pages, and define whether to include or exclude your site from search.

PRACTICE FILES Before you can complete the exercises in this chapter, you need to copy the book's practice files to your computer. The practice files that you'll use in this chapter are in the **Chapter09** practice file folder. A complete list of practice files is provided in "Using the practice files" at the beginning of this book.

IMPORTANT Remember to use your SharePoint site location in place of *http:// wideworldimporters* in the exercises.

Searching your SharePoint site

The new SharePoint search experience is intuitive, engaging, and easy to use. The site search box appears on the top right of most webpages on your site, allowing you to search the current site and any subsites below it.

TIP In a list or a library, there is also a search box on top of the content list so that you can search for content from that list or library.

The search results page combines three main areas. There is a search box that displays your query, the search results list shown below the search box, and the search refiners displayed at the left of the screen that provide additional filters so that you can narrow the search results to help you find what you are looking for.

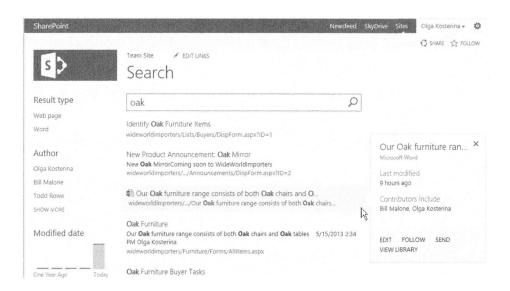

The search results page functionality is provided by three interconnected Web Parts: the **Search Box** Web Part, the **Search Results** Web Part, and the **Refiners** Web Part.

A search result is only helpful when you can act on it. On the search results page, you can act on the search results without opening them; this is done by using the *hover panel*. When you point to a search result, the callout appears to the right of the result, and you can preview the search result content. For example, with a document, the hover panel provides a callout with a live preview, including a deep dive that takes you to the correct part of the document by using deep links. The hover panel also allows you to act on that result with contextual actions based on the result itself. For a document, the menu of actions includes options to edit the document, to follow the document, to send its link to other people, and to open the library where the document resides. For a webpage, the actions include options to open the page or send its link to other people. The search results are security trimmed so only the content and actions that a user has rights to are displayed.

A search result may be displayed with additional indicators, depending on the type. For example, Microsoft Office files, such as Word or Excel, are displayed with the application icon in front of the title of the search result, whereas newsfeed conversations are displayed with the number of replies and the number of **Likes**.

In addition to using a search box on your site, you can also use an **Enterprise Search Center** or a **Basic Search Center** to enter search queries and view the search results. Both **Search Centers** provides an ability to search an entire enterprise, including all SharePoint sites, files shares, and Microsoft Exchange folders, as well as other content sources that are set up by your SharePoint administrator. The **Enterprise Search Center** requires the SharePoint Server 2013 while the **Basic Search Center** is available in all SharePoint 2013 on-premises solutions.

TIP In Microsoft SharePoint Online, a **Search Center** site is automatically available at host_name/search.

The **Enterprise Search Center** provides several pages known as *search verticals*. Search verticals are search pages that are targeted for searching specific content, including **Everything**, for a search across all content; **People**, for specific people searches; **Conversations**, for searching newsfeed conversations; and **Videos**, for searching different types of videos. The list of search verticals is located under the search box in the **Search Center** page. Search verticals provide different search experiences and display search results that are filtered and formatted for content that is specific to this vertical.

The links that let users move quickly between the search verticals are displayed by the **Search Navigation** Web Part. By default, the **Search Navigation** Web Part is set up to show links to the **Everything**, **People**, **Conversations**, and **Videos** search verticals. The **Search Navigation** Web Part gets search results from the **Search Results** Web Part. When users click a link for a search vertical, the search results are displayed according to the search vertical configuration.

The Basic Search Center provides a single search results page, without the search verticals.

In this exercise, you will explore the search results page and use refiners to narrow your search.

 SET UP **Open the SharePoint site that you would like to search. This exercise will use the** *http://wideworldimporters* **site, but you can use whatever SharePoint team site you wish. If prompted, type your user name and password, and then click OK.**

1   In the top-right corner of the home page, in the search box, type a query term, such as **oak**, and then click the magnifying glass icon on the right of the search box, or press **Enter** on the keyboard.

The search results page is displayed. It contains items that match your query term, including documents and webpages. If more than one page of content items matches your query, the total number of pages in the search results appears at the bottom, with each page number representing a link to that page of the overall result set. Notice that the search word, **oak**, is highlighted in the titles of all results.

TROUBLESHOOTING After you have installed a practice site for this chapter, you may need to wait at least 30 minutes for the content to be indexed and shown in the search results page.

2   On the left of the page, in the **Refiners** panel, under **Result type**, click **Word** to display all Microsoft Office Word documents in the search results.

3   Point to the **Oak Chest** document to open its hover panel. Notice that the panel lists information about the document, such as when it was last modified and the names of the contributors. In this example, the contributors are Bill Malone and Olga Kosterina.

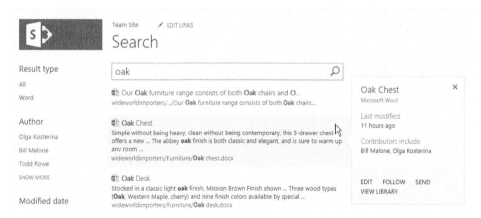

4   You will now display all Word documents authored by Bill Malone. In the **Refiners** panel, under **Author**, click **Bill Malone** to narrow the search results. There are two documents displayed: **Oak Chest** and **Oak Night Stand**.

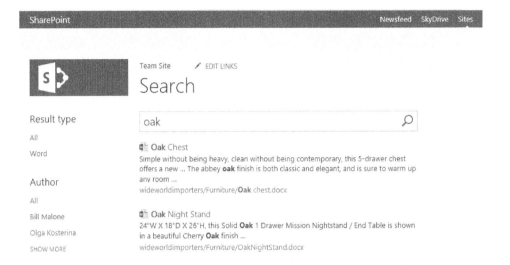

5   Remove the **Author** and the **Result type** refiners by clicking **All** in the **Author** section and the **Result** type section, respectively.

6   You will now display the webpages in the search results. Under **Result type**, click **Web page**. Point to the **Oak Furniture Buyer Tasks - Calendar** search result to display the hover panel. Notice the preview of the live page shown in the callout.

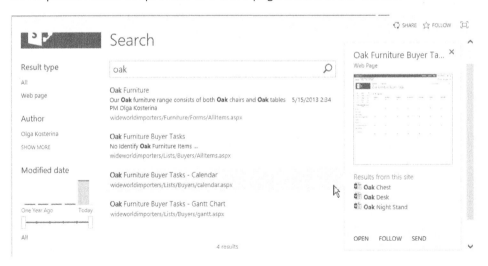

7   Return to the site home page by clicking its link on the top link bar, above the **Search** title.

❌ CLEAN UP **Leave the browser open if you are continuing to the next exercise.**

Using search queries

A *search query* contains one or more words that represent the content that you are trying to find. When executing a query, SharePoint returns a set of content items that form a result set. Your queries are executed against an aggregated database of the content, known as an *index*, which enables SharePoint to respond quickly. You can think of the search index as similar to the index you find at the end of this book. The index is updated periodically using a process called content *crawling*. By default, the content is crawled incrementally once every 20 minutes, but the frequency can be configured differently by your SharePoint administrator. Therefore, when you create new data in your SharePoint site, such as a new announcement, it may not appear immediately in your result set. Similarly, if you delete a document from a document library, it still may appear in the result set, but when you click the link for the document, an error message, "The webpage cannot be found," displays. In this case, the link to the document in the result set is called a *broken link*.

TROUBLESHOOTING If you query to locate information that you know exists, but it doesn't appear in your result set, check the spelling of your search query, wait at least 30 minutes, and repeat the search query. If it still does not appear in the result set, then the index has not been updated; therefore, contact your SharePoint administrator for assistance.

To find information, you may need to enter more than one query term. The more query terms that you enter, the more specific and precise your query becomes, thereby producing a more focused result set. Search queries can include any of the following items:

- A single word
- Multiple words
- A single phrase in quotes
- Multiple phrases in quotes

SharePoint uses an implicit AND query when you search for multiple words or multiple phrases. For example, when you search for the multiple, separate words "oak" and "furniture," the search result set contains only those content items where both words occur. Those words do not have to be side by side, but they do both need to be in the content item somewhere. If a document contains the words "oak" and "chest" but not "oak" and "furniture," that document will not appear in the result set. When you search for the complete phrase "oak furniture," the result set contains only those content items where the two words "oak furniture" appear together.

9

When you use two words or two phrases in your search query and separate them by the word OR, if either word or phrase appears in a document, that document appears in the result set. You can create more complex search queries, such as (chest OR furniture) AND oak. This will return content items that contain the words "oak" and "chest" or the words "oak" and "furniture," but will not return content items that contain the word "chest" and "furniture."

TIP The logical operators in a search query, such as AND and OR, must be uppercase.

In earlier chapters of this book, you used columns on lists and libraries to save list item and document property values, also known as *metadata*. You can use some of these *metadata properties* to help you create powerful search queries, thereby creating a more focused result set. For those metadata properties that store text, in the search box, use the syntax property:value where *value* is a word or phrase. For example, you can use the following default metadata properties for more targeted searches:

- **Author** Use this to find all content items authored by a particular person or persons, such as author:peter.

- **Filename** Use this to find documents by their file name, such as filename:proposal.

- **Filetype** Use this to find specific file types, such as filetype:docx.

- **Title** Use this to find content items based on the value entered in the title column, such as title:"oak chest".

- **Description** Use this to find content items based on the value entered in the description column, such as description:oak.

- **Contenttype** Use to find the content items of a particular type; for example, document, announcement, task.

- **Size** Use this to find files according to their size. For example, size>45000 will find all files greater than 45,000 bytes.

TIP To create targeted search queries, SharePoint 2013 provides a Keyword Query Language (KQL). The query can consist of free-text keywords, property filters, or operators. Keyword queries have a maximum length of 2,048 characters. For more information on KQL syntax, see *msdn.microsoft.com/en-us/library/ee558911(v=office.15).aspx*.

SharePoint Server 2013 supports *managed metadata*, which is a hierarchical collection of centrally managed terms that you can define, and then use as attributes for content items. Consistent use of metadata across sites in your organization helps with content discoverability. As you have seen in the previous exercise, by using a metadata property as a search refiner, a user can filter search results based on metadata.

TIP When you enable managed metadata, the managed metadata service application is automatically created to make it possible to use and share content types across sites on your SharePoint server.

In this exercise, you will use search queries for targeted searches of your site.

➡ SET UP **Open the SharePoint site that you would like to search. This exercise will use the** *http://wideworldmporters* **site, but you can use whatever SharePoint team site you want. If prompted, type your user name and password, and then click OK.**

> **IMPORTANT** Verify that you have sufficient permissions to execute a query in the site that you are using. If in doubt, see Appendix A.

1   In the top-right corner of the home page, in the search box, type a search query such as **Author:"Todd Rowe"** to find all content items authored by Todd Rowe, and then click the magnifying glass icon on the right of the search box, or press **Enter** on the keyboard.

The search results page is displayed showing all content items that were created by Todd Rowe.

2   On the search results page, in the search box, type the search query **Filetype:docx** to find all files with extension .docx, and then either click the magnifying glass or press **Enter**. All files with a .docx extension on your site are listed in the search results panel.

9

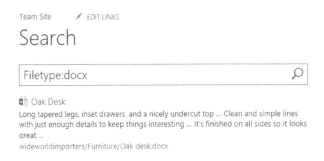

3   You will now search for the items that contain both "oak chairs" and "oak furniture." On the search results page, in the search box, type a search query, **"oak chairs" AND "oak furniture"**, and then either click the magnifying glass or press **Enter**.

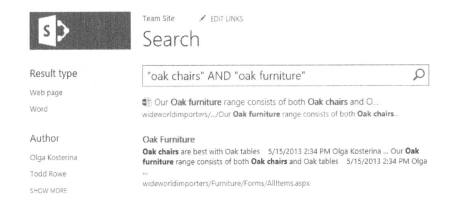

Notice that the search results include a Word document with the title that contains both terms, as well as the webpage of the document library where this document is located.

4   You will now search for the items that contain either "oak chairs" or "oak furniture." On the search results page, in the search box, type the search query, **"oak chairs" OR "oak furniture"**, and then either click the magnifying glass or press **Enter**.

Notice that there are more items returned in the search results than in the previous step. In addition to the items that include both terms, there are also items that include either of the terms.

⊗ CLEAN UP Leave the browser open if you are continuing to the next exercise.

Configuring search behavior

Search functionality is flexible and configurable, and you can tailor the search experience for your site. The **Search Settings** on the **Site Settings** page allow you to specify the search behavior on you site. The search box and the search results page will use these settings.

TIP The search settings that you configure on the site collection level will be inherited by all sites within that site collection, unless you configure other settings for the site that would override the inheritance.

Site Settings › Search Settings

Use this page to configure how Search behaves on this site. The shared Search Box at the top of most pages will use these settings. Note: A change to these settings may take up to 30 minutes to take effect.
Change search behavior for this site collection and all sites within it.

Enter a Search Center URL When you've specified a search center, the search system displays a message to all users offering them the ability to try their search again from that Search Center.	Search Center URL: `[                    ]` Example: /SearchCenter/Pages or http://server/sites/SearchCenter/Pages
Which search results page should queries be sent to? Custom results page URLs can be relative or absolute. URLs can also include special tokens, such as {SearchCenterURL}. This token will be replaced by the value in the "Search Center URL" property. If the value in this property ever changes, any URL using the token will update automatically. Example: {SearchCenterURL}/results.aspx	☑ Use the same results page settings as my parent. ○ Send queries to a custom results page URL. Results page URL: Example: /SearchCenter/Pages/results.aspx or http://server/sites/SearchCenter/Pages/results.aspx ● Turn on the drop-down menu inside the search box, and use the first Search Navigation node as the destination results page.
Configure Search Navigation Search Navigation allows users to move quickly between search experiences listed in the Navigation. Navigation is displayed in the Quick Launch control on search pages, and can also be shown as a drop-down menu from the search box.	Move Up Move Down 🖉 Edit... ✕ Delete 🔗 Add Link... No items found. Selected Item No item currently selected.

Using the **Search Settings**, you can add the link to an Enterprise Search Center, where users can search everything in your company. Then, the search verticals will be shown in the Search Navigation Web Part on the search result pages on your sites. In addition, the search box on your site can include the drop-down list with search verticals from the **Search Center**. The users will be able to choose whether to search your site only, or choose the search verticals to search across all sites and other content sources using the **Search Center**. The default setting for the search box is the site where it is located. You can also add an additional search vertical by using a search navigation configuration for a site. The new link to the vertical will be shown in the Search Navigation Web Part on search result pages, and it can also be shown as a drop-down list in the search box.

In the following exercise, you will configure a Search Center URL, and then test the search behavior on your site. You will need to know the URL of the Enterprise Search Center in your SharePoint environment to complete this exercise.

➜ SET UP Open the SharePoint site where you would like to configure a search. This exercise will use the *http://wideworldmporters* site, but you can use whatever SharePoint team site you want. If prompted, type your user name and password, and then click **OK**.

1   In the top-right corner of the page, click the **Settings** gear icon and select **Site settings**.

2   On the **Site Settings** page, under **Search**, click **Search Settings**.

3   In the **Search Center URL** box, type the URL of the **Search Center** site in your environment. In this example, the Search Center URL is **http://wideworldimporters/search/Pages**, but in your environment, it will be different.

Enter a Search Center URL

When you've specified a search center, the search system displays a message to all users offering them the ability to try their search again from that Search Center.

Search Center URL:

http://wideworldimporters/sites/search/Pages

Example: /SearchCenter/Pages or http://server/sites/SearchCenter/Pages

4   To display the drop-down list of search verticals within the search box, select **Turn on the drop-down menu inside the search box, and use the first Search Navigation node as the destination results page**, if it is not already selected, and then click **OK** to return to the **Site Settings** page.

5   You will now test the search behavior that you've configured. Go to the site home page by clicking its link on the **Quick Launch**.

9

6   In the search box on the top of the page, click the down arrow that opens a drop-down menu of search verticals, and then select **Everything** to search all content via the Enterprise Search Center.

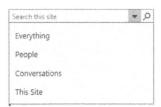

Search this site

Everything

People

Conversations

This Site

7   The search box now shows that the search will search **Everything**. In a search box, type a query text, for example, **oak**.

8 The Search Center results page is displayed. Right under the search box, there is a list of search verticals.

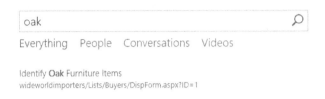

Click the **Back** button in the top-left corner of the browser window to return to the home page of your site.

9 On your site home page, validate that the search box on the top of the page shows **Search this site**, and then type **oak** in the search box. The search results page for your site is displayed.

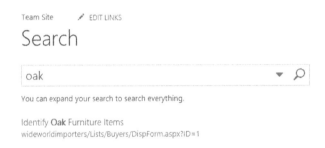

10 Under the search box, click **expand your search**. You are taken to the **Search Center** results page that shows the results of your search across all sites.

❌ CLEAN UP **Leave the browser open if you are continuing to the next exercise.**

Using Advanced Search

SharePoint provides the form to construct search queries in the **Advanced Search** page. Using **Advanced Search**, you can include or exclude words and phrases in the query, filter results by document format, narrow results by language, and filter results by content properties.

In the following exercise, you will construct a query that searches for documents that contain "oak chest", are in English, and have an **Author** property that contains "Bill Malone".

SET UP Open the **Search Center** where you would like to use Advanced Search, if it is not already open. This exercise will use the *http://wideworldmporters/sites/search*, but you can use the **Search Center** site you want. If prompted, type your user name and password, and then click **OK**.

IMPORTANT Verify that you have sufficient permissions to use search in the site that you are using. If in doubt, see Appendix A.

---

1 At the bottom of the **Search Center** page, below the search results, click **Advanced Search**.

2 On the **Advanced Search** page, in the **All of these words** box, type **oak chest**.

3 Select **English** from the list of languages available.

4 In the **Result type** list, select **Word Document**.

5 In the **Add property restrictions** section, in the **Where the Property** list, select **Author**, select **Contains** as a logical operator, and then type **Bill Malone** as a property value.

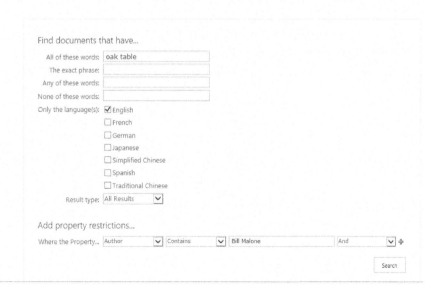

Search Center

Advanced Search

Find documents that have...

All of these words:	oak table
The exact phrase:	
Any of these words:	
None of these words:	
Only the language(s):	☑ English
	☐ French
	☐ German
	☐ Japanese
	☐ Simplified Chinese
	☐ Spanish
	☐ Traditional Chinese
Result type:	All Results

Add property restrictions...

Where the Property... | Author | Contains | Bill Malone | And

Search

9

TIP To add another property, select the logical operator, such as **AND** or **OR**, and then click the **plus sign** (+) to the right of the property line that you've already created.

6 Click **Search**. Only one document, Oak Night Stand, satisfies the search criteria in our example.

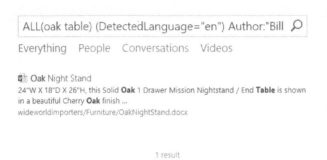

CLEAN UP Leave the browser open if you are continuing to the next exercise.

Setting up search alerts

You can set up a search alert on a search results page so that you receive an email or an SMS text message when the results change for that search query. You can set up alerts on any site search results page, as well as a **Search Center** results page.

Search Center
New Alert ⓘ

Alert Title

Enter the title for this alert. This is included in the subject of the
notification sent for this alert.

Search: ALL(oak table) (DetectedLanguage="er

Delivery Method

Specify how you want the alerts delivered.

Send me alerts by:

◉ E-mail

Change Type

Specify the type of changes that you want to be alerted to.

Only send me alerts when:

◉ New items in search result
◯ Existing items are changed
◯ All changes

When to Send Alerts

Specify how frequently you want to be alerted. (mobile alert is
only available for immediately send)

◉ Send a daily summary
◯ Send a weekly summary

You can choose the type of changes that you'd like to be notified of, such as only when
there are new items in the search results or only when existing items change, or whether
you'd like to be alerted to all changes. You can also set the frequency of alerts to be daily or
weekly.

In the following exercise, you will set up an alert for the advanced search query that you
performed in the previous exercise.

 SET UP **Open the SharePoint site where you would like to set up a search alert, if it is
not already open. If prompted, type your user name and password, and then click OK.**

IMPORTANT Verify that you have sufficient permissions to use search in the site that you are
using. If in doubt, see Appendix A.

1 Run a query that you would like to set an alert for to display the search results page,
if it is not already displayed. At the bottom of the search results page, below the
search results, click **Alert Me**.

2   On the **New Alert** page that appears, specify the name of the query or keep the default, which is the query itself.

3   Define the delivery method as **email**.

4   In the type of changes that you'd like to be notified of, select **All changes**.

5   In the frequency, select **Send a daily summary**, and then click **OK**.

   TIP In SMS alerts, immediate notifications are sent.

You have set up a search alert to be notified by email of changes to the search results on a daily basis.

 CLEAN UP **Close the browser.**

Influencing the relevance rank

When the results of the search are displayed, the search engine calculates the *relevance rank*; in other words, the order in which the search results appear. SharePoint Search uses several *ranking models* that are based on the predefined algorithms that calculate the ranking score of a particular item in the search results. By default, search results are sorted in descending order based on their ranking score. Items with the top score get the top position in search results. *Rank* is the order in which search results are displayed.

Using the search index, the ranking models combine weighted scores for a number of different criteria, including content, metadata, file type, and interaction. For example, depending on your business environment, it may be that some file types are more important from a ranking perspective than others are, and therefore their scores would be higher. Typically, Word and Microsoft Office PowerPoint search results have higher scores than Excel results, and therefore they are displayed higher in the search results page. Another example is an interaction score that is based on the number of times a search result is clicked, and on the queries that led to a result being clicked. For the final ranking score of a search result, all ranking criteria in the ranking model are combined.

TIP The search system automatically uses the appropriate ranking model for the default search verticals: **Everything**, **People**, **Conversations**, and **Videos**.

SharePoint provides a mechanism to influence the ranking of search results by using query rules. A *query rule* consists of a query rule condition and a query rule action. When a query matches a query rule condition, it triggers a query rule action. For example, by using a que-ry rule, you can show a search result above all ranked results. This result is called a *promoted result*. You can also group several results in a result block, and then promote the group in the same way.

For example, you can promote a specific page that contains important information for site visitors to be aware of so that a link to this page appears on top of all search results for a particular period of time—for example, a day. Or you can promote a specific content item to display at the top of the search results when the user searches for particular topics.

TIP A promoted result was called Best Bets in earlier versions of SharePoint.

In the following exercise, you will create a query rule that will promote the **Oak Furniture** library to display at the top of search results when a user searches for "oak" or "furniture."

➜ SET UP **Open the SharePoint site where you would like to configure the search. This exercise will use the *http://wideworldmporters* site, but you can use whatever SharePoint team site you want. If prompted, type your user name and password, and then click OK.**

IMPORTANT Verify that you have sufficient permissions to configure search in the site that you are using. If in doubt, see Appendix A.

1 In the top-right corner of the page, click the **Settings** gear icon and select **Site settings**.

2 On the **Site Settings** page, under **Search**, click **Query Rules**.

3 On the **Manage Query Rules** page, in the **Select a Result Source** list, select **Local SharePoint Results (System)**. This is a prebuilt result source that includes an index for all SharePoint sites in the current farm, with the exception of people.

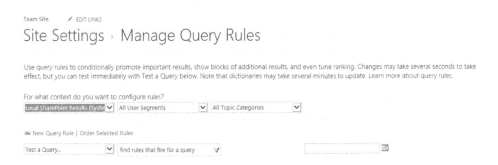

4   Click **New Query Rule**.

5   On the **Add Query Rule** page, in the **General Information** section, in the **Rule name** field, type a name for your query; for example, **MyQueryRule**.

6   In the **Context** section, in the **Query Conditions** section, select **Query Matches Keyword Exactly**, and then in the **Query exactly matches one of these phrases (semicolon separated)** box, type **oak; furniture**.

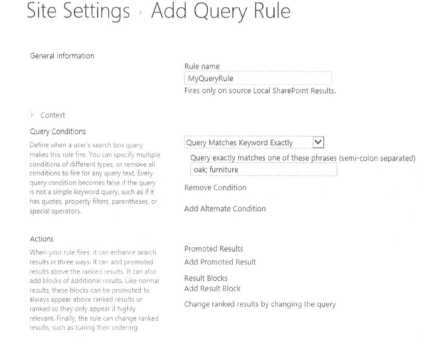

7   In the **Action**s section, click **Add Promoted Result**.

8   In the **Add Promoted Result** dialog, in the **Title** field, type the name that you want to give this promoted result; for example, **Wide World Importers Oak Furniture**. This is a display name that will be shown in the results page.

9   In the **URL** field, type the URL of the result that should be promoted; for example, **http://wideworldimporters/Furniture/AllItems.aspx**.

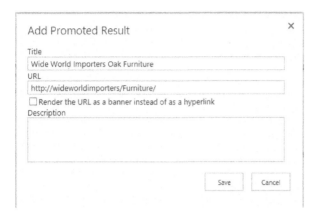

10 Click **Save** to return to the **New Query Rule** page. The new promoted result, **Wide World Importers Oak Furniture**, has been created and is displayed in the **Actions** section on the **News Query Rule** page.

Promoted Results
1 ▾ Wide World Importers Oak Furniture edit remove
Add Promoted Result

11 Click **Save** to save your new query rule and return to the **Manage Query Rules** page.

12 On the **Manage Query Rules** page, validate that your new query is listed under the **Defined for this site** section.

Name	Modified	Conditions	Actions
Defined for this site (1)			
MyQueryRule	5/16/2013	Query Matches Keyword Exactly furniture; oak On Result Source Local SharePoint Results	Add Promoted Results Wide World Importers Oak Furniture

13 You will now test your new query rule. Go to the site home page by clicking its link on the top link bar, just above the page title.

14 In the search box on the top right of the page, type **oak**, and then click the magnifying glass icon, or press **Enter** on the keyboard. In the search results page, validate that the **Wide World Importers Oak Furniture** link is displayed on top of the results set.

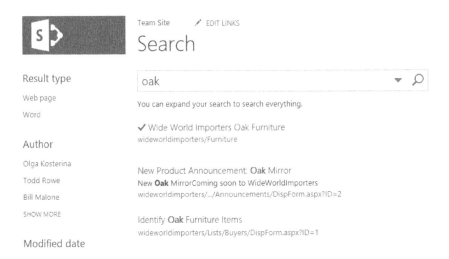

CLEAN UP Leave the browser open if you are continuing to the next exercise.

You will often find that you need to display an item on top of the search results page for all search queries, unconditionally, for a limited period. In the following exercise, you will create a query rule that will display an existing webpage at the top of search results on all search queries, active from today until the end of tomorrow.

SET UP Open the SharePoint site where you would like to configure the search. This exercise will use the *http://wideworldimporters* site, but you can use whatever SharePoint team site you want. If prompted, type your user name and password, and then click **OK**.

> **IMPORTANT** Verify that you have sufficient permissions to configure a search in the site that you are using. If in doubt, see Appendix A.

1   In the top-right corner of the page, click the **Settings** gear icon and select **Site settings**.

2   On the **Site Settings** page, under **Search**, click **Query Rules**.

3   On the **Manage Query Rules** page, in the **Select a Result Source** list, select **Local SharePoint Results (System)**, and then click **New Query Rule**.

4   On the **Add Query Rule** page, in the **General Information** section, in the **Rule name** field, type a name for your query rule; for example, **TodayQueryRule**.

5   In the **Context** section, under **Query Conditions**, click **Remove Condition**. The query condition boxes have been removed. This query rule will fire on any query text.

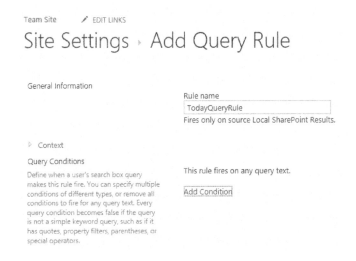

6   In the **Actions** section, click **Add Promoted Result**.

7   In the **Add Promoted Result** dialog, in the **Title** field, type the name that you want to give this promoted result; for example, **Hello World!**. In the **URL** field, type the URL of the result webpage that you'd like to promote; for example, **http://wideworldim-porters/SitePages/HelloWorld.aspx**, and then click **Save**.

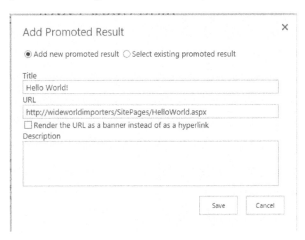

8   Back in the **New Query Rule** page, verify that the new query rule has been created and is listed in the **Actions** section.

9 Expand the **Publishing** section to specify the schedule when the rule will be active. Enter a **Start Date** of today and an **End Date** of tomorrow.

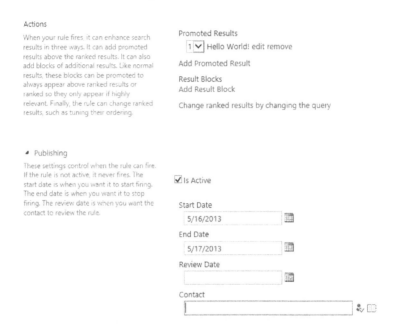

10 Click **Save** to save your new query rule and return to the **Manage Query Rules** page.

11 On the **Manage Query Rules** page, validate that your new **TodayQueryRule** query is listed under the **Defined for this site** section.

12 You will now test the new query rule. Go to the home page by clicking its link on the top link bar, above the page title.

13 In the search box on the top right of the page, type any query text; for example, **chair**. On the search results page, validate that the **Hello World!** link is displayed on top of the results set.

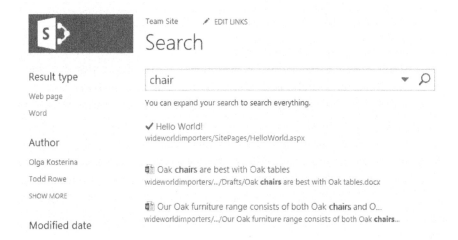

14   You will now compare the rankings for the promoted results. In the search box, type **oak**. Both query rules have fired, and both promoted items are displayed on the top of the list. **Hello World!** is displayed first because it is a more recently promoted result. The ranking model considers the most recent results as more relevant; therefore, **Hello World!** has a higher ranking than the **Wide World Importers Oak Furniture** promoted result, which is displayed second.

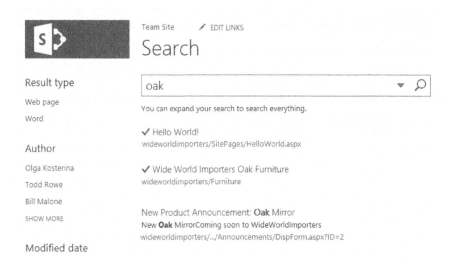

✕ CLEAN UP **Leave the browser open if you are continuing to the next exercise.**

Customizing the search results page

On your site, a user enters search queries into a search box and views the search results using the default search results page. On the Enterprise **Search Center** site, there is a default search page where the search box is located, as well as several search verticals. *Search verticals* are customized search results pages targeted for searching specific content. By default, the Web Parts on the search vertical pages are the same. However, the query in the Search Results Web Part is executed against a particular result source configured differently for each search vertical page. With the **Everything** vertical, for example, the query is executed against the Local SharePoint Results, which is a default result source that covers all content in your SharePoint installation, with the exception of people. For the **People** vertical, the search runs against Local People Results, a result source that defines the search results in the vertical page.

Several Web Part pages provide the search experience in the Enterprise **Search Center** site, including the following:

- **Default.aspx** The **Search Center** home page where users enter their queries.
- **Results.aspx** The default search results page for the **Search Center**; it is also the search results page for the **Everything** search vertical.
- **Peopleresults.aspx** The search results page for the **People** search vertical.
- **Conversationresults.aspx** The search results page for the **Conversations** search vertical.
- **Videoresults.aspx** The search results page for the **Videos** search vertical.
- **Advanced.aspx** The page that provides an **Advanced Search** form.

All of these search results pages are located in the **Pages** library and contain the same Web Parts, as follows:

- **Search Box Web Part** Provides the search box functionality at the top of the search results page

- **Search Results Web Part** Provides the search results in the body of the search results page

- **Refinement Web Part** Provides the refiners, or filters, in the left part of the search results page

- **Search Navigation Web Part** Provides the search verticals navigation links beneath the search box

You can customize Web Parts within the search results pages and configure the different Web Parts settings to modify the pages' behavior. The **Pages** library is configured to require checkout, so you need to check in and publish your changes to the search results pages before other users can see them.

In the following exercise, you will modify the default search results page and configure properties of the **Refinement** Web Part.

SET UP **Open the SharePoint Search Center site where you would like to modify the search results page. This exercise will use the** *http://wideworldmporters/sites/search* **site, but you can use whatever Search Center site you want. If prompted, type your user name and password, and then click OK.**

> **IMPORTANT** Verify that you have sufficient permissions to modify the search results page in the site that you are using. If in doubt, see Appendix A.

1   Open the **Search Center** page, and in the search box, type any search text (for example, **desk**) to display the search results page.

2   On the search results page, click the **Settings** gear icon on the top right of the page, and then select **Edit Page** from the menu. The four Web Parts in the page are displayed.

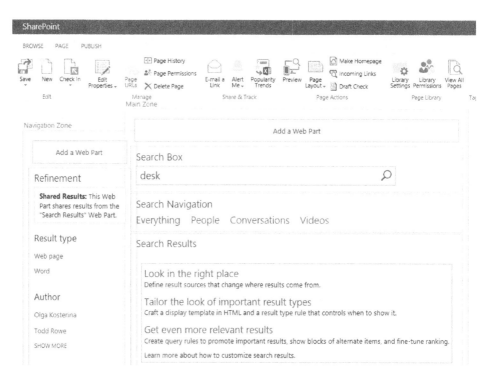

3   On the left of the screen, in the **Refinement** Web Part, hover over the **Refinement** title and click the down arrow that appears on the right to display the Web Part menu. Select **Edit Web Part**.

4   In the Web Part tool pane on the right of the screen, in the **Properties for Search Refinement** section, verify that the **Choose Refiners in this Web Part** option is selected, and then click **Choose Refiners**.

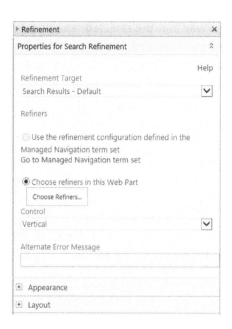

5   You will now remove a refiner that shows when the item was modified. In the
     Refinement configuration dialog, in the **Selected refiners** section on the right, select
     LastModifiedTime, and then click the **Remove** button to move this refiner to the list
     of **Available refiners** on the left.

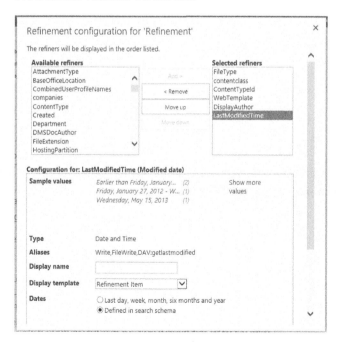

6   You will now change the order of the way that the selected refiners are shown in the Web Part. In the **Selected refiners** section, click the **DisplayAuthor** refiner, and then click the **Move Up** button a few times to position this refiner at the top of the **Selected refiners** section.

7   In the **Refiner** configuration dialog, click **OK**.

8   In the **Web Part** tool pane on the right of the screen, click **Apply**. Verify that your modifications are shown in the **Refinement** Web Part, and then click **OK** in the **Web Part** tool pane to close it.

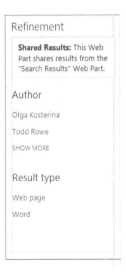

9   In the warning displayed in the yellow bar underneath the ribbon, click **Check In**, and then in the **Comments** dialog, click **Continue**.

10   The empty search results page is displayed. Click **Publish this draft** in the warning
      (displayed in the yellow bar on top of the page) that the recent draft has not been
      published.

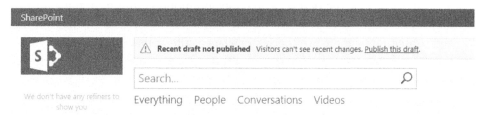

11   The search results page has been published and is redisplayed. Type a query into a
      search box; for example, **furniture**. Press **Enter** to see the search results in the page
      and to test your modifications to the **Refinement** Web Part.

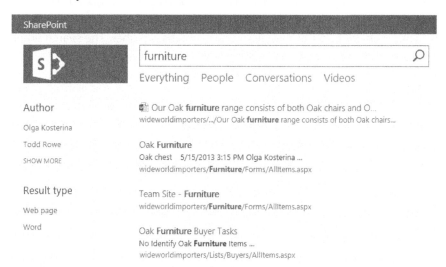

❌ CLEAN UP **Leave the browser open if you are continuing to the next exercise.**

Searching for people

The **People** vertical provides the ability to search for people in your organization against the default result source Local People Results, which is dedicated to people information. The profile store and personal sites are a major source of information for a people search. The profile store is crawled on a regular basis in a similar way to other SharePoint sites, and the content is added to a people-specific index that the search queries in the **People** vertical are executed against. Conceptually, a user profile is treated as a document about that person, with the person's name as the title.

At a basic level, the more search query terms that appear in the person's profile, the more relevant the result. The people search ranking models differ from the information search ranking models. The relevance rank is assigned to search results that are related to people, and subsequently there are specific relevance criteria that include social distance and expertise. On the **People** vertical search results page, you can sort the results by relevance, name, and social distance.

Social distance is computed based on colleague relationship. For example, people who are on the same work team as you will be close to you in regards to social distance. You may also follow other people and content, and other people may follow you. You may participate in conversations with them, and they provide regular comments on your **Newsfeed**. You may also be a member of mailing lists and discussion groups, so you would be considered closer to the members of the same groups than to those who are not members, because your visibility to other people in these groups is higher. The search engine takes this data into consideration when calculating social distance.

Basic expertise information is collected from the user profile; in particular, the **Ask Me About** and **Skills** fields. Other fields are also taken into account, including **Past projects** and **Interests**, and more importantly, the documents that users worked on that are relevant to the search query. To get the best results from a people search, people in your organization should add as much information as they can to their user profiles in the profile store, as well as in their personal sites.

In the next exercise, you will enter information to your user profile, and then explore the **People** vertical search results page.

 SET UP **Open a SharePoint site where you can access your user profile in the profile store. This exercise will use the *http://wideworldmporters* site, but you can use whatever SharePoint team site you want. If prompted, type your user name and password, and then click OK.**

1   To access your user profile, on the top right of the page, click **Newsfeed**, and then in the **Newsfeed** page, click **About Me** on the **Quick Launch**.

2   On the **About Me** page, click **edit** on the top of the page to open your profile for editing.

About Olga Kosterina

⊘ edit your profile

Tell others about yourself and share your areas of expertise by editing your profile.

3   In the **Edit Details**, page, in the **Basic Information** tab, notice that some information has been prepopulated, including your name and when the profile was created by your administrator. Click in the **About Me** field to display the ribbon, and then type some information about yourself. The search engine will crawl this information and use it in the search results page. Your picture from this page will also appear in the search results page in the **People** vertical.

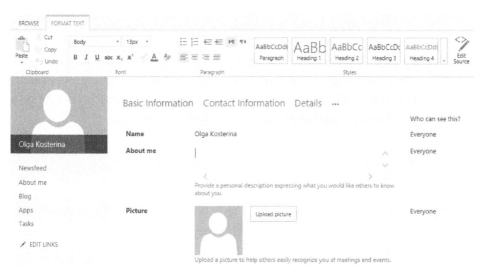

4   At the bottom of the page, fill in your areas of expertise in the **Ask Me About** field. The information from this field will be indexed for the expertise searches and will contribute to expertise relevance rankings.

Ask Me About

Update your "Ask Me About" with topics you can help people with, such as your responsibilities or areas of expertise.

5   Click the **Contact Information** tab and fill in the details, such as your phone number or office location. For some fields, you can choose who will be able to see this data: only you or everyone. Because SharePoint search results are security trimmed, the data that only you can see will not appear in the search results page.

Edit Details

Basic Information   Contact Information   Details   ...

Who can see this?

Mobile phone   Everyone

This number will be shown on your profile. Also, it will be used for text message (SMS) alerts.

Fax   Only Me

Home phone   Only Me

6   Click the **Details** tab and fill in the fields as much as you can. The data in these fields can be used not only for relevance ranking, but also for expertise searches (the **Past projects**, **Skills**, and **Interests** fields) and as an input into computing social distance (the **Schools**, **Past projects**, and **Interests** fields).

		Who can see this?
Past projects		Everyone ▾
	Provide information on previous projects, teams or groups.	
Skills		Everyone ▾
	Include skills used to perform your job or previous projects. (e.g. C++, Public Speaking, Design)	
Schools		Everyone ▾
	List the schools you have attended.	
Birthday		Only Me ▾
	Enter the date in the following format: May 16	
Interests		Everyone ▾
	Share personal and business related interests. We will help you keep in touch with activities related to these interests through events in your newsfeed.	

7 Click on the ellipsis to the right of the **Details** tab to display additional tabs, such as **Newsfeed Settings** and **Languages and Regions**. Both tabs contain information that is indexed by the People search. The **Newsfeed Settings** page, for example, provides a lot of information that can be used in computing the social distance.

		Who can see this?
Followed #Tags		Everyone ▾
	Stay up-to-date on topics that interest you by following #tags. Posts with these #tags will show up in your newsfeed.	
Email Notifications	☑ Someone has started following me ☑ Suggestions for people and keywords I might be interested in ☑ Someone has mentioned me ☑ Someone replied to a conversation that I started ☑ Someone replied to a conversation that I replied to ☑ Someone replied to my community discussion post Pick what email notifications you want to get.	
People I follow	☐ Allow others to see the people you're following and the people following you when they view your profile.	Everyone

Activities I want to share in my newsfeed	☐ Share all of them ⓘ
	  ☐ Following a person
	  ☐ Following a document or site
	  ☐ Following a tag
	  ☐ Tagging an item
	  ☐ Birthday celebration
	  ☐ Job title change
	  ☐ Workplace anniversary
	  ☐ Updating your "Ask Me About"
	  ☐ Posting on a note board
	  ☐ Liking or rating something
	  ☐ New blog post
	  ☐ Participation in communities
	
	Pick the activities you want to tell people about.
		Everyone

9

8   Fill in as much information as you can, and then on the bottom of the **Edit Details** page, click **Save all and close**. In the **Profile Changes** dialog that warns you that the user profile information might not be available right away, click **OK**. Depending on your crawler frequency, it might take a bit of time before your profile is indexed and the data appears in the search results.

9   You will now use the People vertical search. Go to the **peopleresults.aspx** page in the **Search Center** site, and in the search box, type one of the skills you entered in your user profile.

10   Explore the search results page. It displays people in your organization with their photos, where available, in the order of relevance ranking for your query, which is a default for ordering the search results page. You can also display the search results by first name and social distance. On the top of the page, open the drop-down list of ordering options and click **Social Distance** to display the search results by their social distance from you.

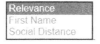

TROUBLESHOOTING If you do not see yourself in the search results page, you may need to wait at least 30 minutes for your user profile data to be crawled and indexed.

✖ CLEAN UP **Leave the browser open if you are continuing to the next exercise.**

Defining your site visibility

By default, all local sites are included in the search results on the **Enterprise Search Center**. The local sites are crawled and their content is indexed and included in the default result source Local SharePoint Results. Sometimes you might need to exclude a site from the search results, even though the users in your organization have access rights to it. For example, when you are redesigning or updating a site, you might want to temporarily exclude this site from showing in search results. The **Search and Offline Availability** page in the **Search** group in **Site Settings** provides an option to define whether the site is indexed, and thus, is visible in the search results. When you exclude your site from search, you also exclude all its subsites.

TIP You can also force reindexing of your site from the **Search and Offline Availability** page. If you force reindexing, the site will be fully reindexed at the next crawl, instead of running a default incremental crawl that picks up the changes since the last crawl.

In the following exercise, you will exclude a site from the search results, and then bring it back again.

SET UP **Open the SharePoint Search Center site that you would like to exclude from the search results. This exercise will use the** *http://wideworldmporters* **site, but you can use whatever SharePoint team site you want. If prompted, type your user name and password, and then click OK.**

> **IMPORTANT** Verify that you have sufficient permissions to configure search in the site that you are using. If in doubt, see Appendix A.

9

1   In the top-right corner of the page, click the **Settings** gear icon and select **Site settings**.

2   On the **Site Settings** page, under **Search**, click **Search and Offline Availability**.

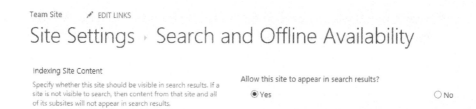

Team Site   ✎ EDIT LINKS

Site Settings ▸ Search and Offline Availability

Indexing Site Content

Specify whether this site should be visible in search results. If a site is not visible to search, then content from that site and all of its subsites will not appear in search results.

Allow this site to appear in search results?

⦿ Yes   ○ No

3   In the **Indexing Site Content** section, under **Allow this site to appear in search results**, click **No**.

4   Click **OK** in the **Search and Offline Availability** page to save your settings and return to the **Site Settings** page. Depending on the crawl frequency in your environment, you may need to wait at least 30 minutes for the changes to take effect.

5   Using steps 2–4 as a guide, reselect the setting to **Yes** to allow your site to be indexed.

 CLEAN UP **Close the browser.**

Key points

- SharePoint 2013 provides a new search engine and an intuitive search experience.

- By using the contextual hover panel on the search results page, you can act on the search results without opening them.

- The search results are security trimmed, so only the content and actions that a user has rights to are displayed.

- For a better way to find what you are looking for, you can target your search by using search queries.

- The **Enterprise Search Center** provides several search verticals that are targeted for searching specific content, such as **Everything**, for a search across all content; **People**, for people-related searches; **Conversations**, for searching newsfeed conversations; and **Videos**, for searching different types of videos.

- You can configure the search behavior and link the search box on your site to the **Search Center**.

- You can set up search alerts to get notified when results of a specific search change.

- Search results are displayed in the order of relevance. Using query rules, you can promote content items to appear at the top of ranked search results.

- The search results pages include four Web Parts: the **Search Box** Web Part, the **Search Results** Web Part, the **Refinement** Web Part, and the **Search Navigation** Web Part. You can customize the search results pages to meet your user requirements.

- The **People** search is based on the information in the profile store and the personal sites in your organization. The relevance model for **People** search includes content, social distance, and expertise.

- You can define whether your site is visible in search results.

9

Chapter at a glance

Work

Working with the timeline, page 347

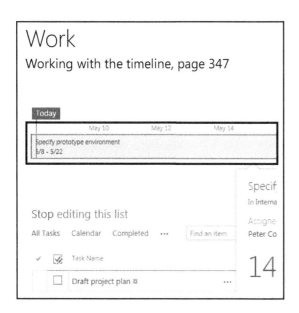

Work

Work with the Project Summary Web Part, page 354

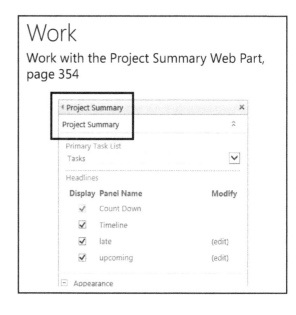

Manage

Manage tasks in one place, page 355

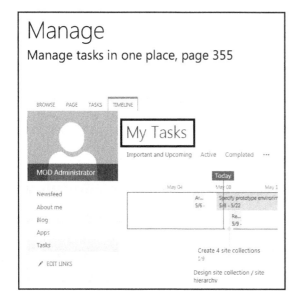

Manage

Manage projects with SharePoint and Project Professional, page 361

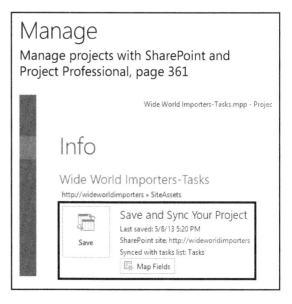

Managing work tasks

IN THIS CHAPTER, YOU WILL LEARN HOW TO

- Create a Project site.

- Work with the timeline, and create and manage subtasks.

- Work with the Project Summary Web Part.

- Manage tasks in one place.

- Manage projects with Microsoft SharePoint and Microsoft Project Professional.

- Use Microsoft Project Server.

Ever since the inception of Microsoft SharePoint, teams have used SharePoint sites to manage work outside a formal project structure. This includes the creation of ad hoc tasks, actions assigned to attendees at meetings, scheduling activities, and the grouping of tasks that are related to one another.

Initially, Microsoft provided an office application, Microsoft Office Project, to assist project managers with developing plans, assigning resources to tasks, tracking progress, managing budgets, and analyzing workloads. Then came Microsoft *Project Server*, which extends the capabilities of Project and provides organizations a central location to store their project information.

Users of SharePoint, Project Professional, and Project Server may find that they have to visit many places to track their tasks and activities. This includes those tasks created in Microsoft Office Outlook, another repository for tasks that can be stored in Microsoft Exchange, if it is used by your organization. To partially alleviate this situation, tasks stored in **Tasks** lists can be managed with Project or Outlook, and you can keep them in sync.

However, SharePoint Server 2013 provides new functionality that aggregates tasks from Microsoft Exchange Server 2013, Microsoft Project Server 2013, and SharePoint Server 2013. Users can view all tasks in their personal site on the **My Tasks** page, which you can find on the **Quick Launch**, on the **Newsfeed** hub. Two-way synchronization lets the user update his tasks using the **My Tasks** page, or he can update the tasks in the products in which they originated.

The task management capabilities within SharePoint 2013 have also vastly improved. You can now have child tasks, known as *subtasks*. Tasks and subtasks can be displayed in a timeline view and you can edit multiple items at once. You can use the **Quick Edit**, view to quickly create task items. There is now a new site template, **Project Site**, which activates all these new task management features by default. In addition to these task management improvements, managing work within a team can be improved with the use of the Microsoft Office OneNote shared notebook.

In this chapter, you will learn how to use the new **Project Site**, the **Timeline** Web Part, and the **Project Summary** Web Part, as well as how to use the **My Tasks** page and how to manage projects with Project Professional.

PRACTICE FILES You don't need any practice files to complete the exercises in this chapter. For more information about practice file requirements, see "Using the practice files" at the beginning of this book.

IMPORTANT Remember to use your SharePoint site location in place of *http:// wideworldmporters* in the following exercises.

Creating a Project site

SharePoint Server 2013 provides a new site template, the **Project Site** template, which lets you create sites in which you can collaborate on lightweight projects. Project managers can quickly get a sense of what is occurring in the project, and members of the project can quickly see how their work fits into the overall context of the project. A Project site includes the following components:

- A Project Summary Web Part
- A visual timeline of the project's tasks
- A project Tasks list
- A library for storing relevant project documents
- A shared calendar for team events
- The ability to connect to Project Professional

There are other components that you may see in a Project site, which are dependent on the installation of other Microsoft server products in you organization:

- If your organization has integrated Microsoft Office Web Apps Server 2013 with SharePoint Server 2013, then a OneNote notebook is created for quickly capturing and organizing information about the project.

- When SharePoint is connected to Exchange Server 2013, a Project site can include a site mailbox for unified communication about the project as it progresses.

- If your Project site is part of a site collection that is associated with Project Server 2013, the Tasks list can be added to the Project Web App (PWA).

TIP In SharePoint 2010, whenever you create a Team site, a Tasks list, and a calendar list are automatically created, thereby allowing you to effectively manage lightweight projects. This is no longer the case in SharePoint 2013.

In SharePoint 2013, when you create a new Team site, you can add a Tasks list app, or on the home page of your team site, you can click on the **Working on a deadline?** tile in the **Get started with our site** Web Part to activate the new task management capabilities. This will activate the **Project Functionality** site feature, which adds a Project Summary Web Part to your team site home page and creates the following list apps:

- Tasks (with a timeline)
- Calendar

TIP The new **Project Site** template automatically activates the **Project Functionality** site feature.

When you click on the **Working on a deadline?** tile, a dialog will subsequently notify you that the project functionality is already installed on the site. It provides you with a link, which if clicked, will display the **Your Apps** page, where you can create other task or calendar list apps.

TIP If you are using Project Server, then whoever manages the project server, usually someone from your organization's *Project Management Office* (PMO), can choose to make SharePoint sites visible in a *Project Web App* (PWA) site.

In this exercise, you will create a Project site.

10

SET UP Open a SharePoint site where you'd like to create, as a subsite, the new project site.

> **IMPORTANT** Verify that you have sufficient rights to create a site. If in doubt, see Appendix A, "SharePoint 2013 user permissions and permission levels."

1 On the **Quick Launch**, click **Site Contents**, and then under **Subsites**, click **new subsite**.

2 In the **Title** box, type **International Contemporary Furniture Fair 2013**, and then, in the Description box, type **Use this Project site to coordinate activities to ensure WWI gets the most benefit from being a Platinum sponsor of ICFF 2013**.

3 In the **URL name** box, type **ICFF13**.

4 Under **Select a template** on the **Collaboration** tab, click **Project Site**, and then click **Create**.

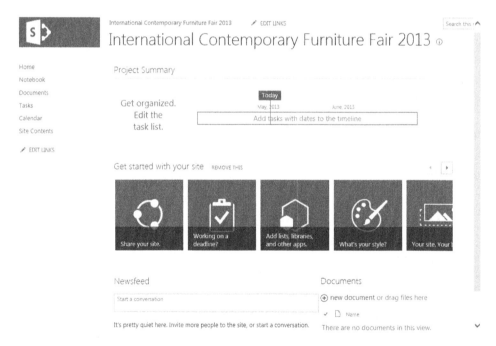

CLEAN UP Leave the browser open if you are continuing to the next exercise.

Working with the timeline

By assigning tasks to other users, you involve them in collaboration activities. When using a **Tasks** list with a timeline view, any task item you add to the **Tasks** list can be added to the timeline, thus providing a graphical interface for viewing important tasks. You can also view your **My Tasks** page, which rolls up tasks across all of your sites.

SEE ALSO Creating and editing items in the Tasks list on a team site is covered in Chapter 3, "Working with documents and information in lists and libraries."

Just like in Project Standard 2013 and Professional 2013, which have timeline views, you can use the timeline view for a Tasks list app. Using either Quick view or Standard view, you can easily add and remove tasks from the timeline. Also, you can remove a task from the timeline by clicking the task to display the callout, and then clicking **REMOVE FROM TIMELINE**.

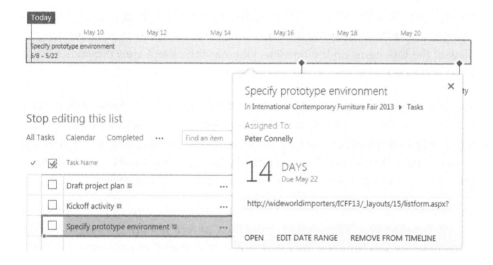

TIP The callout also provides you with more contextual information, such as a countdown to the number of days until the task item is due and a link to where the task item is stored. For PWA projects, the site associated with that project is provided.

You can also apply formatting changes to task items that appear on the timeline. You can change the background color, text color, and font of each task (or subtask), by clicking the task in the timeline and using the commands in the **Font** group on the **Timeline** tab. You can also color the milestone markers.

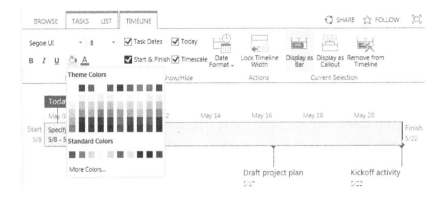

TIP You can re-order the tasks within the timeline view, using a drag-and-drop operation.

You can use commands on the **Timeline** tab to show or hide task dates; to see a pointer to today's date, start and finish dates, and timescales; to change the format of the date; and to lock the current width for all users. In the **Current Selection** group, you can toggle between displaying tasks on the timeline as a bar or as callouts. The timeline provides a high-level overview of the task items on the timeline, whereas the callout view provides a list of task deadlines and calendar events to see specific details.

TIP The Tasks list in SharePoint 2013 contains new views. In SharePoint 2010, when you create a Tasks list, the views **All Tasks**, **My Tasks**, **Due Today**, **Active Tasks**, **By Assigned To**, and **By My Groups** are created. In SharePoint 2013, the following views are created: **All Tasks**, **Late Tasks**, **Upcoming**, **Completed**, **My Tasks**, **Gantt Chart**, and **Calendar**. As with any other list app, you can amend these views and create your own views.

You can also use the **Timeline** Web Part to display a timeline view of task items on other pages. The **Timeline** Web Part is listed under the **Content Rollup** category in the **Web Part** pane. To configure the **Timeline** Web Part, in the **Web Part** tool pane, specify the site where the **Tasks** list is stored. It can be a **Tasks** list from any site within the current site collection or within another site collection. Click **Verify URL**, and then from the **Source** drop-down list, select the **Tasks** list. Each **Tasks** list name is prefixed with the name of the site.

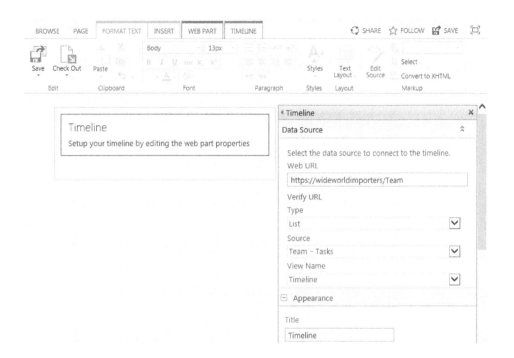

SEE ALSO More information on editing pages and using Web Parts can be found in Chapter 4, "Working with webpages."

In the following exercise, you will add a task item to a **Tasks** list, and then add and format it on the timeline.

SET UP **Open the Project site that you created in the previous exercise, if it is not already open. You can also complete this exercise on any Tasks list by displaying it in Quick Edit view and starting at step 2.**

10

IMPORTANT Verify that you have sufficient rights to create task items. If in doubt, see Appendix A.

1   In the **Project Summary** Web Part, click **Edit** to display the **Quick Edit** view of the Tasks list app.

2   Click in an empty row to create a new task item using the following values, and then press **Enter**:

Column Name	Value
Task Name	Draft project plan
Due Date	Today + 10 days
Assigned To	Type in your name

The first task item is automatically added to the timeline.

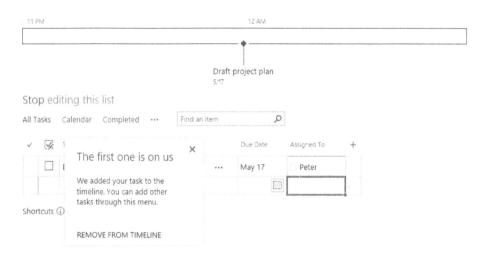

3   Add another new task with the following values, and then press **Enter**:

Column Name	Value
Task Name	Kickoff activity
Due Date	Today + 14 days
Assigned To	Type in your name

4   Right-click the first column to the left of **Kickoff activity**, and then click **Add to Timeline**.

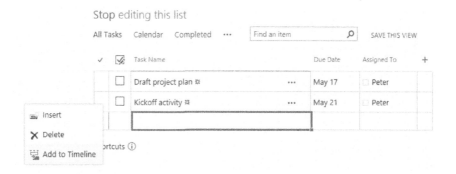

5 Click **Stop**, and then click **new task**. Use the new form to add another new task with the following values, and then click **Save**:

Column Name	Value
Task Name	Specify prototype environment
Start Date	Today
Due Date	Today +14 days
Assigned to	Type in your name

TIP If you like using the **Quick Edit** view of a Tasks list, then you might want to create a new datasheet view, specify it as the default view, and add the columns that you commonly complete when you add new tasks, such as the Start Date.

6 Click to the left of the **Specify prototype environment** task to select the entire row (do not select the check box).

7 On the **Tasks** tab, click **Add to Timeline** in the **Actions** group.

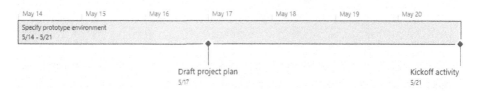

8 On the **Quick Launch**, click **Home** to see the three task items in the **Project Summary** area.

Project Summary

Draft project
plan
due in
10 days

+ ADD TASK ✎ EDIT LIST

May 14   May 15   May 16   May 17   May 18   May 19   May 20

Specify prototype environment
5/14 - 5/21

Draft project plan
5/17

Kickoff activity
5/21

❌ CLEAN UP **Leave the browser open if you are continuing to the next exercise.**

Creating and managing subtasks

When creating a project plan, project managers usually divide the project into a number of tasks, and then breakdown each task into a number of subtasks. In SharePoint 2010, you could not create subtasks. Many organizations tried to mimic subtasks by using related issue items in an issues list or by using two **Tasks** lists—one list containing the primary tasks, and the second list containing subtasks, with a lookup column to show the task title from the primary **Tasks** list. However, neither of the workarounds was satisfactory.

In SharePoint 2013, you can create subtasks, change tasks to subtasks or subtasks to tasks, and have subtasks of subtasks, by using the **Indent** and **Outdent** commands on the **Tasks** tab.

You can also minimize or expand your task hierarchy by using the **Outline** command on the **Tasks** tab or by clicking the arrow to the left of the tasks that contain subtasks.

In this exercise, you will create two subtasks, reorganize the order of the subtasks, and then add them to the timeline.

➡ SET UP **Display the Tasks list that you used in the previous exercise.**

1 Click the ellipsis to the right of **Specify prototype environment** to display the callout, and then click **Create Subtask**.

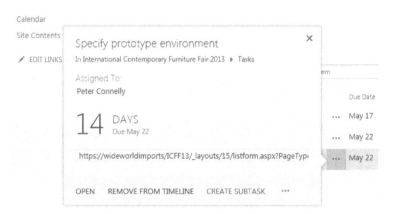

2 In the **Task Name** column, type **Create 4 site collections**. In the **Due Date** column, specify tomorrow's date, and then in the **Assigned To** column, enter your user name. Press **Enter**.

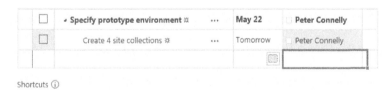

3 In the **Task Name** column, type **Design site collection / site hierarchy**. In the **Due Date** column, specify tomorrow's date, and then in the **Assigned To** column, enter your user name. Press **Enter**.

4 Click the first column to the left of **Design site collection / site hierarchy** to select the whole row, and then on the **Tasks** tab, in the **Hierarchy** group, click **Move Up**.

5 Hold down the **Ctrl** key and click the right column of the two subtasks. On the **Tasks** tab, in the **Actions** group, click **Add to Timeline**.

✖ CLEAN UP Leave the browser open if you are continuing to the next exercise.

10

Working with the Project Summary Web Part

The new SharePoint Server **Project Site** includes the **Project Summary** Web Part, which provides a timeline view and the ability to identify **Late and Upcoming** tasks. This provides an at-a-glance view of the project status. You can then drill down to review the task.

In this exercise, you will configure the **Project Summary** Web Part.

 SET UP **Display the home page of the Project site that you created previously, if it is not already open.**

> **IMPORTANT** Verify that you have sufficient rights to edit the home page. If in doubt, see Appendix A.

1   On the **Page** tab, click **Edit Page**. Click within the **Project Summary** Web Part (for example, click **Today**), and then on the **Web Part** tab, click **Web Part Properties**.

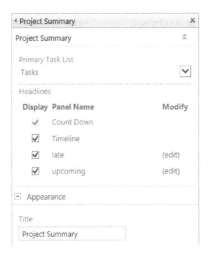

2   In the **Web Part** tool pane, click **(edit)** to the right of **upcoming**. If a **Message from webpage** dialog box is displayed, click **Yes** to save your changes.

3   In the text box in the **Lists to Include in Upcoming Panel** dialog, delete **14** and type **7**.

Lists to Include in Upcoming Panel   ✕

Select which lists you would like to include in the Upcoming panel. Items from the selected lists
that are due today or later will appear in this panel.

☑ Tasks - *Primary Task List*
Show items for the following number of upcoming days: 28

OK   Cancel

4   Click **OK** to close the **Lists to Include in Upcoming Panel** dialog, and then at the bottom of the **Web Part** tool pane, click **OK**.

5   On the **Page** tab, click **Stop Editing**.

✖ CLEAN UP **Leave the browser open if you are continuing to the next exercise.**

Managing tasks in one place

The **Tasks** view in your personal site provides an easily accessible central location where you can manage your tasks. If your SharePoint server administrators have configured something known as the *Work Management Service Application*, and they have completed the integration of Exchange and SharePoint, then tasks assigned to you in SharePoint Server, Outlook, and Project Server are consolidated in a comprehensive work management view.

You can create, update, and delete task items, which are then written back to the original location. You can edit a task item inline or open the task form, and modifications are written back immediately so that other team members are aware of your updates, no matter whether they are viewing the **Tasks** list in Outlook or in Outlook Web App, or using an Outlook task app for a smartphone or in the browser.

SEE ALSO Information on Outlook can be found in Chapter 14, "Using SharePoint with Outlook and Lync."

The **My Tasks** page provides a search box that allows you to search your tasks. It also contains several views that you can use to identify the tasks that are assigned to you. These views are as follows:

- Important and Upcoming
- Active

10

- Completed

- Recently Added

In addition to these views, there are a number of other views that you may also see. If you use Project Web App, the list of views also includes **Timesheet** and **Task Status Reporting**. You will also have a view for each project or site that contains tasks assigned to you.

The **Important and Upcoming** view includes the following:

- **Timeline** This provides an overview of all current and upcoming tasks across approximately a three-week period. You can choose to add and remove tasks from the timeline as required, using the **Timeline** tab that you used with the **Project Summary** Web Part and on the timeline view in a **Tasks** list. You can change the date range for the timeline to show all of your active tasks, using their associated start and due dates to determine the date range. The timeline will begin with the earliest date within all of your tasks, and end with the latest date.

- **Important** The tasks listed in this section have been flagged as **Important**, denoted by the red exclamation mark.

- **Upcoming** This section shows all tasks assigned to you for approximately the next two months. Late tasks are highlighted in red.

Upcoming

◢ International Contemporary Furniture Fair 2013: Tasks

!	☐	Create 4 site collections	···	Tomorrow
!	☐	Design site collection / site hierarchy	···	Tomorrow
!	☐	Draft project plan	···	May 17
!	☐	Kickoff activity	···	May 22
!	☐	Specify prototype environment	···	May 22

◢ Document Center: Tasks

!	☐	Review newly uploaded documents	···	Friday

◢ Finance: Tasks

!	☐	Arrange meeting with head of Finance regarding ICFF13	···	Yesterday

Last updated at 5/8/2013 7:50 PM

In the **Active** view, you can see tasks assigned to you, grouped by project and sites. In this view, you can add and view **Personal Tasks** that will not be seen on any other site, such as planned vacations or personal appointments, which can be synchronized with Exchange, and is therefore visible in Outlook.

The **Completed** view displays tasks that have the **Completed** check box selected. You can mark a task as completed by selecting the check box to the left of the task's name or by using **Mark As Complete** on the **Task** tab. If you mark a task as complete on the **My Tasks** page, it is marked as complete for everyone who is assigned to the task. It is best practice to have only one person assigned to each task; however, that may not always be possible. If you know that other users are working on a task with you, check with them before marking a task as complete on your **My Tasks** page.

When you complete a task, the **% Complete** field will be set to **100%**. For PWA assignments, the **Remaining Work** is set to **0 hours** and the assignment is sent to the task update through the approval loop. You can click the ellipsis to the right of the task item title to display a callout.

The **Recently Added** view displays only those tasks that are within a set number of days. You can change the number of days used to determine which tasks appear in this view.

On the **My Tasks** settings page, you can configure which task items are to be displayed on your **My Tasks** page, thereby preventing your list of tasks from becoming overwhelming. You can also choose to display task items from specific sites and you can change the color of a site's task items when displayed on the timeline. As new sites that have task items are

10

assigned to you, they are automatically assigned a color. You can go to the settings page to change them by clicking **Settings** on the **Tasks** tab.

Old Tasks Limit	☑ Only show the tasks that have been changed within the following number of months: 24
Upcoming Tasks	☑ Only show tasks that were due within this number of days ago: 14 ☑ Only show tasks that are due up to this number of days in the future: 14
Important Tasks	☑ Automatically clear importance from a task if it's been marked as important for more than the following number of days: 14
Recently Added Tasks	Number of days a task will stay in the "Recently Added" view: 1
Default Timeline Range	☑ Set a date range for the timeline. To show all tasks, leave the date fields empty. Start date (number of days before today's date): 7 End date (number of days after today's date): 21
Automatically Hide Empty Filters	☑ Hide a filter which doesn't contain any task for more than the following number of months: 3

Projects	Display Tasks From This Project	Name	Color	Position from Top
	☑	International Contemporary Furniture Fair 2013: Tasks		1 ⌄
	☑	Document Center: Tasks		2 ⌄
	☑	Finance: Tasks		3 ⌄

Save	Cancel

TIP If you have changed the appearance of your timeline to use specific colors for individual tasks, those colors will be used instead of the ones you define as the default colors on the **My Tasks** settings page.

A particularly useful setting is the **Old Tasks Limit** option. Tasks that have not changed in a long time may not be worth keeping on the **My Tasks** page. To hide tasks that have not been changed in a set number of months, select the check box and type the number of months you want to use as a limit; for example, if you do not want to see tasks that have not changed in the last two years, select the check box and type **24** in the box.

In this exercise, you will set a task as **Important** and complete the task (both added to a **Tasks** list on a site) and add a personal task.

SET UP Display the home page of the Project site that you created previously, if it is not already open.

1   Click **Newsfeed** in the top navigation bar, and then on the **Quick Launch**, click **Tasks**.

2   Click **Important and Upcoming**, if this is not the active view.

3   Scroll down to the **Upcoming** section, and then click the **exclamation mark** (!) to the left of **Design site collection / site hierarchy**, which is a task you created in the previous exercise. The exclamation mark should now be red.

4   Refresh the page. The **Design site collection / site hierarchy** task should now be visible in the **Important** section and is not displayed in the **Upcoming** section.

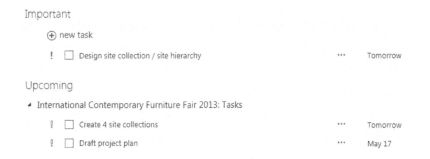

5   On the top of the page, to the right of **Important and Upcoming**, click **Active**.

6   Under **Personal**, click **new task**, and then under **Title**, type **Order foreign currency for holiday**.

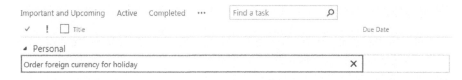

7   Press **Enter**.

▲ Personal
   ⊕ new task
   ! ☐ Order foreign currency for holiday   ··· 🔒

8   Click the ellipsis to the right of **Completed**, and then select the check box to the left of **International Contemporary Furniture Fair 2013** to filter the tasks displayed.

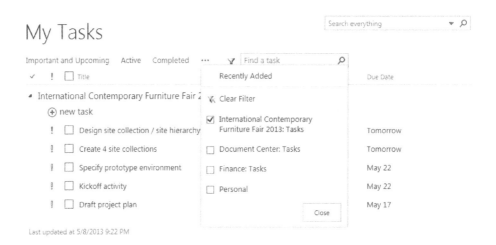

9   Select the check box to the left of **Create 4 site collections** to complete the task.

10   Refresh the page. The completed task is not displayed.

11   At the top of the page, to the right of **Active**, click **Completed** to display the completed **Create 4 site collections** task item.

12   Click **International Contemporary Furniture Fair 2013** to display the home page of the site.

13   On the **Quick Launch**, click **Tasks**. Notice that the **Create 4 site collections** task item is displayed as completed.

❌ CLEAN UP **Close the browser.**

Managing projects with SharePoint and Project Professional

Project Professional 2013 provides rich, out-of-the-box reporting tools on the desktop, with a familiar Excel-like grid to help you quickly and easily measure progress and resource allocation. Project Professional 2013 reports follow industry guidelines, and they include Project Overview, Work Overview, and Burndown.

SEE ALSO You can find information concerning Microsoft Project 2013 quick start training at *blogs.office.com/b/project/archive/2013/04/18/free-project-2013-quick-start-training-available-on-demand.aspx.*

Like many other Office applications, Project includes a set of templates that can be used to jump-start the creation of a project plan. You can also create a project plan from an existing project, an Excel workbook, or from a SharePoint **Tasks** list. Not all project templates are available when you first install Project; some are only available when you are connected to the Internet. When you choose one of these templates, you are provided a preview of the template, a description, and the download size of the template.

Once you have created a project plan, you can synchronize your plan with a **Tasks** list on a SharePoint site at any point. You will see the same timeline and project plan in Project, as well as in the SharePoint site and on your **My Tasks** page. Every time you click **Save in Project**, your project file is saved to the **Site Assets** library and the task items in the **Tasks** list are updated. Now other team members can start updating their progress using SharePoint, Outlook, or a mobile device.

By default, the following fields are synchronized between a SharePoint **Tasks** list and Project: **task name**, **start date**, **finish (due) date**, **% Complete**, **resource name**, and **predecessors**. However, if you want to map additional fields to be synced between Project and SharePoint, on the backstage **Info** page, click **Map Fields**, and select the fields that you would like to sync. You or your team members can now report on custom fields or generate reports based on nondefault SharePoint **Tasks** list columns.

In this exercise, you will create a new project plan, and then you will synchronize your plan with a **Tasks** list on a SharePoint site.

10

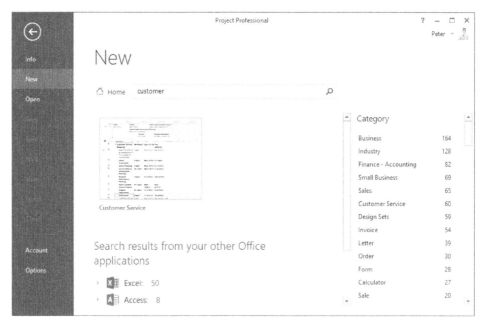 **SET UP** Start Microsoft Project 2013. Remember to use your SharePoint site location in place of *http://wideworldimporters* in the following exercise. You will need access to the Internet to complete this exercise.

IMPORTANT Verify that you have sufficient rights to create items in a Tasks list and that you can upload a file in the **Site Assets** library. If in doubt, see Appendix A.

1   Below the **Search for online templates** text box, type **customer**, and then press **Enter**.

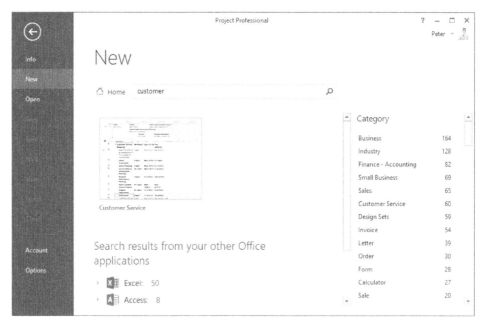

2   Click **Customer Service**, and then click **Create**.

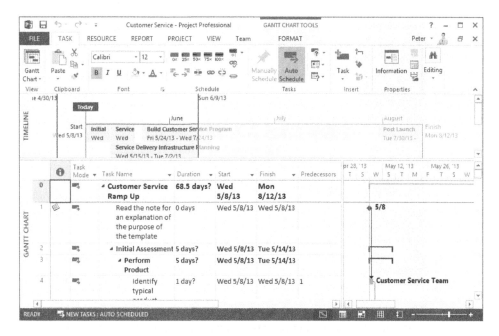

3   Click **File** to display the backstage **Info** page, and then click **Save As**.

4   In the middle pane, under **Save and Sync**, click **Sync with SharePoint**. In the right pane, under **Sync with**, select **Existing SharePoint site**.

5   In the **Site Address** text box, type the URL of the SharePoint site, such as **http://wideworldimporters**.

6   Click **Verify Site**, and then under **Tasks List**, select a Tasks list that you want to link to the project plan, such as **Tasks**, or type the name of a new Tasks list.

10

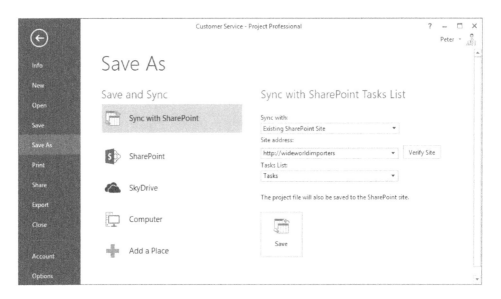

TROUBLESHOOTING If no Tasks lists are displayed in the **Tasks List** drop-down list, then the site that you connected to does not contain a Tasks list.

7 Click **Save**, and then wait while SharePoint and Project are updated.

8 Click **OK** to any Microsoft Project dialog box.es that appear. You may also need to provide a user name and password.

9 Click **File** to display the backstage **Info** page.

10 In the **Save and Sync Your Project** section, click the link to the right of **SharePoint site** to open the site in which you saved your project plan.

11   On the **Quick Launch**, click the name of the Tasks list, such as **Tasks**.

Tasks

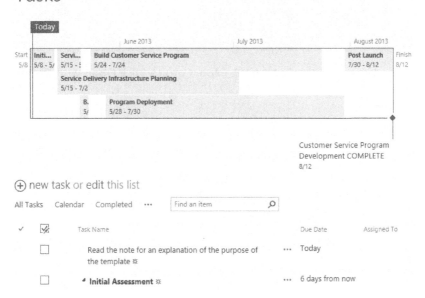

12   Click **Site Contents**, and then click **Site Assets** to check that the project plan uploaded.

✖ CLEAN UP **Close the browser.**

Synchronizing a Tasks list with Project

10

Many projects may begin by using task items in a **Tasks** list on a SharePoint site. Team members can view and track the progress of their tasks easily in the browser. They do not need to have Project installed. However, the project manager may want to manage the progress in Project. You can sync your **Tasks** list with Project by using the browser.

In this exercise, you will sync a **Tasks** list with Project.

SET UP Display the Tasks list that you used previously in this chapter.

IMPORTANT Verify that you have sufficient rights to upload a file in the **Site Assets** library. If in doubt, see Appendix A.

1 On the **List** tab, in the **Connect & Export** group, click **Open with Project**.

2 You may have to provide a user name and password to open your Tasks list and the timeline view in Project Professional.

3 In Project, on the **View** tab, click **Gantt Chart** to see the task items.

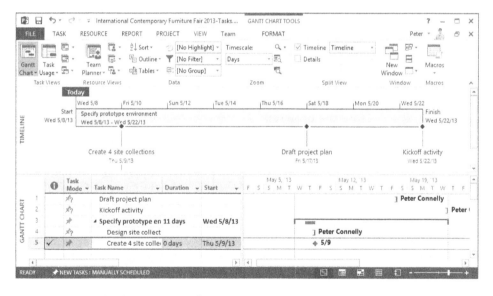

TIP You can now use the backstage **Info** page to save and sync to the SharePoint site.

CLEAN UP Exit Microsoft Project. Click No in the warning dialog and close the browser.

Key points

- The task management capabilities within SharePoint Server 2013 are vastly more improved than earlier versions. They include tasks, subtasks, a timeline view, a Timeline Web Part that can display the timeline of Tasks lists from other sites, and a Project Summary Web Part that can aggregate the timeline tasks from Tasks lists in one site.

- A new site template called **Project Site** activates all the new task management features by default.

- You can use the **Quick Edit** view of a Tasks list app to quickly create task items.

- SharePoint Server 2013 provides new functionality that also aggregates tasks from Exchange 2013 and Project Server 2013.

- Users can view all tasks in their personal site on the **My Tasks** page, which you can find on the **Quick Launch**, on the **Newsfeed** hub.

- Two-way synchronization lets users update their tasks using the **My Tasks** page, or they can update a task in the Microsoft Office product in which it originated.

10

Chapter at a glance

Configure

Configure a workflow, page 374

Work with

Work with a workflow, page 380

Manage

Manage workflows, page 384

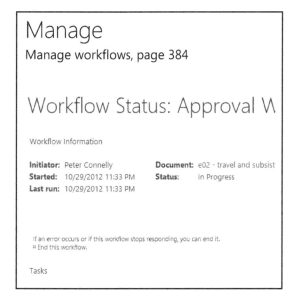

Manage with Outlook

Manage workflow tasks within Outlook 2013, page 387

Working with workflows

IN THIS CHAPTER, YOU WILL LEARN HOW TO

- Automate business processes using SharePoint.

- Understand the built-in workflows of SharePoint.

- Configure and work with workflows.

- Manage workflows using the browser and within Outlook 2013.

- Terminate workflows.

- Remove workflows from lists and libraries.

- Associate workflows with content types.

The workflow technology included in Microsoft SharePoint Foundation 2013 and Microsoft SharePoint Server 2013 can help you automate new and existing business processes. In the past, creating a workflow was typically a task for developers. Most companies have many different types of workflows, and hiring a developer to create workflows can be time-consuming and expensive. SharePoint provides you with a number of built-in workflows that you can configure using the browser.

You can add SharePoint workflows to lists, libraries, and content types. You can also use site workflows; however, adding workflows to lists or libraries will probably still be the most popular type of SharePoint workflow.

In this chapter, you will learn the fundamentals of the workflow architecture and what workflows are provided by default when you install either SharePoint Foundation or SharePoint Server. You will learn how to create, delete, and modify workflows, and how to track the status of workflows that are currently running using the browser and within Microsoft Outlook 2013. You will also learn how to associate workflows with content types.

PRACTICE FILES You don't need any practice files to complete the exercises in this chapter. For more information about practice file requirements, see "Using the practice files" at the beginning of this book.

Automating business processes using SharePoint

Automating frequently run or time-consuming business processes helps you to make efficient use of your time and the time of people on your team. Also, with the introduction of SharePoint in an organization, the initial productivity boom can be transformed into a management burden as more content is added to the SharePoint installation and the amount of work that users will need to do to maintain the content on a day-to-day basis increases. SharePoint can help you with your old and new business processes.

In previous chapters, you were introduced to how SharePoint can help you complete your work with the use of the following:

- RSS feeds, for finding information from a variety of sources on an ad-hoc basis

- Alerts, for regular notifications of new, modified, or deleted content

- Content approval, which along with versioning, helps you to manage content and who can see content that is classified as draft

However, none of these three methods helps you automate business processes beyond a one-step process. You could combine these methods, such as using content approval with alerts to provide a lightweight workflow that sends you emails when your team members change documents. However, such a solution can help solve only a small number of your business processes. You might want to route a document or a webpage to a number of people before publishing it.

SharePoint provides two other methods to help automate processes:

- **User-centric workflows** Used to automate and track processes that require human intervention, such as notifying users when their action is required to move the process forward. Such processes could take days, weeks, or months to complete and may need to wait for an event or another process to complete.

- **Fully automated workflows, which developers know as event receivers** Used to automate processes that require no human intervention, such as moving job applications from one document library to a series of other document libraries for some purpose.

Workflows and event receivers cannot automate a task unless time is taken to define exactly how the task should be automated, nor can they track the status of information stored on paper documents. They also cannot force users to perform a particular task. You must have a clear understanding of how the business process operates. If you do not understand how to complete a business process manually, you will not be able to describe the business process in sufficient detail to automate that process.

Therefore, some planning and startup tasks are needed to automate a process. You do not necessarily want to automate every little process in your organization. You want to automate processes that are predictable and those where the startup cost of creating a workflow and ensuring that your team is happy with the new process will be offset by the productivity improvement that the automated process will provide. You must also understand what SharePoint has to offer.

Understanding the built-in workflows of SharePoint

SharePoint provides a number of built-in workflows that you can configure using the browser. Additional workflows can be created using Microsoft SharePoint Designer 2013, Microsoft Visual Studio 2012, or Microsoft Visio 2013 in combination with SharePoint Designer 2013. Event receivers can be created only using Visual Studio 2012.

TIP SharePoint Designer is a free product found at *www.microsoft.com/en-us/download/search.aspx?q=sharepoint+designer+2013*.

You can think of a workflow as a series of tasks that produce an outcome. In the same way that you base a new site, list, or library on a template, you can base a new workflow on a workflow template. These templates are implemented as features that can be activated or deactivated at the site or site collection level by using the browser or by using applications. A workflow template is available only when a workflow feature is activated.

Many SharePoint workflows are created by associating a workflow template with a list, library, or content type. Such workflows are focused on documents; however, not all workflows are like that. To cater to other scenarios, you can create site workflows by associating a workflow template at the site level.

Site workflows operate within the context of a SharePoint site instead of being attached to a specific list and operating on a specific list item. Site workflows are started manually or programmatically, but a user cannot use the browser to configure a site workflow to start automatically. SharePoint 2013 does not come with any workflow templates that you can associate at the site level; therefore, to create site workflows, you must use either Visual Studio 2012 or SharePoint Designer 2013.

SharePoint 2013 allows you to run the same type of workflows that you may have used in SharePoint 2010, known as SharePoint 2010 workflows. However, SharePoint Server 2013 introduces a new, highly scalable workflow framework that is implemented by using a new piece of software, Workflow Manager, which allows you to run SharePoint 2013 workflows. Workflow Manager is installed separately from SharePoint 2013 by your server administrators. Workflow Manager can only be used with SharePoint Server and does not interact with SharePoint Foundation, and therefore you cannot use SharePoint 2013 workflows with a SharePoint Foundation installation. SharePoint Server contains no SharePoint 2013 workflow templates. To create SharePoint 2013 workflows, you must use either Visual Studio 2012 or SharePoint Designer 2013.

SharePoint Foundation ships with only one generic SharePoint 2010 workflow template, the Three-state workflow template that can be used across multiple scenarios. On the other hand, SharePoint Server contains additional SharePoint 2010 workflow templates:

- **Approval – SharePoint 2010** Provides an approval mechanism for documents.

- **Collect Feedback – SharePoint 2010** Provides a feedback mechanism for documents.

- **Collect Signatures – SharePoint 2010** Provides a mechanism for collecting digital signatures for completing a document.

- **Publishing Approval** Similar to the Approval workflow template, this workflow is commonly used with the Pages library on publishing sites to approve publishing pages. More information on publishing sites and pages can be found in Chapter 15, "Working with content management."

- **Disposition Approval** Provides an expiration and retention mechanism that allows you to decide whether to retain or delete expired documents. This workflow can be started only by using the browser.

- **Group Approval** Similar to the Approval workflow; however, it is available only in East Asian versions of SharePoint Server.

- **Translation Management** Provides a mechanism for document translation by creating copies of documents to be translated, and also assigns tasks to translators. This workflow is available when activated by your SharePoint server administrators using Windows PowerShell. You can then create a SharePoint Server Translation Management library, a Languages And Translators list, and a Translation Management workflow. More information on the Translation Management workflow can be found at *office.microsoft.com/en-us/sharepoint-server-help/use-a-translation-management-workflow-HA010154430.aspx*.

SEE ALSO More information about the workflows included in SharePoint can be found at *office.microsoft.com/en-us/sharepoint-help/about-the-workflows-included-with-sharepoint-HA102771434.aspx*.

Not all workflow templates are automatically available within sites on all site collections. Your site collection administrator may need to activate a site collection feature for you to use a workflow template; for example, to use any of the workflow templates that have SharePoint 2010 appended to their name, your site collection administrator would need to active the Workflow site collection feature. Table 11-1 details which workflow templates are active on which sites.

11

Table 11-1 *Workflow site collection features*

Site collection feature	Publishing sites	Collaboration sites
Disposition Approval Workflow	Active	Active
Publishing Approval Workflow	Active	Deactivated
SharePoint 2007 Workflows	Deactivated	Deactivated
Three-state Workflow	Deactivated	Active
Workflows	Active	Deactivated

TIP The Microsoft Office SharePoint Server 2007 workflows are only available on sites that were upgraded from SharePoint Server 2007 to Microsoft SharePoint Server 2010, and then upgraded to Microsoft SharePoint Server 2013.

The workflow templates that have SharePoint 2010 appended to their name are reusable workflows, and therefore can be modified by using SharePoint Designer 2013. They also contain a Microsoft Visio visualization of the workflow.

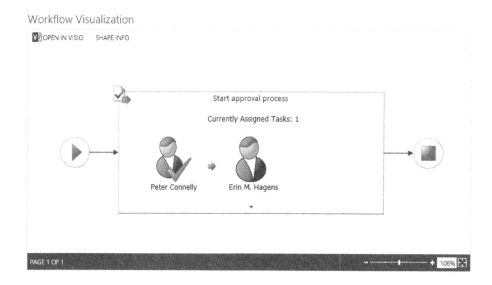

TROUBLESHOOTING Visio visualizations of SharePoint 2010 workflows are only available when your organization is using the Enterprise edition of SharePoint Server and your server administrator has configured Visio Services. The SharePoint Server Enterprise feature also needs to be active at the site collection and site levels. Visio visualizations can also be seen in the SharePoint Online Enterprise (E3 & E4) and SharePoint Online Small Business.

Configuring a workflow

Each of the built-in workflow templates can be customized in a limited fashion to define the exact process necessary to meet your business needs. An instance of a workflow uses the configured workflow template as a blueprint, which defines the conditions that should be tested to decide which tasks to complete to produce the outcome.

For example, you can configure the Three-state workflow template to define an expense-approval workflow process. Members of your team create an expense form, and when they upload it into a document library, you want the document to progress through the expense-approval workflow process.

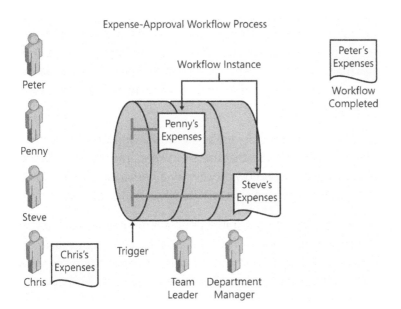

Expense-Approval Workflow Process

The workflow process always has a start and an end. The trigger for entering the process is uploading the document into the document library. An instance of workflow is created when a workflow event is triggered. Each expense form must be approved by Approver #1 (stage 1) and Approver #2 (stage 2), in sequence. Once the expense form has completed both stages, it is approved (stage 3). When the workflow instance reaches the end of the workflow process, it is set to Completed. The workflow process then does no other work until a new workflow instance is created.

To maintain the status of the document as it progresses through the workflow, you must create a Choice column that can store the three states of the workflow and helps you track the progress of the document through the workflow.

The Three-state workflow can be triggered in the following ways:

- Manually, using the browser or using SharePoint Server from a Microsoft Office 2010 or Microsoft Office 2013 application. You can restrict who can start workflow instances manually to those users who have the Manage Lists permissions.

- Automatically, when you create a list item or document.

11

Other SharePoint Server workflows can have other trigger events. For example, the Approval workflow template can be configured for any of the following:

- Changing an item or file will automatically start the workflow.

- Starting a workflow instance automatically when publishing a major version of an item or file. Choosing this option, a workflow instance will not automatically start when a minor version of a file is saved. Therefore, to use this option the library must be configured with major and minor versioning enabled. See Chapter 6, "Making lists and libraries work for you," for more information on how to configure a library to use major and minor versions.

Workflows can use both a Task list and History list as the workflow process executes. A workflow can add task items to a Task list so that users can keep track of all the work that needs to be finished to complete the workflow process for a particular workflow instance. The workflow could send emails to users when a task item is assigned to them.

The History list keeps track of the workflow instances that are running or that have been completed for a given list item or document. This is a hidden list and is not shown on the Site Content webpage. You can display this list in the browser by appending */lists/workflow history/* to your site's Uniform Resource Locator (URL); for example, *http://wideworldimporters/lists/workflow history/*.

TIP You could export the contents of the Workflow History list to Microsoft Office Excel and create reports to analyze the workflow process. However, you should not rely on items in the workflow history lists for auditing purposes. Items in the Workflow History list are purged every 60 days, or deleted when workflow templates are removed from lists, libraries, or sites.

There are four distinct workflow roles:

- The person who creates workflow templates is usually a business analyst or power end-user, who knows the business process that they wish to automate and is known as the *workflow creator*.

- The person who associates the workflow template with a content type, site, list, or library is known as the *workflow author*. To associate a workflow template with a list or library, the workflow author must be mapped to the Manage List or Web Designer permission rights on the list or library. To associate a workflow template with a site or content type, the workflow author must be a member of the Site Owners group on the SharePoint site. When the default workflow templates do not meet business needs, the business analyst or power end-user could use SharePoint Designer to build a workflow to automate the business process; alternatively, a developer could be involved to use Visual Studio 2012.

- The *workflow initiator* is the person who starts a workflow instance on a document or list item. They must have Edit Item permission rights on the list item or file to manually start a workflow instance or to terminate a workflow instance.

- Users who interact with a workflow instance are known as *workflow participants*. They complete the task items that support the workflow instances.

In the following exercise, you will add a site column to a document library that gives you a choice for each workflow state. You will then associate a workflow template with the document library.

 SET UP **Open a Team SharePoint site where you would like to associate a workflow template with a document library. This exercise will use the *http://wideworldimporters* site, but you can use whatever SharePoint Team site you want. If prompted, type your user name and password, and then click OK.**

> **IMPORTANT** Verify that you have sufficient rights to manage the document library. If in doubt, refer to Appendix A, "SharePoint 2013 user permissions and permission levels."

1   On the **Quick Launch**, click the document library where you want to associate a workflow template.

2   On the **Library** tab, click **Create Column** in the **Manage Views** group.

3   In the **Column Name** box, type **Workflow States** and select the **Choice** option.

4   In the **Type each choice on a separate line** box, enter three choices: **Submitted to Approver #1**, **Submitted to Approver #2**, and **Approved**. Be sure to delete the three predefined generic choices first. Then click **OK**.

> **TIP** You can create more than one Choice list column, and a Choice list can have more than three choices. However, the Three-state workflow can be configured to use only three values.

Once the new column is created, you can create the new workflow.

11

5   On the **Library** tab, in the **Settings** group, click the arrow to the right of **Workflow Settings**, and then click **Add a Workflow**.

6   On the **Add a Workflow** page, select **Three-state**, and then in the **Name** section, type a new name for this workflow, such as **Approval Workflow**.

TROUBLESHOOTING If the Three-state workflow does not appear, then you may need to activate the Three-state workflow feature at the site collection level. See Chapter 5, "Creating and managing sites," for more information on features.

7   In the **Select a task** list, select a Tasks list if one is already created, or **Tasks (new)** if one has not been created.

TIP The name of the new Task list will take the format of *workflow name* Tasks, such as Approval Workflow Tasks. You should create a new Task list if you will have many documents or list items progressing through a workflow.

8   In the **Start Options** section, leave the selections at their default settings.

Workflow

Select a workflow to add to this document library. If a workflow is missing from the list, your site administrator may have to publish or activate it

Select a workflow template:

*Disposition Approval

*Three-state

Description:
Use this workflow to track items in a list.

*Denotes a SharePoint 2010 template.

Name

Enter a name for this workflow. The name will be used to identify this workflow to users of this document library.

Enter a unique name for this workflow:

Approval Workflow

Task List

Select the name of the task list to use with this workflow, or create a new one.

Select a task list:

Tasks

Description:
Task list for workflow.

History List

Select the name of the history list to use with this workflow, or create a new one.

Select a history list:

Workflow History

Description:
History list for workflow.

Start Options

Specify how this workflow can be started.

☑ Allow this workflow to be manually started by an authenticated user with Edit Item permissions.
  ☐ Require Manage Lists Permissions to start the workflow.

☐ Start this workflow to approve publishing a major version of an item.

☐ Creating a new item will start this workflow.

9   Click **Next** to display the second workflow settings page, known as the association page.

10 In the **Workflow states** section, the new column that you added to the document library automatically appears with the three choices that you entered for the three states of the workflow. If it does not appear, from the **Select a choice field** list, click **Workflow States**, and enter the initial, middle, and final states in the three fields, if needed.

11 In the **Specify what you want to happen when a workflow is initiated** section, in the **Tasks Details** area, leave the selections at their default settings, and in the **E-mail Message Details** area, clear the **Send e-mail message** check box.

Workflow states:

Select a 'Choice' field, and then select a value for the initial, middle, and final states. For an Issues list, the states for an item are specified by the Status field, where:
Initial State = Active
Middle State = Resolved
Final State = Closed
As the item moves through the various stages of the workflow the item is updated automatically.

Select a 'Choice' field:
Workflow States

Initial state
Submitted to Approver #1

Middle state
Submitted to Approver #2

Final state
Approved

Specify what you want to happen when a workflow is initiated:

For example, when a workflow is initiated on an issue in an Issues list, Microsoft SharePoint Foundation creates a task for the assigned user. When the user completes the task, the workflow changes from its initial state (Active) to its middle state (Resolved). You can also choose to send an e-mail message to notify the assigned user of the task.

Task Details:
Task Title:

Custom message: Workflow initiated:

☑ Include list field: Approval Status

The value for the field selected is concatenated to the custom message.

Task Description:

Custom message: A workflow has been initiate

☑ Include list field: Approver Comments

☑ Insert link to List item

Task Due Date:

☑ Include list field: Created

Task Assigned To:

◉ Include list field: Created By

○ Custom:

E-mail Message Details:

☐ Send e-mail message

12   Repeat step 11 for the **Specify what you want to happen when a workflow changes to its middle state** section, and then click **OK**.

❌ CLEAN UP **Leave the browser open if you are continuing to the next exercise.**

Working with workflows

Once a workflow template is associated with a list or library and customized to define the process as required to meet your business needs, a list item or document can be sent through the process.

In the following exercise, you manually start a workflow instance for a document and complete the tasks for the workflow process.

SET UP Go to the document library where you associated the workflow template. Make sure that you have at least one document in the library before you start this exercise.

1   Click to the left of the document that you want to start a workflow, and then on the **Files** tab, in the **Workflows** group, click **Workflows**.

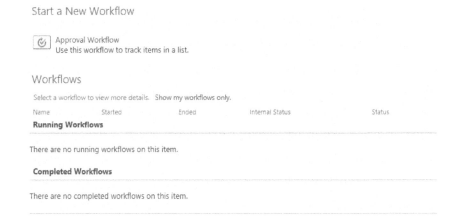

2   On the **Start a New Workflow** page, under **Start a New Workflow**, click **Approval Workflow** to display the default view of the library containing the two new columns: **Workflow States** and **Approval Workflow**.

11

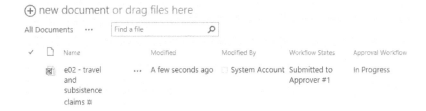

TIP When you manually start a workflow, some workflows will present you with a form where you can enter information. This page is known as the *initiation page*, and may have similar fields to the association form.

3   In the **Approval Workflow** column, click **In Progress** to display the **Workflow Status** page.

Notice that this page is divided into three parts: **Workflow Information**, **Tasks**, and **Workflow History**. In the **Tasks** section, one task item is listed as being assigned to you, with a status of **Not Started**. In the **Related Content** column, there is a link to the document with which the workflow instance is associated. There is also a link to the document in the **Workflow Information** section. In the **Workflow History** section, there is one entry with an **Event Type of Workflow Initiated**.

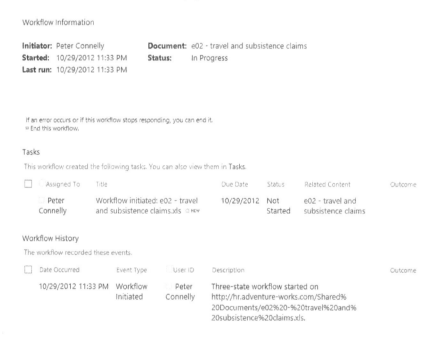

Workflow Status: Approval Workflow

Workflow Information

Initiator: Peter Connelly   **Document:** e02 - travel and subsistence claims
Started: 10/29/2012 11:33 PM   **Status:**   In Progress
Last run: 10/29/2012 11:33 PM

If an error occurs or if this workflow stops responding, you can end it.
□ End this workflow.

Tasks

This workflow created the following tasks. You can also view them in Tasks.

	Assigned To	Title	Due Date	Status	Related Content	Outcome
□	Peter Connelly	Workflow initiated: e02 - travel and subsistence claims.xls ○NEW	10/29/2012	Not Started	e02 - travel and subsistence claims	

Workflow History

The workflow recorded these events.

	Date Occurred	Event Type	User ID	Description	Outcome
	10/29/2012 11:33 PM	Workflow Initiated	Peter Connelly	Three-state workflow started on http://hr.adventure-works.com/Shared%20Documents/e02%20-%20travel%20and%20subsistence%20claims.xls.	

4   In the **Tasks** section, under **Title**, click **Workflow initiated** to display the task item.

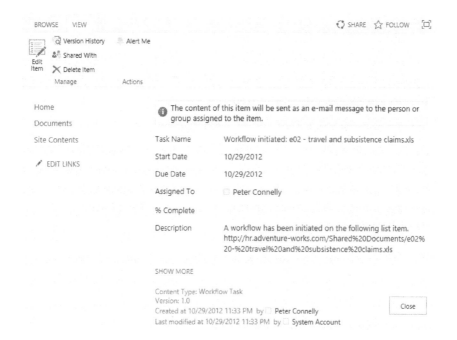

BROWSE   VIEW   SHARE   FOLLOW

Version History   Alert Me

Edit   Shared With
Item   Delete Item

Manage   Actions

Home

Documents

Site Contents

EDIT LINKS

The content of this item will be sent as an e-mail message to the person or group assigned to the item.

Task Name   Workflow initiated: e02 - travel and subsistence claims.xls

Start Date   10/29/2012

Due Date   10/29/2012

Assigned To   Peter Connelly

% Complete

Description   A workflow has been initiated on the following list item.
                   http://hr.adventure-works.com/Shared%20Documents/e02%
                   20-%20travel%20and%20subsistence%20claims.xls

SHOW MORE

Content Type: Workflow Task
Version: 1.0
Created at 10/29/2012 11:33 PM by Peter Connelly   Close
Last modified at 10/29/2012 11:33 PM by System Account

5   On the **View** tab, click **Edit Item** to display the task input form.

6   In the **Status** list, select **Completed**. You may have to scroll down and click **SHOW MORE** to see the **Status** list. Then, on the **Edit** tab, in the **Commit** group, click **Save** to close the task input form and display the **Workflow Status** page.

     Notice that the Tasks section contains two task items; the first is **Completed**, and the second is **Not Started**. The Workflow History section has two entries: **Workflow Initiated** and **Task Completed**.

     TROUBLESHOOTING If the two tasks do not appear in the **Tasks** section and in the **Workflow Information** section, a message in red text states that due to heavy loads, the latest workflow operation has been delayed. Refresh the page and click **OK** in the message box that appears.

7   Under **Tasks**, to the right of the sentence that starts **You can also view them in**, click the link to the **Tasks** list.

8   In the default view of the **Tasks** list, click the task item with a title of **Review task**, and repeat steps 5 and 6.

     The **All Tasks** page refreshes again, and the two task items related to the workflow have a status of **Completed**.

11

9   On the **Quick Launch**, click the document library with which you are working in this exercise to display the default view of the library.

Notice that the **Workflow States** column has a value of **Approved**, and the **Approval Workflow** column has a value of **Completed** for the document that you started a workflow instance in step 2.

10   In the **Approval Workflow** column, click **Completed**.

On the **Workflow Status: Approval Workflow** page, in the **Workflow Information** section, the workflow instance has a status of **Completed**. In the **Tasks** section, the two tasks have a status of **Completed**, and in the **Workflow History** section, there are four events: a **Workflow Initiated** event, two **Task Completed** events, and a **Workflow Completed** event.

✖ CLEAN UP **Leave the browser open if you are continuing to the next exercise.**

Managing workflows

As you use the workflow process, you may find that it does not match your business requirements. Therefore, you will need to modify the workflow as time progresses, perhaps to change the person who does the first stage or second stage of the process.

In the following exercise, you modify a workflow process for a document library, complete both of the tasks for the workflow process, and then terminate the workflow instance.

➜ SET UP **Open the default view of the document library where you associated the workflow template.**

IMPORTANT Verify that you have sufficient rights to modify the workflow process for the document library. If in doubt, refer to Appendix A.

1   On the **Library** tab, click **Workflow Settings** in the **Settings** group to display the **Workflow Settings** page.

Settings ▸ Workflow Settings ⓘ

Workflows

Show workflow associations of this type:

This List	⌄

Select a different type to see its workflows.

☑ Workflow Name (click to change settings)   Workflows in Progress

SharePoint 2013 Workflows
    There are no SharePoint 2013 Workflows associated with this list.

SharePoint 2010 Workflows
    Approval Workflow   0

    ▫ Add a workflow
    ▫ Remove, Block, or Restore a Workflow

2   Under **Workflow Name**, click **Approval Workflow** to display the **Change a Workflow** page.

3   In the **Start Options** section, select the **Creating a new item will start this workflow** check box, and then click **Next**.

4   On the **Customize the Three-state Workflow** page, in the **Specify what you want to happen when a workflow is initiated** section, in the **Custom message** box, type **Review Stage 1**, and under **Task description**, in the **Include list field**, select **Version**.

5   Under **Task Assigned To**, select **Custom**, and then in the **Custom** box, enter the user name of a person to approve the document. Click the **Check Name** icon to the right of the **Custom** box to verify that you have entered a valid user name.

    TIP By specifying a person to assign a task to, you have not modified the permissions of the **Task** list. You have configured the workflow to store the user name in the **Assign To** column on the Task list. If you want that person to complete the task, he will need access to the list. Any user who has Full Control on the list can complete the task item.

6   Click **OK** to return to the default view of the library.

7   Click the new document to display the **Add a document** dialog box, and then click **Browse**.

8   In the **Choose File to Upload** dialog box, browse to the file that you would like to upload. Click **Open**, and then click **OK** to open a dialog displaying **Workflow States** on **Submitted To Approver #1**.

11

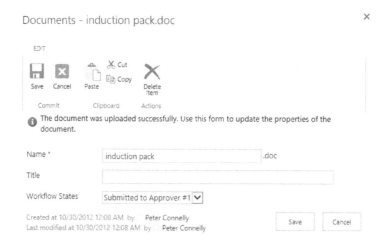

Documents - induction pack.doc

EDIT

Save | Cancel | Paste | Cut | Copy | Delete Item

Commit | Clipboard | Actions

The document was uploaded successfully. Use this form to update the properties of the document.

Name *   induction pack   .doc

Title

Workflow States   Submitted to Approver #1

Created at 10/30/2012 12:08 AM by   Peter Connelly
Last modified at 10/30/2012 12:08 AM by   Peter Connelly

Save | Cancel

9   Click **Save**.

The default view of the document library refreshes, with the new document that you uploaded listed on the page with an Approval Workflow status of In Progress.

10   Click the ellipsis to the right of the document you uploaded in step 8. In the hover card, click the ellipsis, and then on the list item menu, click **Workflows**.

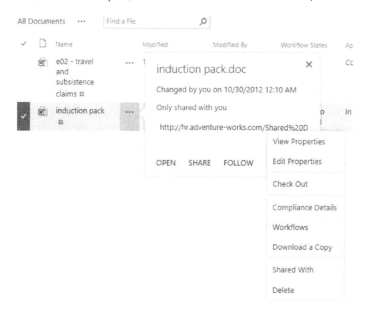

All Documents   ⋯   Find a file

✓   Name   Modified   Modified By   Workflow States   Ap

e02 - travel and subsistence claims ✿   ⋯

induction pack ✿   ⋯

induction pack.doc   ✕

Changed by you on 10/30/2012 12:10 AM

Only shared with you

http://hr.adventure-works.com/Shared%20D

OPEN   SHARE   FOLLOW

View Properties
Edit Properties
Check Out
Compliance Details
Workflows
Download a Copy
Shared With
Delete

The **Workflows:** *document name* page is displayed and in the **Workflows** section, there is a running workflow for the **Approval Workflow**, with a status of **In Progress**. The **Approval Workflow** is not listed in the **Start a New Workflow** section.

TIP If the **Approval Workflow** is not listed in the Start a New Workflow section, you cannot start another workflow instance for that workflow until the running workflow instance has completed.

11   Under **Running Workflows**, click **Approval Workflow**.

On the **Workflow Status** page, in the **Tasks** section, there is a task assigned to the user you specified in step 5.

12   Click **Review Stage 1** to open the **Approval Workflow Tasks** page.

In the **Description** field, the version number of the document is displayed along with a message box with the text, "A workflow has been initiated on the following list item," and a link to the document.

13   Click **Close** to return to the **Workflow Status** page.

❌ CLEAN UP **Leave the browser open if you are continuing to the next exercise.**

Managing workflow tasks within Outlook 2013

Workflow tasks are assigned to participants by using a Tasks list. You can use Outlook 2007, Outlook 2010, or Outlook 2013 as a place to receive workflow-related notifications and complete workflow tasks.

TIP More information on using Outlook 2013 with SharePoint can be found in Chapter 14, "Using SharePoint with Outlook and Lync."

In the following exercise, you will manage workflow tasks in Outlook 2013.

➡ SET UP **Open the Workflow Status page for the document you used in the previous exercise, if it is not already open.**

IMPORTANT Verify that you have sufficient rights to manage tasks in the Approval Workflow Tasks list. If in doubt, refer to Appendix A.

1   In the **Tasks** section, to the right of the sentence that starts **You can also view them in**, click the link to the **Tasks** list so that you can see the task named "**Review Stage 1: *document name*"** with a status of **Not Started**, which you created in the previous exercise.

2   On the **List** tab, in the **Connect & Export** group, click **Connect to Outlook**.

3   Click **Allow** to confirm that you want to open Outlook, and then click **Yes** to connect the Task list to Outlook. In the Outlook Tasks navigation pane, under **Other Tasks**, the **Tasks** list that you associated with the workflow is selected, and in the detail pane, the **Review Stage 1: *document name*** task is listed.

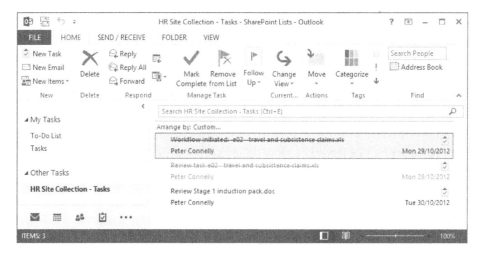

4   Click the task, and on the **Home** tab, click **Mark Complete**.

    The text of the task, Review Stage 1: *document name*, is struck through, denoting that the task is completed.

5   Press **F9**. In the detail pane, a second task, Review task *document name*, is added.

6   Double-click the task to open the Review task *document name* Task form. The task contains two links to the document: the task item in the **Tasks** list and a link to the **Tasks** list. By using these links, you can open, review, and modify the document's contents.

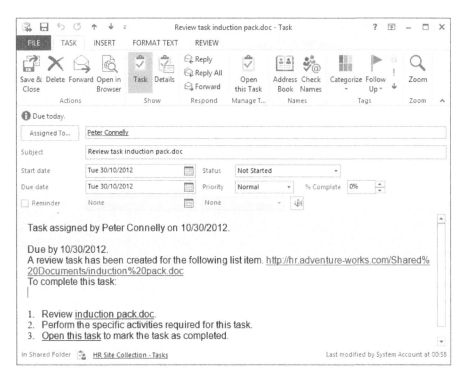

7   From the **Status** drop-down list, select **Completed**, and then on the **Task** tab, click **Save & Close**. The text of the Review task: *document name* task is struck through.

8   In Outlook, in the **Tasks** navigation pane, under **Other Tasks**, click the **Tasks** list that you associated with the workflow, and on the **Folder** tab, click **Open in Web Browser** in the **Actions** group to display the **Tasks List** page with the two completed tasks.

9   In the browser, on the **Quick Launch**, click the library you associated with the workflow. In the *workflow name* column for the document on which you started, the workflow appears with a status of **Completed**.

✕ CLEAN UP Close Outlook. Leave the browser open if you are continuing to the next exercise.

11

Terminating workflows

From time to time, you may need to terminate a workflow instance. For example, a person may have left your organization, and you have used a different business process to pay expenses to him or her. In the following exercise, you will start a workflow instance on a document; you will then terminate that workflow instance.

 SET UP **Open the All Documents view of the document library where you associated the workflow template.**

IMPORTANT Verify that you have sufficient rights to create and delete workflow instances on a document. If in doubt, refer to Appendix A.

1 Start a workflow on a document, and then in the *workflow name* column, click **In Progress**.

2 In the **Workflow Information** section, click **End this workflow**.

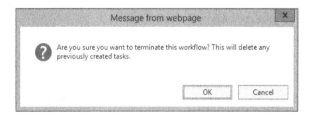

Workflow Information

Initiator: Peter Connelly   **Document:** interview rating summary
Started: 10/30/2012 1:11 AM   **Status:**   In Progress
Last run: 10/30/2012 1:11 AM

If an error occurs or if this workflow stops responding, you can end it.
▣ End this workflow.

A **Message from webpage** dialog box opens, asking if you are sure that you want to terminate this workflow.

3 Click **OK**.

The **Workflow Status** page refreshes, and in the **Workflow Information** section, the workflow has a status of **Canceled**. There are no task items listed in the **Tasks** section, and in the **Workflow History** section, the last event in the list has an event type of **Workflow Canceled**.

4   On the **Quick Launch**, click the document library with which you are working to display the default view of the library. The *workflow name* column for your document is set to **Canceled**.

✖ CLEAN UP **Leave the browser open if you are continuing to the next exercise.**

Removing workflows from lists and libraries

When an automated business process is no longer needed, you should remove the workflow from the list or library. This will prevent confusion for users who use that list or library. In the following exercise, you will remove a workflow from a document library.

➔ SET UP **Open the All Documents view of the document library where you associated the workflow template.**

> **IMPORTANT** Verify that you have sufficient rights to remove a workflow from the document library. If in doubt, refer to Appendix A.

1   On the **Quick Launch**, click the document library or list where you associated a workflow template.

2   On the **Library** tab, in the **Settings** group, click **Workflow Settings** to display the **Workflow Settings** page.

11

3   Click **Remove, Block, or Restore a Workflow** to display the **Remove Workflows** page.

Settings · Remove Workflows ⓘ

SharePoint 2013 Workflows

Select the workflows to remove
from this document library.
Removing a workflow association
cancels its running workflows.
Select No New Instances to allow
running workflows to complete.

Workflow	Instances	Allow	No New Instances	Remove

SharePoint 2010 Workflows

Select the workflows to remove
from this document library.
Removing a workflow association
cancels its running workflows.
Select No New Instances to allow
running workflows to complete.

Workflow	Instances	Allow	No New Instances	Remove
Approval Workflow	0	◉	○	○

[OK] [Cancel]

4   Select **Remove**, and then click **OK**.

TIP When there are a number of instances in progress for the workflow, select **No New** Instances, and then return to this task in a day or two, allowing the people on your team to complete the outstanding tasks for these workflow instances.

The **Workflow Settings** page is displayed, showing that the workflow is no longer associated with the list or library.

✖ CLEAN UP **Leave the browser open if you are continuing to the next exercise.**

Associating workflows with content types

Content types are designed to help users define a reusable collection of settings that can include columns, workflows, and other attributes. They can be associated with their own document template and with their own workflow and retention policies. Content types and site columns can be defined at the site or site collection level, or within the content type hub if your organization is using Managed Metadata Service. When created at the site collection level, they can be used by lists and libraries, or by any site within the site collection hierarchy. When created at the site level, they can be used only by lists and libraries within that site and any child sites.

If you need to use the same workflow process with a particular type of list or library, or a specific document type, then you should consider associating a workflow template with a content type and customizing it to define the process necessary to meet your business needs. This will reduce the amount of rework you would otherwise need to complete to achieve this consistency.

You may want the same approval process on every document library in a site or site collection, so users can send a document through the approval process manually when needed. To create this solution, you would amend the document content type in the content type hub or at the top of the site collection, and select the **Update All Content Types That Inherit From This Type With These Workflow Settings** option.

TIP When a site collection contains many sites, it may take some time for the content type configuration to be applied to all child sites. If you are creating a new site hierarchy, then create all of your content types and site columns before creating any child sites.

Another example could be the need to have two types of announcements—team announcements that must be approved and announcements that need no approval. To meet this business need, you could create a new announcement content type based on the original content type, so that you get all the same functionality of the built-in announcement list and a workflow. Site owners can then choose to associate the new content type with their announcement list, so they are able to create the two types of announcements.

IMPORTANT The Three-state workflow needs a column to store the three states. All columns in a content type must be a site column; therefore, if you associate the Three-state workflow with a content type, you must add a **Choice site** column to store the three states.

In the following exercise, you will create a new content type, add a site column to the content type, associate a workflow template with the content type, and configure its settings.

 SET UP **Open the SharePoint Team site that you used in the previous exercise, if it is not already open.**

IMPORTANT Verify that you have sufficient rights to create a content type. If in doubt, refer to Appendix A.

11

1   Click the **Settings** gear icon, and then click **Site settings** to display the **Site Settings** page.

2   Under **Web Designer Galleries**, click **Site Content Types**, and then on the **Site Content Types** page, click **Create** to display the **New Site Content Type** page.

3   In the **Name** box, type **Team Announcements**, and in the **Description** box, type **Use this content type to create new lists where the team can create team announcements**.

4   In the **Select parent content type from** list, select **List Content Types**, and in the **Parent Content Type**, select **Announcement**, if it is not already selected.

5   In the **Group** section, select **New Group** and type **WideWorldImporters**.

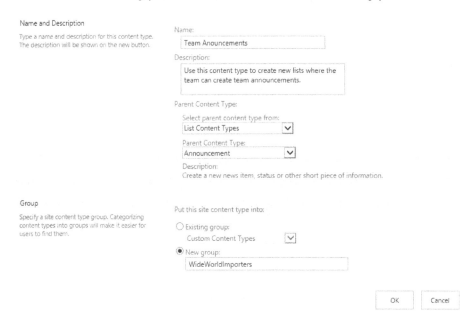

6   Click **OK** to display the **Team Announcements** page.

7   In the **Columns** section, click **Add from existing site columns** to display the **Add Columns** page.

8   In the **Available columns** list, scroll down and select **Status**, and then click **Add**. The **Status** column appears in the Columns To Add list.

Site Content Type ▸ Add Columns ⓘ

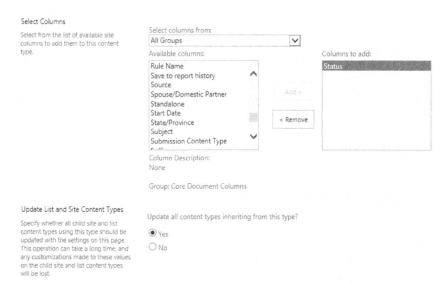

Select Columns

Select from the list of available site columns to add them to this content type.

Select columns from:

All Groups

Available columns:

Rule Name
Save to report history
Source
Spouse/Domestic Partner
Standalone
Start Date
State/Province
Subject
Submission Content Type

Columns to add:

Status

Add >

< Remove

Column Description:
None

Group: Core Document Columns

Update List and Site Content Types

Specify whether all child site and list content types using this type should be updated with the settings on this page. This operation can take a long time, and any customizations made to these values on the child site and list content types will be lost.

Update all content types inheriting from this type?

◉ Yes
◯ No

9   Click **OK** to display the **Team Announcements Site Content Type** page. **Status** is listed in the **Columns** section, with the **Source** column blank. This indicates that the **Status** column was added to this content type and not inherited from a parent content type.

11

Site Content Types ▸ Site Content Type

Site Content Type Information

Name: Team Anouncements
Description: Use this content type to create new lists where the team can create team announcements.
Parent: Announcement
Group: WideWorldImporters

Settings

▫ Name, description, and group
▫ Advanced settings
▫ Workflow settings
▫ Information management policy settings
▫ Delete this site content type

Columns

Name	Type	Status	Source
Title	Single line of text	Required	Item
Body	Multiple lines of text	Optional	Announcement
Expires	Date and Time	Optional	Announcement
Status	Choice	Optional	

▫ Add from existing site columns
▫ Add from new site column
▫ Column order

10 In the **Settings** section, click **Workflow settings**, and then on the **Workflow Settings** page, click **Add a workflow**.

11 On the **Add a Workflow** page, in the **Workflow** section, select **Three-state**. Then, in the **Name** section, type a new name for this workflow, such as **Announcement Approval**. Leave the other sections at their default settings, and then click **Next**.

12 In the **Workflow states** section, the site column that you added to the content type automatically appears with the three choices—**Not Started**, **Draft**, and **Reviewed**— for the three states of the workflow. If this column does not appear, from the **Select a Choice field** list, click **Status** and enter the initial, middle, and final states in the three lists as needed.

Workflow states:

Select a 'Choice' field, and then select a value for the initial, middle, and final states. For an Issues list, the states for an item are specified by the Status field, where:

Initial State = Active
Middle State = Resolved
Final State = Closed

As the item moves through the various stages of the workflow, the item is updated automatically.

Select a 'Choice' field:

| Status | ⌄ |

Initial state

| Not Started | ⌄ |

Middle state

| Draft | ⌄ |

Final state

| Reviewed | ⌄ |

13 Leave the other sections at their default settings, and then click **OK**. You can now associate this content type with any list and the workflow will be automatically associated with that list.

✖ CLEAN UP **Close the browser.**

Key points

- Workflows can help to automate and track long-running, repetitive processes that require human interaction, after someone has defined exactly what form that automation will take.

- Plan your workflows and involve the people who will use the workflow.

- You can use the same workflows that you may have used in SharePoint 2010, known as SharePoint 2010 workflows.

- SharePoint Server 2013 introduces a new, highly scalable workflow framework that is implemented by using a new piece of software, Workflow Manager, which allows you to run SharePoint 2013 workflows.

- Workflow Manager is installed separately from SharePoint 2013 by your server administrators.

- A workflow template is available only when a workflow feature is activated.

- Workflow templates can be associated with sites, lists, libraries, or content types.

- Each of the built-in workflow templates can be customized in a limited fashion to define the exact process necessary to meet your business needs.

11

- To maintain the status of a document through a Three-state workflow process, you must create a **Choice** column that stores the three states of the workflow.

- The workflow name is used as the name of a column; therefore, do not give the workflow the same name as an existing column.

- You cannot start two instances of the same workflow on a list item or document.

- A workflow's progress is recorded in a **Workflow History** list, and workflow tasks are assigned to participants by using a **Tasks** list.

- You can receive an email notification when a workflow task is created.

- Outlook 2013 serves as a place to receive workflow-related notifications and to complete workflow tasks.

- Workflow templates can be associated with content types. This reduces the amount of rework you would otherwise need to complete to provide consistent workflows across multiple lists, libraries, and sites.

Chapter at a glance

Import

Import data from an Excel spreadsheet to a list in SharePoint, page 402

Export

Export data to a SharePoint list, page 408

Build

Build an Access app, page 413

Import and Link

Import data from a SharePoint list, page 432
Link to a SharePoint list, page 435

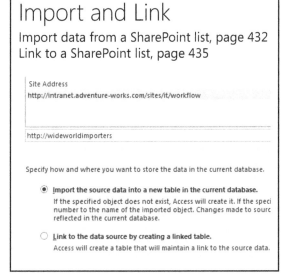

Using SharePoint with Excel and Access

12

IN THIS CHAPTER, YOU WILL LEARN HOW TO

- Import data from an Excel spreadsheet to a list in SharePoint.

- Export a SharePoint list to an Excel spreadsheet.

- Export an Excel table to a SharePoint site.

- Build an Access app.

- Create a table in an Access app.

- Work with Access apps in the browser.

- Export data from an Access desktop database to a list.

- Import data from a list, and link to a list.

- Move data from a desktop database to a list, and work offline.

Microsoft SharePoint 2013 provides the collaborative backbone to the Microsoft Office 2013 system. This chapter focuses on the integration of SharePoint 2013 with Microsoft Office Excel 2013 and Microsoft Office Access 2013.

Similar to previous versions, with Excel 2013 you can export and import data to and from SharePoint lists and provide one-way synchronization from SharePoint lists to Excel spreadsheets so that you can take the data offline, and then synchronize with the SharePoint lists when you reconnect.

The combination of SharePoint 2013 and Access 2013 makes it easy for you to build a ***desktop database*** against SharePoint. Ever since Microsoft Windows SharePoint Services 3.0, you could move away from storing your Access desktop database files on file shares. You can store an Access database in a SharePoint library, which lets you and your team collaborate easily with the Access database solution. You can also move data held in Access tables to SharePoint lists, exposing the lists in the Access database as linked tables that allow updates in SharePoint lists to be reflected in the Access table, and vice versa. If you do not possess the skills or privileges to be a Microsoft SQL Server database administrator, you can still obtain the manageability and stability benefits of storing data on the server while retaining the use of Access. Also, the data in the linked tables is stored locally on your computer so that you can work offline with data, and then synchronize the changes when you reconnect.

However, there are some performance issues with this approach. It does not allow you to model some of the more complex scenarios built using Access; therefore, new with the Enterprise edition of Microsoft SharePoint Server 2010 is the ability to create a SharePoint site based on an Access database, known as an *Access web database*. This ability is extended in SharePoint Server 2013, with a new, completely rewritten *Access Services* service application, where Access 2013 databases are published to SharePoint Server 2013 as an *Access web app*, also known as *Access apps*. Access apps are excellent when you wish to rapidly create end-to-end web-based business solutions, including those that involve custom forms.

This chapter details the integration of SharePoint with Excel 2013 and Access 2013 apps, as well as desktop databases. Although you can complete many of the desktop database-related tasks documented in this chapter using previous versions, the steps and screen shots in this chapter were created using Excel 2013 and Access 2013. If you use Microsoft Office Excel 2010 or Microsoft Office Access 2010, your steps and screen shots will be slightly different. See *Microsoft SharePoint Foundation 2010 Step by Step* by Olga Londer and Penelope Coventry (Microsoft Press, 2010) for steps on using Access 2010 with SharePoint.

PRACTICE FILES Before you can complete the exercises in this chapter, you need to copy the book's practice files to your computer. The practice files you'll use in this chapter are in the **Chapter12** practice file folder. A complete list of practice files is provided in "Using the practice files" at the beginning of this book.

IMPORTANT Remember to use your SharePoint site location in place of *http:// wideworldimporters* in the following exercises.

Importing data from an Excel spreadsheet to a list in SharePoint

In many situations, you might already have data within a spreadsheet, but later you find that you need to share the data with other members of your team. SharePoint can import data from an Excel spreadsheet into a SharePoint list. Those users who have appropriate permissions may read the SharePoint list, whereas others may even revise the list or enter additional data. You can choose to import all the data held on a worksheet, in a *range* of cells, in a *named range*, or in an *Excel table*.

In the following exercise, you will use your browser to create a SharePoint custom list that contains data imported from an Excel spreadsheet.

SET UP **This exercise uses the Furniture_Price.xlsx file in the Chapter12 practice folder. Open the SharePoint site where you would like to import data from the Excel spreadsheet. Remember to use your SharePoint site location in place of *http://wideworldimporters* in the exercises.**

> **IMPORTANT** Verify that you have sufficient rights to add an app. If in doubt, see Appendix A, "SharePoint 2013 user permissions and permission levels."

1   On the **Settings** menu, click **Add an app**. Then in the **Find an app** box, type **excel** and press **Enter**.

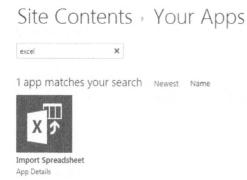

2   Click **Import Spreadsheet**, and then on the **New** page, in the **Name** box, type **FurniturePrice**.

TIP Any Uniform Resource Locator (URL) in SharePoint is limited to 260 characters. The name that you type here is used to create both the URL and the title of the list. Later in this exercise, you will change the title to a user-friendly name.

3   In the **Description** box, type **This list contains the furniture items in stock together with their unit prices**.

4   Click **Browse**.

5   In the **Choose File to Upload** dialog box, go to the Chapter12 practice folder and double-click **Furniture_Price.xlsx**.

6   On the **New** page, click **Import**.

Site Contents › New

Name and Description
Type a new name as you want it to appear in headings and links throughout the site. Type descriptive text that will help site visitors use this list.

Name:

FurniturePrice

Description:

This list contains the furniture items in stock together with their unit prices.

Import from Spreadsheet
Specify the location for the spreadsheet you want to use as the basis for this list.

File location:

\PracticeFiles\Furniture_Price.xlsx   Browse...

Import   Cancel

Excel 2013 opens **Furniture_Price.xlsx** and displays the **Import to Windows SharePoint Services list** dialog box.

7   From the **Range Type** list, check that **Table Range** is selected, and then in the **Selected Range** list, select **Stock!FurniturePriceTable**.

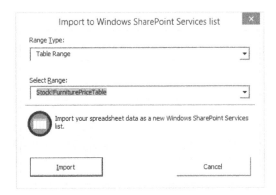

8   Click **Import** to create the **FurniturePrice** list and to display it in the browser.

TIP If you import a range of cells from an Excel spreadsheet and want the Excel column names to become the SharePoint list column names, you should first edit the spreadsheet and convert the range of cells to an Excel table.

FurniturePrice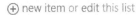

⊕ new item or edit this list

All Items   •••   [Find an item   🔍]

✓	Furniture Name		Furniture Range	Material	In Stock	Unit Price	Total
	Tall unit ✳	•••	Bianca	steel	5	$25.00	$125.00
	Base unit with drawers ✳	•••	Bianca	steel	99	$20.00	$1,980.00
	Wall unit ✳	•••	Bianca	steel	10	$115.00	$1,150.00
	Corner unit ✳	•••	Bianca	steel	5	$75.00	$375.00
	Slimline base unit ✳	•••	Bianca	steel	ppp	$64.00	#VALUE!
	3-seater sofa ✳	•••	Milan	Material	25	$95.00	$2,375.00
	Armchair ✳	•••	Milan	Material	10	$83.00	$830.00
	Dining chair ✳	•••	Boston	Leather	45	$53.00	$2,385.00

9. To change the title of the list, click the **List** tab, and then in the **Settings** group, click **List Settings**.

10. Under **General Settings**, click **List name, description and navigation**.

11. On the **General Settings** page, in the **Name** box, type a user-friendly name, such as **Furniture Price**.

12. In the **Navigation** section, click the **Yes** option to display this list on the **Quick Launch**.

13. Click **Save** at the bottom of the webpage, and then on the breadcrumb, click the **Furniture Price** to display the **All Items** view of the list.

❌ CLEAN UP **Leave the browser open if you are continuing to the next exercise.**

Exporting a SharePoint list to an Excel spreadsheet

12

You can export the contents of SharePoint lists, the results of a survey, or document libraries to an Excel spreadsheet. In Excel, changes that you make to data in your Excel worksheet do not synchronize with the list on the SharePoint website; that is, only a one-way synchronization occurs from the SharePoint site to Excel. The exported list or library is connected to a web query, which when run, updates the spreadsheet with changes made to the original list on your SharePoint site. The Excel spreadsheet maintains this connection to the SharePoint list, and therefore becomes a *linked object*.

The export process exports only the columns and rows contained in the list's current view. If none of the views contain the data that you want to export, then you must create a new view to meet your needs. Alternatively, you can choose one of the existing views, export the list to a spreadsheet, and then delete the unwanted data.

TIP The columns in Excel retain the data types from the exported SharePoint list; they do not retain the formulas of a calculated column.

When you export a SharePoint library to an Excel spreadsheet, Excel represents the documents in the list with hyperlinks that point to the documents on the SharePoint site. Similarly, attachments on list items are replaced with a hyperlink. In the Excel spreadsheet, click this link to open the file.

TIP You should make a habit of renaming your tables in Excel so that you recognize the data that they contain. This process helps make the formulas that summarize table data much easier to understand. To rename an Excel table, first ensure that the **Design** contextual tab is active, and then, in the **Properties** group, edit the value in the **Table Name** field.

In this exercise, you will export a list from a SharePoint site to an Excel 2013 spreadsheet. You will add data to the spreadsheet, and then synchronize the data in the spreadsheet with the contents of the list on the SharePoint site.

 SET UP **In the browser, open the SharePoint site, if it is not already open, where you have a list whose contents you want to export to an Excel spreadsheet. This exercise uses the list that you created in the previous exercise.**

IMPORTANT Verify that you have sufficient rights to edit items in the list. If in doubt, see Appendix A.

1   On the **Quick Launch**, click **Furniture Price**. Click the **List** tab, and then click **Export to Excel** in the **Connect & Export** group.

2   If you get a browser message asking whether you want to open or save owssvr.iqy, click **Open**.

Excel 2013 opens a new workbook that contains one worksheet, named **owssvr**. A **Microsoft Excel Security Notice** dialog box appears, warning you that data connections have been blocked.

3   Click **Enable** to display the results of the Excel query. Each column in Excel contains an AutoFilter arrow in the header row, and the Design contextual tab is active.

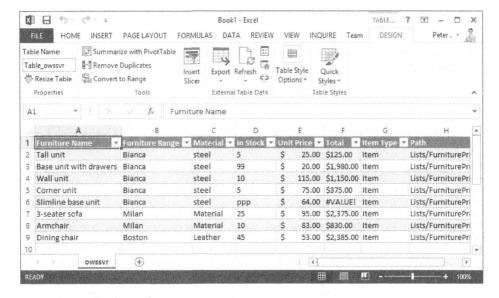

4   Click cell **A10**, type **Antique**, and then press **Tab**. Type **Bi**, and then press **Tab** so that IntelliSense completes the word *Bianca* for you.

5   Type **wood**, and then press **Tab**. Type **5**, and then press **Tab**. Type **10**, and then press **Enter**. Excel places a dollar sign ($) before the number 10.

6   On the **Data** tab, in the **Connections** group, click **Refresh All**.

The spreadsheet is updated with a copy of the data from the Furniture Price list on the SharePoint website. Your changes to data in the Excel spreadsheet are lost.

12

7   Click cell **A2**, and then, in the **Connections** group on the **Data** tab, click **Properties** to display the **External Data Properties** dialog box. You can use this dialog box to alter the behavior of the refreshed activity.

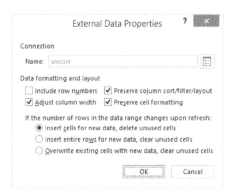

8   Click **Cancel**.

CLEAN UP **Close the browser and exit Excel 2013. You do not need to save the spreadsheet.**

Exporting an Excel table to a SharePoint site

Creating a SharePoint list from within Excel is known as *exporting* an Excel table. Once the table data is placed on the SharePoint site, users can see the Excel data without opening Excel. As in the first exercise of this chapter, you can maintain a link between the SharePoint list and the Excel data, but any changes in the Excel spreadsheet are not reflected in the SharePoint list. You can only synchronize changes in the SharePoint list to the Excel spreadsheet.

The export to SharePoint process uses a two-step wizard. When you export an Excel table to SharePoint, Excel checks the data in each column to ensure that the data belongs to a data type supported by SharePoint. If it doesn't, Excel usually applies the Text data type to each column. Excel also checks whether each column contains only one type of data. If a column contains a mixture of data types, such as numbers and text, then Excel chooses Text as the data type. Once Excel completes its check, the second step of the wizard appears, which identifies the data types that will be used to create the columns in SharePoint, and identifies cells that contain different data values than the rest of the cells in a column. Any formulas are also removed.

Once the export process is complete, the spreadsheet contains two extra columns, **Item Type** and **Path**. On the **Design** contextual tab, you can use commands in the **External Table** data group to alter the properties of a range of cells, open the connected SharePoint list in a browser, or unlink a list.

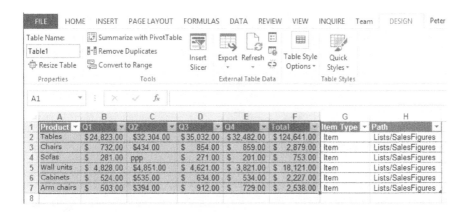

IMPORTANT When you export an Excel table to SharePoint, the new SharePoint list does not appear on the **Quick Launch**.

In the following exercise, you will export a spreadsheet to a SharePoint list.

➡ SET UP **You will use the Sales_Figures.xlsx file, located in the Chapter12 practice folder. Start Excel 2013 before beginning this exercise, and then open the Sales_Figures. xlsx document.**

IMPORTANT Verify that you have sufficient rights to edit items in the list. If in doubt, see Appendix A.

1   In Excel 2013, in the **Protected View** notification area, click **Enable Editing**, if displayed, and then click any cell within the data. If you are using an Excel spreadsheet other than the practice file, and the data that you want to export is already found within an Excel 2010 table, skip to step 4.

2   On the **Home** tab, in the **Styles** group, click **Format as Table**, and then select a table style.

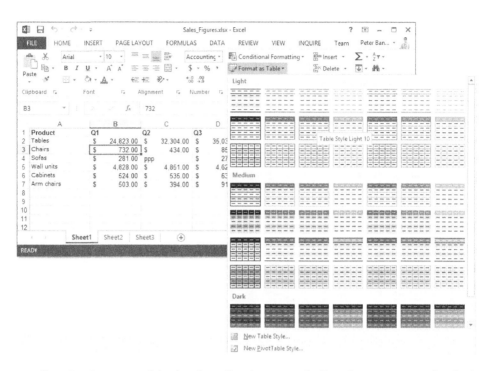

TIP By selecting one cell in the data, Excel automatically selects a range of cells that contain data; however, you can select a different range of cells to use when creating a table. In addition, if your data does not contain headers, Excel creates them for you and labels them as Column1, Column2, and so on.

3 When the **Format As Table** dialog box appears, click **OK**.

The data is converted into a table and the **Design** tab on the **Table Tools** tab set appears.

4 On the **Design** tab, in the **External Table Data** group, click **Export**, and then, from the drop-down list, click **Export Table to SharePoint List**.

TROUBLESHOOTING If the table is not active on the worksheet, the **Design** tab disappears. To export a table, it must be active on the worksheet. To make a table active, click any cell in the table.

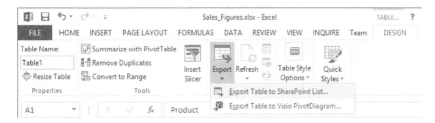

The first step of the two-step **Export Table to SharePoint List** wizard appears.

5   In the **Address** box, type the name of the site where you want to export the data, such as **http://wideworldimporters**.

6   Select the **Create a read-only connection to the new SharePoint list** check box.

> **IMPORTANT** If the **Create a read-only connection to the new SharePoint list** check box is selected, the spreadsheet is linked to the SharePoint list and you can synchronize updates from the SharePoint list to the spreadsheet. However, once the SharePoint list is created, you cannot link the spreadsheet to the SharePoint list. Therefore, if you wish to synchronize updates between the list and the spreadsheet, be sure to select this check box now.

7   In the **Name** box, type **SalesFigures**, and in the **Description** box, type **This list contains furniture sales for this year**.

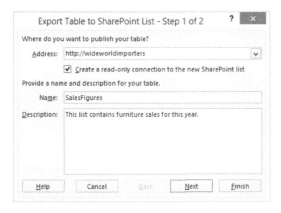

8   Click **Next** to display the second step of the wizard.

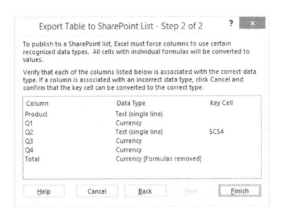

In the Key Cell column, notice that cell C4 in the Q2 column contains a different data type from the rest of the cells in that column. Also, the formulas are removed from the Total column. If you have the region and language format (also known as the date, time, or number format) of your operating system set to English (United States), then columns Q1, Q3, Q4, and Total have a data type of Currency; otherwise, they will have a data type of Number.

TIP At this point, you can click **Cancel**, correct the erroneous data, and then restart the export process. Also, because Excel removes formulas during the export process, you may consider deleting the **Total** column and creating a calculated column once you have completed the export process and the data is on your SharePoint site.

9   Click **Finish**. A **Microsoft SharePoint Foundation** dialog box appears with the URL of your new SharePoint list.

10   Click the URL of your new SharePoint list. A new browser window opens, displaying the new SharePoint list.

SalesFigures ⓘ

Stop editing this list

All Items   ···   Find an item   🔍

✓	📄	Product		Q1	Q2	Q3	Q4	Total	+
	📄	Tables ※	···	$24,823.00	$32,304.00	$35,032.00	$32,482.00	$124,641.00	
	📄	Chairs ※	···	$732.00	$434.00	$854.00	$859.00	$2,879.00	
	📄	Sofas ※	···	$281.00	ppp	$271.00	$201.00	$753.00	
	📄	Wall units ※	···	$4,828.00	$4,851.00	$4,621.00	$3,821.00	$18,121.00	
	📄	Cabinets ※	···	$524.00	$535.00	$634.00	$534.00	$2,227.00	
	📄	Arm chairs ※	···	$503.00	$394.00	$912.00	$729.00	$2,538.00	

❌ CLEAN UP **Close all browser windows, and close the SharePoint Foundation dialog box by clicking OK. Exit Excel and save the changes to the spreadsheet.**

Building an Access app

SharePoint Server 2013 provides the following two methods of building end-to-end web-based business solutions. Both require the purchase of SharePoint Server Enterprise Client Access Licenses (CALs).

- **Access web database** These cannot be created using Access 2013. You can still view and edit a previously created web database by using Access 2010 and SharePoint Server 2010, and you can republish it to SharePoint Server 2013 using Access 2010. Web databases are exposed as a SharePoint site. Data held in Access tables is moved to SharePoint lists, and forms and reports are created as webpages. You cannot automatically convert a web database to an Access web app; however, you can manually convert a web database to an Access web app by importing the data from the web database into a new Access app, and then re-create the user interface and business logic.

  SEE ALSO An Office visual instruction on creating web databases with Access 2010 and Access Services can be found at *msdn.microsoft.com/en-us/library/ff402351(office.14).aspx.*

12

- **Access apps** These apps are SharePoint apps, which can be deployed to the Share-Point Store. You use the browser to view and edit data, and you use Access 2013 to design the Access app. Data and Access objects for each Access app is saved in its own Microsoft SQL Server 2012 database; it is not saved in SharePoint lists. This SQL-integrated approach improves the performance, manageability, and scalability of the business solution. Also, this makes it possible for SQL Server developers to extend the solution by directly connecting to the tables in the database, including building reports with Desktop Access Reports, Excel, and Power View.

SEE ALSO An example of how to visualize your Access app data in Excel can be found at *blogs.office.com/b/microsoft-access/archive/2013/01/22/visualize-access-data-in-excel.aspx*.

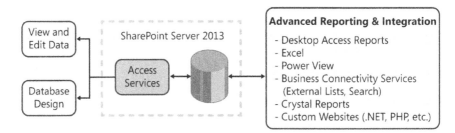

However, as the data is not stored in SharePoint, some functionality is lost when com-pared to creating a SharePoint integrated forms solution by using Microsoft InfoPath 2013 Designer. For example, you cannot create or initiate a SharePoint workflow on data in Access apps, nor can you have unique permissions at the table or row level. Also, the data stored inside the Access app is not indexed by the SharePoint search engine. The rest of this section describes the creation of Access apps.

Access 2013 includes a set of templates that can be used to jump-start the creation of Access apps. Any template with a global icon and that does not contain the word *desktop* can be used to create an Access app. These templates include **Custom web app**, **Asset tracking**, **Contacts**, **Issue tracking**, **Project management**, and **Task management**.

The **Asset tracking**, **Contacts**, **Issue tracking**, **Project management**, and **Task manage-ment** templates are not available when you first install Access. They are available when you are connected to the Internet. When you choose one of these templates, you are provided a preview of the home webpage, a description, and the download size of the template.

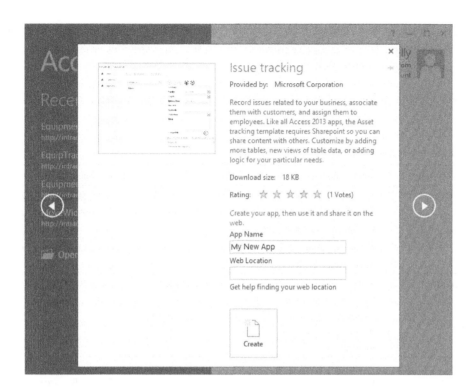

Your Access app can contain tables, views (known as forms), queries, and data macros. When you create an Access app based on the Custom Web App template, it contains no tables, views, queries, or data macros; and when the Access app appears in the browser, the webpage displays a link to open the app within Access so that you can start adding tables.

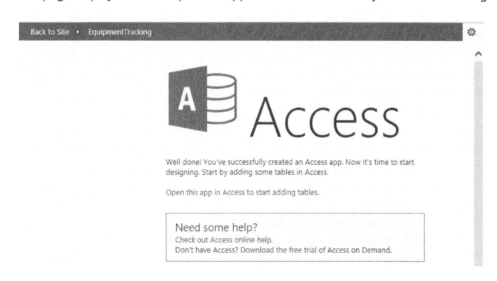

NOTE You can create an Access app by using the **Your Apps** page, which appears when you click **Add an app** from the **Settings** gear icon in the browser. This creates an Access app using the Custom Web App template.

The Access app templates available for download over the Internet are summarized in Table 12-1.

Table 12-1 *Access app templates*

Template name	Description	Tables	Views
Asset Tracking	Track equipment used by your business and assigned to employees.	Assets, Categories, Employees	List, Datasheet, By Category, By Group
Contacts	Manage individual and corporate relationships.	Contacts	List, Datasheet, By Group
Issue Tracking	Record issues related to your business, associate them with customers, and assign them to employees	Issues, Customers, Employees, Issue Comments, Related Issues	List, Datasheet, By Status, By Group
Project Management	Manage projects by breaking work items into tasks, associating them with customer, and assigning them to employees.	Projects, Employees, Customers, Tasks	List, Datasheet, By Status, By Group

The name of the SQL Server 2012 database that is created when you add an Access app to your site can be found when you open the Access app in Access and click the **File** tab to display the backstage **Info** page. The database name will be of the format db_*guid*, where *guid* is an automatically generated number. The name of the site where the Access app was added appears in the title of the Access window.

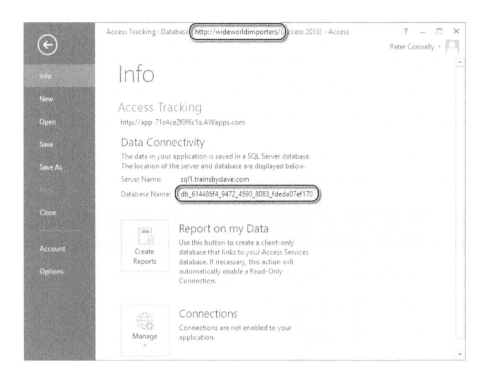

The tables, views, queries, and macros are all stored in the database. Whenever you enter data or modify the design of the Access app, you are interacting with the database; however, the user interface gives no indication of this.

Although the server name and database name is of little interest to you, it is important to advanced users who wish to directly connect to the database. You can control external connections to your Access app database by using the **Manage** split button at the bottom of the backstage **Info** page. The default configuration of the Access app database is not to allow any external connections. Another group of interested users is your IT department, who may wish to schedule operational procedures, such as backup and maintenance on the database.

TIP You can make your own backups of the Access app database by creating an *App Package file*, and restoring the Access app by using the app package on any SharePoint 2013 site. More information on how to complete such a task is documented at *blogs.office. com/b/microsoft-access/archive/2012/09/27/moving-and-backing-up-your-access-2013-web-apps.aspx*.

Whichever template you use, when an Access app is created, it inherits the permissions and branding from the site where the app was added. You cannot change the permissions or

12

branding within the Access app. Users who design the Access app using Access must be mapped to the Full Control permission level at the site where the app was added. Users who use the browser to run the Access app must be mapped to either the Read or Contribute permission level, depending whether you wish them to just view the data or want them to create, update, and delete the data.

In this exercise, you will create an app from a template.

 SET UP **Start Access 2013. Remember to use your SharePoint site location in place of** *http://wideworldimporters* **in the following exercise.**

IMPORTANT Verify that you have sufficient rights to add an app. If in doubt, see Appendix A.

1   In the middle pane, click **Custom web app**.

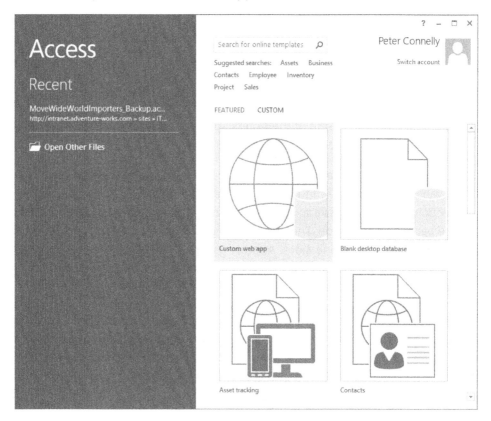

2   In the **Custom web app** dialog, in the **App Name** text box, type **EquipmentTracking**, and then in the **Web Location** text box, type the URL of the SharePoint site where you want to add the Access app, such as **http://wideworldimporters**.

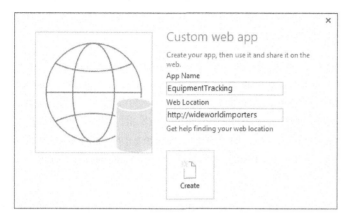

3   Click **Create** to create the app and to display the app in Access.

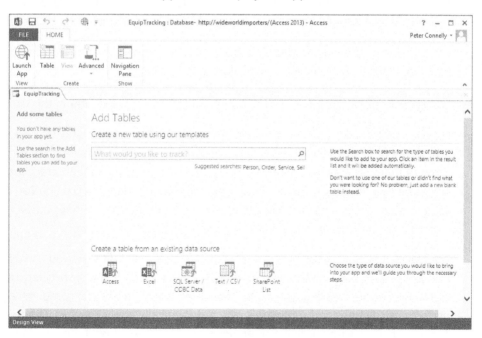

✖ CLEAN UP Leave Access open if you are continuing to the next exercise.

Creating a table in an Access app

With an Access app, you use the browser to add, edit, view, and delete data, and you use Access 2013 to design the Access app. This means that Access 2013 is used to create and customize tables, views, queries, and macros.

Each Access table is created as a SQL Server table, which has the same name that it was given in Access, as are the fields (columns) you create in the Access. Access data types are mapped to SQL Server database data types. For example, text fields map to nvarchar; number fields use decimal, int, or float; and image fields are stored as varbinary (MAX). However, in many instances, you will not need to create tables and add fields to those tables, because Access provides a number of table templates (nouns), which you can use as a basis for your new tables.

When you select a table template, other related tables may be added to the Access app; for example, when you add the **Assets** table, the **Categories** table is added, which allows you to group and organize your assets. The Orders template provides an **Orders** table, as well as tables to track related **Customers**, **Employees**, **Products**, **Suppliers**, and **Categories**.

You can also create linked tables; for example, you can connect to and display real-time data from SharePoint lists, including external lists.

SEE ALSO Creating linked tables to SharePoint lists is discussed later in this chapter.

For each table, two views are automatically generated: **List** and **Datasheet**. Each can be likened to the views on SharePoint internal lists and libraries. These are the pages in the browser that users see when they go to the Access app, and use to interact with the data. There are two other types of views, Summary and Blank views, which you can use to develop custom views. The Summary view allows you to group data rows based on a value in a column or, alternatively, calculate a sum or an average of a column.

The **Datasheet** view in the browser is similar to the **Quick Edit** view you use on lists and libraries. If your users find that they extensively use the same filters, sorts, or column hiding, you may consider creating queries for the Access app. Queries can combine related tables, perform calculations and summaries, and automatically apply changes. Queries in the Access app are created as SQL Server views or as a table-valued function (TVF), if the query has parameters.

To automate common tasks, you can create macros. A *macro* is a miniature program that you create and store in an Access app. Access apps do not support the Visual Basic (VB) programming language. There are two types of macros:

- User interface macros, which perform actions, such as navigating to another view, or showing or hiding controls. They can be attached to command buttons or combo boxes.

- Data macros, which are created by selecting **Data Macros** from the **Advanced** split button in the **Create** group on the **Home** tab. These macros are used to implement business rules at the data level, and therefore can be used to create, edit, and delete records.

To create views, macros, and queries, use the **Advanced** split button in the **Create** group on the **Home** tab within Access.

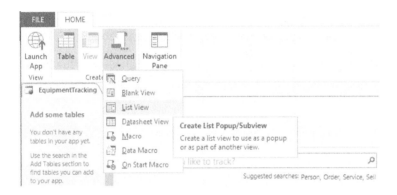

In this exercise, you will create a table in an Access app.

SET UP **Start Access 2013 and open the Equipment Tracking Access app that you created in the previous exercise, if it is not already open. You can use your own Access app if you wish.**

IMPORTANT Verify that that the user ID you are using is mapped to the Full Control permission level in the site where the Access app was added.

1 On the **Add Tables** screen, under **Create a new table using our templates**, type **equipment**, and then click the search icon to the right of the text box to search through the list of table templates.

12

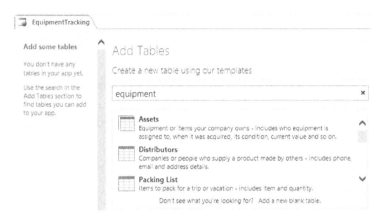

2   Click **Assets** to create the Assets, Categories, and Employees tables.

3   In the left navigation pane, click **Assets** to display the design view of the home page of the Access app.

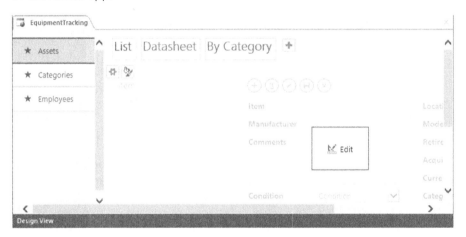

⊗ CLEAN UP **Leave Access open if you are continuing to the next exercise.**

Working with an Access app in the browser

Once you have designed the Access app in Access, it can be used in the browser to create, read, update, and delete the data associated with your app. Users mapped to the Contribute permission level on the site where the app was added can complete these tasks; these users will not need to have Access installed on their computers to work with the data.

In the browser, the Access app page is divided into a number of sections. Depending on the view and the relationship between the tables, not all of these sections will be shown in all views:

- **Table list** Each table is presented by a link in the table list. Using Access, you can rearrange the order that the tables appear, and hide those tables that you do not want to be displayed in the browser.

- **View selector** Lets you select a specific view of items stored in a table.

- **Search and filter text box** Lets you search and filter the items displayed in the view.

- **Action Bar** Lets you add, delete, edit, save, and cancel changes. The **Action Bar** is the same in each view. You can customize the **Action Bar** in Access by replacing the five default commands with custom commands. You can even hide it, if you prefer.

- **Item pane** Lets you browse the items displayed in the view. For each item, up to three properties can be displayed. In the list view of the **Employees** table, the primary field is the **First Name** and **Last Name**, and the secondary field is the **Company**. No property is assigned to the thumbnail field.

- **Item Detailed pane** Lets you view, create, modify, and delete the properties of an item.

- **Related items** Displays items from other tables that are related to the item displayed in the Item Detailed pane.

12

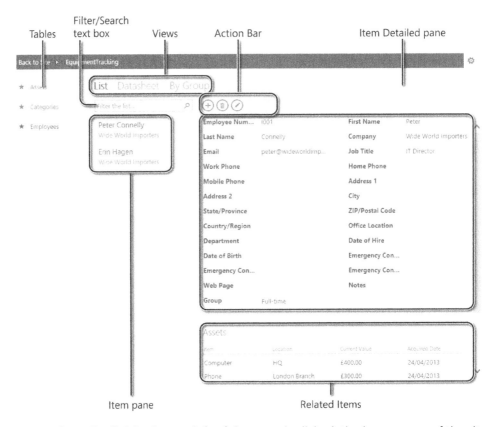

Tables   Filter/Search text box   Views   Action Bar   Item Detailed pane

Item pane   Related Items

When the **Back to Site** link in the top left of the page is clicked, the home page of the site where you added the Access app is displayed. Click the cog icon in the top right of the page to customize the app in Access.

To display the Access app within Access, on the **Home** tab, click **Launch App**, or you can use the browser by going to the **Site Content** page and clicking the app. In the browser, if the background color of the Access app is not solid red, but the text below the name of the app—**We're adding your app**—is red, then SharePoint is still creating the Access app.

You can use the following keyboard shortcut keys when working with the Access app in the browser:

Action	Keyboard shortcut
Browse between the table list, view selector, filter/search text box, Action Bar, and controls in the data pane.	Tab, Shift+Tab, or Arrow keys
Create a new item.	Ctrl+N

Action	Keyboard shortcut
Delete an item.	Delete
Edit an item.	Ctrl+E
Save an item.	Ctrl+S
Cancel an action.	Escape
Edit a filter.	/
Close a dialog.	Escape

In this exercise, you will add data to an Access app using the **List** and **Datasheet** views.

 SET UP **Start Access 2013 and open the Equipment Tracking Access app that you cre-ated in the previous exercise, if it is not already open. You can use your own Access app if you wish.**

IMPORTANT Verify that you have sufficient rights to edit data in the app. If in doubt, see Appendix A.

1   On the **Home** tab, in the **View** group, click **Launch App** to open the app in the browser.

2   In the table list, click **Employees**, and create a new employee item using the values in the following list:

Label	Value
Employee Number	I0001
First Name	Peter
Last Name	Connelly
Company	Wide World Importers
Email	peter@wideworldimporters.com
Job Title	IT Director

12

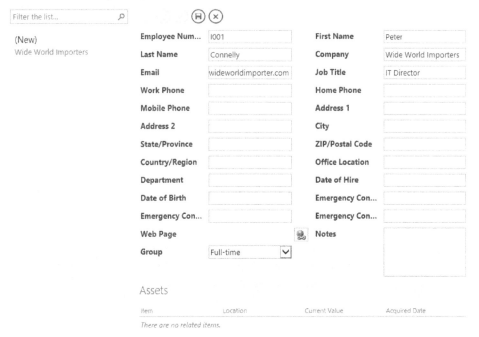

3   Click the **Save** control on the **Action Bar**.

4   In the table list, click **Categories**, and then click **Datasheet** in the view selector.

5   Under **Title**, type **Desktop**, and then press **Enter** to go to the next row.

6   Repeat the previous step to create two other categories: **Tablet** and **Smartphone**.

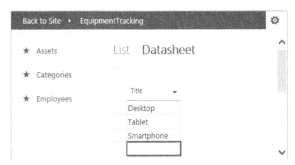

7   In the table list, click **Assets** and create two new asset items using the values in the following table. To save each item, click the **Save** control on the **Action Bar**, and click the **Add** control on the **Action Bar** to display the form to add the second item.

Label	Asset 1	Asset 2
Item	Computer	Phone
Location	HQ	London Branch
Manufacturer	Contoso	Adventure Works
Model	C0369	A0123
Acquired Date (use the data picker)	Today's date	Today's date
Current Value	400	300
Condition	Good	New
Category	Desktop	Smartphone
Owned By	Peter Connelly	Peter Connelly

TIP As you type the values for the **Category** and **Owned By** fields, the controls display a list of items from the **Categories** and **Employees** tables to help ensure data integrity.

8 With **Assets** still selected in the table list, in the view selector, click **By Category** to summarize the assets by category.

9 Under **Item**, click **Computer** to display a dialog to view all the properties associated with the computer asset.

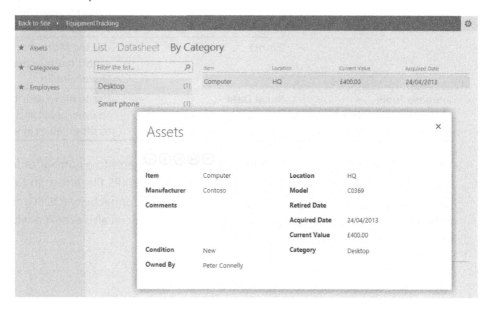

❌ CLEAN UP **Close Access and all browser windows.**

Exporting data from an Access desktop database to a list

Traditionally, Access uses database objects to manipulate and display data, tables, reports, and queries, where the Access database is stored on a file system or in a SharePoint library and requires the use of Access on the computer. When you create such a database with Access 2013, the same file format that was used with Microsoft Office Access 2007 or Access 2010 is created—an .accdb file; these files are known as a *desktop database*.

SEE ALSO More information on changes in Access 2013 can be found at *technet.microsoft. com/en-us/library/cc178954.aspx*.

Access consists of a number of tabs, many of which provide a quick way to work with SharePoint websites and lists, as summarized in the following table.

In the following table, note that "External Data" in column 1 goes with both row 2 and row 3, that is, "External Data" applies to both "Import & Link" in column 2 and "Export" in column 2.

Tab	Group	Description
External Data	Import & Link	Use the **More** drop-down list to import from or link to data on a SharePoint list.
	Export	Use the **More** drop-down list to export the selected object as a SharePoint list.
Database Tools	Move Data	Use to move your tables to a SharePoint list and create links to those tables in your database.

Access allows you to export a table or other database objects to a number of formats, such as an external file, an Excel workbook, a text file, a PDF or XPS file, email, an Extensible Markup Language (XML) document, an Open Database Connectivity (ODBC) data source, or a Hypertext Markup Language (HTML) document. You can also export a table to a SharePoint site, where a new list is created.

TIP Access 2013 does not support linking, importing, or exporting using the Installable Indexed Sequential Access Method (ISAM) for Lotus 1-2-3, Paradox, Microsoft Jet 3.x, or Microsoft Jet 2.x. This means that you can no longer open a Microsoft Office Access 97 database in Access 2013. You'll need to upgrade the file using either Access 2010 or Access 2007, and save it in the .accdb file format, which can then be used in Access 2013. More information on discontinued features and modified functionality in Access 2013 can be found at *office.microsoft.com/en-us/access-help/discontinued-features-and-modified-functionality-in-access-2013-HA102749226.aspx.*

To export the data to a SharePoint list, you use a wizard that builds an export query, which Access uses to query the Access table for data, and it then copies the data to the SharePoint list. You can save the export query, which you can do without using the wizard. Your saved exports can be found under the **External Data** tab in the **Export** group. Similarly, you can save your export as a Microsoft Office Outlook task, which you can then configure to remind you to run the export query.

When a SharePoint list is created from an Access table, the list does not automatically appear on the **Quick Launch**. To create a link to the list on the **Quick Launch**, you need to go to the **General Settings** page by clicking **List name, description and navigation** on the list's **Settings** page.

In the following exercise, you will export a table from within an Access 2013 desktop database into a SharePoint site by creating a new SharePoint list, and then save the export query.

 SET UP **This exercise uses the ExpImpWideWorldImporters.accdb Access database file, located in the Chapter12 practice folder; you could use any Access database that contains data in a table. Start Access 2013 and open the ExpImpWideWorldImporters.accdb database. Remember to use your SharePoint site location in place of *http://wideworldimporters* in the following exercise.**

> **IMPORTANT** Verify that you have sufficient rights to create a list. If in doubt, see Appendix A.

1   Under **Tables**, click **FurniturePrices**, if it is not already selected, and then, on the Access ribbon, click the **External Data** tab. In the **Export** group, click **More**, and then click **SharePoint List**.

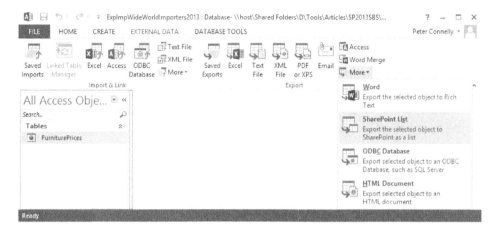

2   In the **Export - SharePoint Site** dialog box, in the **Specify a SharePoint site** area, select the site where you want to export the table, or type the URL in the text box; for
example **http://wideworldimporters**.

3   In the **Specify a name for the new list** box, type **exportFurniturePrices**.

4   Leave the **Open the list when finished** check box selected.

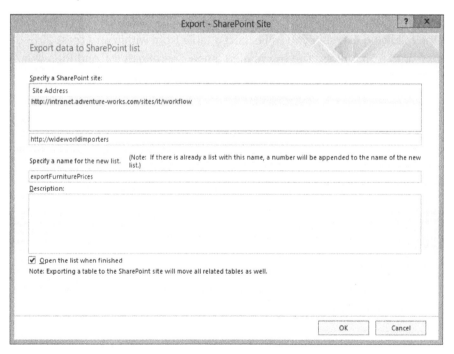

5   Click **OK** to export the data and display the newly created list, **exportFurniturePrices**.

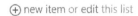

exportFurniturePrices

⊕ new item or edit this list

All Items ···   Find an item   🔍

✓	StockID	StockNo	Furniture Name	Furniture Range	Furniture Type	Country of Origin	Material	In Stock	Unit Price	Total
	1	W0001	Tall unit	Bianca	Bathroom	German	steel	5	$25.00	$125.00
	2	W0002	Base unit with drawers	Bianca	Bathroom	German	steel	99	$20.00	$1,980.00
	3	W0003	Wall unit	Bianca	Bathroom	German	steel	10	$115.00	$1,150.00
	4	W0004	Corner unit	Bianca	Bathroom	German	steel	5	$75.00	$375.00
	5	W0005	Slimline base unit	Bianca	Bathroom	German	steel	2	$64.00	$128.00

TROUBLESHOOTING If you mistype the website name in the **Site** text box, Access 2013 displays a warning dialog box, stating that it can't find the website. If this occurs, verify the website address and try again.

6   Return to the **Save Export Steps** page of the **Export - SharePoint Site** dialog box in Access.

7   Select the **Save export steps** check box to display the **Save As** and **Description** text boxes, as well as the **Create an Outlook Task** areas.

12

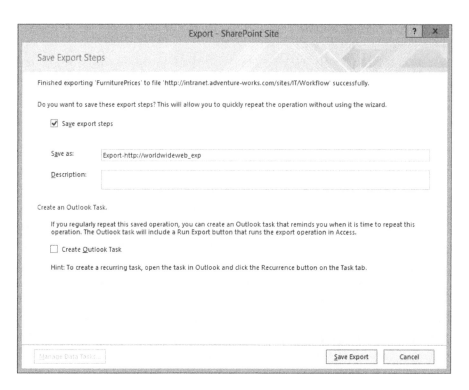

8   Click **Save Export** to close the **Export - SharePoint Site** dialog box.

❌ CLEAN UP **Exit the ExpImpWideWorldImporters.accdb database and close the browser. Choose No if prompted to save the changes.**

Importing a list

By using Access, you can create a new table in either an Access app or an Access desktop database by importing data from an external data source, such as an Excel workbook, an ODBC data source, or a SharePoint website. The new table becomes an integral part of your database, and the data is not affected by subsequent changes made to the data source after it is imported.

When you import data from a SharePoint list, the imported data is based on a view, and only those columns and rows shown in the view are imported. The **Get External Data** wizard lets you select the required view from the **Items To Import** drop-down list.

Once the table is created and the data imported from the list into the table, you can edit the data in the table. Such changes will not be reflected back in the list on the SharePoint website.

IMPORTANT Changes to the SharePoint list are not copied to the Access table, nor are changes to the Access table reflected in the SharePoint list. A linked object is not created as part of this process.

In this exercise, you will import data from a SharePoint list.

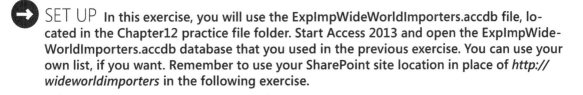 SET UP **In this exercise, you will use the ExpImpWideWorldImporters.accdb file, located in the Chapter12 practice file folder. Start Access 2013 and open the ExpImpWide-WorldImporters.accdb database that you used in the previous exercise. You can use your own list, if you want. Remember to use your SharePoint site location in place of *http:// wideworldimporters* in the following exercise.**

IMPORTANT Verify that you have sufficient rights to read list items. If in doubt, see Appendix A.

1   On the Access ribbon, click the **External Data** tab. In the **Import & Link** group, click **More**, and then click **SharePoint List** to display the **Get External Data - SharePoint Site** dialog box.

2   In the **Specify a SharePoint site** area, select the site that contains the list with the data that you want to import into the database.

    TROUBLESHOOTING If the URL for the SharePoint site does not appear, type the URL in the text box.

3   Select the **Import the source data into a new table in the current database** option.

12

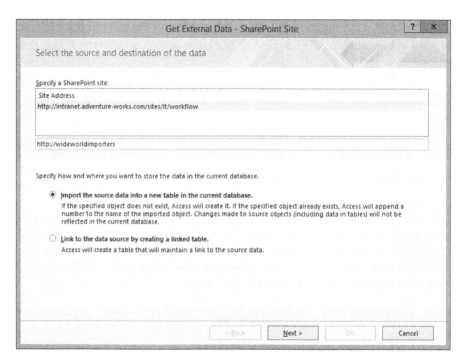

4　Click **Next** to display the **Import data from list** page of the **Get External Data - SharePoint Site** dialog box.

5　Select the check box to the left of the list from which you want to import the data, such as **exportFurniturePrices**.

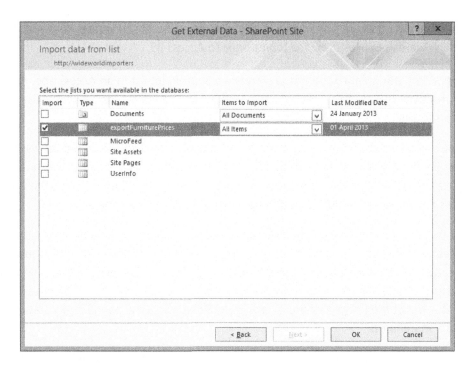

6   Click **OK**, and then click **Close**.

7   Under **Tables**, in the **Access** navigation pane, double-click **exportFurniturePrices** to open the **exportFurniturePrices** table in Datasheet view.

TROUBLESHOOTING If a table is not created from your SharePoint list, then a table called **Web Compatibility Issues** is created, which lists incompatibilities. Correct the issues and repeat this exercise.

✖ CLEAN UP **Leave Access open if you are continuing to the next exercise. Close any open browser windows.**

Linking to a list

Data was copied in the previous section so that the same data could be stored in both a list on a SharePoint site and either an Access app or an Access desktop database. If you do not want to maintain two copies of that data, but you do need to refer to the data within the Access app or an Access desktop database, then Access provides methods of accessing external data that are physically located outside an Access database, known as *linked tables*, which were known as *attached tables* prior to Access 95.

TIP When using linked tables to reference a SharePoint list in an Access app, Access 2013 currently only supports read-only connections to SharePoint lists. Also, the list must be in the site where the Access app was added.

The easiest way to reference a SharePoint list externally is to use linked tables. You should use linking rather than importing if the data is maintained by either a user or a separate application on the SharePoint website. Also, to set up a connection to a list, the user who creates the linked table must have Change permissions rights to the list.

With a desktop database, the data from the linked tables is cached in local tables when the user is online with SharePoint, thereby improving large list performance. When server connectivity is lost, the database automatically goes into offline mode. When connectivity is restored, Access automatically synchronizes data changes for you. Text in the far right of the status bar at the bottom of the Access window indicates the connectivity status of Access with SharePoint.

With an Access app, the data is not displayed in Access; it is displayed in the browser and data is directly accessed from the tables in the app's database.

TIP External content types can be used to reveal external data in Office 2013 and Microsoft Office 2010 applications, including Access 2013 and Outlook 2013. Information on how to create External content types and how to use them in Access 2013 can be found in Chapter 22, "Working with external content," in *Microsoft SharePoint 2013 Inside Out*, by Darvish Shadravan, Penelope Coventry, Thomas Resing, and Christina Wheeler (Microsoft Press, 2013).

In this exercise, you will link a table to a SharePoint list, enter data in Access, and check that the data appears in the list.

 SET UP **Start Access 2013 and open the ExpImpWideWorldImporters.accdb database that you used in the previous exercise, if it is not already open. You can use your own Access database if you wish. Remember to use your SharePoint site location in place of** *http://wideworldimporters* **in the following exercise.**

> **IMPORTANT** Verify that you have sufficient rights to edit items in the list. If in doubt, see Appendix A.

1   On the Access ribbon, click the **External Data** tab. In the **Import & Link** group, click **More**, and then click **SharePoint List**. If an Access dialog box opens, stating that all objects must be closed prior to continuing this operation, click **Yes** to close the objects.

2   On the **Get External Data - SharePoint Site** dialog box, in the **Specify a SharePoint site** area, select the site that contains the list to which you wish to link.

    TROUBLESHOOTING If the URL for the SharePoint site does not appear, type the URL in the text box.

3   Check that the **Link to the data source by creating a linked table** option is selected, and then click **Next**.

4   On the **Choose the SharePoint lists you want to link to** page, select the check box to the left of the list to which you wish to link, such as **exportFurniturePrices**.

5   Click **OK**.

6   Under **Tables**, right-click the linked **exportFurniturePrices1** table, and then select **More options**.

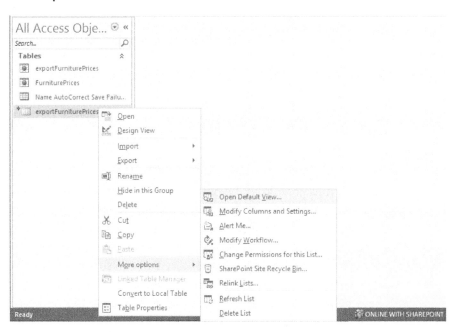

7   Click **Open Default View** to display the **exportFurniturePrices** list in the browser.

12

8   Switch back to Access. Under **Tables**, double-click **exportFurniturePrices1** to open the linked table in Datasheet view, and then click the cell in the first row under the **Furniture Name** column, and type **Base Unit**.

9   Click the cell in the second row under the **Furniture Name** column.

> **IMPORTANT** By moving to another row, Access automatically synchronizes changes to the SharePoint list.

10   Switch back to the browser, click **Refresh**, and then verify that the first row has been modified.

11   On the ribbon, click the **Items** tab, and then click **New Item** in the **New** group.

12   In the **StockNo** text box, type **W0033**, and then click **Save** to add the W0033 list item to the list.

     TIP To see the new item in the browser, you will need to scroll to the bottom of the list and click the right arrow to display the next page.

13   Switch back to Access. On the **Home** tab, in the **Records** group, click **Refresh All**.

❌ CLEAN UP **Exit the ExpImpWideWorldImporters.accdb database and close any open browser windows.**

Moving data from a desktop database to a list

Many Access applications grow from the need to manage and aggregate data. These data-centric applications often prove useful to more than one person in an organization, and thus the need to share them increases. However, Access is not truly meant for concurrent use. As Access desktop database applications grow and become more complex, it is necessary to consider upsizing them to a data repository that can support more users while increasing availability, reliability, and manageability. Beginning with Access 2000, various tools and wizards have helped with this process. Starting with Access 2007, you can upsize your Access desktop database to SharePoint, which is known as *moving* your Access database.

When you move data from an Access desktop database to a SharePoint site, this process creates a SharePoint list for each Access table. Data from Access tables is moved into these

SharePoint lists, and each data row becomes a list item in a SharePoint list. Tables in the desktop database are replaced with linked tables that point to the newly created SharePoint list or lists. The Access database now becomes a user interface to the data by retaining views, reports, and relationships between tables.

TIP Unlike in Access 2007, saving the Access database in a SharePoint library cannot be completed as part of the move process. When an Access database is saved to a SharePoint list, and users open the database in Access to make design changes, the last person who uploads the changed database back to the SharePoint library overwrites changes by other users. Therefore, use the checkout and check-in functionalities of SharePoint libraries when making database design changes.

Because the data is now in SharePoint, you can use SharePoint functionality. For example, you can restore deleted list items from the **Recycle Bin** and apply workflow rules to data items. If you choose to save the desktop database in the library, users who want to use the desktop database can go to the library in a browser, where the desktop database can be opened in Access.

Prior to Access 2007, multiple users kept their own copies of an Access database and amended it separately, often not viewing others' amendments until they were included in official documents, and the need to amalgamate the changes was recognized. To allow users to keep their own copy of a database, a business process would need to be introduced to maintain the data integrity of the database and distribute updates to the appropriate users. By using the process outlined here, users can add and modify data by using either SharePoint or the linked tables within the Access database. New views, data relationships, and reports maintained in the desktop database file can be managed as any other document when saved in SharePoint, including check-in and checkout facilities. Security on the data and the desktop database can be maintained using SharePoint security. To take advantage of these features, you must move your data from your desktop database to SharePoint.

SEE ALSO More information on developing Access hybrid applications can be found at *blogs.msdn.com/b/access/archive/2010/07/20/the-access-show-developing-access-2010-hybrid-apps-with-dick-moffat.aspx*. Although this example uses Access 2010 and SharePoint 2010, it is still relevant to Access 2013 and SharePoint 2013.

12

In the following exercise, you will move data from within an Access desktop database to a SharePoint site, and then save the desktop database in a library.

➜ SET UP **This exercise uses the MoveWideWorldImporters.accdb file, located in the Chapter12 practice file folder. Start Access 2013 and open the**

MoveWideWorldImporters.accdb database. Remember to use your SharePoint site location in place of *http://wideworldimporters* in the following exercise.

IMPORTANT Verify that you have sufficient rights to create lists. If in doubt, see Appendix A.

1   On the Access ribbon, click the **Database Tools** tab. In the **Move Data** group, click **SharePoint** to display the **Export Tables to SharePoint Wizard**.

2   In the **What SharePoint site do you want to use?** text box, type the name of your SharePoint site, such as **http://wideworldimporters**.

3   Click **Next** to start the move operation.

4   When the message stating that "Your tables have been successfully shared" appears, select the **Show Details** check box to check which lists were created and the name of the database backup.

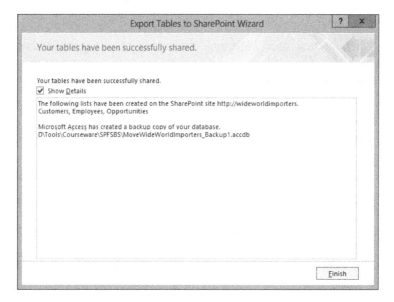

5   Click **Finish**, and then click **File** to display the backstage view of Access.

6   In the left navigation pane, click **Save As**. Under **File Types**, verify that **Save Database as** is selected, and then in the right pane, in the **Advanced** section, select **SharePoint**.

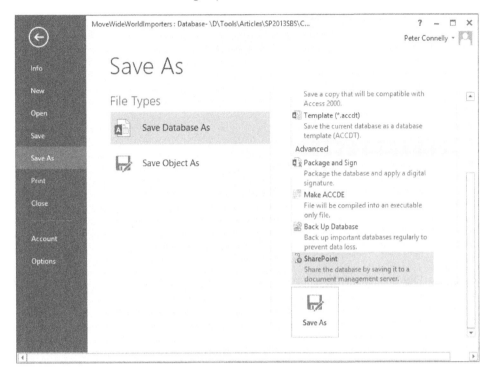

7   Click **Save As**.

8   In the **Save to SharePoint** dialog box, in the **File name** box, type the URL of the SharePoint site that contains the library where you wish to save your desktop database, such as **http://wideworldimporters**, and then press **Enter** to display the libraries of the SharePoint site.

12

9   Double-click **Documents**, and then click **Save** to complete the save process.

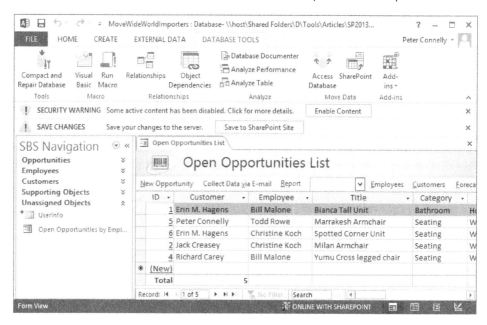

✖ CLEAN UP Leave Access open if you are continuing to the next exercise.

Working offline

In the previous section, you moved data from an Access desktop database to a SharePoint site, and you created linked tables pointing to a SharePoint list where the list items can be viewed and updated using Access. In these tables, the data is stored outside Access. However, you might still like to access the data in a disconnected environment. When using Access 2007, Access 2010, or Access 2013, you are able to cache SharePoint list data locally in an offline mode. The data that is held locally is not independent of the data in the SharePoint list. You may synchronize changes back to the SharePoint site any time that you want.

To switch from working online to offline, on the **External Data** tab, click **Work Offline**—the first command in the **Web Linked Lists** group. The command changes to **Work Online** and the previously inactive **Synchronize** and **Discard Changes** commands are enabled. All data is cached within the desktop database, and links to the SharePoint lists are cut temporarily. However, Access behaves much as it did online. The only indication that it is offline is the Access status bar at the bottom of the Access window, which reads **OFFLINE WITH SHAREPOINT.**

In Access, when you are online with a SharePoint website and you modify data within a row in a table, moving out of the row causes Access to synchronize changes. However, when you are working offline, a dimmed pencil icon in the first column of the row that you have amended indicates that you have made changes to the row and synchronization has not occurred.

> **IMPORTANT** If you provide a copy of an offline Access database, the data in the database will be visible to users who may not have permissions to view the data on the SharePoint site. This could be a security risk.

In this exercise, you will explore synchronizing data with a table linked to a SharePoint list when working offline. This exercise uses the linked tables that were created during the move operation in the previous exercise. You can use your own tables that are linked to a SharePoint list, if you want.

 SET UP **Start Access 2013 and open the MoveWideWorldImporters.accdb database that you saved in the Shared Documents library in the previous exercise.**

12

IMPORTANT Verify that you have sufficient rights to edit items in the lists linked to the Access tables. If in doubt, see Appendix A.

1   Under the **Supporting Objects** group, click the double down arrow, and then right-click **Opportunities**. Select **More Options**, and then click **Open Default View** to open the **Opportunities** list in browser, so that you can verify changes to the list later in the exercise.

2   Switch back to Access. On the Access ribbon, click the **External Data** tab, and in the **Web Linked Lists** group, click **Work Offline**.

3   Under the **Supporting Objects** group, double-click **Opportunities** to display the contents of the table in Datasheet view.

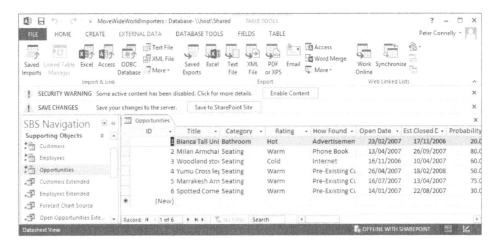

4   Click the cell in the first row under the **Title** column, and then type **Bianca Corner Unit**. Click a cell in the second row.

TROUBLESHOOTING If an Access dialog box opens, stating that a value must be greater than 1/1/1900, click **OK** to close the dialog box. Press the **Esc** key to discard your changes. On the **External Data** tab, in the **Web Linked Lists** group, click **Work Online**, and then repeat steps 1, 2, and 4.

5   Switch back to the browser. Click **Refresh**, and then verify that the first row has not been modified.

6   In the browser, click the cell in the first row under **Title**, type **Woodland Bench**, and then click a cell in the second row.

7 Switch back to Access. On the **External Data** tab, in the **Web Linked Lists** group, click **Synchronize** to force Access to temporarily connect to the SharePoint list to synchronize changes.

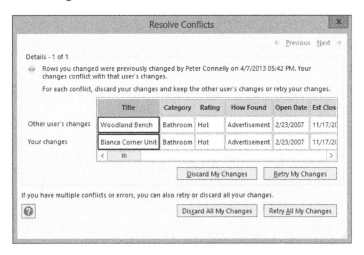

8 In the **Resolve Conflicts** dialog box, click **Discard My Changes**.

9 Under **Supporting Objects**, double-click **Opportunities** to open the table in Datasheet view, and verify that the **Title** column of the first row contains the text **Woodland Bench**.

10 In the Datasheet view of the **Opportunities** table, click the cell in the first row under the **Title** column and type **Bianca Corner Unit**. Click a cell in the second row.

11 On the **External Data** tab, in the **Web Linked Lists** group, click **Work Online**.

12 Switch back to the browser. Click **Refresh**, and then verify that the first row contains the text **Bianca Corner Unit**.

13 On the ribbon, on the **List** tab, in the **Manage Views** group, click **Create Column**.

14 In the **Column name** box, type **Advertisement** and select the **Yes/No** option. Click **OK**.

15 Switch back to Access. Under **Supporting Objects**, right-click **Opportunities**, click **More options**, and then click **Refresh List**.

16 Open the **Opportunities** table, if necessary, and check that the **Advertisement** column is visible.

✖ CLEAN UP **Exit the MoveWideWorldImporters.accdb database and close the browser.**

12

Key points

- You can create a custom list from the browser by importing data from an Excel spreadsheet.

- You can create an Excel spreadsheet from the browser and export data into it from a SharePoint list.

- From within Excel, you can export data from an Excel table into a newly created SharePoint list.

- You can synchronize changes between a SharePoint list and an Excel spreadsheet. This is a one-way synchronization process.

- Integration with SharePoint makes Access 2013 a great collaboration tool, while also permitting data to be stored on enterprise servers for better manageability.

- In Access 2013, databases can be published to SharePoint Server 2013 as an Access web app, also known as an Access app, where data is stored in its own SQL Server 2012 database. The browser is used to view and edit data, and Access 2013 is used to design the Access app.

- In Access 2010, databases can be published as an Access web database. These can only be created using Access 2010 and Access Services 2010.

- Both Access apps and Access web database can only be used when SharePoint Server Enterprise Client Access Licenses (CALs) have been purchased. You can integrate Access desktop databases with any edition of SharePoint 2013.

- When using an Access desktop database, you can export data from a table to SharePoint lists. Data in the Access table is not affected by subsequent changes made to the SharePoint list because there is no synchronization process between Access and a SharePoint site.

- Using either an Access app or a desktop database, you can use linked tables. This lets you take advantage of SharePoint features such as workflow, security, and searching.

- At the time that this book was written, data from a linked table in an Access app is read-only; however, in a desktop database, two-way synchronization is provided and you can maintain a cache to use when working offline.

- You can move an Access desktop database to a SharePoint site. Data is moved into SharePoint lists, and if you want, you can save the desktop database in a library.

Chapter at a glance

Create

Create a PowerPivot Gallery, page 453

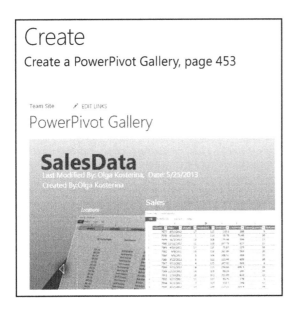

Work

Work with data models, page 462

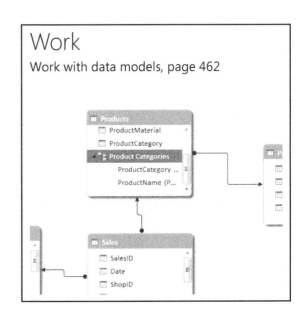

Publish

Publish PowerPivot dashboards, page 479

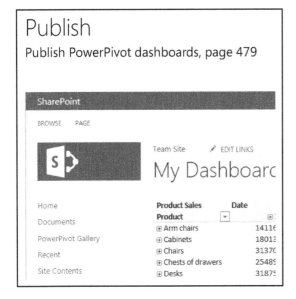

Build

Build Power View visualizations, page 485

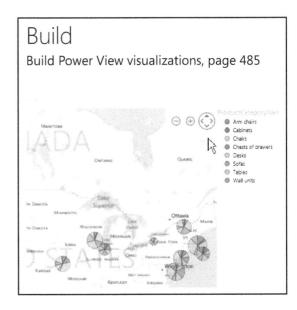

Working with business intelligence

13

IN THIS CHAPTER, YOU WILL LEARN HOW TO

- Understand SharePoint BI capabilities and components.

- Use Excel Services.

- Work with data models.

- Create and publish PowerPivot dashboards.

- Publish PowerPivot dashboards using Excel Web Part.

- Build visualizations with Power View.

- Create and use Power View reports with multiple views.

- Display a Power View report in a Web Part.

Business intelligence (BI) is a set of tools and capabilities that work together to turn large amounts of data into meaningful information for better decision making. SharePoint 2013 provides a BI platform that puts power in the hand of the users with self-service capabilities delivered through Microsoft SharePoint and Microsoft Office Excel. You can use SharePoint BI capabilities for collaborative browser-based data exploration, visualization, and presentation experiences that provide better and deeper insights for making decisions.

In Chapter 12, "Using SharePoint with Excel and Access," you learned how to import lists from Excel into SharePoint. The integration between SharePoint and Excel goes even deeper with the BI functionality. With Microsoft Office Excel 2013, you can build data models and create a wide range of scorecards and dashboards that can be published to SharePoint, where you can share workbooks with others using Excel Services capabilities. Excel Services is a Microsoft SharePoint 2013 component that you can use to display all or part of an Excel workbook in a browser so that people in your organization can explore and analyze data in the workbook. You can use Microsoft PowerPivot in Excel to mashup data from multiple sources, and to build Microsoft PivotChart and Microsoft PivotTable reports for information analysis that you can publish to SharePoint. You can view, sort, filter, and interact with PivotTables and PivotCharts in the browser as you would by using the Excel client.

One of the major BI capabilities in SharePoint 2013 is Microsoft Power View, which is an ad hoc reporting tool that you can use to build highly interactive and intuitive browser-based data exploration, visualization, and presentation experiences for people in your organization. You can create a variety of interactive charts and tables, and add timeline controls, filters, and slicers so that users may drill further into the data. Power View was introduced in Microsoft SQL Server 2012, and you can use its intuitive reporting to visually explore data through interactive reports and animations.

In SharePoint 2013, the self-service BI goes beyond individual insight. All self-service BI capabilities are extended into a collaborative BI platform for sharing insights and working together to develop insights even further. In addition to Excel Services, BI in SharePoint supports Microsoft Office Visio Services and Microsoft PerformancePoint Services. However, PerformancePoint Services are not available in Microsoft Office 365 and Microsoft SharePoint Online.

TIP Full BI capabilities are included in SharePoint 2013 Enterprise, which is installed with SQL Server 2012 Enterprise in on-premises deployments. Office 365 and SharePoint Online support many, but not all, BI capabilities. However, the gap between the online and on-premises SharePoint BI is narrowing as more SharePoint Online updates become available. For more information on the BI features supported by SharePoint Online, go to *technet. microsoft.com/en-us/library/dn198235.aspx.*

In this chapter, you will learn about SharePoint BI components, use Excel Services, work with data models, create and publish PowerPivot dashboards, build and explore Power View visualizations, work with Power View reports with multiple views, and display Power View reports in a Web Part.

PRACTICE FILES Before you can complete the exercises in this chapter, you need to copy the book's practice files to your computer. The practice files you'll use in this chapter are in the **Chapter13** practice file folder. A complete list of practice files is provided in "Using the practice files" at the beginning of this book.

IMPORTANT Remember to use your SharePoint site location in place of *http:// wideworldimporters* in the exercises.

Understanding SharePoint BI components

There are a number of BI tools and components in SharePoint 2013 that work together so that you can explore, visualize, and share information in interactive reports, scorecards, and dashboards. They include SharePoint server-side services, as well as sites, libraries, and content types that are specifically designed for providing self-service BI functionality. In addition, the **Enterprise Search Center** site includes a built-in vertical search results page, named **Reports**, that searches the index of BI-related reports and provides previews of the search results in the hover panel for quick reference.

There are three server-side SharePoint services that provide features and functionality to support SharePoint business intelligence applications: Excel Services, PerformancePoint Services, and Visio Services.

Using Excel Services, you can view and interact with data in Excel workbooks that have been published to SharePoint sites. You can explore and analyze data in a browser in the same way that you do in the Excel client. For example, you can point to a value in a Pivot chart or table and the mouse tip will suggest ways to view additional information. Excel Services in SharePoint 2013 connect to SQL Server 2012 Analysis Services (SSAS) and SQL Server 2012 Reporting Services (SSRS) servers to provide PowerPivot and Power View capabilities.

SEE ALSO For more information on deploying SQL Server 2012 BI features for SharePoint 2013, refer to *technet.microsoft.com/en-us/library/jj218795.aspx*. For a list of software requirements for installing BI capabilities on SharePoint 2013, refer to *technet.microsoft. com/en-us/library/jj219634.aspx*.

Using PerformancePoint Services, you can create centrally managed interactive dashboards that display key performance indicators (KPIs) and data visualizations in the form of score-cards, reports, and filters. PerformancePoint dashboards can be viewed and interacted with on iPad devices using the Safari web browser. PerformancePoint Services is only available in the on-premises implementations of SharePoint Server 2013.

Using Visio Services, you can share and view visual diagrams to SharePoint sites. You can create and publish diagrams that are connected to data sources and that can be configured to refresh data to display up-to-date information. The diagrams can be viewed on your local computer and on mobile devices. This allows you to view Visio documents without having the Visio client installed on your device. In addition to viewing, you can add comments to the Visio Drawing (*.vsdx) diagrams in the browser in fullpage rendering mode. Visio diagrams can also be rendered within the Microsoft Visio Web Access Web Part.

13

In addition to the server-side service applications, SharePoint BI components provide site and library templates that provide you with the BI self-service capabilities, including the Business Intelligence Center site, the PowerPivot site, and the PowerPivot Gallery library.

The Business Intelligence Center is an enterprise SharePoint site that has been designed to support enterprise-wide BI applications. Using Business Intelligence Center, organizations can centrally store and manage data connections, reports, scorecards, dashboards, and Web Part pages. In SharePoint 2013, Business Intelligence Center is optimized and streamlined. It provides multiple libraries, Web Parts, and content types that are optimized for BI self-service applications.

The PowerPivot site is a collaboration SharePoint site that includes Excel Services capabilities with PowerPivot and Power View features. It is similar to the Team site, but in addition to the default Documents library, it also provides a PowerPivot Gallery, which is a documents library with additional functionalities that are designed to support Excel Services BI applications. PowerPivot site is available as part of PowerPivot for SharePoint 2013.

TIP PowerPivot for SharePoint 2013 is available as a free add-in to SQL Server 2012 Enterprise. It is also included in SQL Server 2012 SP1. It can be downloaded from *www.microsoft.com/en-us/download/details.aspx?id=35577.*

When PowerPivot for SharePoint 2013 is deployed on the SharePoint farm and enabled in the site collection, the PowerPivot site template becomes available in the **New SharePoint Site** page when you create a new site in this site collection.

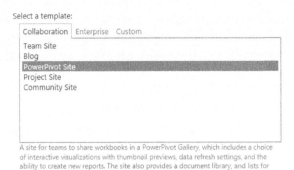

Template Selection

Select a template:

Collaboration | Enterprise | Custom

Team Site
Blog
PowerPivot Site
Project Site
Community Site

A site for teams to share workbooks in a PowerPivot Gallery, which includes a choice of interactive visualizations with thumbnail previews, data refresh settings, and the ability to create new reports. The site also provides a document library, and lists for managing announcements, calendar items, tasks, and discussions.

The PowerPivot Gallery is deployed as a part of a PowerPivot site and is displayed on its **Quick Launch**. However, you can also add the **PowerPivot Gallery** to your existing Team site. When PowerPivot for SharePoint 2013 is deployed in a site collection, the **PowerPivot Gallery** app is added to the list of available apps for all sites in this site collection. You can add the PowerPivot Gallery from **Your Apps** page by using the **Add app** command.

Home

Documents

PowerPivot Gallery

Site Contents

TIP At the time of writing, the PowerPivot site and PowerPivot Gallery are not available in Office 365 and SharePoint Online. In SharePoint Online, the Documents library in the Business Intelligence Center provides functionality that is similar to the PowerPivot Gallery.

In this exercise, you will create a PowerPivot Gallery library on your site, upload the Excel workbook in the PowerPivot Gallery, and explore the library views.

IMPORTANT You will use the **SalesData.xslx** practice file, located in the Chapter13 practice file folder.

13

➡ SET UP Open the SharePoint site where you would like to create a PowerPivot Gallery. This exercise will use the *http://wideworldmporters* site, but you can use whatever SharePoint team site you want. If prompted, type your user name and password, and then click OK.

1   On the **Quick Launch**, click **Site Contents**, and then on the **Site Contents** page, click **add an app** to display the **Your Apps** page.

2   In the search box at the top of **Your Apps** page, type **PowerPivot**, and then click the magnifying glass at the right of the search box to locate the **PowerPivot Gallery** app. Alternatively, scroll down the page till you find the **PowerPivot Gallery** app.

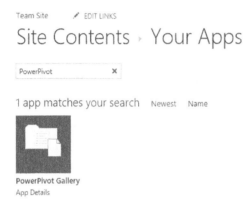

3   Click the **PowerPivot** app to add a new PowerPivot Gallery on your site.

4   In the Adding PowerPivot Gallery dialog box, in the **Name** box, type the name for your new gallery, such as **PowerPivot Gallery,** and click **Create**.

5   You are taken back to the **Site Contents** page that now shows the new **PowerPivot Gallery**. You will now create a permanent link to this library on the **Quick Launch**. On the **Quick Launch**, below the list of links, click **EDIT LINKS**.

6   Drag the **PowerPivot Gallery** link up and position it above the **Recent** section, where it is currently located. Click **Save** on the **Quick Launch** to save the new **Quick Launch** layout.

Home
Documents
PowerPivot Gallery
Recent
Site Contents

✎ EDIT LINKS

7   On the **Quick Launch**, click the **PowerPivot Gallery** link to open it.

8   The new gallery is displayed. If Silverlight is not installed on your machine, the **Install Microsoft Silverlight** message box appears, prompting you to install Silverlight. Click the message box to download and install Silverlight on your computer.

PowerPivot Gallery ⓘ

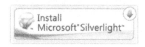

9   In the download confirmation bar at the bottom of the screen, click **Run** to start the Silverlight installation.

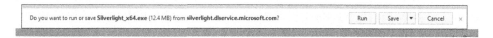

10   Click **Yes** in the **User Account Control** message box, if it appears, to confirm that you'd like to allow the installation.

13

11   The Silverlight setup wizard starts. On the **Install Silverlight** wizard page, click **Install now.**

12   In the **Installation Successful** dialog, click **Close**, and then press **F5** on the keyboard to refresh the **PowerPivot Gallery** page in the browser. This is the new gallery, so the page is empty.

13   You will now upload the **SalesData** workbook into the **PowerPivot Gallery**. Click the **Files** tab on the top left of the page to open the ribbon, and then in the **New** section, click **Upload Document.**

14   In the **Add a document** dialog, click **Browse** and go to the **Chapter13** practice folder, select **SalesData.xslx**, and click **Open**. Then, in the **Add a document** dialog, click **OK** to upload the workbook. In the document properties dialog **Power Pivot Gallery - SalesData.xslx** (if it appears), click **Save.**

15   The workbook has been uploaded to the **PowerPivot Gallery**. It is displayed in the Gallery view that allows you to preview the worksheets within the workbook. The first worksheet is in focus and is displayed in the left pane, larger than the others. You can bring any worksheet in focus by pointing at it. You move to the worksheets that are not displayed in the screen by using the left and right navigation buttons, as well as

by clicking the navigation dots, located at the bottom of the workbook view. Browse through the worksheets to familiarize yourself with the Gallery view of the workbook.

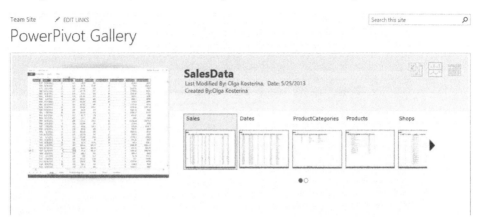

You will now explore other available PowerPivot Gallery views.

16   On the **Library** ribbon, in the **Manage Views** section, under **Current View**, open the drop-down list of views.

17   Select the **Carousel** view to switch to it. The workbook is displayed in the Carousel view, where you can browse through the worksheets using left and right arrows. The worksheet in focus is displayed in the center, whereas the worksheets to the left and to the right of it are dimmed. Use the left and right navigation buttons to go through the worksheets in the workbook.

PowerPivot Gallery

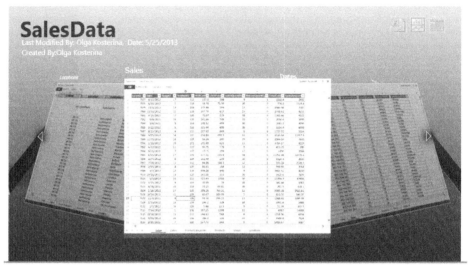

18   Once again, on the **Library** ribbon, open the drop-down list of views, and this time
      select the **Theater** view. The worksheet in focus is displayed on top of the view, in the
      stage section. You can browse through the worksheets using left and right navigation
      buttons in the worksheets lineup under the stage, and you can bring them into focus
      on the stage by pointing at them.

PowerPivot Gallery

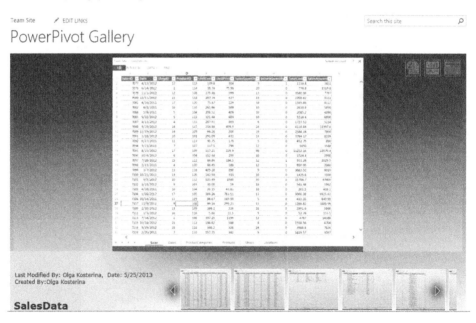

19 Finally, open the drop-down list of views and switch to the **All Documents** view to display the library as the list of documents. This view can be useful for managing files in the library.

20 Switch back to the **Gallery** view that is the default view for all PowerPivot Galleries.

✖ CLEAN UP **Leave the browser open if you are continuing to the next exercise.**

Using Excel Services

Excel Services in SharePoint 2013 is a shared service in which you can publish Excel workbooks on SharePoint to view all or parts of an Excel workbook in the browser. You can directly save the Excel workbooks and publish reports to a library on a SharePoint site. Excel Services will then process and render the data in the workbook in the browser, so that you can share the workbook with others and they can interactively explore and analyze the data it contains. Access to the published workbooks can be managed and secured on SharePoint using user access permissions and permissions levels in the same way as any other file within a library.

For example, in the previous exercise, Excel Services enabled the preview of the workbook in the PowerPivot Gallery views. Although Excel Services is available in previous versions of SharePoint, in SharePoint 2013, there is a higher level of parity between the browser and the Excel client.

IMPORTANT You can interact with Excel workbooks in a browser through Excel Services; however, the workbooks cannot be edited in the browser by using Excel Services.

TIP Excel Services is available only in SharePoint Server 2013 Enterprise.

In the following exercise, you will use Excel Services in the PowerPivot Gallery library to explore the SalesData workbook and to sort, filter, and search the data it contains.

13

SET UP **Open the SharePoint site that you used in the previous exercise, if it is not already open. If prompted, type your user name and password, and then click OK.**

IMPORTANT Verify that you have sufficient permissions to view the workbook in a library on the site that you are using. If in doubt, see Appendix A.

1   On the **Quick Launch**, click **PowerPivot Gallery** to open the PowerPivot Gallery, if it is not already open.

2   In the **SalesData** workbook displayed in the **Gallery** view, click the worksheet that you'd like to view; for example, **Sales**. Excel Services opens the workbook in the browser and displays the worksheet that you have chosen.

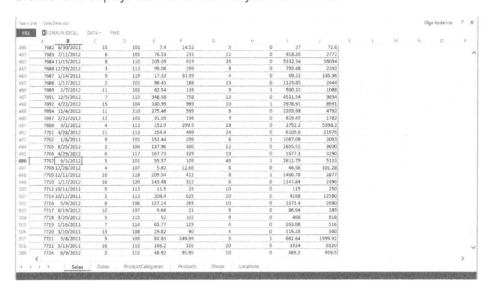

3   Explore the workbook. It contains five tables in five worksheets: Sales, Dates, Products, ProductCategories, Shops, and Locations. The worksheet tabs are shown at the bottom of the Excel Services page, as they would be in an Excel client.

The Sales worksheet lists sales transactions in Wide World Importers stores located in cities in the United States for the years 2011 and 2012. The Products worksheet lists assorted items of furniture that were sold during this period. Each product belongs to a product category. The product categories are listed in the ProductCategories worksheet. The Stores worksheet lists the Wide World Importers stores where the products were sold, and the Locations worksheet lists the cities and the states where the stores are located. Finally, the Dates worksheet is a reference table that provides a list of dates by the year, half year, quarter, and month.

After you have browsed through all the worksheets to familiarize yourself with the data, click the **Sales** tab at the bottom of the screen to return to the Sales worksheet.

4   You will now sort a Sales table by date in descending order. In the **Date** column header, click the down arrow to display a menu of sort and filter options, and then select **Sort Descending**.

5   The Sales table has been sorted in descending order by date. Notice that the button in the Date header now shows a down arrow that identifies that this column is sorted in descending order.

You will now display sales transactions from a Seattle store. There are one thousand transactions in the **Sales** worksheet, so locating specific transactions by scrolling through the table is difficult. It would be good to filter the table by Seattle store transactions. However, in the Sales table, the stores are identified by their numeric ID in the ShopID column, so first you need to find out the ShopID for the Wide World Importers shop in Seattle.

6   Open the **Shops** tab and locate the Seattle store in the **ShopName** column, and then look up its ID in the **ShopID** column. The ID for the Wide World Importers shop is 1.

7   Go back to the **Sales** table by clicking its tab. Click the down arrow in the **ShopID** column header, click **Number Filters**, and then select **Equals**. In the **Custom Filter** dialog, type **1**, and then click **OK**.

8   The transactions with the ShopID of 1 are displayed. You will now locate a specific transaction in the displayed list of transactions. Click **Find** at the top of the worksheet

13

page. To search for a transaction that took place on September 3, 2012, go to the **Find** dialog, and in the **Find what** box, type a date of September 3, 2012, in the data format used in your setup (for example, **9/3/2012**), and then click **OK**.

9   The cell that contains the search term is identified by the green box around it, and its row is brought into view.

152	7384	9/8/2012	1	103	59.32	129	9	0	533.88	1161
158	278	9/3/2012	1	107	269.48	586	12	0	3233.76	7032
161	7427	9/1/2012	1	120	155.89	339	36	1	5456.15	11865
202	557	7/29/2012	1	106	321.44	699	12	1	3535.84	7689

10   Having explored the workbook and the data that it contains, you will now close the **Excel Services** page. In the top-right corner of the workbook, to the right of your user name, click **X** to exit Excel Services and to return to the PowerPivot Gallery page.

TIP There are two **X** icons that are located in the top-right area of your screen: one to exit the workbook and another one to close the browser. Make sure that you click the correct **X** to exit the workbook and leave the browser open.

❌ CLEAN UP **Leave the browser open if you are continuing to the next exercise.**

Working with data models

With *data models* in Excel Services for SharePoint 2013 and Excel 2013, you can bring data from a variety of sources into one cohesive data set, and then use it to create charts, tables, reports, and dashboards. A data model is essentially a collection of data from multiple sources with relationships between different fields, which you can create and organize by using PowerPivot for Excel. Typically, a data model includes one or more tables of data. To build a data model, you can sort and organize the data and create relationships between different tables.

After you have created a data model in Excel, you can use it as a source to create multiple charts, tables, and reports. For example, you can use Excel 2013 to create interactive PivotChart reports and PivotTable reports. Or, you can use Power View to create interactive visualizations such as pie charts, bar charts, bubble charts, line charts, and many others.

Using Excel Services in SharePoint Server 2013, you and others can view and use workbooks that have been published to SharePoint Server, including workbooks that contain data models. You collect data in a data model, and then use it as a source for reports and scorecards that you can publish and share. Excel Services retains connectivity to external data sources and refreshes the data so that the reports, scorecards, and workbooks remain up to date. You can use SharePoint permissions to control who can view and use the reports, scorecards, and workbooks that you have published.

When you create a data model in Excel, in addition to data that is native to Excel, you can also combine data from one or more external data sources. Excel Services supports a subset of the external data connections that you can create with Excel. The external data connections that are supported in Excel Services in SharePoint Server 2013 include connections to the following data sources:

- SQL Server tables
- SQL Server Analysis Services cubes
- OLE DB and ODBC data sources

SEE ALSO For more information on data sources that are supported in Excel Services in SharePoint 2013, refer to *technet.microsoft.com/en-us/library/jj819452.aspx*.

The following are external data sources that you can connect to from Excel, but are not supported in Excel Services in SharePoint Server 2013:

- XML files
- Text files
- Access databases
- Website content
- Windows Azure Marketplace data

TIP If you want to use data from external data sources that are not supported in Excel Services, you might be able to import the snapshot of data into Excel, and then use it in your data model as the data native to Excel.

To build a data model, use the PowerPivot add-in for Excel that is included in Excel 2013. With PowerPivot for Excel, you can import the data from external sources, if needed, and build relationships between disparate data so that you can work with the data as a whole.

By default, the PowerPivot add-in for Excel is not enabled. In the following exercise, you will enable the PowerPivot add-in for Excel 2013.

➡ SET UP **Open Excel 2013 on your computer.**

1   Click **File**, and then select **Options**.

2   In the **Excel Options** dialog, select **Add-ins**.

3   In the **Manage** drop-down list, select **COM Add-ins**, and then click **Go**.

4   In the **COM Add-ins** dialog, select **Microsoft Office PowerPivot for Excel 2013** from the list of available add-ins, and then click **OK**.

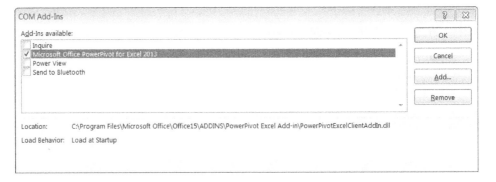

5   In Excel, validate that PowerPivot has been enabled by verifying that there is now a **PowerPivot** tab displayed on the ribbon.

✖ CLEAN UP **Leave Excel open if you are continuing to the next exercise.**

The PowerPivot add-in provides the data-modeling engine in Excel 2013 that is used to create data relationships and hierarchies to design your data model according to your business requirements.

In the following exercise, you will work with a data model using PowerPivot in Excel. You will enhance the existing data model that is based on the tables in the SalesData workbook. You will add a relationship to the model and create two hierarchies, one of which will contain a calculated column that you will add to a table. The data model that you create in this exercise will be used in the rest of the exercises in this chapter.

IMPORTANT You will use the **SalesData.xslx** practice file, located in the Chapter13 practice file folder.

 SET UP **Open Excel 2013 on your computer, if it is not already open.**

1   Click **File**, select **Open,** click **Computer**, and then click **Browse**.

2   Go to the **Chapter13** practice folder, select **SalesData.xslx**, and then click **Open**.

    The SalesData workbook opens in Excel. You are already familiar with the tables in this workbook and the data they contain from the exercise in the previous section in this chapter. You will now open the data model in this workbook, and then explore and enhance it.

3   Click the **PowerPivot** tab on the ribbon, and then click the **Manage** button to open the PowerPivot window and to work with the data model.

4   The **PowerPivot** window opens in the Data View. In the **View** group on the ribbon, click **Diagram View** to display the diagram of the data model.

5   Explore the data model diagram that is displayed. It shows five tables in this work-
     book, with the names of the columns in each table and the links between the tables.

     Point to an arrow that links the **Sales** table and the **Shops** table. The related columns
     in the linked tables are shown in blue boxes. Notice that the **ShopID** in the **Sales** ta-
     ble, which you had to look up in the **Shops** table in the previous exercise, is mapped
     to the **ShopID** in the **Shops** table so that the data can be retrieved without having to
     look it up manually.

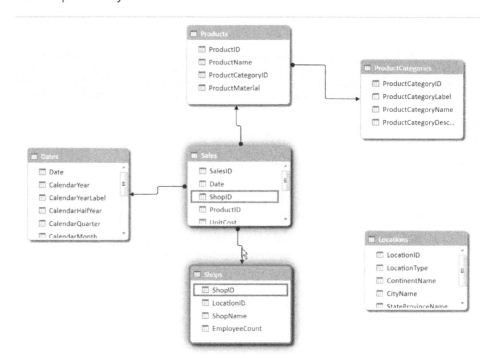

6   Point to the link between the **Sales** table and the **Dates** table to see the related col-
     umns named **Date**. Point to the link between the **Sales** table and the **Products** table
     to see the related columns named **ProductID**. Finally, point to the link between the
     Products table and the **ProductCategories** table to see the related columns named
     ProductCategoryID.

7   You will now create a relationship between the **Shops** table and the **Locations** table
     using the **LocationID** columns, which both tables contain. Drag the **LocationID** col-
     umn in the **Shops** table to the **LocationID** column in the **Locations** table. PowerPivot
     draws a line between the two columns, indicating that the relationship has been
     established.

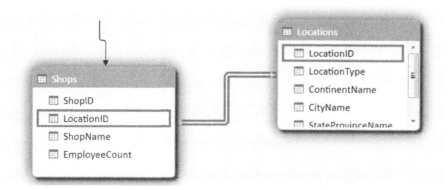

8   You will now create a hierarchy of columns in the **Dates** table. It contains the columns for date, month, quarter, half year, and year. A date is a part of a month, which, in turn, is a part of a quarter, which, in turn, is a part of half of a year, which, in turn, is a part of a year. A hierarchy will establish these relationships between the columns. In the **Dates** table, hold down the **Ctrl** key while you click the **Date**, **CalendarMonth**, **CalendarQuarter**, **CalendarHalfYear**, and **CalendarYear** columns to select them.

TIP When you create a hierarchy, you create a new object in your model. You do not move the columns into a hierarchy; instead, additional objects are created in the data model.

9   Right-click one of the selected columns to open the context menu, and then select **Create Hierarchy**.

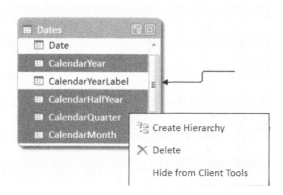

10 A parent hierarchy level is created at the bottom of the table, and the selected columns are copied under the hierarchy as child levels. Type **Calendar** to name your new hierarchy. Scroll down and resize the table box to view the entire new hierarchy.

13

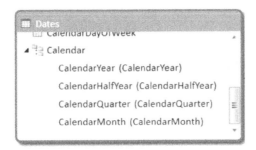

11   You will now create another hierarchy in the **Products** table with the **ProductCategory** as the parent node, and **ProductName** as the child node. However, because the **ProductCategory** column is not a part of the **Products** table but of the **ProductCategories** table, you will first create a related **ProductCategory** column in the **Products** table, which will be calculated and filled in by the model. You can create a calculated column using Data View in the PowerPivot window.

In the **View** group on the ribbon, click **Data View.**

12   At the bottom of the Data View window, click the **Products** tab to display the **Products** table, and then click **Add Column** in the header row to the right of the table.

13   In the formula bar, type = **RELATED(ProductCategories[ProductCategoryName])**, and then press **Enter** on the keyboard. The RELATED function has returned values for each cell in the new column from the **ProductCategoryName** column in the **ProductCategories** related table. The new column has been populated.

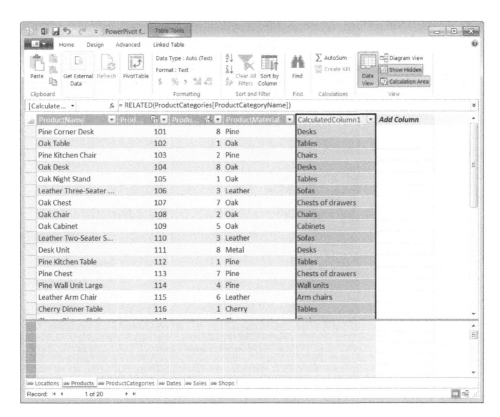

14 To rename the new column from its default name, **CalculatedColumn1**, right-click the header of the new column, select **Rename Column**, and then type **ProductCategory** as the column name. Press **Enter**.

15 You will now use this column in a hierarchy in the **Products** table. In the **View** group on the ribbon, click **Diagram View** to display the data model diagram. Verify that the **Products** table now lists the **ProductCategory** calculated column that you have created.

16 In the **Products** table, hold down the **Ctrl** key while you click the **ProductName** and **ProductCategory** columns to select them, and then right-click one of the selected columns and select **Create Hierarchy** from the context menu.

17 Type **Product Categories** as the name of the new hierarchy.

13

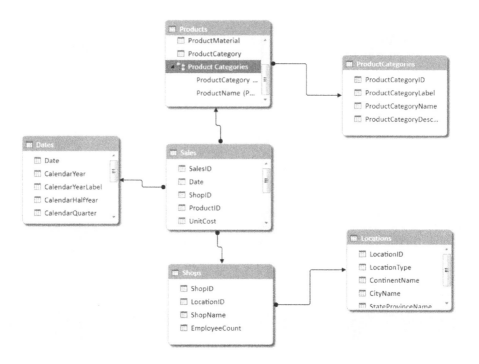

18   In the top left of the PowerPivot window, click **Save** to save your data model. The PowerPivot window is minimized and the Excel workbook is displayed.

❌ CLEAN UP **Leave Excel open if you are continuing to the next exercise.**

Creating and publishing PowerPivot dashboards

After you create a data model, you can use it to build PivotTables and PivotCharts in the Excel workbook. The workbook can then be published to a SharePoint site, where the PowerPivot server components provide server-side query processing of PowerPivot data in Excel workbooks, which you access from SharePoint sites. Excel Services in SharePoint 2013 includes data model functionality to enable interaction with a PowerPivot workbook in the browser.

TIP The server-side processing, collaboration, and document management support for the PowerPivot workbooks that you publish to SharePoint is enabled by Microsoft SQL Server 2012 PowerPivot for SharePoint, which needs to be installed by your SharePoint server administrator.

When you publish a workbook with PowerPivot data to a PowerPivot Gallery, the preview images are created for Excel workbooks that contain embedded PowerPivot data or have a connection to PowerPivot data that is published in a different workbook in the same gallery.

In the following exercise, you will use Excel to create a PivotTable report and a PivotChart report based on the data model you created in the previous exercise. You will then publish the reports into the PowerPivot Gallery on the SharePoint site to create an interactive PowerPivot dashboard.

 SET UP **In Excel, open the SalesData workbook that you used in the previous exercise, if it is not already open.**

> **IMPORTANT** Verify that you have sufficient permissions to publish a document in the PowerPivot Gallery in the site that you are using. If in doubt, see Appendix A.

1   Open the **Sales** worksheet by clicking its tab at the bottom of the Excel window. Click the **Insert** tab on the ribbon, and then click the **Pivot Table** button.

2   In the **Create PivotTable** dialog box, under **Choose the data that you want to analyze**, select **Use an external data source**, and then click **Choose Connection**.

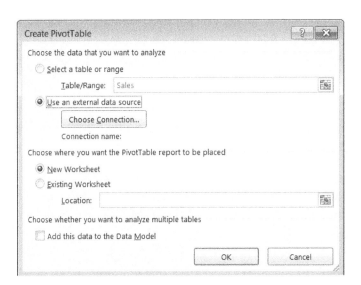

3   In the **Existing Connections** dialog box, on the **Tables** tab, under **This Workbook Data Model**, select **Tables in Workbook Data Model**, and then click **Open**.

4   In the **Create PivotTable** dialog box, under **Choose where you want PivotTable report to be placed**, verify that **New Worksheet** is selected, and then click **OK**.

The new worksheet opens and shows a PivotTable Fields list containing all the tables in the workbook data model. You will now create a PivotTable to analyze the SalesAmount by products and product categories and by dates and periods. You will use the Product Categories hierarchy for rows and the Calendar hierarchy for columns.

5   In the **PivotTable Fields** pane, expand the **Dates** table, and then drag the **Calendar** hierarchy into the **Columns** area. Expand the **Products** table and drag the **Product Categories** hierarchy into the **Rows** area.

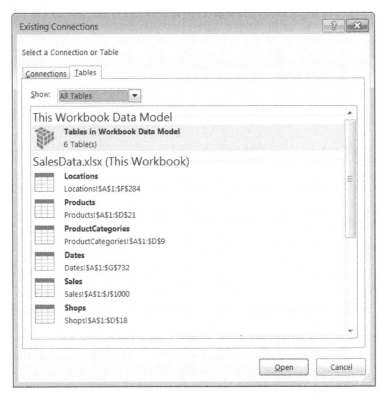

6   Expand the **Sales** table, scroll down to the **SalesAmount** field, and drag it to the **Values** area. The PivotTable is built in the worksheet.

7   In the **PivotTable**, click **Sum of SalesAmount** in the top left of the table, and type **Product Sales** to change the title.

13

8 Click **Row Labels** and replace the text with **Products**. Click **Column Labels** and re-place the text with **Date**.

9 Click anywhere within the **PivotTable**, and then click the **Analyze** tab on the ribbon. In the **PivotTable Name** box on the left of the ribbon, type **Product Sales**.

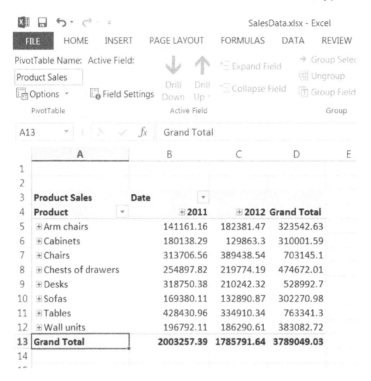

10 You will now add a PivotChart report. Position your cursor where you would like to create the PivotChart, click the **Insert** tab on the ribbon, click the **PivotChart** button, and then select **PivotChart** from the drop-down list.

11 In the **Create PivotChart** dialog box, under **Choose the data that you want to ana-lyze**, select **Use an external data source**, and then click **Choose Connection**. In the **Existing Connections** dialog box, on the **Tables** tab, under **This Workbook Data Model**, select **Tables in Workbook Data Model** and click **Open**, and then click **OK** in the **Create PivotChart** dialog box.

12 In the **PivotChart** stencil, click the default title, **Chart 1**, and type **Sales 2011-2012** to name the chart.

13   In the **PivotChart Fields** pane, expand the **Dates** table, and then drag the **Calendar** hierarchy into the **Legend (Series)** area. Expand the **Products** table, and then drag the **Products Categories** hierarchy into the **Axis** area. Finally, expand the **Sales** table, scroll down to the **SalesAmount** field, and then drag it to the **Values** area.

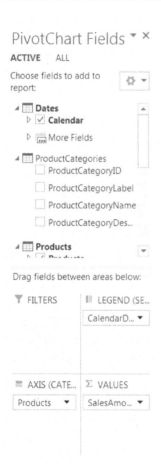

14   The PivotChart has been built in the worksheet. In the top left of the PivotChart, right-click the **Sum of SalesAmount**. Click on **Value Field Settings**. In the **Value Field Settings** dialog box, in the **Custom Name** box, change the name to **Product Sales**, and then click **OK**.

13

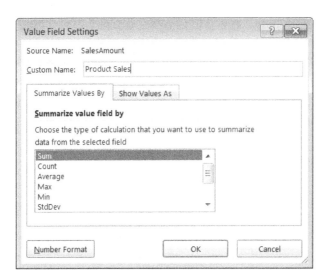

15   Click anywhere within the chart, and then click the **Analyze** tab on the ribbon. In the **Chart Name** box on the left of the ribbon, type **Sales 2011-2012**.

16   You will now prepare the workbook for publishing. Click the **File** tab, and then click **Browser View Options** to set up the parts of the workbook that will be visible on the SharePoint site.

17   In the **Browser View Options** dialog box, on the **Show** tab, in the drop-down list, select **Items in the Workbook**, and then select the **Products Sales** PivotTable. Select the **Sales 2011-2012** chart from the list of available items, and then click **OK**.

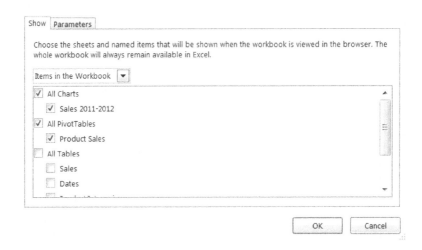

18   Click the **Save** option on the menu at the left side of the screen to save your workbook, and then exit Excel.

19   In the browser, open the PowerPivot Gallery where you would like to publish your PowerPivot reports, if it is not already open. Click the **Files** tab, and then on the ribbon, click **Upload Document**.

20   In the **Add a document** dialog, click **Browse** and go to the location where you saved the SalesData workbook, such as the **Chapter13** practice folder. Select **SalesData.xslx**, and then click **Open**. Then, in the **Add a document** dialog, click **OK** to upload the workbook. In the **Power Pivot Gallery - SalesData.xslx** document properties dialog (if it appears), click **Save**.

21   After the workbook has been uploaded, note from the preview that all worksheets are hidden from view. Only the PivotTable and the PivotChart are available, each on a separate page. Click the **PivotTable** preview page to open the dashboard in Excel Services.

TROUBLESHOOTING If you don't see the preview images, switch to the **Gallery** view.

22   You can analyze the data in the **Products Sales** table and drill down into the dates and the products using the plus and minus buttons, respectively, to expand and contract the sections. For example, expand the years **2011** and **2012** to display the sales amounts by the half-year periods. Then, expand the **Chairs** category to see the sales by individual products in this category, and further expand **H1 2011** to display the sales of the Chairs products by month in Q2 2011.

Notice that there are options on the left of the page that allow you to save, download, or print the dashboard. You can also open the workbook in Excel for editing.

23   In the dashboard, you can browse between pages using their preview images in the View pane. Click on the preview image for the **Sales 2011-2012** chart to display the chart page.

24   You will now analyze the Sales data using the chart. For example, double-click the **Desks** category, and then in the **Query and Refresh Data** confirmation message, click **Yes** to confirm that you would like to refresh the workbook, if it appears.

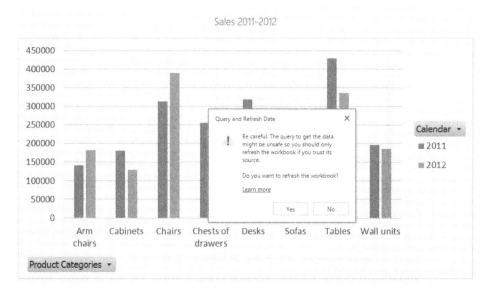

25   The chart is refreshed and displays the product sales in the Desks category by year.

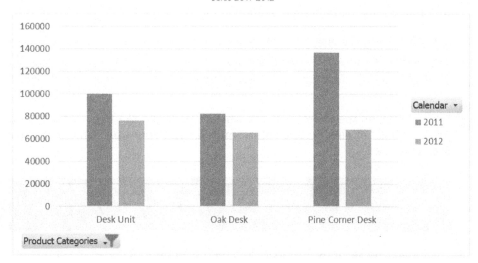

Sales 2011-2012

26   You can choose a variety of product and date filter combinations by using the Product Categories drop-down list for the horizontal axis, and the Calendar drop-down list for the vertical axis. Try different combinations in the chart, if you want, and then exit Excel Services to return to the PowerPivot Gallery page.

✖ CLEAN UP Leave the browser open if you are continuing to the next exercise.

Publishing PowerPivot dashboards using Excel Web Part

Having published a PivotTable and a PivotChart to the SharePoint site, you can display them in a webpage using an Excel Web Part.

SEE ALSO Web Parts are server-side controls that run inside the context of SharePoint site pages and provide additional features and functionalities. For an in-depth discussion on Web Parts, refer to Chapter 4 "Working with webpages."

You can create a dashboard-style webpage by adding several Excel Web Parts to the same page, which will display different PowerPivot reports side by side. Each Web Part is independent, and filters applied in one report do not affect another. PowerPivot reports

13

displayed in Web Parts on the same page can be from different Excel workbooks, but all workbooks must be published to SharePoint.

In the following exercise, you will create a PowerPivot dashboard. You will first create a new page in the SharePoint site, and then add two Excel Web Parts to this page, displaying the PivotTable and the PivotChart that you worked with in the previous exercises.

 SET UP **Open the SharePoint site where you would like to create a PowerPivot dashboard, if it is not already open. If prompted, type your user name and password, and then click OK.**

> **IMPORTANT** Verify that you have sufficient permissions to create pages in the site that you are using. If in doubt, see Appendix A.

1 Click the **Settings** gear icon, and then select **Add a page**.

2 In the **Add a page** dialog, in the **New page name** box, type **My Dashboard**, and then click **Create.** The new page opens for editing.

3 To insert the Web Part into the page, position your cursor within the box outlined on the page, and on the **Insert** tab, in the **Parts** group, click **Web Part** to display the **Parts** pane.

4 In the **Categories** list on the left of the page, select the **Business Data** category.

5 In the **Parts** list, select the **Excel Web Access** Web Part.

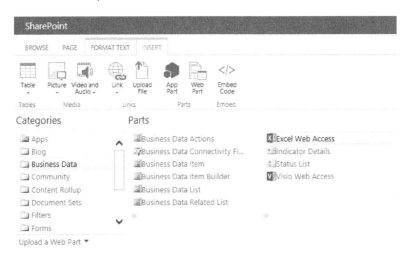

6 Click **Add** to add the **Excel Web Access** Web Part to the page.

7 On the **My Dashboard** page, in the **Excel Web Access** Web Part, click **Click here to open the tool pane**.

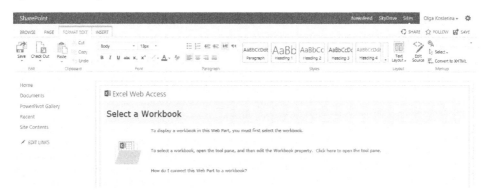

8 The tool pane for the Excel Web Access Web Part opens on the right of the page. In the **Excel Web Access** tool pane, in the **Workbook Display** section, at the right of the **Workbook** text box, click the ellipsis button.

9 In the **Select an Asset** dialog, browse to **SalesData.xslx** in the **PowerPivot Gallery** library, and click to select it. Notice that the URL for your selection is displayed in the **Location (URL)** box at the bottom of the dialog, and then click **Insert**. The URL has been inserted into the **Workbook** text box.

13

10. In the **Excel Web Access** tool pane, in the **Workbook Display** section, in the **Named Item** textbox, type **Product Sales**.

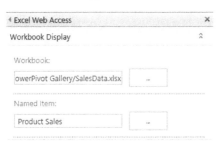

11. In the **Toolbars and Title Bar** section, in the **Type of Toolbar** list, select **None**.

12. Expand the **Appearance** section and set up the following parameters:

   a. In the **Height** section, select **Yes** to set a fixed height, and then type **300** to set the height to 300 pixels.

   b. In the **Chrome Type** list, select **None**.

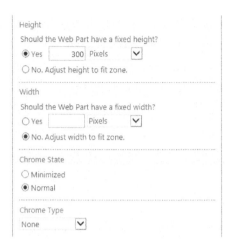

Height

Should the Web Part have a fixed height?

◉ Yes   300 Pixels   ☑

○ No. Adjust height to fit zone.

Width

Should the Web Part have a fixed width?

○ Yes   Pixels   ☑

◉ No. Adjust width to fit zone.

Chrome State

○ Minimized

◉ Normal

Chrome Type

None   ☑

13 In the **Excel Web Access** tool pane, click **OK** to confirm your settings and close the tool. The Excel Web Part displays the **Product Sales** table.

14 On the **Page** tab, click **Save** to save the webpage. After the webpage has been saved, the ribbon closes and the webpage is displayed in browse mode. If there is a delay in displaying the PivotTable report, refresh the page.

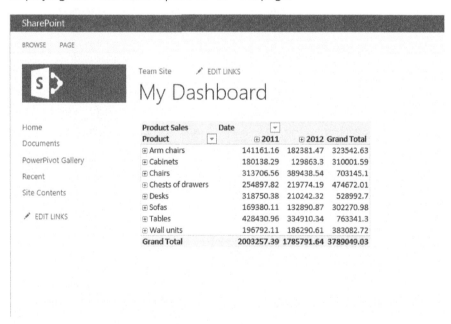

SharePoint			
BROWSE PAGE			

Team Site   ✎ EDIT LINKS

My Dashboard

Home

Documents

PowerPivot Gallery

Recent

Site Contents

✎ EDIT LINKS

Product Sales	Date	⊞ 2011	⊞ 2012	Grand Total
Product ▾		⊞ 2011	⊞ 2012	Grand Total
⊞ Arm chairs		141161.16	182381.47	323542.63
⊞ Cabinets		180138.29	129863.3	310001.59
⊞ Chairs		313706.56	389438.54	703145.1
⊞ Chests of drawers		254897.82	219774.19	474672.01
⊞ Desks		318750.38	210242.32	528992.7
⊞ Sofas		169380.11	132890.87	302270.98
⊞ Tables		428430.96	334910.34	763341.3
⊞ Wall units		196792.11	186290.61	383082.72
Grand Total		**2003257.39**	**1785791.64**	**3789049.03**

13

You will now insert another Excel Web Part and set it up to display the PivotChart that you created in the previous exercise.

15   In the **Settings** menu, select **Edit page**. Using steps 3–13 as a guide, insert the second Excel Web Part. Type **Sales 2011-1012** in the **Named Item** box in step 10.

16   On the **Page** tab, click **Save** to save your new My Dashboard webpage. After the webpage has been saved, the ribbon closes and the webpage is displayed in browse mode. If there is a delay in displaying the PivotTable and PivotChart reports, refresh the page.

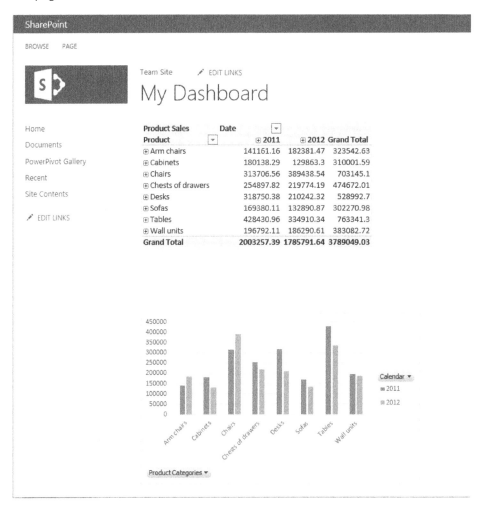

17   Verify that the interactive capabilities are available within the Web Parts. For example, in the PivotTable, expand the year **2012**, and then expand the **Desks** product category.

❌ CLEAN UP **Leave the browser open if you are continuing to the next exercise.**

Building visualizations with Power View

Power View is a browser-based Silverlight application. Using Power View, you can present and share insights with others in your organization through interactive presentations. Power View in SharePoint 2013 provides a highly interactive, browser-based data exploration, visualization, and presentation experience. With Power View, you can create interactive reports with intuitive charts, grids, and filters that provide the ability to visually explore data and easily create interactive visualizations to help define insights.

Power View is available as a stand-alone version in SharePoint and as a native feature in Excel 2013. Both versions of Power View require Silverlight to be installed on the local machine.

TIP In SharePoint, Power View is a feature of the SQL Server 2012 Service Pack 1 Reporting Services Add-in for Microsoft SharePoint.

Power View reports provide views of data from data models based on PowerPivot workbooks published in a PowerPivot Gallery, or models deployed to SSAS instances. Each page within a Power View report is referred to as a *view*. In Power View, you can quickly create a variety of interactive and intuitive visualizations, including tables and matrices, as well as pie, bar, and bubble charts and sets of multiple charts.

Power View uses the metadata in the underlying data model to compute the relationships between the different tables and fields. Based on these relationships, Power View provides the ability to filter one visualization, and at the same time, highlight another visualization in a current view. In addition to the filters, you can use slicers to compare and evaluate your data from different perspectives. When you have multiple slicers in a view, the selection for one slicer filters the other slicers in the view.

Power View in SharePoint has two presentation modes: a reading mode and a full-screen mode. In the presentation modes, the ribbon and other design areas are hidden to provide more space for the reports that are still fully interactive.

IMPORTANT Power View reports on SharePoint are separate files with the .rdlx file format. In Excel, Power View sheets are part of an Excel .xlsx workbook. The .rdlx file format is not compatible with the .xlsx format. In other words, you cannot open a Power View .rdlx file in Excel. Equally, SharePoint cannot open Power View sheets in an Excel .xlsx file. The .rdlx file format is also not compatible with the .rdl files that you create in SQL Server 2012 Report Builder or SQL Server 2012 Reporting Services (SSRS). You cannot open .rdl reports in Power View, and vice versa.

13

In the following exercise, you will create a Power View report in SharePoint 2013 that will provide a view of the Wide World Importers stores in the United States on a map, and show their respective sales performance. You will then create a pie chart for each of the stores that will be displayed on the map and show the stores' sales performance by a product category. Finally, you will switch to reading mode and explore the data using the visualization that you've built.

> **IMPORTANT** To be able to complete this exercise, you need to be connected to the Internet, because the map capabilities are provided by the Bing search service on the Internet.

 SET UP **Open the SharePoint site where you would like to create a Power View report, if it is not already open. If prompted, type your user name and password, and then click OK.**

> **IMPORTANT** Verify that you have sufficient permissions to create a report in the library on the site that you are using. If in doubt, see Appendix A.

1   On the **Quick Launch**, open the **PowerPivot Gallery** with the **SalesData** workbook, if it is not already open.

2   In the top-right corner of the **SalesData** workbook gallery view, click the **Create Power View Report** icon to open its data model in the Power View design environment, and then create a Power View report.

3   Explore the Power View design environment. The main part of the page displays the view area, which is empty for the time being. In the view area, there is a design surface to create a new view, and the Filters area, which displays the filters in the view. To the right of the page, a Fields List area shows all the tables in the data model. You can drag the tables and filters to the view, or select the fields to appear there.

> **TIP** In the top-left corner of the Power View page, above the ribbon, there are the **Undo** and **Redo** icons that allow you to undo or redo the last action, respectively.

You will now create a table with the data for your visualization.

4   In the **Fields List**, open the **Sales** table, and then drag the **SalesAmount** field to the design surface in the view. Power View draws the table in the view, displaying actual data and adding a **SalesAmount** column heading.

5   In the **Fields List**, open the **Locations** table and drag the **CityName** field to the **SalesAmount** table in the view. When the table area becomes highlighted, release the mouse to add the **CityName** field to the table. Power View calculates the data and displays a new table with two columns: **SalesAmount** and **CityName**.

6   On the **Design** tab on the ribbon, in the **Visualizations** group, select **Map**. If a privacy warning appears in the yellow bar under the ribbon, stating that some of the data needs to be geocoded by sending it to Bing, click **Enable Content** to confirm that you would like to proceed.

7   A map visualization appears in the view. Resize the visualization area by dragging its corner so that you can see the map with the blue circles, the size of which indicates the sales performance for the individual stores.

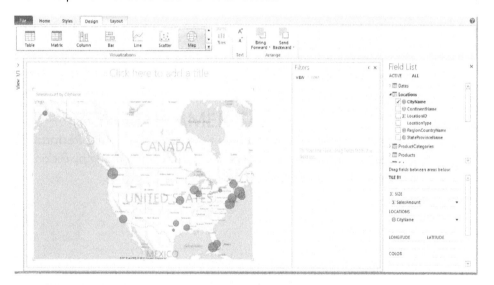

While this visualization is already quite informative, you can bring even more insights to your map visualization with only a few clicks. You will now replace the blue circles with pie charts that will not only indicate the sales performance of a store, but will also show the sales by product categories.

13

8   In the **Field List**, open the **ProductCategories** table and drag the **ProductCategoryName** field into the **Color** area, located at the bottom of the **Field List** pane.

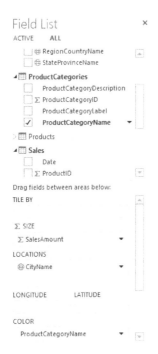

The map is redisplayed with the pie charts for each store location. In addition, a legend appears on the top right of the map. It lists the product categories, with the colors that identify them, in the pie charts.

9   On top of the map, click within the title area and type **Sales Performance**. To make it easier to interact with your report, switch to reading mode by clicking the **Home** tab, and then selecting **Reading Mode** in the **Display** group.

10   The map visualization is displayed in reading mode. Hover over the map to display map controls in the top-right corner of the map window. The controls allow you to adjust the map view by zooming in or out and moving the map up, down, to the right, or to the left. You can also drag the map within the window to bring different areas into view.

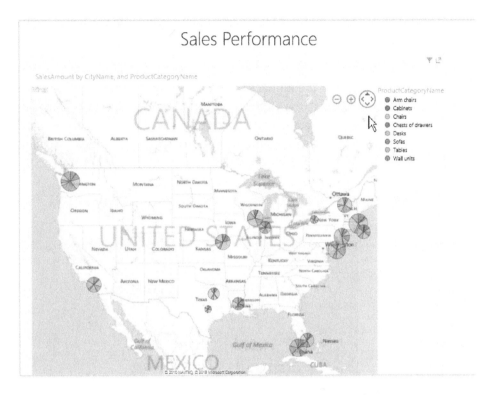

TIP You can increase the map area to include the title area of the chart by clicking the **Pop Out** icon in the top-right corner of the chart area. To redisplay the title, click the icon again.

11 Point to a chart on the map. The chart increases in size and the mouse tip appears, showing the location of the shop, the name of the product category you happen to point to on the chart, and the sales amount for this category.

12 To call out a particular product category, click this category in the legend; for example, **Tables.** The colors for other categories in the pie charts are dimmed, allowing the

13

sales performance for the Tables category to stand out and to be easily identifiable for all locations.

13   You will now work with the filters that are displayed in the **Filters** area. If the Filters area is empty, click the funnel icon in the top-right corner of the chart area to display the available filters in the **Filters** area. Open the **CityName** filter and select a city; for example, **Boston**. The report is filtered by the city name, Boston, and only the chart for Boston store is displayed on the map, allowing you to focus on the sales performance for this particular location.

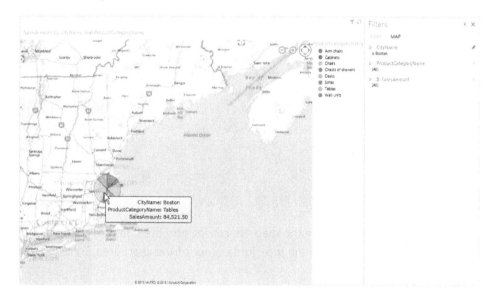

14   Open the **CityName** filter again and clear the selection for Boston to redisplay the map with the sales performance charts for all stores.

15   Click **Edit Report** to return to the design mode, and then on the **File** menu, click **Save As** to save the Power View report to the PowerPivot Gallery. In the **Save As** dialog box, type **SalesPerformance** and click **Save**.

TIP A Power View report is saved as an .rdlx file, which is separate from the .xslx workbook that contains the data model that the report is based on.

TIP When you save a Power View report, you have the option to include the preview images of the report, which can be displayed in the PowerPivot Gallery in SharePoint Server 2013. By default, the preview images are enabled and saved with the report.

16 Click the **Back** button in the top-left corner of the browser window to return to the PowerPivot Gallery. Verify that the **SalesPerformance** report is saved in the gallery and that the preview image of the map visualization is shown.

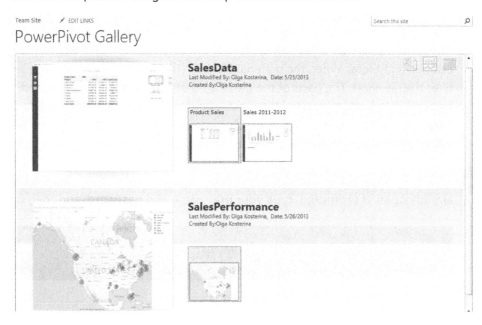

CLEAN UP Leave the browser open if you are continuing to the next exercise.

Creating and using Power View reports with multiple views

A Power View report in SharePoint 2013 can contain multiple views that are all based on the same data model. However, each view has its own visualizations and filters. In design mode, you can copy and paste between the views, and you can also duplicate views.

To move between the different views in a report in design mode, you can click the preview images in the **View** pane located on the left of the screen. In the reading and the full-screen modes, in addition to the navigation arrows on the bottom right of the screen, a view chooser icon is available on the bottom left of all views. The view chooser icon displays a row of clickable preview images on the bottom of the **Power View** page, providing navigation in the report.

In the following exercise, you will add a new view to the **SalesPerformance** report. In the new view, you will create two connected visualizations, so that when a filter is chosen in one visualization, you can filter and highlight the other one. The first visualization is a pie chart that displays the sales amount by product category for all stores, sliced by year, to complement the pie charts for individual stores in the first view. The second visualization is a bar chart that displays the sales amount by the product material, such as Oak, Pine, Cherry, Leather, and Metal. When the material filter is selected in the bar chart, the selection will filter the pie chart. The parts of the pie chart that correspond to the selected material will be highlighted, and the rest of the pie will be dimmed. You will then validate that the filters only apply within a view. In other words, visualizations and filters in the first view have no influence on the second view, and vice versa.

 SET UP Open the SharePoint site that you used in the previous exercise, if it is not already open. If prompted, type your user name and password, and then click OK.

> **IMPORTANT** Verify that you have sufficient permissions to create a report in the library on the site that you are using. If in doubt, see Appendix A.

1   On the **Quick Launch**, open the **PowerPivot Gallery** with the **SalesPerformance** report, if it is not already open, and then click the **SalesPerformance** preview image to open the report in the Power View design environment.

2   Click **Edit Report**, and then on the **Home** tab on the ribbon, in the **Insert** group, click **New View** to add a new view page. Power View creates an empty view. Notice that the View pane on the left of the screen has expanded to show the preview images for both views. Click the small left arrow icon on the top left of the **View** pane to hide it, so that you have more space to work with the visualizations in the view.

3   To build a table that will provide a basis for your pie chart visualization, in the **Fields List**, open the **Sales** table, locate the **SalesAmount** field, and then drag it to the view. Power View creates a table with the **SalesAmount** table heading and the actual value displayed.

4   In the **Fields List**, open the **ProductCategories** table, locate the **ProductCategoryName** field, and then drag it to the **SalesAmount** table in the view. When the table is highlighted, release the mouse to add the field to the table. Power View calculates the data and displays a new table with two columns: **SalesAmount** and **ProductCategotyName**.

5   On the **Design** tab on the ribbon, in the **Vizualizations** group, open a drop-down list of available virtualizations. In the **Charts** section, click **Pie**. Power View creates a pie chart that shows the product category sales.

    TIP The Power View choice of virtualizations is contextual. It only displays those virtualizations that can be used with the selected data. For example, all charts become unavailable if there are no aggregated numeric values in the data.

6   To slice the pie sectors by a year, in the **Fields List**, open the **Dates** table, locate the **CalendarYear** field, and then drag it to the **Slices** area on the bottom of the **Field List** pane.

13

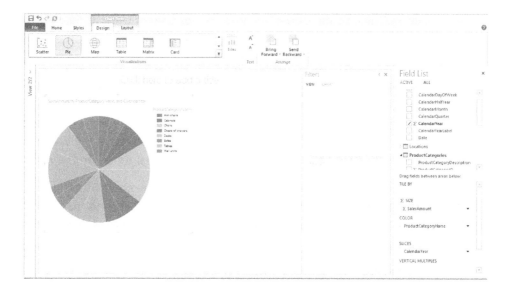

7   To build a table that will provide a basis for the bar chart visualization, in the **Fields List**, open the **Sales** table, locate the **SalesAmount** field, and then drag it to an empty area in the view. Power View creates a table with the **SalesAmount** table heading and the actual value displayed.

8   In the **Fields List**, open the **Products** table, locate the **ProductMaterial** field and drag it to the **SalesAmount** table in the view. When the table is highlighted, drag the field. Power View calculates the data and displays a new table with two columns: **SalesAmount** and **ProductMaterial**.

9   On the **Design** tab on the ribbon, in the **Visualizations** group, open a drop-down list of available visualizations. In the **Charts** section, click **Bar**. Power View creates a bar chart that shows the sales amount by product material.

10 On the top of the view, in the title area, type **Sales Comparison**.

11 In the bar chart, click a bar for a material; for example, **Oak**. Other bars in the bar chart become dimmed. The pie chart displays only the parts that apply to the Oak furniture, with the other parts dimmed. You have filtered one visualization (the pie chart) based on the selection in another virtualization (the bar chart) in the same view.

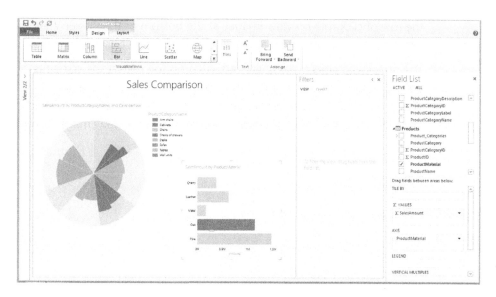

12 Expand the **View** pane to see the preview images for both views, and click on the first view to display it. Verify that the visualization in the first view is unchanged and displays the pie chart diagrams for all product materials, with no highlights. In other words, the first view has not been affected by the ProductMaterial filter in the second view.

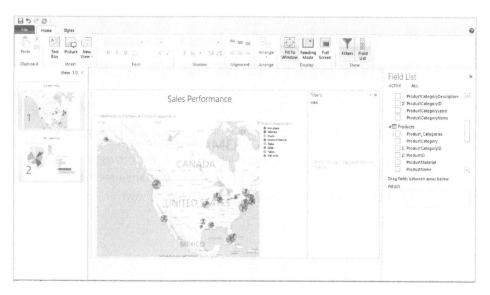

13 Switch to reading mode by clicking **Reading Mode** on the **Home** tab on the ribbon, and then click the view chooser icon, in the bottom-left corner of the page, to display

the row of clickable preview images at the bottom of the Power View window, which provides the navigation capability in the report.

The preview images are highlighted, whereas the rest of the screen is dimmed. When you point to a preview image, it is displayed in the main page area that is dimmed. When you click the preview image, its corresponding view is displayed in the full page, which is no longer dimmed, and the row of preview images is removed from display.

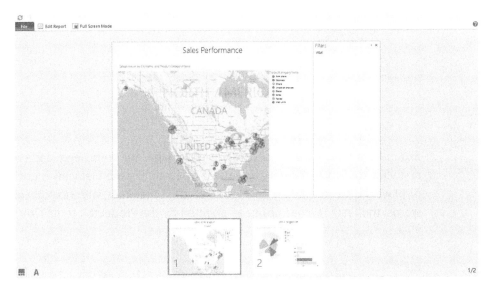

14   Close the **Filters** pane to provide more space for visualizations.

15   Click **Edit Report**, and then on the **File** menu, click **Save** to save the Power View report to the PowerPivot Gallery. Alternatively, you can click the **Save** icon on the top left of the page. If a **Confirm Save** dialog appears, click **Save**.

16   Click the **Back** button in the top-left corner of the browser window to return to the PowerPivot Gallery. Verify that the **SalesPerformance** report is saved in the gallery and that the preview images of both views are shown.

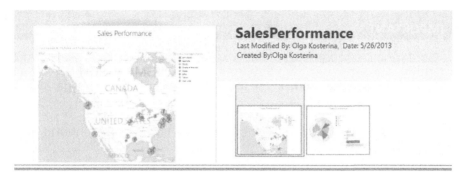

 CLEAN UP **Close the browser.**

Displaying a Power View report in a Web Part

Power View reports can be integrated into a SharePoint site page using Web Parts. Two generic Web Parts provided by SharePoint 2013 can be used to display the Power View reports on the webpage: the **Page Viewer** Web Part and the **Silverlight Web Part**.

The **Page Viewer** Web Part is a general purpose Web Part that retrieves and displays a webpage using a hyperlink. You can easily add this Web Part to new and existing pages to display Power View reports.

> **IMPORTANT** The **Page Viewer** Web Part uses the HTML *<IFRAME>* element, and therefore cannot be used in browsers that don't support IFrames.

In the following exercise, you will create a new page in the SharePoint site, add a **Page Viewer** Web Part to the page, and then configure the Web Part to display the Power View report that you worked with in the previous exercises.

 SET UP **Open the SharePoint site where you would like to add a page with a Power View report displayed in the Web Part. If prompted, type your user name and password, and then click OK.**

13

1   Click the **Settings** menu in the top right of your SharePoint page, and then select **Add a page** from the menu.

2   In the **Add a page** dialog, in the **New name** box, type **Hello World**, and then click **Create**.

3   The new page opens for editing. To insert the Web Part into the page, position your cursor within the box outlined on the page, and click the **Insert** tab on the ribbon. Then, in the **Parts** group, click **Web Part** to display the **Parts** pane.

4   In the **Categories** list on the left of the page, select the **Media and Content** category.

5   In the **Parts** list, select the **Page Viewer** Web Part.

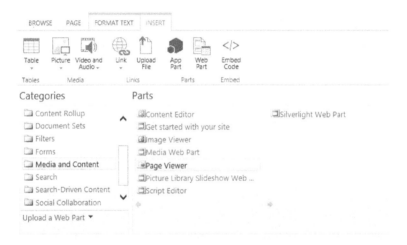

6   Click **Add** to add the **Page Viewer** Web Part to the page.

7   On the **Hello World** page, in the **Page Viewer** Web Part, click **open the tool pane**. If a message box appears, asking you to save your changes before continuing, click **OK**.

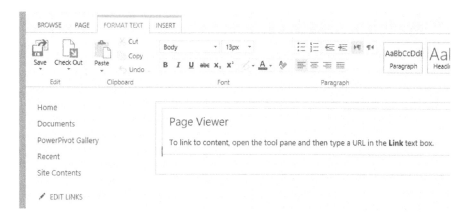

8   The tool pane for the **Page Viewer** Web Part opens on the right side of the page. The next task is to specify the URL of the Power View report in the **Link** box in the **Page Viewer** tool pane.

To identify the report URL, open a new tab or a new window in the browser, go to **PowerPivot Gallery**, where the Power View report is located, and click a preview image to open the Power View environment.

9   In the Power View environment, set up the view in a way that you would like it to appear in the Web Part. On the **Home** tab on the ribbon, click **Reading Mode** to switch to the presentation mode so that the ribbon and other design tools are not displayed. In the multiple page reports, display the view that you want to be displayed in the Web Part when it first appears on the page; for example, the map visualization in the SalesPerformance report. Then, in the browser address bar, highlight the URL to select it, right-click the selection, and then click **Copy** on the context menu.

13

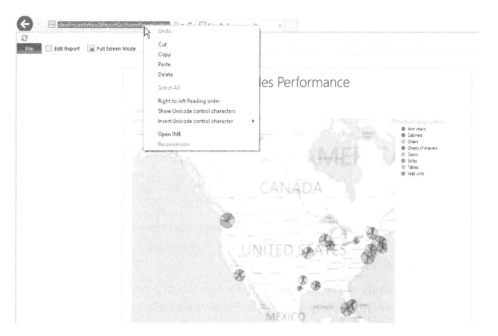

10   Return to the browser that displays the **Hello World** page, with the **Page Viewer** tool pane open on the right side of the page. In the **Page Viewer** tool pane, on the right side of the **Link** text box, click the ellipsis button to open the **Text Editor** dialog box, in which you can edit the URL.

11 Clear any text in the **Text Editor** dialog box, and then paste the Power View report URL into the **Text Editor** by right-clicking in the text box and selecting **Paste** from the menu.

In our scenario, the URL is as follows:

http://wideworldimporters/_layouts/15/ReportServer/AdHocReportDesigner.aspx?Relati veReportUrl=%2fwideworldimporters%2fPowerPivot%2520Gallery%2fSalesPerforman ce.rdlx&ViewMode=Presentation&ReportSection=ReportSection.

In your environment, the server path part of the URL will be different from the **wideworldimporters**. However, the rest of the URL will be similar because it is programmatically generated by SharePoint.

12 You will now add a parameter to the URL that will instruct the Power View to hide the top toolbar that displays the **Edit Report** and the **Full Screen** options, as well as the **File** menu. Unless you want users to edit the report from within the Web Part, hiding the toolbar will provide a better user experience.

In the **Text Editor** window, position your cursor at the end of the URL, immediately after **ReportSection** parameter, and type the following string: **&PreviewBar=False**.

The URL looks like the following, as long as you replace **wideworldimporters** with your server path as before:

http://wideworldimporters/_layouts/15/ReportServer/AdHocReportDesigner.aspx?Relati veReportUrl=%2fwideworldimporters%2fPowerPivot%2520Gallery%2fSalesPerforman ce.rdlx&ViewMode=Presentation&ReportSection=ReportSection&PreviewBar=False.

13

```
Text Editor -- Webpage Dialog                  x

http://wideworldimporters/_layouts/15/Repor
tServer/AdHocReportDesigner.aspx?RelativeRe
portUrl=%2fwideworldimporters%2fPowerPivot%
2520Gallery%2fSalesPerformance.rdlx&ViewMod
e=Presentation&ReportSection=ReportSection&
PreviewBar=False




                              OK      Cancel
```

13   Click **OK** to insert the URL string into the **Link** text box in the **Page Viewer** tool pane, and then click **Test link**, located just above the **Link** text box. The link is tested in the new browser tab. Validate that the Power View report successfully opens. If the Power View report is not rendering, check the URL and repeat steps 9–13, if necessary.

14   Click the browser tab that is displaying the **Hello World** page, and then in the **Page Viewer** tool pane, in the **Appearance** section, set the following parameters:

a.   In the **Title** box, remove the **Page Viewer** title to clear the box.

b.   In the **Height** section, select **Yes** to set a fixed width, and then type **600** to set the width to 600 pixels.

C.   In the **Width** section, select **Yes** to set a fixed height, and then type **600** to set the height to 600 pixels.

d.   In the **Chrome Type** list, select **None**.

15. In the **Page Viewer** tool pane, click **OK** to confirm your settings and close the tool.

16. On the **Format Text** tab on the ribbon, in the **Edit** group, click **Save** to save your new Hello World webpage. After the webpage has been saved, the ribbon closes and the webpage is displayed in browse mode. If there is a delay in displaying the Power View report, refresh the page.

13

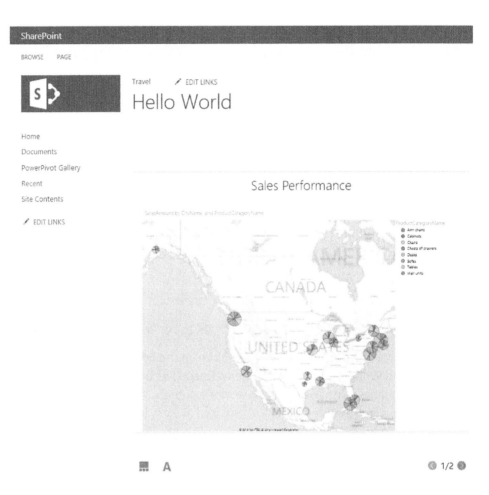

17   In the **Power View** report, verify that the interactive capabilities are available within the Web Part. For example, in the **Sales Performance** view, point to a pie chart and verify that the mouse tip provides information about the sales performance of a product category in the location that you are pointing at.

In the bottom left of the Power View report, click the view chooser icon. Go to the **Sales Comparison** view and click a bar in the bar chart to filter the pie chart by product category.

CLEAN UP **Close the browser.**

13

Key points

- SharePoint 2013 provides intuitive, powerful, self-service BI capabilities for exploring and visualizing data to facilitate better decision making.

- BI server-side components include Excel Services, Visio Services, and Performance-Point Services. Excel Services and SQL Server 2012 provide server-side capabilities for PowerPivot and Power View support.

- There are a number of sites, libraries, and content types that are optimized for providing support to BI applications, including the Business Intelligence Center site, the PowerPivot site, and the PowerPivot Gallery library.

- PowerPivot in Excel 2013 provides a data-modeling engine that brings together various data from multiple data sources. PowerPivot workbooks can be published to SharePoint, where the server-side components recognize the data models and provide functionality for exploring, analyzing, and visualizing data in the browser.

- You can publish interactive PowerPivot dashboards on the SharePoint site so that users can explore and analyze data, and collaborate and share insights. You can add PivotTables and PivotCharts to a webpage using the Excel Web Part.

- Power View in SharePoint 2013 provides an easy-to-use environment to build data visualizations and mashups so that you can explore data from many perspectives using different filters and slicers.

- A Power View report can include multiple views. Visualizations and filters apply within each view. You can create connected visualizations within a view but not between the views.

- Power View reports are .rdlx files that are not compatible with either Excel .xslx or Report Builder .rdl file formats.

- You can display a Power View report within a Web Part on a webpage.

Chapter at a glance

Sync

Sync your tasks with Outlook, page 511

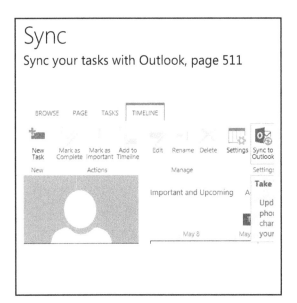

View

View SharePoint Calendar list apps in Outlook, page 523

Use

Use Lync Presence with documents in libraries, page 537

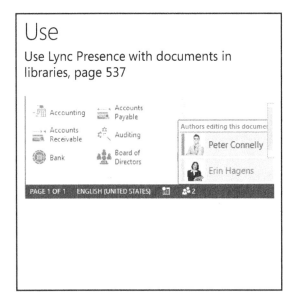

Create

Create a site mailbox, page 541

Using SharePoint with Outlook and Lync

14

IN THIS CHAPTER YOU, WILL LEARN HOW TO

- Sync your tasks with Outlook.

- Connect a SharePoint Contacts list app to Outlook.

- Move an Outlook contact to a SharePoint Contacts list.

- Copy SharePoint contacts into Outlook.

- Send an email using a SharePoint Contacts list.

- View SharePoint calendars and personal calendars in Outlook.

- Take SharePoint content offline.

- Manage SharePoint alerts in Outlook.

- Configure an RSS feed.

- Use Lync Presence with documents in libraries.

- Use site mailboxes.

For many years, Microsoft SharePoint Server has integrated with the Microsoft Office Outlook client application to allow you to aggregate and manage all of your tasks in one place, whether you created them within Outlook, in a SharePoint Tasks list, or within Microsoft Office OneNote. Microsoft Office Outlook 2013 and Microsoft SharePoint 2013 provide the same functionality; in addition, similar access is available with Microsoft Exchange Server 2013 and Microsoft Outlook Web App.

With Outlook 2013, like Microsoft Office Outlook 2010, you can keep a local copy of your team's Calendars, Tasks, and Contacts lists, as well as libraries. You can synchronize information in two directions for items in Contacts lists, calendars, Tasks lists, and discussion boards. A local copy of SharePoint data is available offline when you are not connected to the network, and it can be synchronized with the SharePoint site manually or automatically when you next connect. Outlook also supports Really Simple Syndication (RSS) feeds so that you can subscribe to and stay updated on the latest news sites and blogs. You can also manage all of your SharePoint alerts from one Outlook dialog box.

IMPORTANT In Microsoft SharePoint 2010, you can create a **Meeting Workspace** site by using the browser or Outlook. A **Meeting Workspace** is slightly different from a Team site. It has no **Quick Launch**, and the pages are Web Part pages and not wiki pages. In SharePoint 2013, any of the Meeting Workspace site templates are deprecated, as is the Document Workspace and the Group Work site templates. If you have upgraded from SharePoint 2010, any sites you created from these site templates will continue to function. You should not create any new Meeting Workspaces, Document Workspaces, or Group Work site templates, however. For the **Group Calendar** and **Resource Reservation** features added to the traditional calendar, the better long-term replacement is to use Outlook and Exchange Server features.

When Microsoft Lync Server 2013 is installed with Lync Web Access, much of the application's functionality can also be accessed straight from within Office client applications, Microsoft Office Web Apps, or SharePoint. Similar to the way Lync offered connectivity in the past by providing "presence" information, you can see whether another user is online, offline, or busy. You can start an instant message or a web conference call.

You will also encounter a more unified search experience when SharePoint Server 2013 is used in conjunction with Microsoft Exchange Server 2013 and Microsoft Lync Server 2013. Whether you use the browser to display a SharePoint site or you use Microsoft Outlook Web App, you can find content sitting in your Exchange Server site mailbox, your Exchange Server archive, SharePoint document libraries, SharePoint lists, your Lync instant message conversations, and even content that is stored on a Windows network share. In addition, SharePoint Server 2013 and Exchange Server 2013 provide a suite of features, such as site mailboxes and enterprise Electronic Discovery (eDiscovery).

SEE ALSO Information on search can be found in Chapter 9, "Searching for information and people." Information on records management and compliance, which include eDiscovery, are discussed in Chapter 15, "Working with content management."

The Microsoft SharePoint Server 2010, Microsoft Exchange Server 2010, and Microsoft Lync Server 2010 products provide much of this functionality; however, with the tight integration of SharePoint Server 2013, Exchange Server 2013, and Lync Server 2013, along with Office Web Apps, you no longer have to think about which device you are on—regardless of whether you use a Windows computer, a Mac laptop, a Windows 8 tablet, an Apple iPad or iPod, an Android tablet, a mobile phone, or whatever system you are configured to for access to documents, and whether or not you have the Lync client installed.

In this chapter, you will learn how to sync your tasks with Outlook, and how to copy and move Outlook contacts to and from a SharePoint Contacts list. You will also learn how to connect SharePoint Calendar lists to Outlook, how to view SharePoint calendars side by side with personal calendars, how to edit SharePoint calendar items offline, how to manage SharePoint alerts in Outlook, and how to subscribe to a SharePoint list RSS feed. You will then create and use a site mailbox.

Although you can complete many of the tasks documented in this chapter by using Microsoft Office Outlook 2010, the steps and screen shots in this chapter were created using Outlook 2013. If you use Outlook 2010, your steps and screen shots will be slightly different. See *Microsoft SharePoint Foundation 2010 Step by Step*, by Olga Londer and Penelope Coventry (Microsoft Press, 2011), for steps on using Outlook 2010.

PRACTICE FILES Before you can complete the exercises in this chapter, you need to copy the book's practice files to your computer. The practice files that you'll use in this chapter are in the **Chapter14** practice file folder. A complete list of practice files is provided in "Using the practice files" at the beginning of this book.

IMPORTANT Remember to use your SharePoint site location in place of *http://wideworldmporters* in the following exercises.

Syncing your tasks with Outlook

You can sync your tasks with Outlook from your **My Tasks** page or from any Tasks list. A **Sync Tasks with Microsoft Outlook** dialog appears, where you must select the **Sync Tasks** check box if you want to view your tasks within the Outlook client application or the Outlook Web App.

14

This functionality relies on the installation of Exchange Server 2013 within your organization. If you try to complete the **Sync to Outlook** activity, but Exchange Server 2013 is not installed, when you click **OK** on the **Sync Tasks with Microsoft Outlook** dialog, an error message appears, stating that you are not able to sync your tasks because your mailbox is on an Exchange Server that isn't supported.

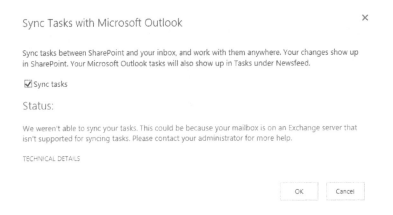

In the following exercise, you will sync your tasks from your **My Tasks** page with Outlook.

> **SEE ALSO** The **My Tasks** page is available from the **Newsfeed** hub. The **My Tasks** page and the **Newsfeed** hub are discussed in Chapter 7, "Getting social."

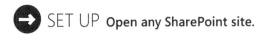 SET UP **Open any SharePoint site.**

1   In the global navigation bar, click **Newsfeed**, and then on the **Quick Launch**, click **Tasks**.

2   On the **Tasks** tab, in the **Settings** group, click **Sync to Outlook**.

3   On the **Sync Tasks with Microsoft Outlook** dialog that appears, select **Sync tasks**, and then click **OK**.

4   Open **Outlook Web App** or the **Outlook** client, and at the bottom of the **Navigation** pane, click **Tasks**.

5   Complete a task; for example, in Outlook Web App. Hover over the task that you wish to complete so that icons appear to the right, and then click the **Mark Complete** icon.

6   The task that you completed is no longer displayed in Outlook.

7   In the browser, go to your **My Tasks** page, and note that the task that you completed in Outlook is now displayed in the **Completed** view and not in the **Active** view.

❌ CLEAN UP   **Close the browser and exit Outlook, if it is open.**

14

Connecting a SharePoint Contacts list app to Outlook

To initiate the integration between SharePoint lists and libraries and Outlook, you need to connect the list or library. You can connect most SharePoint lists, as well as all SharePoint library types, to Outlook. The following list and library types are not supported for connection to Outlook:

- Survey
- Issue Tracking
- Announcements
- Links
- Custom Lists
- Solutions Gallery
- List Templates Gallery
- Web Part Gallery

When you connect a list or library to Outlook, the list or library appears in the respective areas of the Outlook Navigation pane. Calendars appear in the **Calendar** pane under **Other Calendars**, tasks appear in the **Tasks** pane under **Other Tasks**, and contacts appear in the **Contacts** pane under **Other Contacts**.

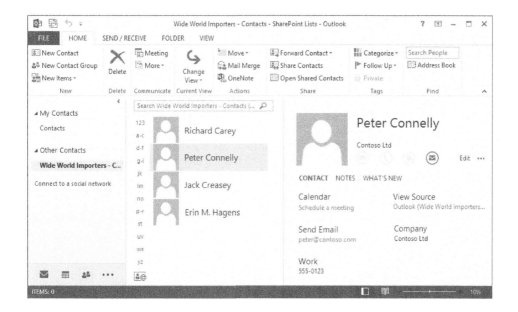

TIP Outlook contains built-in technology (*Exchange ActiveSync Support* and *Social Connector*) that allows you to receive emails, appointments, and contacts from Outlook.com and Hotmail, as well as updates from social networks; therefore, the default view in Outlook 2013 for contacts is not the Business Card view, as it is in Outlook 2010. The People view is the new default view for contacts. The Business Card view now aggregates information about the same person from multiple contacts sources.

Discussion lists and libraries appear in a folder in the **Mail** pane, under **SharePoint Lists**. When you connect external lists to Outlook, they are created in the **SharePoint External Lists** folder.

Once a list is connected to Outlook, you can modify that list within Outlook at any time, whether you are online or offline. When you connect to a library to modify a file, double-click the file to open it in the appropriate program. You can also share the connection with others by right-clicking the list or library name in Outlook, and then clicking **Share This Folder**.

14

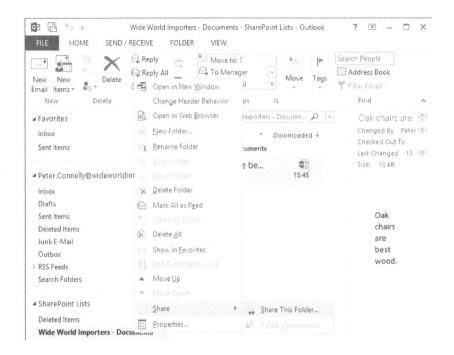

SharePoint permissions carry over when using SharePoint resources in Outlook. For example, if you have permission to edit a document or list item on the SharePoint site, you can also edit the document or list item within Outlook.

When you modify a document from a library that you have connected to Outlook, you will be modifying an offline copy of that document, known as a *cached copy*, by default. You can choose to send the document to the SharePoint library when you have completed your modification. During your offline editing, another user could modify the same document, so it is recommended to always check out your document before you edit it. You can turn off offline editing by using **Options** in the Microsoft Office Word backstage view.

SEE ALSO More information on document management and coauthoring can be found in *Microsoft SharePoint 2013 Inside Out*, by Darvish Shadravan, Penelope Coventry, Thomas Resing, and Christina Wheeler (Microsoft Press, 2013).

Deleting a connected SharePoint list folder from Outlook does not delete the SharePoint list or its data from the SharePoint server; however, the data in that list is no longer available offline from within Outlook. An alternative method of managing connected SharePoint lists or libraries is to click the **File** tab to switch to the backstage view of Outlook. Then, under **Account Information**, click **Account Settings**, and then click **Account Settings** in the drop-down list to display the **Account Settings** dialog box. Click the **SharePoint Lists** tab, click the SharePoint list or library that you want to manage, and then click **Remove** or **Change**.

TIP Removing connected lists or libraries from Outlook helps you focus on current projects.

In the following exercise, you will connect to Outlook from a Contacts list on a SharePoint site. You can use the same technique to connect to other SharePoint lists or libraries.

SET UP **Open a SharePoint site, such as one created from the practice .wsp file for this chapter. If you have not created a site based on this chapter's .wsp file, then you will need a Contacts list to complete this exercise. You can create a Contacts list by following the steps in the exercise in Chapter 3, "Working with documents and information in lists and libraries," which explains how to create a list.**

> **IMPORTANT** Verify that you have sufficient rights to read the items in the Contacts list. If in doubt, see Appendix A, "SharePoint 2013 user permissions and permission levels."

1   On the **Quick Launch**, under the **Lists** section, click **Contacts**.

2   On the **List** tab in the **List Tools** contextual tab set, within the **Connect & Export** group, click **Connect to Outlook**.

> **TROUBLESHOOTING** If the **Connect to Outlook** command is inactive, press **F5** to reload the page. Many of the collaboration sites in SharePoint 2013 use a new technology, known as *Minimal Download Strategy*, so that pages can load faster; however, the **Connect to Outlook** command is dimmed when the page is first loaded.

14

3   If an **Internet Explorer - Security Warning** dialog box appears, asking "Do you want to allow this website to open a program on your computer?," click **Allow**.

4   If another Internet Explorer - Security Warning dialog box appears, stating that, "A website wants to open web content using this program on your computer," click **Allow**. A **Microsoft Outlook** dialog box appears, stating that, "You should only connect lists from sources you know and trust."

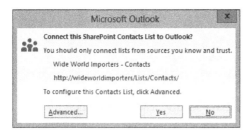

5   Click **Advanced** to open a **SharePoint Lists Options** dialog box, and in the **Folder Name** text box, type **WideWorldImporters - Contacts**.

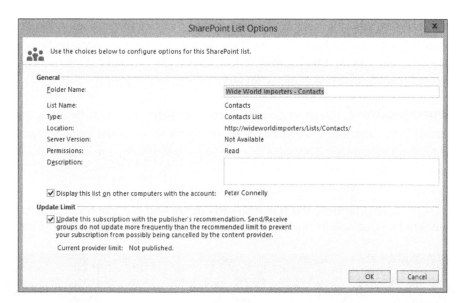

6   Click **OK**, and in the **Microsoft Outlook** dialog box, click **Yes** to display the Contacts list in Outlook.

❌ CLEAN UP **Close the browser. Leave Outlook open if you are continuing to the next exercise.**

Moving an Outlook contact to a SharePoint Contacts list app

By connecting a SharePoint Contacts list to Outlook, you are creating an Outlook Contacts folder. You can copy the contact information in your Outlook Contacts folder back into the SharePoint Contacts list. The new contacts within the Outlook Contacts folder are added to the SharePoint Contacts list the next time Outlook synchronizes with SharePoint, and you can then share the contact information with users who visit your SharePoint site. Any other users who also connected the SharePoint Contacts list to their copy of Outlook will observe the new contacts within their Outlook Contacts folder when they next synchronize with SharePoint. Also, a **Microsoft Outlook** dialog box will appear, stating that any incompatible content will be removed during the next synchronization, and that the original version of each affected item will be preserved in the Local Failures folder.

14

In this exercise, you will move contact information from your Outlook Address Book to a Contacts list on a SharePoint site. You can use the same technique to move calendar items from a SharePoint Calendar list to your Calendar folder, as well as to move task and event items into their respective Outlook folders.

TROUBLESHOOTING You cannot move a recurring series of events by using the steps detailed in this exercise. Instead, open the recurring series or the individual occurrence from a recurring series within Outlook. Click the **File** tab to display the backstage, and then click **Move to Folder**.

 SET UP **Open Outlook, if it is not already open. You can use the Contacts list that you connected to Outlook in the previous exercise, or you can use another Contacts list.**

> **IMPORTANT** Verify that you have sufficient rights to create new list items in the Contacts list. If in doubt, see Appendix A.

1   In the Outlook **Navigation** pane, under **My Contacts**, select **Contacts**.

2   Select two or more users that you want to move by holding down the **Shift** key or the **Ctrl** key while clicking the left mouse button.

    TIP Press **Ctrl+A** to select all contacts.

3   On the **Home** tab, in the **Actions** group, click **Move**, and then click **Other Folder**.

4   Scroll down the **Move Items** dialog box. To the left of the **SharePoint Lists** folder, click the arrow icon, and then select **WideWorldImporters - Contacts**.

5   Click **OK** to display the **Contacts** folder, under **My Contacts**, without the contacts that you selected.

> **TIP** To move a single contact, select the contact, and then press **Ctrl+Shift+V** to open the **Move Items** dialog box. Alternatively, while holding down the mouse button, drag the contact to **WideWorldImporters - Contacts** in the Outlook **Navigation** pane. You can also use these techniques to move more than one contact.

✖ CLEAN UP **Leave Outlook open if you are continuing to the next exercise.**

Copying SharePoint contacts into Outlook

You can copy any single contact or event item from a SharePoint list to Outlook. Once the contact item is copied into the Contacts folder, the contact item in the Contacts folder and the contact item on the SharePoint Contacts list are independent of each other—that is, there is no link between them. Therefore, amendments made to the contact in the Outlook Contacts folder are completed on the contact item in the SharePoint Contacts list. To ensure that your contact information does not become outdated, you should assign a definitive location for a specific contact by maintaining it as a contact item on either a SharePoint Contacts list or in your Outlook Contacts folder, but not both. If contact information is to be shared among a team, then a SharePoint Contacts list is the preferred location.

An alternative method to copy contacts is to select one or more contacts, and while holding down the **Ctrl** key and the mouse button, drag the contacts to the **Contacts** folder in the Outlook **Navigation** pane.

14

TROUBLESHOOTING You cannot copy a recurring series of events by using the steps detailed in the following exercise. Instead, copy a recurring series or an individual occurrence from a recurring series by opening it within Outlook. On the **Appointment Series** tab, in the **Actions** group, click **Copy to My Calendar**.

In the following exercise, you will copy contacts from a Contacts list in a SharePoint site into Outlook. You can also copy a calendar, an event, or task items by using the same technique.

 SET UP **Open Outlook, if it is not already open. You can use the Contacts list that you connected to Outlook in a previous exercise, or you can use another Contacts list. Ensure that there are contact items added to the list.**

> **IMPORTANT** Verify that you have sufficient rights to read the items in the Contacts list. If in doubt, see Appendix A.

1   In the Outlook **Navigation** pane, under **Other Contacts**, select **WideWorldImporters - Contacts**.

2   Select the users that you want to copy by holding down the **Shift** key or the **Ctrl** key when selecting the users.

3   Right-click one of the contacts that you selected, click **Move**, and then click **Copy to Folder**.

4   Scroll to the top of the **Copy Items** dialog box that appears. Select **Contacts**, and then click **OK** to add the contacts to your **Outlook Contacts** folder.

TROUBLESHOOTING If the name or email address of the contact already exists in your Outlook Contacts folder, the **Duplicate Contact Detected** dialog box appears so that you can resolve the conflict.

 CLEAN UP **Leave Outlook open if you are continuing to the next exercise.**

Viewing SharePoint calendars in Outlook

You can work with multiple calendars when using Outlook, thereby enabling you to create calendars for specific purposes, such as having one for work and one for your personal life. By using Outlook, you can view several calendars at the same time. When you view and scroll multiple calendars, they all display the same date or time frame. This feature is particularly useful if you have connected a SharePoint Calendar list to Outlook. By doing so, you are creating an Outlook Calendar folder in which a copy of the data from the SharePoint list is stored locally. In this way, you can keep track of any calendar items in a SharePoint list from the Outlook Calendar folder, even if you are not connected to the network.

Your personal Outlook calendar appears side by side with the connected SharePoint Calendar list. The background color of the Calendar folder name matches the color on the displayed calendar, so that you can discern between the two calendars. You can use *overlay mode*, where the two (or more) calendars are merged; however, the two calendars remain color-coordinated, as do the appointments in both calendars.

In the following exercise, you will connect to a SharePoint Calendar list to view your personal Outlook calendar and a connected SharePoint Calendar list, side by side in overlay mode.

➡ SET UP **In the browser, open the SharePoint site where the Calendar list is located.**

> **IMPORTANT** Verify that you have sufficient rights to read the items in the Contacts list. If in doubt, see Appendix A.

1 On the **Quick Launch**, under the **Lists** section, click **Calendar**, and then, on the **Calendar** tab, in the **Connect & Export** group, click **Connect to Outlook**.

2 If an Internet Explorer – Security Warning dialog box opens, asking, "Do you want to allow this website to open a program on your computer?," click **Allow**.

14

3   Outlook opens. In the Outlook dialog box, click **Advanced** to open a **SharePoint Lists Options** dialog box.

4   In the **Folder Name** text box, type **WideWorldImporters - Calendar**, and then click **OK**. Then, in the **Microsoft Outlook** dialog box, click **Yes**. You might be asked to supply your user name and password.

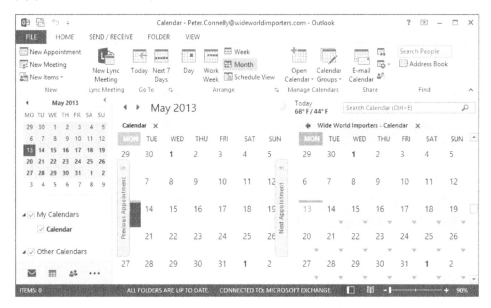

5   Click the arrow on the **WideWorldImporters - Calendar** tab to view the two calendars in *overlay* mode.

     TIP Once a Calendar list is connected to Outlook, use the check box to the left of the calendar name to control the number of calendars that you want to view side by side. Also, information on how to change the calendar Weather Bar forecast city can be found at *office.microsoft.com/en-us/outlook-help/change-the-calendar-weather-bar-forecast-city-HA102749748.aspx*.

✕ CLEAN UP **Leave Outlook open if you are continuing to the next exercise.**

Taking SharePoint content offline

Connecting lists to Outlook enables you to aggregate all of your list items in one place. For example, you can view all the calendar events in the Calendar window or all of your tasks in the Tasks windows, or you can view tasks assigned only to you on the **To-Do** bar. When you connect a SharePoint list or library, including external lists to Outlook, a local copy of the SharePoint content is stored locally on your computer.

TIP The **Archive** feature in Outlook cannot be used with the SharePoint List folder, or with any connected lists or libraries.

Connected SharePoint content can be used online or offline; however, it is important to understand the following synchronization processes:

- **Online** Once a list or library is connected, edits made in Outlook are synchronized automatically with the master content on the SharePoint site, depending on the **Send/Receive** settings.

  The default—**Send/Receive Group, All Accounts**—is configured for your mail items, and it also controls the updates to subscribed RSS feeds and SharePoint lists. The All Accounts group schedules an update to occur every 30 minutes. You can force synchronization to all Outlook connections immediately by clicking the **Send/Receive All Folders** command on the **Send/Receive** tab or by pressing **F9** on the keyboard. You can create new Send/Receive groups, which contain all or only a subset of your SharePoint connected lists or libraries, with their own synchronization schedules.

  Once the SharePoint list or library is updated, your changes are synchronized with other users who are connected to them in Outlook when they click the SharePoint list or library in the Outlook Navigation pane. If those users have the list or library open in the Outlook details pane, then they will not see the updates until the next synchronization schedule.

- **Offline** When you are offline, the Outlook status bar displays a red circle with a white X, and the message "Working Offline" appears. You can view and edit cached copies of the SharePoint content, but your modifications are not synchronized with the master content on the SharePoint site. To synchronize the content, you must go online.

When connected to Outlook, External Lists (meaning that the data is external to SharePoint) are created in the SharePoint External Lists folder, which is not controlled by the **Send/Receive** settings. External Lists are synchronized by default every 6 hours. When you right-click an **External List** in Outlook, you can learn the synchronization status and the time that

14

the data was last refreshed from the external system. You can then force synchronization. Data that is presented in an **External List** may or may not be available offline, depending on how the External Content Type for that **External List** is configured.

SEE ALSO Information on External Lists and External Content Types can be found in Chapter 22, "Working with external content," in *Microsoft SharePoint 2013 Inside Out*.

In this exercise, you will make Calendar list content available offline, and then edit an appointment offline.

 SET UP **Open Outlook, if it is not already open, and show the Calendar list that you connected to Outlook in a previous exercise.**

IMPORTANT Verify that you have sufficient rights to modify the items in the Calendar list. If in doubt, see Appendix A.

1   On the **Send/Receive** tab, in the **Preferences** group, click **Work Offline**.

    TROUBLESHOOTING If the **Work Offline** command does not appear in the **Preference** group, verify that your account is configured for **Cached Exchange Mode**. This can be configured in the backstage view by clicking **Account Settings**, and then, from the drop-down list, clicking **Account Settings**. On the **E-mail** tab, select the relevant account, and then click **Change**. Select the **Use Cached Exchange Mode** option. You will need to close Outlook and reopen it for the changes to take effect.

2   Click the **WideWorldImporters - Calendar** tab, and then, on the **Home** tab, click **New Appointment** to open a new, untitled appointment form.

3   On the form status bar, hover over the icon, or hover over the link to the right of **In Shared Folder** so that a tooltip appears with the date that the Calendar list was last updated.

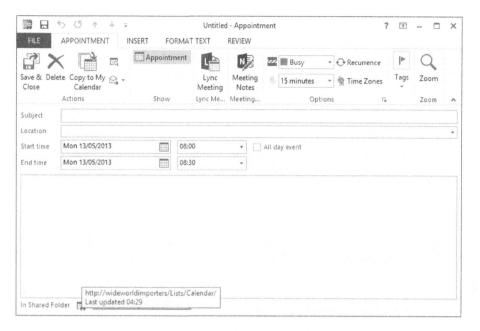

4   In the **Subject** box, type **SharePoint team meeting**, and then, on the **Appointment** tab, click **Save & Close** to display the new appointment in the details pane. If a **Reminder** dialog box appears, click **Dismiss**.

TROUBLESHOOTING   You may have to arrange the calendars to show the Daily view to see the new appointment.

5   In the **Navigation** pane, under **Other Calendars**, right-click **WideWorldImporters - Calendar**, and click **Open in Web Browser**.

In the browser, notice that the appointment that you added in Outlook does not appear in the SharePoint Calendar list, and then close the browser.

6   In Outlook, on the **Send/Receive** tab, in the **Preferences** group, click **Work Offline** so that the Offline icon disappears from the Outlook status bar.

7   Press **F9** to force an immediate synchronization.

8   In the **Navigation** pane, under **Other Calendars**, right-click **WideWorldImporters - Calendar**, and then click **Open in Web Browser** to confirm that the appointment that you added in Outlook appears in the SharePoint Calendar list.

✖ CLEAN UP **Close the browser. Leave Outlook open if you are continuing to the next exercise.**

Managing SharePoint alerts in Outlook

When you create an alert for an item, such as a document, list item, document library, list, survey, or search result, you immediately receive a confirmation email message notifying you that the alert was created successfully. This message indicates that the alert process is working. The confirmation message also contains information about the alert and provides links to the SharePoint site where the item is located. When someone makes a change to the item, you receive an email message alert that indicates what was changed, who made the change, and when the change was made. You should create an alert when content has changed and you need (or want) to take notice of it.

To avoid alerts swamping your inbox, you should carefully choose the SharePoint content about which you wish to be alerted. Ideally, you should select only important content that you want to monitor. Consider subscribing to RSS feeds to monitor other SharePoint content that is not as important and that does not need your close supervision.

By default, Microsoft SharePoint Foundation does not provide an alert aggregation capability for all of your alerts across every SharePoint site. To manage your alerts by using the browser, you would have to visit each site that has an alert set. To help manage your alerts, you could save the email notifying you that an alert was created successfully. You could then use the email to go to those sites on which the alerts are set.

In an environment where many SharePoint sites exist, managing your alerts could be a daunting task if they are monitored and organized merely by the links in your email alert messages and by memory. With the **Outlook Rules and Alerts** dialog box, you can manage email alerts received from all SharePoint intranet sites and trusted websites, including any or all of the following options:

- **Alter the properties of an alert.** The **Alert Properties** dialog box provides a link to the SharePoint site, a **Modify Alert** button and a **View Item** button, and a link to the **Alerts** management page on the SharePoint site.

- **Select multiple alerts by using the Shift key or Ctrl key when you click an alert.** You can then click **Delete** to delete all the alerts that you selected. Click **Yes** on the **Microsoft Outlook** warning dialog box that appears, asking whether you want to delete the selected rows.

- **Use Outlook E-mail Rules to manage your alerts.** You can create **E-mail Rules** so that a notification window pops up, a sound is played, the alert email message is moved to a specified folder, or some other action is performed on receipt of an alert message.

  SEE ALSO Chapter 3 and Chapter 6, "Making lists and libraries work for you," both cover additional information on managing alerts on lists and documents from the browser.

In the following exercise, you will use Outlook to create a new alert.

14

SET UP Open Outlook, if it is not already open. The exercise will use the SharePoint Contacts list that you used earlier in this chapter, but you can use another Contacts list if you want.

IMPORTANT Verify that you have sufficient rights to create an alert on the Contacts list. If in doubt, see Appendix A.

1 Click the **File** tab to display the backstage, and then click **Manage Rules & Alerts** at the bottom of the middle pane. You may need to scroll down.

2 In the **Rules and Alerts** dialog box that appears, click the **Manage Alerts** tab.

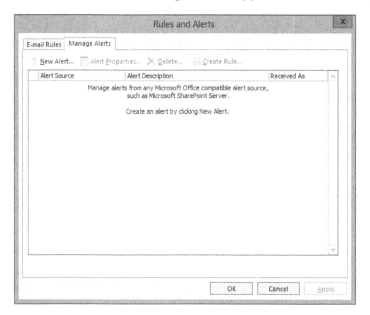

3 Click **New Alert** to display the **New Alert** dialog box, and in the **Web site Address** box, type the Uniform Resource Locator (URL) of a SharePoint site that contains a Contacts list.

4   Click **Open** to display the **New Alert** page in the browser, and then select **Contacts**.

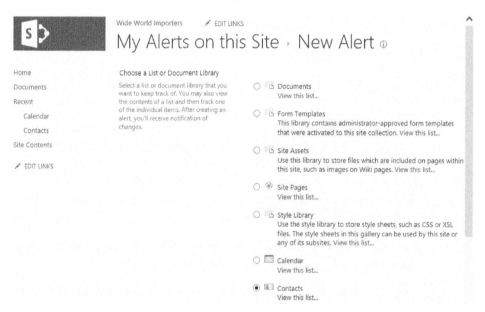

5   Scroll down and click **Next** to display the second **New Alert** page.

14

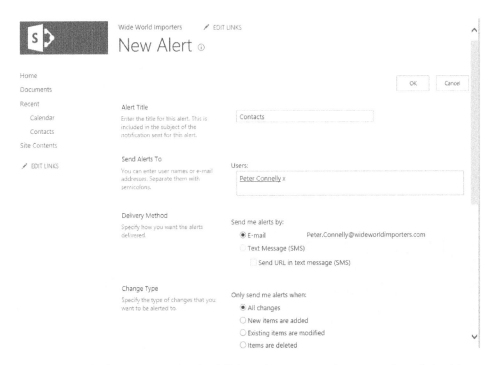

TIP The **Send Alerts To** section is visible only to users who are assigned the Manage Lists permissions for the list. This section allows users who manage the list to configure alerts for other users.

6 In the **Send Alerts To** section, type your email address, if it doesn't already appear, and then review the other settings.

7 Click **OK** to display the **My Alerts On This Site** page, where under the **Frequency: Immediate** area, the alert named **Contacts** is listed.

TROUBLESHOOTING If your SharePoint server is not configured to send email, an **Error** page will appear. Only a server administrator can configure email settings for a SharePoint installation.

8 Close all browser windows and switch to Outlook, where the **Rules and Alerts** dialog box should still be visible. A new alert, **Contacts: All items (All Changes)**, should be listed.

TROUBLESHOOTING If the alert does not appear in the **Rules and Alerts** dialog box, click **OK**, and then click **Manage Rules & Alerts**. If the new alert still does not appear, then exit Outlook. Restart Outlook, and then reopen the **Rules and Alerts** dialog box.

CLEAN UP Close all Outlook dialog boxes. Leave Outlook open if you are continuing to the next exercise.

Configuring an RSS feed

In the previous section, you learned how to manage alerts, which are notifications received via email that notify you when content has changed in a SharePoint list or library. Alerts are a "push" method of notification. SharePoint pushes content automatically to you based on specific criteria at predefined intervals, which you select.

Outlook supports RSS (this acronym previously meant *Rich Site Summary*), which is another method of notifying you when something has changed or new content is published within a SharePoint site. RSS is a "pull" method of notification. You decide when to use an RSS reader to read content exposed as RSS feeds. You will not be automatically notified when there is any new content or changed content; therefore, most people will use RSS to stay updated on the latest news on websites and blogs, but it can also be used by sites to distribute pictures or audio or video content.

Sites that expose their content via RSS are said to have an RSS feed. Outlook allows you to syndicate this content, and such programs are called *RSS readers*. You can manage your RSS feeds in Outlook just like other mail by flagging them for follow-up, assigning them a specific color, or automating any process by using **E-mail Rules**.

You can create an RSS feed on content stored in a SharePoint list. Therefore, very simple business processes can be handled by alerts. RSS suits ad hoc queries or processes. More complex business processes can be managed using the built-in workflows or by using Microsoft SharePoint Designer 2013 or Microsoft Visual Studio 2012.

SEE ALSO More information on built-in workflows can be found in Chapter 11, "Working with workflows."

In this exercise, you will add an RSS feed to Outlook.

SET UP Open the browser and display the SharePoint list or library with which you would like to subscribe to the RSS feed. The exercise will use the *http://wideworldimporters* site and the Documents library, but you can use whatever site and list or library you want.

14

1   On the **Library** or **List** tab, in the **Share & Track** group, click **RSS Feed** to display information about files in the Documents page as an RSS feed.

2   Right-click **Subscribe to this feed**, and then click **Copy Shortcut**.

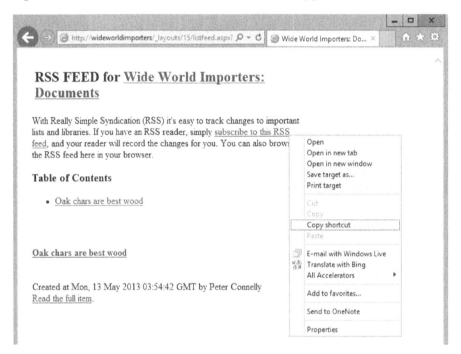

TIP You can also copy the URL of the RSS feed from the browser address box.

3   Open Outlook, if it is not already open. On the navigation bar, under your mail folders, right-click **RSS Feeds**, and then click **Add a New RSS Feed**.

4   In the **New RSS Feed** dialog box, in the **Enter the location of the RSS Feed** box,
    press **Ctrl+V** to paste the shortcut that you copied in step 2.

5   Click **Add** to close the **New RSS Feed** dialog box. A **Microsoft Outlook** dialog box
    appears.

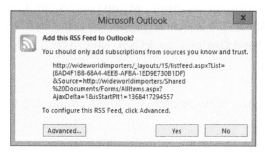

6   Click **Advanced** to open the **RSS Feed Options** dialog box.

7   In the **General** section, in the **Feed Name** box, type **WideWorldImporters:
    Documents**.

14

8   Click **OK** to close the **RSS Feed Options** dialog box, and then click **Yes** to close the **Microsoft Outlook** dialog box.

The RSS feed, **WideWorldImporters: Documents**, appears as a folder. The details pane displays an entry for each document in the Documents library.

TIP You can change the properties of the RSS Feed as follows: Click the **File** tab to display the backstage, and then click **Account Settings**. From the drop-down list, click **Account Settings** to display the **Account Settings** dialog box. Click the **RSS Feeds** tab, and then select the RSS Feed whose properties you wish to modify. Click **Change** to display the **RSS Feed Options** dialog box, where you can change the **RSS Feed** properties.

✖ CLEAN UP **Exit Outlook. Leave the browser open if you are continuing to the next exercise.**

Using Lync Presence with documents in libraries

With Lync Server 2013 installed, you can see a user's presence. You can click a user's name in many applications to start an instant message, a web conference, a persistent chat, or an audio or video conversation, as well as content sharing. Or, when you look at a document stored in SharePoint (on-premises or SharePoint within Microsoft Office 365) or SkyDrive, and you click the name of the author of the document, you can initiate communication with that person. This method of collaboration is also available when you open an office document using one of the Office client applications, including Microsoft Visio 2013.

TIP With the Lync Server 2013 Persistent Chat Server, you can organize or participate in real-time discussions in virtual rooms. These discussions are searchable and persist. Persistent Chat is not available in Microsoft Lync Online.

The Lync Server 2013 client user interface has been redesigned to be intuitive and touch-friendly, which provides availability across a large number of devices. You can start communication with other users, whether you or they are using, for example, a mobile phone, and if the phone has video capabilities, a video call can be made. The Microsoft Lync Web App allows PC and Mac users to join a Lync meeting from within an HTML5-capable browser, and delivers a full Lync meeting experience, including high-definition video, voice over IP, instant messaging, and the integration with desktop applications, such as with Microsoft Office PowerPoint sharing.

Other improvements include the use of high-definition pictures, with its integration with Exchange Server, and enhanced contact cards, which you see consistently through all Office client applications, Office Web Apps, and SharePoint.

A presence status is provided by Lync, even when telecommuting. Presence shows your availability and that of other members of your team, and your willingness to communicate. You can manually change your presence status, but it can also be changed based on device activity, an integrated calendar, your mobile status, and your call or meeting status. The presence states are as you would imagine: with text and a color image; for example, **Available** is a green square, **Away** is an orange square, and **Busy** is a red square.

TIP Your organization can also create custom presence states.

You can optionally share your location, or it can be set automatically to your organization's network elements, which are mapped to a physical address or manually entered, thereby

14

keeping you and other users informed. When privacy or confidentiality is a concern, you can modify your settings to show presence updates only to those contacts on your buddy list.

Your presence can be federated with other public networks, such as Skype, AOL, and Google Talk, and between other organizations using Lync Server, Lync Online, or Microsoft Office Communication Server.

The use of Lync enhances the collaboration functionality of SharePoint. This is very useful if you are taking advantage of coauthoring functionality, which enables multiple users to work on a file at any time, without interfering with each other's changes. Coauthoring can only be used in libraries where versioning is enabled and checkout is not used. You can coauthor Microsoft Office application files, such as those created in Word 2010 and Word 2013, Excel 2010 and Excel 2013, PowerPoint 2010 and PowerPoint 2013, OneNote 2010 and OneNote 2013, and Visio 2013 using one of the Office client applications or one of the Office Web Apps.

For example, when more than one user is editing a Visio file, and that file is stored in SharePoint, the Visio client application displays an icon on the status bar that indicates the number of users editing the file. When the icon is clicked, the list of authors appears. By hovering over the author names, a callout displays contact information, along with the options to start an instant message, a call, or a video call, or to send an email.

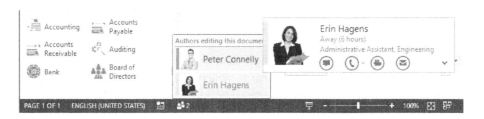

You can see similar information in the backstage view, on the **Info** tab.

WideWorldImporters Sales Process.vsdx - Visio Professional

Info

WideWorldImporters Sales Process

http://wideworldimporters » Shared Documents

Send a Message ▾

People Currently Editing

Last updated today at 6:51 PM

Peter Connelly

Erin Hagens

In this exercise, you will initiate an instant message using a contact card from a file in a library.

 SET UP **Open a SharePoint site, and go to a library that contains a document uploaded by another user who is available for you to start an instant message.**

1 Hover over the person's name in the **Modified By** column to display the callout.

2 Click the down arrow in the bottom-right corner to display the contact card.

14

Documents

⊕ new document or drag files here

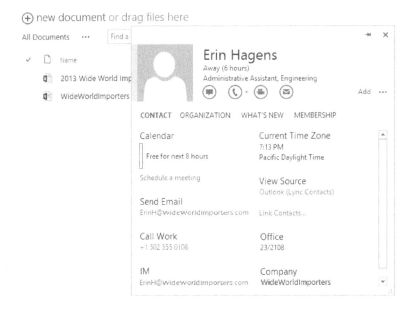

All Documents ⋯   Find a

✓ ▢ Name

   ▣ 2013 Wide World Imp

   ▣ WideWorldImporters

Erin Hagens
Away (6 hours)
Administrative Assistant, Engineering

CONTACT ORGANIZATION WHAT'S NEW MEMBERSHIP

Calendar

Free for next 8 hours

Schedule a meeting

Send Email
ErinH@wideworldimporters.com

Call Work
+1 502 555 0108

IM
ErinH@wideworldimporters.com

Current Time Zone
7:13 PM
Pacific Daylight Time

View Source
Outlook (Lync Contacts)

Link Contacts...

Office
23/2108

Company
WideWorldImporters

Add ⋯

3   Under **IM**, click the person's email address to display a **Pop Out Conversation** dialog box.

4   Type, **Can we have a chat about this document?**, and then press **Enter**.

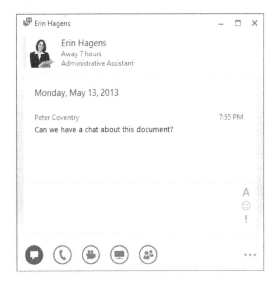

Erin Hagens

Erin Hagens
Away 7 hours
Administrative Assistant

Monday, May 13, 2013

Peter Coventry   7:55 PM
Can we have a chat about this document?

CLEAN UP Close the Pop Out Conversation dialog box. Leave the browser open if you are continuing to the next exercise.

Creating site mailboxes

Site mailboxes allow you to work with content from both Exchange Server and SharePoint Server. The contents of site mailboxes remain in their original locations—that is, email remains on the Exchange Server, and documents remain within their SharePoint sites; however, you can see and work with them from either Outlook or SharePoint.

When SharePoint Server and Exchange Server are configured by your server administrator to use site mailboxes, and the **Site Mailbox** site feature is activated, a site mailbox can be created for a site through SharePoint. To create a site mailbox, add a Site Mailbox app to your site, and then on the **Site Content** page, click **Site Mailbox**, which creates the site mailbox. It may take a while for the site mailbox creation process to complete. When the site mailbox is fully configured, an email message is sent to everyone in the site's Owners and Members groups. You can use your SharePoint site while the site mailbox is created.

TROUBLESHOOTING If your SharePoint Server and Exchange Server environment has not been configured to use site mailboxes, when you click **Site Mailbox** on the **Site Contents** page, a page appears, stating that your SharePoint Server configuration is not supported. If this is the case, you will not be able to complete the following exercise. The **Site Mailbox** feature at the site level must also be activated.

Wide World Importers
Site Mailbox

Your SharePoint Server configuration is not supported

Your organization's SharePoint Server configuration is not supported. Please contact your system administrator for more information.

Correlation ID: 1cba1a9c-1d5a-5067-249a-27fa172e0714, Error Code 103

Sunday, May 12, 2013 8:56:18 AM

The first time you open the site mailbox, you will be prompted to set up the language and time zone options.

14

Outlook Web App

Choose your preferred display language and home time zone below:

Language:

| English (United Kingdom) | ∨ |

Time zone:

| (UTC) Dublin, Edinburgh, Lisbon, London | ∨ |

⊘ save

Once created, users who belong to either the site's Members group or Owners group can see and work with the content in the site mailbox. If you do not have sufficient permissions to view the content in a site mailbox, or you have only recently been given access to a site mailbox, then an **Almost there!** page appears.

Almost there!

This site mailbox is all set up, but it looks like you don't have permission to access this site mailbox. Double-check to make sure that your name appears in the site's default owners or default members group. If you were recently added, it may take up to one day to receive access.

Once a site mailbox is created for your site, a new email account is created, which uses the name of your site. For example, if your site has the title, "Wide World Importers," spaces will be removed and the email address for that site mailbox will be *WideWorldImporters@wide-worldimporters.com*. This email address cannot be changed; therefore, when you create a site, you should choose a name that works well as an email address.

Site mailboxes improve collaboration and user productivity by allowing access to both SharePoint Server and Exchange Server using the same interface. They help team members keep relevant information in a single place. New team members can use the site mailbox as an easy way to learn about a new project.

SEE ALSO More information on using site mailboxes can be found at *blogs.technet.com/b/exchange/archive/2012/08/22/site-mailboxes-in-the-new-office.aspx*.

In this exercise, you will add the Site Mailbox app to a SharePoint site. You will review the site mailbox in Outlook.

➡ SET UP **Open a SharePoint site where you would like to create a Site Mailbox app.**

IMPORTANT Verify that you have sufficient rights to create a Site Mailbox app. If in doubt, see Appendix A.

1 From the **Settings** gear icon, click **add an app**, and then on the **Your Apps** page, click **Site Mailbox**.

2 On the **Site Contents** page, click **Site Mailbox**.

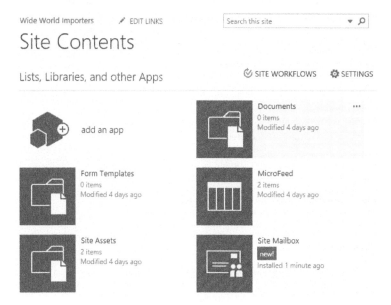

3 The Outlook Web App opens. Select the language and time zone for your site's mailbox, and then wait for the site mailbox setup to complete.

14

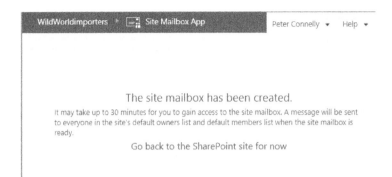

The site mailbox has been created.

It may take up to 30 minutes for you to gain access to the site mailbox. A message will be sent to everyone in the site's default owners list and default members list when the site mailbox is ready.

Go back to the SharePoint site for now

4   On **The site mailbox has been created** page, click **Go back to the SharePoint site now** to return to your SharePoint site, and then wait for the site mailbox to be created. It may take several minutes to several hours.

5   Open Outlook 2013, if it is not already open. You should have received an email stating that your site has a new mailbox.

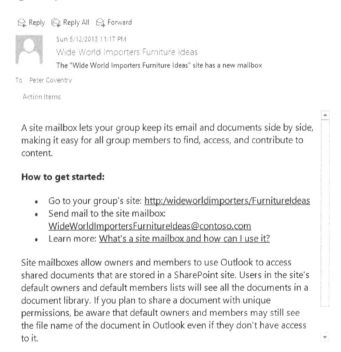

6   In the folder pane, expand your site mailbox and review the folders.

7   In the folder pane, click **Documents** and review the list of documents already in the document library on your SharePoint site.

TROUBLESHOOTING If the Documents folder does not display, exit Outlook, and then reopen it.

✖ CLEAN UP **Close any open browser windows and exit Outlook.**

Key points

- You can copy contacts listed in your personal Outlook Contacts folder both to and from a SharePoint Contacts list.

- You can copy and move SharePoint list items both to and from Outlook.

- You can connect any SharePoint Contacts list, Calendar, Tasks list, and discussion board to Outlook. This action creates a folder in Outlook that you can synchronize with the SharePoint list or that synchronizes automatically every 20 minutes.

- In Outlook, you can view multiple calendars side by side. These calendars can be connected to SharePoint Calendar lists.

- You can aggregate and manage all of your tasks in one place whether you created them within Outlook, in a SharePoint Tasks list, or within OneNote.

- You can manage all of your SharePoint alerts from the **Rules and Alerts** dialog box in Outlook.

- You can manage your RSS feeds in Outlook, just like your other mail, by flagging them for follow-up, assigning them a specific color, or by automating any process through **E-mail Rules**.

- The use of Lync enhances the collaboration functionality of SharePoint.

- With site mailboxes, you can work with content from both Exchange Server and SharePoint Server.

- The contents of site mailboxes remain in their original locations—that is, email remains on the Exchange server and documents remain within their SharePoint sites; however, you can see and work with them from either Outlook or SharePoint.

- Users must be added to the site's Members group or Owners group to see and work with the content in the site mailbox.

14

Chapter at a glance

Work

Work with Document Sets, page 552

Organize

Organize content, page 557

Create

Create a page layout, page 579

Define

Define a SharePoint site policy, page 594

Working with content management

15

IN THIS CHAPTER, YOU WILL LEARN HOW TO

- Work with Document IDs and Document Sets.

- Organize content.

- Create a Records Center and manage records.

- Configure in place records management.

- Create publishing sites.

- Create and manage page layouts.

- Use reusable content and product catalogs.

- Define a SharePoint site policy.

Microsoft SharePoint Server is an Enterprise Content Management (ECM) system. It contains a core set of enterprise document management features that can store millions and millions of documents, which can be accessed at a high retrieval rate. It includes record sets and electronic records management features that are becoming more critical to organizations. It provides mechanisms for the authoring, branding, and the controlled publishing of web content, known as *Web Content Management* (WCM). As you can see, ECM is a broad subject area that this chapter can only introduce you to.

Microsoft SharePoint Server 2010 has many of the basic ECM components that remain in place in Microsoft SharePoint Server 2013, including major and minor versioning; check-in and checkout; content approval; version trimming; multiple file uploads; an explorer view of libraries; the synchronization of offline files; and the ability to define data (metadata) at the site, site collection, and enterprise levels using site columns, content types, enterprise content types, keywords, and term sets.

SharePoint Server 2010 also provides many site templates that you can use as a basis for managing content, such as the Document Center and the Records Center. With the records management mechanism, you can enforce content control specified by external pressures, such as those from legislators, regulators, auditors, and legal processes. Not only can you place holds on records and associate them with retention and expiration policies, Microsoft SharePoint Server 2013 now includes two methods for search and locating files: using the Records Center's eDiscovery features and creating sites from the eDiscovery Center site template.

Any library can make use of these features, including Document IDs and the Content Organizer, which automatically move documents to the libraries where they should be stored.

With SharePoint 2010, WCM functionality mainly consists of WCM pages, known as *publishing pages*, which are based on page layouts. The WCM feature uses document management capabilities to manage pages so that you can check pages in and out, as well as use the Approval workflow.

Content authors usually add static content to pages and dynamically displayed data from lists or libraries by using the Content Query Web Part (CQWP); however, those lists and libraries have to be stored within sites in the same site collection.

SharePoint Server 2013 introduces additional WCM functionality that is based on displaying content using search, as well as the structure of the site. Navigation can be organized by managed metadata. WCM pages can roll up content from anywhere within your SharePoint implementation using cross-site collection publishing (XSP) and the Content Search Web Part (CSWP). This scenario is particularly suited for an organization that needs to provide information on a range of products, and SharePoint Server provides a new site template, Product Catalog, which can be used as a basis for such a scenario.

TIP To use many of the ECM features, you need to activate these features at either the site collection or site level. Chapter 5, "Creating and managing sites," contains information on features.

In this chapter, you will learn how to configure Document IDs, how to create a Document Set, how to use the Content Organizer, how to create a Records Center site, how to manage records, and how to use in place records management. You will also learn how to create a publishing site, as well as how to create and manage page layouts. You will then activate the cross-site collection feature and define a site policy.

IMPORTANT Remember to use your SharePoint site location in place of *http:// wideworldmporters* in the following exercises.

Working with Document IDs

When you upload a file to a library, it is assigned a web address based on the library URL and the file name. When a file is moved to a different library, it is assigned a new web address; therefore, links that were created when the file was stored in the first location no longer work now that the file has been moved. Similarly, when you submit content to a repository, a new web address is created again, and you will not find it later using the original URL if it has been moved from its original location. In these scenarios, you may consider using the Document ID feature, which is a site collection level feature. Once activated at the site collection level, all documents in all libraries in the site collection automatically receive a unique ID.

Document IDs consist of the following two parts:

- A prefix, which is randomly generated, so that Document IDs are unique in your SharePoint installation. You can specify the prefix using the **Document ID** settings page. You should ensure that every site collection that uses the **Document ID** feature has a unique prefix; otherwise, you could end up with duplicate IDs.

- Two numbers, which consist of the ID of the list that the document was first created in and the ID of the item in that list.

An example Document ID is SP13SBS-4-2. When you use a library view or the properties view of a file, the **Document ID** column can be displayed.

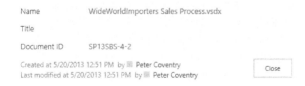

Name	WideWorldImporters Sales Process.vsdx
Title	
Document ID	SP13SBS-4-2

Created at 5/20/2013 12:51 PM by Peter Coventry
Last modified at 5/20/2013 12:51 PM by Peter Coventry

Close

TIP You can display the **Document ID** column on any library in the site collection, so that you can see the Document ID assigned to the files. This is useful if you need to reference a file elsewhere.

The Document ID column is a URL with a format like *http://wideworldimporters/_layouts/ DocIdRedir.aspx?ID=SP13SBS-4-2*. When you click this URL, search is used to find the file, and therefore the URL is valid, even if the document has been moved to another location.

IMPORTANT When documents are copied, new Document IDs are assigned. Because finding documents using their Document IDs is search dependent, when you copy a document, it cannot be found based on its new Document ID until the library you have copied it to is indexed. When you move or cut and paste documents, Document IDs are retained as long as the site collection that contains the destination library has the **Document ID Service** feature activated.

When you activate the **Document ID Service** site collection feature, new hidden site columns are added to the site collection, and those site columns are added to the Document content type and the Document Set content type. Then, a content type pushdown is triggered to all libraries that use those content types, and Document IDs are assigned to existing documents. Also, when the feature is activated, the **Find by Document ID** Web Part is made available under the **Search** category on the **Insert Web Part** pane. By referencing a Document ID in this Web Part, you can display the properties of the document. This Web Part will only look for documents in its current site collection; therefore, if you move a document to another site collection, it will not be found by the Document ID Web Part.

TIP SharePoint is configured, by default, to run Document ID–related jobs nightly. Until the jobs are run, the **Document ID Service** is not fully activated, and the existing documents in your site collection will not be assigned Document IDs immediately.

Deactivating the **Document ID Service** feature removes the link to **Document ID Settings** on the **Site Settings** page and stops the assignment of Document IDs. The **Document ID** columns remain so that, even after deactivation, existing Document IDs are preserved. After the feature is deactivated, users who try to use a static URL to look up an item by its Document ID see an error message indicating that, "This site collection is not configured to use Document IDs."

In this exercise, you will activate and configure the **Document ID Service** feature.

SET UP **Open the top level site of a site collection in which you want to activate the Document ID Service feature.**

> **IMPORTANT** Verify that you have sufficient rights to enable a site collection feature and to amend library settings. If in doubt, see Appendix A, "SharePoint 2013 user permissions and permission levels."

15

1   On the **Settings** menu, click **Site settings**. Under **Site Collection Administration**, click **Site collection features**, and to the right of **Document ID Service**, click **Activate**, if it is not already active.

> **TROUBLESHOOTING** If you do not see the **Site Collection Administration** section, then you are not a site collection administrator. If you see **Go to top level site settings**, you are not at the top level site of the site collection.

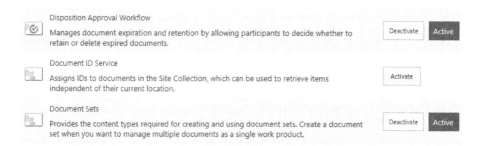

2   On the breadcrumb, click **Site Settings**, and then under **Site Collection Administration**, click **Document ID settings**.

> **TROUBLESHOOTING** If the **Document ID Settings** link is not displayed, check that the **Document ID Service** site collection feature is activated.

3   In the **Begin IDs** text box, type **SP13SBS**.

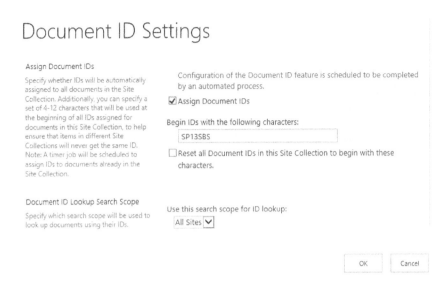

Document ID Settings

Assign Document IDs

Specify whether IDs will be automatically assigned to all documents in the Site Collection. Additionally, you can specify a set of 4-12 characters that will be used at the beginning of all IDs assigned for documents in this Site Collection, to help ensure that items in different Site Collections will never get the same ID. Note: A timer job will be scheduled to assign IDs to documents already in the Site Collection.

Configuration of the Document ID feature is scheduled to be completed by an automated process.

☑ Assign Document IDs

Begin IDs with the following characters:

SP13SBS

☐ Reset all Document IDs in this Site Collection to begin with these characters.

Document ID Lookup Search Scope

Specify which search scope will be used to look up documents using their IDs.

Use this search scope for ID lookup:

All Sites ▼

OK   Cancel

4   Click **OK**.

❌ CLEAN UP **Leave the browser open if you are continuing to the next exercise.**

Creating Document Sets

As part of a business process, you may find that you always have three or four related files, such as a new product proposal created in Microsoft Office PowerPoint, a Microsoft Office Excel file with supporting financial information, and a product sheet created with Microsoft Office Word. You could use the metadata in a column to group them together, or you could use a folder. With SharePoint Server, you can group different files as one item or as a set by using the **Document Sets** site collection feature. With Document Sets, you can standardize the production of proposals, project documentation, and other content that has multiple files.

Document Sets can share metadata with their contents, making it easier to tag and manage content. Workflows can be run on individual items within a set, or on the Document Set as a whole. For example, you may have a Document Set that defines legal cases. You can specify that when a legal case is closed, the Document Set that represents that legal case can be routed, with all of its content, to a Records Center site for storage and eventual disposition.

You can use versioning with Document Sets. When you change the version of a document within the Document Set, the version number of the document is incremented, but the version number of the Document Set remains unchanged. To change the version number of the Document Set, on the **Manage** tab, in the **Manage** group, click **Capture Version**. Capturing a version of a Document Set is similar to taking a snapshot. The current properties of the documents within the documents are saved. You have the choice to include only the current major version of the documents within the Document Set or the latest minor version.

SEE ALSO There are many settings that you can use to customize your Document Set; for example, each Document Set comes with its own Welcome page, which is like the home page for your Team site. More information can be found at *technet.microsoft.com/en-us/library/ff603637.aspx*.

In this exercise, you will enable the **Document Sets** site collection feature, if it is not already activated, create a Document Set content type and add it to a library, and then create a Document Set.

 SET UP **Open the top level site of a site collection where you want to activate the Document Set feature. This exercise uses two files, ProductProposalPresentation.pptx and ProductSheet.docx, in the Chapter15 practice folder; you could use any files.**

> **IMPORTANT** Verify that you have sufficient rights to enable a site collection feature and to amend library settings. If in doubt, see Appendix A.

1   From the **Settings** menu, click **Site settings**. Under **Site Collection Administration**, click **Site collection features**, and to the right of **Document Sets**, click **Activate**, if it is not already active.

    TIP If you create a new site collection, this feature is automatically enabled; for example, if you used the Team Site template to create the top level site. However, if you have upgraded from SharePoint 2010, you may need to activate the feature.

2   Go to the site where you want to create the Document Set content type. From the **Settings** menu, click **Site settings**, and then under **Web Designer Galleries**, click **Site content types**.

3   On the **Site Content Types** page, click **Create** to display the **New Site Content Types** page.

4   In the **Name** box, type **Product Proposals**.

5   In the **Select parent content type from** list, select **Document Set Content Types**, and in the **Parent Content Type** list, select **Document Set**.

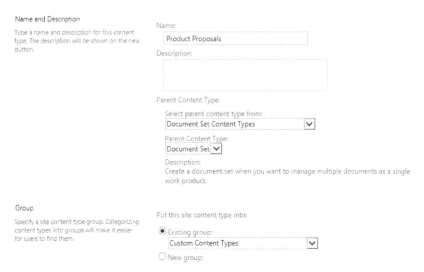

6   Click **OK** to display the **Site Content Type** page, and then under **Settings**, click **Document Set settings**.

7   On the **Document Set Settings** page, in the **Default Content** section, click **Browse** to the right of **File name**, and then go to the **Chapter15** practice folder. Click **ProductProposalPresentation**, and then click **Open**.

8   Click **Add new default content** and repeat step 7 to use **ProductSheet**.

Site Content Type ▸ Document Set Settings

Allowed Content Types

Select from the list of available site content types to add them to the Document Set.

Select site content types from:

All Groups ▾

Available Site Content Types:

| Html Page Layout ^ |
| Image |
| Item Display Template |
| JavaScript Display Template |
| Link to a Document |
| List View Style |
| Master Page |
| Master Page Preview ▾ |
| Page |

Add >

Remove

Content types allowed in the Document Set:

Document

Description:
Article Page is a system content type template created by the Publishing Resources feature. It is the associated content type template for the default page layouts used to create article pages in sites that have the Publishing feature enabled.

Group: Page Layout Content Types

Default Content

If you want new Document Sets that are created from this content type to include specific items, upload those items here and specify their content types. To create a folder in the document set where one or more items will be stored, type or paste a name in the Folder box.

Content Type	Folder	File Name		
Document ▾		/ \Documents\ProductProposalPresentation.pptx	Browse...	⊞ Delete
Document ▾		/ 55\Users\Public\Documents\ProductSheet.docx	Browse...	⊞ Delete

Add new default content ...

☑ Add the name of the Document Set to each file name

9 At the bottom of the page, click **OK** to redisplay the **Site Content Type** page.

10 On the **Quick Launch**, click **Site Contents**, and then click the library where you want to add the Document Set content type that you have just created.

11 On the **Library** tab, in the **Settings** group, click **Library Settings**.

12 On the **Settings** page, under **General Settings**, click **Advanced settings**, and then under **Allow management of content type**, select **Yes**, if it is not already selected. At the bottom of the page, click **OK**.

13 On the **Settings** page, under **Content Types**, click **Add from existing site content types**.

14 On the **Add Content Types** page, under **Select site content types from**, select **Custom Content Types**, and then under **Available Site Content Types**, select **Product Proposals**. Click **Add**.

Settings › Add Content Types ⓘ

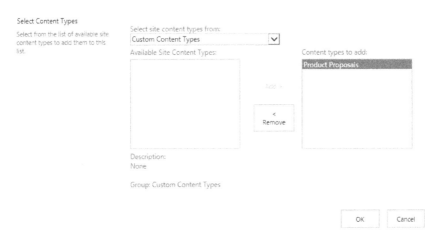

Select Content Types

Select from the list of available site content types to add them to this list.

Select site content types from:

Custom Content Types

Available Site Content Types:

Content types to add:

Product Proposals

Add >

<
Remove

Description:
None

Group: Custom Content Types

OK   Cancel

15   Click **OK**, and then in the breadcrumb, click the library name.

16   On the **Files** tab, click the **New Document** down arrow.

17   Click **Product Proposals**, and then in the **Name** box, type **2014 Madrid Kitchen Furniture**.

New Document Set: Product Proposals

✎ Spelling...

Name *   2014 Madrid Kitchen Furniture

Description

A description of the Document Set

Save   Cancel

18   Click **Save** to display the welcome page for the **2014 Madrid Kitchen Furniture** Document Set.

Documents ▸ 2014 Madrid Kitchen Furniture

2014 Madrid Kitchen Furniture

View All Properties
Edit Properties

⊕ new document or drag files here

Find a file   🔍

✓	🗋	Name		Modified	Modified By
	📊	2014 Madrid Kitchen Furniture - ProductProposalPresentation ✻	•••	A few seconds ago	🔲 Peter Connelly
	📄	2014 Madrid Kitchen Furniture - ProductSheet ✻	•••	A few seconds ago	🔲 Peter Connelly

✖ CLEAN UP **Leave the browser open if you are continuing to the next exercise.**

Organizing content

The Content Organizer not only allows you to automatically route documents to different libraries, and folders within those libraries, you can also use it, for example, to make sure that any folder within a library contains no more than, say, 2,500 items. When file number 2,501 is added to the library, the Content Organizer can automatically create a new folder and put the file in that folder. All of this routing and folder creation can be handled automatically without requiring user intervention. After a document is uploaded and the required metadata applied, the upload form displays the URL to the location that the document has been routed; therefore, you know where to find it in the future. The Content Organizer uses the same routing engine as the Records Center site.

TIP The Content Organizer cannot route documents to a Document Set, nor does it redirect pages. However, you can move a Document Set as long as the content type is added to the destination library. SharePoint will zip the Document Set to do this.

To use the Content Organizer, the **Content Organizer** site feature must be activated, and it will only work with content types based on the Document content type. Once the Content Organizer site feature is activated, a new library, the **Drop Off Library**, is created. Two new links are provided under **Site Administration** on the **Site Settings** page: **Content Organizer Settings** and **Content Organizer Rules**.

Documents are routed as follows:

- Documents with the correct content type, metadata, and matching rules are automatically routed to the destination library or folder. The Content Organizer will move the content to the new location whether or not the contributing user has access to the destination location. The user ID of the contributing user will be used for the **Modified By** property on the destination document.

- Documents that lack the metadata required to match a rule, or that are missing required metadata, are stored in the **Drop Off Library** so that the metadata can be entered.

- When you create a rule that uses content types, the first time that you add a rule for that content type, the content type is automatically added to the **Drop Off Library**.

- Content types are not automatically added to the destination library; you must manually add them if they are required.

Use the **Content Organizer Settings** page to configure whether to route documents that are added to the site based on rules. Any changes made here affect routing for the entire site. The **Content Organizer Settings** page consists of the following seven sections:

- **Redirect Users to the Drop Off Library** Select this check box to redirect files that are uploaded to libraries with rules to the Drop Off Library. Files loaded into libraries that have no rules are unaffected. When a file is uploaded, the document properties window for Drop Off Library appears, which you can use to enter the metadata properties. Once the routing rules are applied to the document, you will be shown the destination URL for the file. If the check box is cleared, you can bypass the organizer and upload the files directly to a library or folder.

- **Sending to Another Site** Select this check box to allow rules for directing uploads in the current site to route to other sites. The destination site must also have the **Content Organizer** site feature installed and activated. You can only route files to other sites in site collections within a SharePoint web application.

Site Settings › Content Organizer: Settings ⓘ

Redirect Users to the Drop Off Library

When this setting is enabled, users are redirected to the Drop Off Library when they try to upload content to libraries in this site that have one or more content organizer rules pointing to them.
If this setting is disabled, users can always bypass the organizer and upload files directly to a library or folder.

Users will never be redirected to the Drop Off Library when organizing pages.

☑ Require users to use the organizer when submitting new content to libraries with one or more organizer rules pointing to them

Sending to Another Site

If there are too many items to fit into one site collection, enable this setting to distribute content to other sites that also have content organizers.

☐ Allow rules to specify another site as a target location

- **Folder Partitioning** Select this check box to create a threshold limit on the number of files that can be stored in a library. Once the limit is reached, the organizer will create subfolders. You can create very large document libraries by nesting folders.

- **Duplicate Submissions** Select this check box to decide what happens when you upload a file that already exists in the library. You can decide to create a new version, if versioning is enabled in the library, or to append unique characters to the end of the file name.

Folder Partitioning

The organizer can automatically create subfolders once a target location exceeds a certain size.

☐ Create subfolders after a target location has too many items

Number of items in a single folder: 2500

Format of folder name: Submitted after %1

%1 is replaced by the date and time the folder is created.

Duplicate Submissions

Specify what should occur when a file with the same name already exists in a target location.
If versioning is not enabled in a target library, the organizer will append unique characters to duplicate submissions regardless of the setting selected here.

◉ Use SharePoint versioning
○ Append unique characters to the end of duplicate filenames

- **Preserving Context** Select this check box to save the original audit logs and properties of the files. This is particularly important when using Records Center sites, so that all the historical information about a file is retained. If this information is retained, you can view it by clicking **Compliance Details** in the **View Properties** page.

- **Rule Managers** Use this section to add the users or groups that you want to manage the Content Organizer rules. These users must have Manage Web Site permission to edit rules.

- **Submission Points** Use this section for information on configuring how other sites or email messaging software sends content to the site. By default, email integration with Content Organizer is not enabled; your SharePoint server administrator will need to active this feature. Once activated, you can create a rule to route information submitted by an email. On the **New Rule** page, in the **Submission's Content Type** section, in the **Type** list, select **E-mail Submission**. In the **Conditions** section, you can choose email fields such as **Subject**, **To**, **From**, and **CC**.

Preserving Context

The organizer can save the original audit logs and properties if they are included with submissions. The saved logs and properties are stored in an audit entry on the submitted document.

☐ Save the original audit log and properties of submitted content

Rule Managers

Specify the users who manage the rules and can respond when incoming content doesn't match any rule.

Rule Managers must have the Manage Web Site permission to access the content organizer rules list from the site settings page.

☑ E-mail rule managers when submissions do not match a rule
☑ E-mail rule managers when content has been left in the Drop Off Library
Enter users or groups separated by semicolons:

Peter Connelly

Number of days to wait before sending an e-mail: 3

Submission Points

Use this information to set up other sites or e-mail messaging software to send content to this site.

Web service URL: http://wideworldimporters/_vti_bin/OfficialFile.asmx
E-mail address:

Use the **Content Organizer Rules** page to create the rules that are used for routing documents. Any rules created here are used to route individual files based on metadata attributes that you choose. The **New Rule** page consists of the following five sections:

- **Rule Name** Enter the name that you wish to give the rule.

- **Rule Status And Priority** Use this section to specify the priority of the rule and whether the rule should run on incoming files. The priority can range from 1 (highest priority) to 9 (lowest priority). This is useful when you have more than one rule, and you can select which rule should be applied first to the uploaded files.

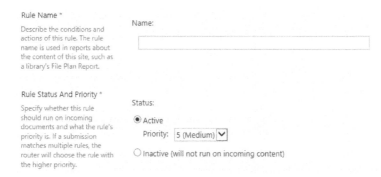

Rule Name *
Describe the conditions and actions of this rule. The rule name is used in reports about the content of this site, such as a library's File Plan Report.

Name:

Rule Status And Priority *
Specify whether this rule should run on incoming documents and what the rule's priority is. If a submission matches multiple rules, the router will choose the rule with the higher priority.

Status:
◉ Active
    Priority: 5 (Medium) ▾
○ Inactive (will not run on incoming content)

- **Submission's Content Type** Use this section to select a content type whose properties can be used in the conditions of the rule. The drop-down list box only shows the content types that are based on the Document content type. With the **Alternate names** check box, you can define existing content types that are named differently in other sites.

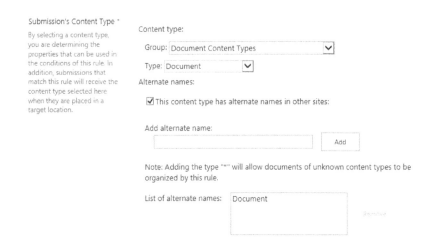

Submission's Content Type *

By selecting a content type, you are determining the properties that can be used in the conditions of this rule. In addition, submissions that match this rule will receive the content type selected here when they are placed in a target location.

Content type:

Group: Document Content Types

Type: Document

Alternate names:

☑ This content type has alternate names in other sites:

Add alternate name:

[   ] [Add]

Note: Adding the type "*" will allow documents of unknown content types to be organized by this rule.

List of alternate names: | Document
Remove

- **Conditions** This is the section where the real power of the feature lies. You can create up to six conditions where the properties of the items must meet certain values.

Conditions

In order to match this rule, a submission's properties must match all the specified property conditions (e.g. "If Date Created is before 1/1/2000").

Property-based conditions:

Property: Name

Operator: begins with

Value: SBS

X

(Add another condition)

- **Target Location** Select a destination library or folder to route the file when the preceding conditions are met. It could be on the same site, or a different library on a different site. You can also create a folder for each unique value of a property.

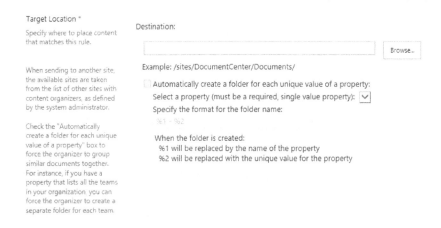

Target Location *

Specify where to place content that matches this rule.

When sending to another site, the available sites are taken from the list of other sites with content organizers, as defined by the system administrator.

Check the "Automatically create a folder for each unique value of a property" box to force the organizer to group similar documents together. For instance, if you have a property that lists all the teams in your organization, you can force the organizer to create a separate folder for each team.

Destination:

[   ] [Browse...]

Example: /sites/DocumentCenter/Documents/

☐ Automatically create a folder for each unique value of a property:

Select a property (must be a required, single value property): [∨]

Specify the format for the folder name:

%1 - %2

When the folder is created:
%1 will be replaced by the name of the property
%2 will be replaced with the unique value for the property

In the following exercise, you will enable the **Content Organizer** site feature.

SET UP **Open a SharePoint site where you'd like to use the Content Organizer.**

IMPORTANT Verify that you have sufficient rights to manage a site. If in doubt, see Appendix A.

1   On the **Settings** menu, click **Site settings**, and then under **Site Actions**, click **Manage Site Features**.

2   To the right of **Content Organizer**, click **Activate**, if it is not already active.

3   In the breadcrumb, click **Site Settings**. Under **Site Administration**, click **Content Organizer Rules**, and then click **new item**.

4   On the **New Rule** page, in the **Name** box, type, **Holiday Files**.

5   In the **Submission's Content Type** section, in the **Group** list, select **Document Content Types**, and in the **Type** list, select **Document**.

6   In the **Condition** section, in the **Property** list, select **Name**. In the **Operator** list, select **begins with**, and then in the **Value** box, type **Holiday**.

7   In the **Target Location** section, click **Browse**. Go to the library where you wish to route files that match this rule, and then click **OK**.

8   On the **Quick Launch**, click **Site Contents**, and then click **Drop Off Library**. Click **new document**. In the **Submit Document** dialog, click **Browse**, and then go to the **Chapter15** practice folder. Click **Holiday budget planner**, and then click **Open**.

9   Click **OK**. Once the document has been uploaded, the properties form appears, warning that the document will be moved.

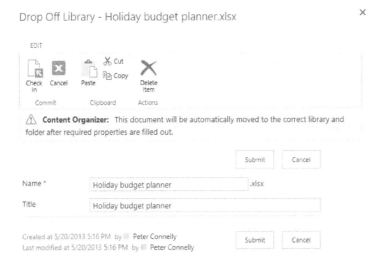

Drop Off Library - Holiday budget planner.xlsx ✕

EDIT

Check In | Cancel | Paste | ✂ Cut | 🗐 Copy | ✕ Delete Item

Commit | Clipboard | Actions

⚠ **Content Organizer:** This document will be automatically moved to the correct library and folder after required properties are filled out.

Submit | Cancel

Name * | Holiday budget planner | .xlsx

Title | Holiday budget planner

Created at 5/20/2013 5:16 PM by ▪ Peter Connelly
Last modified at 5/20/2013 5:16 PM by ▪ Peter Connelly

Submit | Cancel

10   Click **Submit** to display the **Saved to Final Destination** page. Click **OK**.

✖ CLEAN UP **Leave the browser open if you are continuing to the next exercise.**

Creating a Records Center

A *record* is a document or other electronic or physical entity that serves as evidence of an activity or transaction performed by an organization and that requires retention for some time frame. *Records management* is the process by which an organization does the following:

- Determines the type of information that should be considered a record.

- Determines how active documents (that are to become records) should be handled while they are being used, and determines how they should be collected after they are declared as records.

- Determines the manner in which and the amount of time that each record type should be retained to meet legal, business, or regulatory requirements.

- Researches and implements technological solutions and business processes to help ensure that the organization complies with its records management obligations in a cost-effective and nonintrusive way.

- Performs records-related tasks (such as disposing of expired records, or locating and protecting records) that are related to external events, such as lawsuits.

TIP Records management is not a trivial activity. It needs careful planning and the creation of a *file plan*. Information on records management planning can be found at *technet.microsoft.com/en-us/library/ff363731.aspx*.

SharePoint Server can be used in a records management solution. Records can be declared in place, or files can be archived to a records repository where they can be managed as records. You can configure a records repository as a top level site of a site collection or as a subsite by using the Records Center site template.

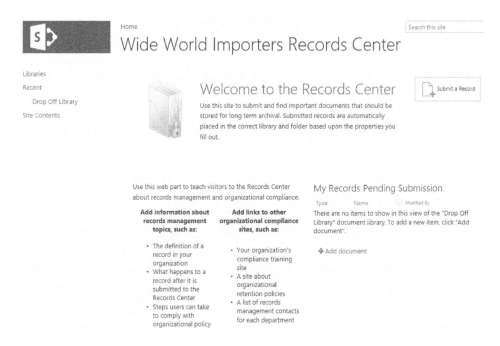

TIP A SharePoint server administrator can configure **Send To** links to send files to a Records Center site by using the Central Administration website or Windows PowerShell.

In this exercise, you will create a Records Center site.

SET UP Open a SharePoint site where you'd like to create, as a subsite, the new Records Center.

> **IMPORTANT** Verify that you have sufficient rights to create a site. If in doubt, see Appendix A.

1   Click the **Settings** gear icon, and then click **Site contents**.

2   Scroll to the bottom of the **Site Content** page, and then under **Subsites**, click **new subsite**.

3   In the **Title** text box, type **Wide World Importers Records Center**, and in the **Description** text box, type **This site is to be used as the records repository for Wide World Importers**.

4   In the **URL name** text box, type **RecordsCenter**.

5   Click the **Enterprise** tab, if it is not already active, and then click **Records Center**.

6   Leave the default settings for the options in the **Permissions** and **Navigation Inheritance** sections, and then click **Create**.

CLEAN UP Leave the browser open if you are continuing to the next exercise.

Introducing eDiscovery features

With the eDiscovery capabilities in SharePoint, legal teams can discover and export content from a variety of sources, such as documents, microblogs, wiki pages, social feeds, instant messages, and emails. The Discovery Center is completely redesigned in SharePoint Server 2013 and has a new site template, which you can use to create the top level site of a site collection; however, you can use core eDiscovery features in a Records Center.

Cases

Site Contents

Welcome to the eDiscovery Center

Use this site to create, manage and work on eDiscovery Cases. With eDiscovery Cases you can manage the identification and in-place hold of Exchange mailboxes, SharePoint sites, and other sources of content. You can also create and manage search queries to identify relevant content and then export the search results.

Create new case

Get Started

1. Grant your legal users permissions to access content across your SharePoint deployment. We recommend creating a security group that contains your legal team members.
2. To discover Exchange mailboxes, ensure your administrator has installed the Exchange Web Services Managed Client on all SharePoint servers and have your administrator configure

In-Place Hold, Search, & Export

- With in-place holds you can specify SharePoint sites and mailboxes to place on hold. When content is modified or deleted it will be stored in-place until you need to export it.
- In-place eDiscovery search allows you to search across SharePoint sites, file shares, and

A Discovery Center is usually deployed as a single, centralized enterprise-wide portal in which individual users who have access rights are able to create and manipulate discovery cases across multiple SharePoint farms and in Microsoft Exchange. All of the data managed by the Discovery Center can be exported into the industry-standard Electronic Data Reference Model (EDRM) XML format, so that it can be imported into a review tool.

The eDiscovery features in SharePoint Server 2013 have been specifically reengineered for managing eDiscovery cases and holds, as follows:

- An eDiscovery set is a combination of sources, queries, and potentially in place holds. An eDiscovery set source could include Exchange mailboxes, SharePoint sites, and Microsoft Lync conversations.

- A *hold* is a method to preserve content, which is especially useful when the content is needed in legal proceedings or in regulatory reviews, such as an audit. This content is usually identified by an organization as a record. By placing a hold on content, you prevent the deletion of content from any retention or expiration policies.

    TIP In any review process, it is important that reviewers have the ability to find content. With eDiscovery features, you can focus queries by using filters and exporting the results of those queries.

In SharePoint Server 2010, you can place documents, pages, and list items on hold, which prevents users from deleting or editing them. SharePoint Server 2013 provides in place holds, which can be used to preserve sites and Exchange mailboxes. An in place hold also makes it possible for users to continue to edit or even delete preserved content, thereby allowing users to continue working on the content without realizing that a hold has been placed on the content. This is important when you do not want it to be obvious to users that the content is being reviewed.

An in place hold is applied at the site level. When an in place hold is applied, a copy of the content is preserved as it was at the time the hold was initiated. Initially, the content is preserved in its original location. When a user first attempts to modify or delete content, because a hold was applied, a copy is preserved in a preservation hold library.

The preservation hold library is only visible to site collection administrators or users, who at the web-application level, have been given permissions to see all content in all site collections within the web application. Also, SharePoint Server search has special permissions to crawl content in the preservation hold library.

When content in the preservation hold library does not match at least one of the eDiscovery set filters, it is deleted.

Managing records

When a Records Center is first created, the only library that exists is the **Drop Off Library**. You will need to create libraries and lists to store each record that is specified in your file plan. Each record will be associated with different types of data, and therefore you will create content types, add site columns to those content types, and associate the content types with the lists and libraries in your Records Center. You will then specify information retention policies and configure the Content Organizer to route each record type to the appropriate location.

Information management policies help your organization control its records. There are two ways of configuring and applying compliance and retention rules on a SharePoint site:

- Use an information management policy for a content type, and as the content types are applied to records, the policies are applied to the records. However, you cannot specify an information management policy for content types that are installed when a site collection is created. You must create a content type that is based on one of the default core content types and apply an information management policy to your content type.

- Associate policies with records based on location; that is, if you associate a policy to a list, library, or folder, the policy is applied to any record stored in them.

    TIP You must be a member of the Owners group for the Records Center site to create and manage policies.

An information management policy can consist of one or more policy features: labels, auditing, expiration, and barcodes.

Once your Records Center is configured, you can then convert active content to records by using one of the following techniques:

- Manually declaring a document to be a record. It is very rare that your organization would manually let users declare records. Records are usually declared using the other options in this list.

- Defining a policy that declares a document to be a record or that sends a document to a Records Center site at a specified time.

- Creating a workflow that sends a document to a Records Center site.

- Using a custom solution.

    TIP When an item is declared as a record, a padlock is added to its icon.

You can use the **Compliance Details** dialog box to view the important business information about a record, including the name, content type, and folder path of a document; any retention policies on a document (and their recurrence); and exemption status and hold status. You can also add or remove holds and records, and generate audit log reports.

In this exercise, you will create a location-based retention policy.

 SET UP **Open the Records Center that you created in the previous exercise.**

> **IMPORTANT** Verify that you have sufficient rights to edit the home page of this site. If in doubt, see Appendix A.

1   On the **Quick Launch**, click **Libraries**, and then click **add an app**.

2   On the **Your Apps** page, click **Document Library** and type **Contracts**. Click **Create**.

3   On the **Site Contents** page, click **Contracts**. On the **Library** tab, click **Library Settings**.

4   Under **Permissions and Management**, click **Information management policy settings** to display the **Information Management Policy Settings** page.

Settings · Information Management Policy Settings ⓘ

Library Based Retention Schedule

By default, a library will enforce the retention schedule set on its content types. Alternatively you can stop enforcing content type schedules and instead define schedules on the library and its folders.

Source of retention for this library: **Content Types** (Change source)

Content Type Policies

This table shows all the content types for this library, along with the policies and expiration schedules for each type. To modify the policy for a content type, click its name.

Content Type	Policy	Description	Retention Policy Defined
Document	None		No
Folder	None		No

5   To the right of **Content Types**, click **Change source** to display the **Library Based Retention Schedule** page.

Edit Policy: Library Based Retention Schedule

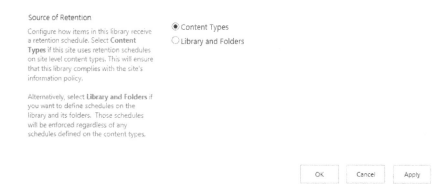

Source of Retention

Configure how items in this library receive a retention schedule. Select **Content Types** if this site uses retention schedules on site level content types. This will ensure that this library complies with the site's information policy.

Alternatively, select **Library and Folders** if you want to define schedules on the library and its folders. Those schedules will be enforced regardless of any schedules defined on the content types.

◉ Content Types
○ Library and Folders

OK   Cancel   Apply

6   Select **Library and Folders**. A dialog box appears, warning that when library and folder retention schedules are used, all content type retention schedules are ignored and that you may be overwriting policies defined by your site administrator.

7   Click **OK**. The page redisplays, showing a **Library Based Retention Schedule** section.

8   In the **Description** box, type **Declare contracts as records when they are finalized**, and then click **Add a retention stage** to open the **Stage** properties dialog.

9　　To the right of Created, type **7**, and in the **Action** list, select **Permanently Delete**.

10　　Click **OK** to close the dialog.

11　　Click **Apply**, and then click **OK**.

❌ CLEAN UP **Leave the browser open if you are continuing to the next exercise.**

Configuring in place records management

In addition to the Records Center as a central repository for document retention, SharePoint Server site owners can configure in place records management. Once a library is configured to allow the manual declaration of records, any document in the library can be declared as a record, and is then protected from changes or deletion.

The following are some additional benefits of using an in place records management system:

- Records can exist and be managed across multiple sites. An organization may want certain documents and wikis to be declared as records without moving them to a Records Center.

- With versioning enabled, maintaining versions of records is automatic.

- eDiscovery search can be executed against records and active documents at the same time.

- There is broader control over what a record is in your organization and who can create a record.

The first step in configuring an in place records management system is to activate the feature at the site collection level. Activating the feature enables the **Declare/Undeclared Record** command on the ribbon. You can then configure record declaration at the site collection level or at the list or library level.

On the **Record Declaration Settings** page, you can place a restriction on what can be done to items that are declared as records, and choose whether the manual declaration of records should be available in lists and libraries by default.

Record Declaration Settings

Record Restrictions

Specify restrictions to place on a document or item once it has been declared as a record. Changing this setting will not affect items which have already been declared records. Note: The information management policy settings can also specify different policies for records and non-records.

○ No Additional Restrictions
  Records are no more restricted than non-records.
○ Block Delete
  Records can be edited but not deleted.
● Block Edit and Delete
  Records cannot be edited or deleted. Any changes will require the record declaration to be revoked.

Record Declaration Availability

Specify whether all lists and libraries in this site should make the manual declaration of records available by default. When manual record declaration is unavailable, records can only be declared through a policy or workflow.

Manual record declaration in lists and libraries should be:

○ Available in all locations by default
● Not available in all locations by default

Declaration Roles

Specify which user roles can declare and undeclare record status manually.

The declaration of records can be performed by:

● All list contributors and administrators
○ Only list administrators
○ Only policy actions

Undeclaring a record can be performed by:

○ All list contributors and administrators
● Only list administrators
○ Only policy actions

Manual record declaration can be configured at the site collection level and be overridden in each list or library within the site collection. By configuring record declarations for a list or library, you have more control over where items are declared as records. Also, you can have items automatically declared as records when they are added to the list or library.

In this exercise, you will configure in place records management and declare an in place record.

➜ SET UP **Open the top level site of a site collection that contains sites in which you want to use in place records management.**

> **IMPORTANT** Verify that you have sufficient rights to activate a site collection feature. If in doubt, see Appendix A.

1 From the **Settings** menu, click **Site settings**. Under **Site Collection Administration**, click **Site collection features**, and to the right of **In Place Record Management**, click **Activate**, if it is not already active.

   TROUBLESHOOTING If you do not see the **Site Collection Administration** section, then you are not a site collection administrator. If you see **Go to top level site settings**, you are not at the top level site of the site collection.

2 Go to the library that you want to use in place records management, and then on the **Library** tab, click **Library Settings**.

3 Under **Permissions and Management**, click **Record declaration settings**.

4 In the **Manual Record Declaration Availability** section, select **Always allow the manual declaration of records**.

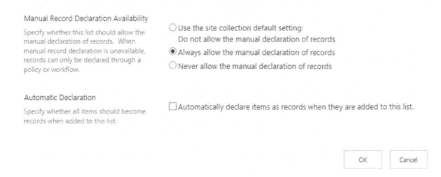

Library Record Declaration Settings ⓘ

Manual Record Declaration Availability
Specify whether this list should allow the manual declaration of records. When manual record declaration is unavailable, records can only be declared through a policy or workflow.

○ Use the site collection default setting:
  Do not allow the manual declaration of records
◉ Always allow the manual declaration of records
○ Never allow the manual declaration of records

Automatic Declaration
Specify whether all items should become records when added to this list.

☐ Automatically declare items as records when they are added to this list.

[OK]   [Cancel]

5   Click **OK**, and then on the breadcrumb, click the library name. If the library has no file, click **new documents** and upload a document.

6   Click to the left of the document that you want to declare as a record so that a check mark appears, and then on the **Files** tab, in the **Manage** group, click **Declare Record**.

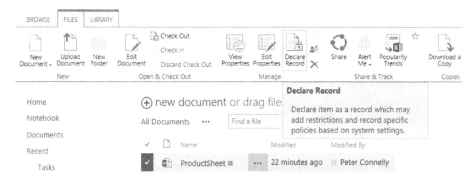

7   Click **OK** to confirm that you want to declare the selected documents as records.

8   Click the ellipsis to the right of the document you declared as a record. Click the ellipsis in the callout, and then click **Compliance Details**.

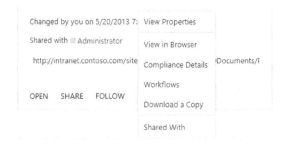

The **Compliance Details** dialog box appears.

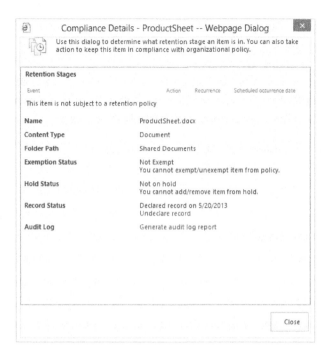

Compliance Details - ProductSheet -- Webpage Dialog   [x]

Use this dialog to determine what retention stage an item is in. You can also take action to keep this item in compliance with organizational policy.

Retention Stages

Event	Action	Recurrence	Scheduled occurrence date

This item is not subject to a retention policy

Name	ProductSheet.docx
Content Type	Document
Folder Path	Shared Documents
Exemption Status	Not Exempt You cannot exempt/unexempt item from policy.
Hold Status	Not on hold You cannot add/remove item from hold.
Record Status	Declared record on 5/20/2013 Undeclare record
Audit Log	Generate audit log report

Close

9   Click **Close**.

❌ CLEAN UP **Leave the browser open if you are continuing to the next exercise.**

Creating a publishing site

In SharePoint Server 2013, you have two methods of providing and controlling web content. You can create publishing pages based on page layouts, or you can display web content based on information that has been indexed by SharePoint Server or has been tagged using the Terms Store, which is part of the Managed Metadata Service (MMS). In reality, many of your Internet and intranet sites will use a combination of these two methods. Whichever method your organization chooses to use, you will need at least one publishing site.

Publishing sites can be created as a top level site of a site collection or a subsite. Publishing functionality is available when the **SharePoint Server Publishing** site feature is activated, which, in turn, depends on functionality available when the **SharePoint Server Publishing Infrastructure** site collection feature is activated.

The **SharePoint Server Publishing Infrastructure** site collection feature adds a number of objects to the top level site of your site collections. These objects include the following

SharePoint groups: Approvers, Designers, Hierarchy Managers, Restricted Readers, and Style Resource Readers; and several new libraries: Pages, Site Collection Documents, Style Library, and Site Collection Images. They also include the Content and Structure reports and **Reusable Content** lists. In addition, the **Publishing Infrastructure** feature adds new Web Parts, site columns, and content pages, and replaces the top link bar with a global navigation menu. It also adds a number of new links to the **Site Settings** page.

SharePoint Server provides the following publishing sites templates:

- Publishing Portal

- Publishing Site

- Publishing Site with Workflow

- Enterprise Wiki

- Product Catalog

SEE ALSO Information on using an Enterprise Wiki site can be found in Chapter 8, "Working with wikis and blogs."

Typically, publishing sites are created as subsites (or child sites) in a site collection, which was created, for example, by using the Publishing Portal or Product Catalog site templates. The Publishing Portal is typically used for creating multiple publishing sites that contain many publishing pages. The Product Catalog can be used when you want to use search to display content and manage navigation.

The Publishing Portal, Product Catalog, and Enterprise Wiki site templates can only be used to create the root site of a site collection. These three site templates automatically activate the **SharePoint Server Publishing Infrastructure** feature.

All publishing site templates automatically activate the **SharePoint Server Publishing** site feature. This site feature automatically creates the Pages library. Site owners can activate features to extend the functionality of their sites. Therefore, it is possible for a site based on the Team Site template to be turned into a publishing site by activating the **SharePoint Server Publishing** feature.

On a site based on the **Publishing Site with Workflow** template, both content approval and the approval workflow are enabled so that a page will move from content creator to an approver. Also, on any publishing site, by configuring **Manage Item Scheduling**, you can place the page in a scheduled state, whereby the page is not visible until a particular date is reached. You can also configure an end date with the option to automatically send the page's contact an email message when the page expires. You can also configure scheduled reviews of publishing pages, as well an information management policy on the Pages library to manage the retention and deletion of pages.

To maintain a large Internet or intranet site, you will need people who have the following roles:

- **Site Owners** For a large site that contains many child sites, this may be a team of people who decide the site structure and governance, and manage centrally stored resources, such as images. Within each child site, a person or team may decide on the lists and libraries that the site contains, or the pages required. This team produces wire diagrams that represent how each component on the page should be laid out.

- **Page Layout designer** This person uses Design Manager or Microsoft SharePoint Designer 2013 to create and maintain page layouts. You might need a developer, depending on the complexity of the requirements.

- **Content creator** These users create and modify publishing pages based on page layouts, or enter data into product catalogs. Users who are placed in the Members SharePoint groups can amend items, documents, and publishing pages. Therefore, most installations will create an additional SharePoint group, so they can differentiate between users who can edit and modify publishing pages and those, for example, who can upload and approve files in other document libraries, such as the Site Collection Documents and Site Collection Images library or items in the **Reusable Content** list.

- **Approver** These users moderate, edit, and approve publishing pages. This special SharePoint group is created automatically and, on a site created from the **Publishing Site with Workflow** template, is linked to the Page Approval workflow on the Pages library. Users in this group can approve any item or document in any list or library that has Content Approval enabled.

- **Visitor** These users have read-only access to pages.

In this exercise, you will create a publishing site with workflows, and include yourself in the Approvers SharePoint group.

TROUBLESHOOTING To create a publishing subsite, **the SharePoint Server Publishing Infrastructure** site collection feature must be activated. This feature is automatically activated if the top level site of a site collection was created using a publishing site template. Normally, this site collection feature is not activated on site collections where the top level site was created using a Team site; therefore, you usually cannot create a publishing site as a subsite of a Team site.

 SET UP **Open a SharePoint site where you'd like to create, as a subsite, the new publishing site.**

> **IMPORTANT** Verify that you have sufficient rights to create a site. If in doubt, see Appendix A.

1   On the **Quick Launch**, click **Site Contents**, and then at the bottom of the **Site Content** page, under **Subsites**, click **new subsite**.

2   In the **Title** text box, type **Wide World Importers Job Vacancies**, and in the **Description** text box, type **This site contains job vacancies that anyone within Wide World Importers can apply for.**

3   In the **URL name** text box, type **JobVacancies**.

4   Click the **Publishing** tab, if it is not already active, and then click **Publishing Site with Workflow**.

   TROUBLESHOOTING If the **Publishing** tab is not displayed, check that the **SharePoint Server Publishing Infrastructure** site collection feature is activated. Information on activating site collection features can be found in Chapter 5.

5   Leave the default settings for the options in the **Permissions** and **Navigation Inheritance** sections, and then click **Create**.

CLEAN UP **Leave the browser open if you are continuing to the next exercise.**

Creating page layouts

One of the key constructs of publishing sites is the ability to control the strict layout of content on a page by using a page layout. Each publishing page is based on a page layout. Each page layout is associated with a master page so that the branding and navigation are the same on publishing pages as they are on ordinary content pages. You can restrict the content shown in different areas of a page by placing controls on the page layout. The content displayed in these controls are saved in the columns of the Pages library. The page layout controls are responsible for retrieving the content from the Pages library of a site, and shows that content to the users.

TIP When a page is created from a page layout, you can include Web Parts or app parts by adding at least one Web Part zone to the page layout. If a page layout contains no Web Part zones, then no Web Parts or app parts can be added to a publishing page.

Each page layout is based on a content type, which consists of a number of site columns. When the content type is associated with the Pages library, the site columns, in turn, specifies the field controls (columns) that the page layout can use. For example, you might want to create new publishing pages when new vacancies arise in your organization. You therefore create a site column for information about job vacancies, such as Job Reference, Job Title, Department, Location, Salary, Job Type, and Pay Band. You then create a content type, Job Vacancy, and add to it the site columns that you created. You create your page layout based on the Job Vacancy content type. This allows you to decide with field controls (site columns) how to add to the page layout.

SEE ALSO Information on site columns and content types can be found in Chapter 6, "Making lists and libraries work for you."

SharePoint Server comes with the following built-in page-layout content types:

- **Page** This content type is used when you want to create your own page layout.

- **Article Page** This content type is based on the Page content type and is used to create Article page layouts. SharePoint Server provides four **Article Page** page layouts; for example, the **Image on right** page layout is used for presenting an article (as in a magazine article) on a website. It contains a **Page Image** field control and a **Page Content** field control to capture data and a few other simple field controls.

- **Catalog-Item Reuse** This content type is used when you want to create article pages that can be easily reused or republished across site collections.

- **Enterprise Wiki Page** This is the default content type in the Pages library of an Enterprise Wiki site. It provides a basic content area, as well as ratings and categories field controls.

- **Error Page** This page layout is used to create error pages and is associated with every Pages library.

- **Project Page** This content type is associated with the Pages library on the Enterprise Wiki site. It provides basic information to describe a project, including a project status column and a contact name column.

- **Redirect Page** This content type is used to create a *variations* page layout to direct users to the variations home page when the variations settings are configured.

- **Welcome Page** This content type is based on the Page content type and is used to create the Blank Web Part page, and Splash and Summary Link page layouts.

All page layouts are stored in the Master Page Gallery in the top level site of a site collection. Although the Master Page Gallery has all the features of a normal document library because of its importance to the whole site collection, it is secured to limit the rights of most users. As a page layout designer, you must have Design permission levels or higher to work with the files in this library. Such permission levels are automatically assigned to you if you are a member of the Designers SharePoint group. To protect the contents of the Master Page Gallery further, content approval and minor and major versioning is enabled by default; therefore, for a user to see pages based on your page layouts, the page layouts must be published as a major version and approved. To facilitate this process, you might consider enabling the approval workflow for the Master Page Gallery.

You can create a page layout by using a Design Manager in the browser or by using SharePoint Designer 2013. The Design Manager is new in SharePoint Server 2013. It is available on the **Settings** menu on publishing sites and provides a step-by-step approach for creating design assets that you can use to brand sites. Field controls and other components can be added, moved, and deleted from your page layout using the Design Manager.

IMPORTANT Whenever you create a page layout, you must create a page to check that the page layout is as designed. To create a publishing page, you must have Contribute rights on the Pages document library. To approve publishing pages, you must be a member of the Approvers SharePoint group.

In this exercise, you will create site columns and a content type, associate the site columns with a content type, and then using the Design Manager, you will create a page layout based on that content type.

 SET UP **Open the publishing site that you created in the previous exercise, if it is not already open.**

> **IMPORTANT** Verify that you have sufficient rights to create page layouts and content types. If in doubt, see Appendix A.

1   From the **Settings** menu, click **Site Settings**, and then under **Site Collection Administration**, click **Go to top level site settings**.

> **TROUBLESHOOTING** If you do not see the **Site Collection Administration** section, then you are not a site collection administrator, in which case you need to open the top level site of the site collection, and then go to the **Site Settings** page of that site.

2   Under **Web Designer Galleries**, click **Site content types**. Create and use the following values, and then press **OK**.

Label	Value
Name	Job Vacancy
Description	Use this content type to create the job vacancy page layout.
Select parent content type from	Page Layout Content Types
Parent Content Type	Article Page
New Group	WWI HR

3   On the **Site Content Type** page, at the bottom of the page, click **Add from existing site column** to display the **Add Columns** page.

4   In the **Select Columns** section, add the two site columns, **Job Title** and **Location**, so that they appear in the **Columns to add** list. Click **OK**.

5 On the **Site Content Type** page, at the bottom of the page, click **Add from new site column**, and then select the **Create Column** page to create the following two site columns.

Column Name	Column type
Job Description	Full HTML content with formatting and constraints for publishing.
Closing Date	Date and Time

Target Audiences	Audience Targeting	Optional	System Page
Hide physical URLs from search	Yes/No	Optional	System Page
Page Image	Publishing Image	Optional	Article Page
Page Content	Publishing HTML	Optional	Article Page
Summary Links	Summary Links	Optional	Article Page
Byline	Single line of text	Optional	Article Page
Article Date	Date and Time	Optional	Article Page
Image Caption	Publishing HTML	Optional	Article Page
Browser Title	Single line of text	Optional	Page
Meta Description	Single line of text	Optional	Page
Meta Keywords	Single line of text	Optional	Page
Hide from Internet Search Engines	Yes/No	Optional	Page
Job Title	Single line of text	Optional	
Location	Single line of text	Optional	
Job Descriptions	Publishing HTML	Optional	
Closing Date	Date and Time	Optional	

▫ Add from existing site columns
▫ Add from new site column
▫ Column order

6 On the **Site Content Type** page, under **Columns**, click each of the following columns: **Contact E-Mail Address**, **Contact Name**, **Contact Picture**, **Page Image**, **Page Content**, **Summary Links**, **Image Caption**, and **Byline**. On the **Change Content Type Column** page, in the **Column Setting** section, select **Hidden (Will not appear in forms)**, and then click **OK**.

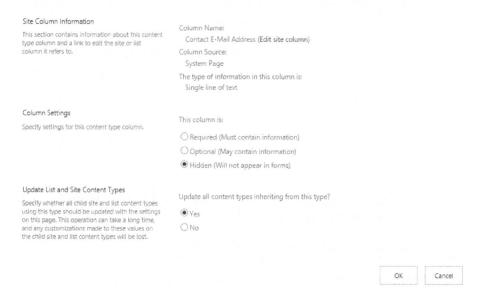

Site Content Type › Change Content Type Column ⓘ

Site Column Information

This section contains information about this content type column and a link to edit the site or list column it refers to.

Column Name:
Contact E-Mail Address (**Edit site column**)

Column Source:
System Page

The type of information in this column is:
Single line of text

Column Settings

Specify settings for this content type column.

This column is:

○ Required (Must contain information)

○ Optional (May contain information)

◉ Hidden (Will not appear in forms)

Update List and Site Content Types

Specify whether all child site and list content types using this type should be updated with the settings on this page. This operation can take a long time, and any customizations made to these values on the child site and list content types will be lost.

Update all content types inheriting from this type?

◉ Yes

○ No

[OK]   [Cancel]

---

7   On the **Site Content Type** page, under **Columns**, click each of the following columns: **Job Title**, **Location**, and **Job Description**. On the **Change Content Type Column** page, in the **Column Setting** section, select **Required (Must contain information)**, and then click **OK**.

8   From the **Settings** menu, click **Design Manager**.

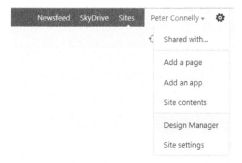

| Newsfeed | SkyDrive | Sites | Peter Connelly ▾ | ⚙ |

⟨ Shared with...

Add a page

Add an app

Site contents

Design Manager

Site settings

9   On the **Quick Launch**, click **Edit Page Layouts**.

EDIT LINKS

Design Manager: Edit Page Layouts

1. Welcome
2. Manage Device Channels
3. Upload Design Files
4. Edit Master Pages
5. Edit Display Templates
6. Edit Page Layouts
7. Publish and Apply Design
8. Create Design Package

Page layouts define the look and feel of a set of pages by styling page fields and web part zones within the common elements of a master page. You can use the network drive you mapped earlier to edit your page layouts using any HTML editor. To preview your page layout, click on its file name or status. While previewing your HTML page layout, use the Snippet Gallery to get code snippets for SharePoint functionality that you can copy and paste into your HTML file.

• Create a page layout

   Name   Status   Associated Content Type   Approval Status

There are no files in the view "Html Page Layouts".

10   Click **Create a page layout**. In the **Create a Page Layout** dialog, in the **Name** text box, type **Job Vacancy page layout**. Leave the Master Page settings as is.

11   In the **Content Type** list, select **Job Vacancy**.

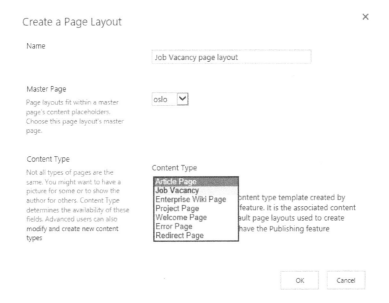

TROUBLESHOOTING If the **Job Vacancy** content type is not displayed, check that you created it at the top level of the site collection. If you did create the site columns and content type on a subsite, delete them and go to step 1.

584   Chapter 15 Working with content management

12   Click **OK** to display the **Edit Page Layouts** page.

	Name	Status	Associated Content Type	Approval Status
	Job Vacancy page layout ※	··· Conversion successful.	Job Vacancy	Draft

13   Under **Name**, click **Job Vacancy page layout** to display a preview of the page layout.

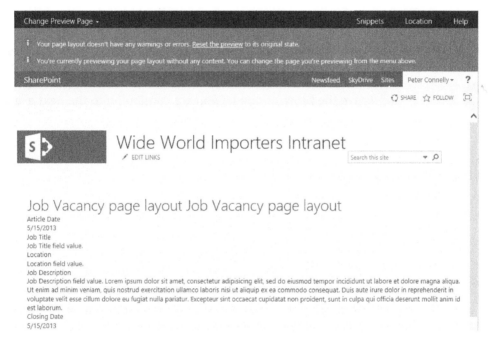

14   Click the **Back** button on the browser toolbar to display the **Edit Page Layout** page. For the **Job Vacancy** page layout to be listed on the page, you may have to click the **Refresh** button on the browser toolbar.

15   Click the ellipsis to the right of **Job Vacancy page layout**, and then in the bottom right of the callout, click the ellipsis to open the menu. Click **Publish a Major Version**.

- Create a page layout

☐ Name

Job Vacancy page layout   ...
※

Job Vacancy page layout.ht...   ×

Changed by you on   View Properties   al Status

Shared with lots of p   Edit Properties

http://wideworldim

Check Out

OPEN   SHARE   Publish a Major Version

Version History

Compliance Details

16   In the **Publish Major Version** dialog, click **OK** to display the **Edit Page Layouts** page
        where the Job Vacancy page layout now has an approval status of Approved.

 CLEAN UP **Leave the browser open if you are continuing to the next exercise.**

Managing page layouts

Using a browser, you can configure each site within a site collection to display all or some
of the page layouts. Therefore, if you create page layouts that are specific to the Human
Resources department, you can limit the Human Resources site to use only the Human
Resources page layouts, and any child site of the Human Resources site can be configured
to inherit the preferred layouts from its parent site.

In this exercise, you will set the default page layout, and then you will create a page to
check that the page is using the default page layout.

 SET UP **Display the publishing site that you created earlier in this chapter, if it is not
already displayed.**

IMPORTANT Verify that you have sufficient rights to manage page layouts. If in doubt, see
Appendix A.

1   From the **Settings** menu, click **Site settings**, and then under **Look and Feel**, click **Page Layouts and site templates**.

2   In the **New Page Default Settings** section, select **Select the default page layout**, and from the list, select **(Job Vacancy) Job Vacancy page layout**.

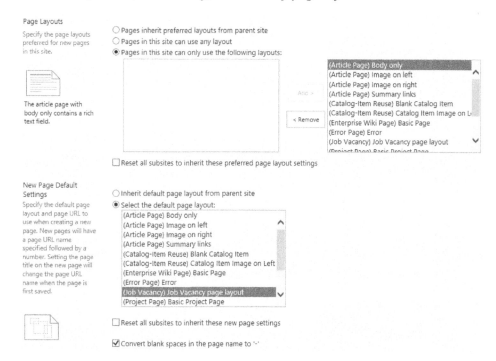

3   At the bottom of the page, click **OK**.

4   On the **Settings** menu, click **Add a page**. In the **Add a page** dialog, type **IT Support vacancy**, and then click **Create**.

5   In the **Job Title** text box, type **IT Technician**, and in the **Location** text box, type **London**.

IT Support vacancy ✏ EDIT LINKS   Search this site

Edit Item IT Support vacancy

⚠ **Checked out to you** Only you can see your recent changes. Check it in.
⚠ **Publication Start Date:** Immediately

Title

    IT Support vacancy

Article Date

                          ▦

Job Title

    IT Technician

Location

    London

Job Description

                Click here to add new content

Closing Date

                          ▦

6   On the **Page** tab, in the **Edit** group, click **Save**.

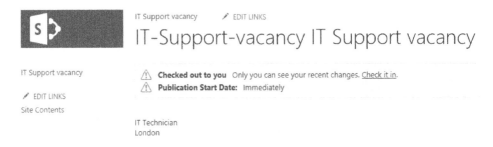

IT Support vacancy ✏ EDIT LINKS

IT-Support-vacancy IT Support vacancy

IT Support vacancy

✏ EDIT LINKS

Site Contents

⚠ **Checked out to you** Only you can see your recent changes. Check it in.
⚠ **Publication Start Date:** Immediately

IT Technician
London

✖ CLEAN UP **Leave the browser open if you are continuing to the next exercise.**

Using reusable content

When creating content on a publishing page, you may find that you are typing the same content again and again. SharePoint Server provides the capability to reuse content items by creating the Reusable Content list. This list is created at the top level site of a site collection and automatically gets created when the **SharePoint Server Publishing Infrastructure** site collection feature is activated.

Use reusable content in the following scenarios:

- You have text within your organization that is very standardized and should never change, such as in a corporate mission statement, an executive bio, or a product description. This text should always be written exactly the same way when displayed. There may also be content that needs to be displayed in multiple locations. Reusable content minimizes the effort associated with maintenance because you can update the text in a single list and push all changes out to each page in the site collection where the content appears.

- You have text that acts as a template to demonstrate to page creators how content should be formatted. This could be an outline for a product, which acts as a starting point to help minimize the time it takes to add content to the page. The page creator can add more defined and relevant information.

You must have Contributor permissions to add items to the **Reusable Content** list. You can create categories and folders within the list to help you organize these items. Once items are added to the **Reusable Content** list, you can add those items to the content area of a publishing page by using the **Reusable Content Picker**.

Each item of reusable content can consist of either HTML or plain text and can be designated as either automatically updated or not. Reusable content that consists of HTML can contain text and HTML elements, such as images, tables, and lists. These HTML elements can be styled or formatted as needed. Reusable content that consists of plain text can contain only use unformatted, unstyled text. If a reusable content item is designated as automatically updated, the content is inserted into webpages as a read-only reference, and the page content is updated if the item is changed.

If the reusable content item is not designated as automatically updated, the content is inserted as a copy in the webpage, and the content is not updated if the item is changed.

In this exercise, you will create a new content category and add a reusable content item.

SET UP **Open the publishing page that you created in the previous exercise, if it is not already open.**

1   From the **Settings** menu, click **Site settings**, and then under **Site Collection Administration**, click **Go to top level site settings**.

2   On the **Quick Launch**, click **Site Contents**, and then click **Reusable Content**.

3   On the **List** tab, in the **Settings** group, click **List Settings**, and then under **Columns**, click **Content Category**.

4   On the **Edit Column** page, under **Type each choice on a separate line**, delete **None**, if it exists, and then type **Copyright** and **Furniture** on separate lines. At the bottom of the page, click **OK** to display the **Settings** page.

5   In the breadcrumb, click **Reusable content**, and then click **new item**. In the **Title** text box, type **Wide World Importers copyright**, and in **Content Category** list, select **Copyright**, if it is not already selected.

6   Leave the **Automatic Update** check box selected, and then in the **Reusable HTML** section, click **Click here to add new content**.

7   Type **Wide World Importers**, and then if you have a keyboard that contains a numeric keyboard, click the **Num Lock** key so that it is selected. Hold down the **Alt** key and type **0169** on the numeric keyboard to include a copyright symbol. Then type **copyright 2013**.

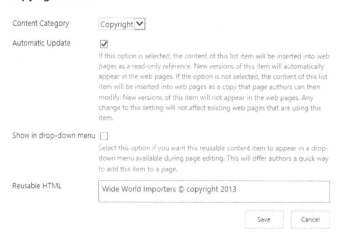

8   Click **Save**.

9   Go to the publishing page where you want to use the reusable content, such as the **IT Support vacancy** page that you created in the previous exercise.

10   On the **Page** tab, click **Edit**, and then in the **Job Description** text box, type **Desktop skills are required**.

11   On the **Insert** tab, click **Reusable Content**, and then click **Wide World Importers copyright**.

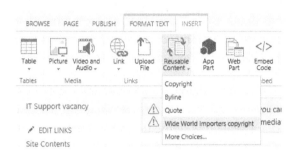

12   On the **Page** tab, click **Save**.

❌ CLEAN UP **Leave the browser open if you are continuing to the next exercise.**

Using a product catalog

Previously in this chapter, you created content on publishing pages. You can use this content as static data or you can dynamically display content from lists and libraries by using the Content Query Web Part (CQWP), where lists and libraries have to be stored within sites in the same site collection. However, in SharePoint Server 2013, you can use cross-site collection publishing (XSP) to create one authoring site collection, whose content is displayed on pages in multiple publishing site collections without the need to redeploy the content to those site collections.

SEE ALSO XSP is not explained in depth in this section; it is an advanced WCM technique. More information can be found in Chapter 12, "Designing web content management sites," in *Microsoft SharePoint 2013 Inside Out*, by Darvish Shadravan, Penelope Coventry, Thomas Resing, and Christina Wheeler (Microsoft Press, 2013).

To achieve this, you need to use catalogs to publish content across site collections; in other words, without catalogs, you cannot use XSP. To use XSP, the **Cross-Site Collection Publishing** site collection feature must be activated. Using this feature, you can share lists and libraries—including the **Pages** library—as catalogs so that other sites and site collections can use the catalog content on their pages. For example, content stored in libraries and lists in an authoring site collection can be displayed across three separate publishing site collections by using the CSWP.

When the **XSP** site collection feature is activated, on the list or library **Settings** page, under **General Settings**, there is a new link named **Catalog Settings**. When you click this link, the **Catalog Settings** page is displayed, where you can suggest how friendly URLs are created. You can choose up to five columns in the list or library that, when combined, uniquely identify an item in the list. In the **Catalog Navigation** section, select the column you created earlier that maps to a term set. You can also choose to enable anonymous access.

TIP Before configuring a list or library as a catalog, you should add a column to the list or library so that you can tag items from an MMS term set. You should add at least one item to the list or library, and then tag it against one of the terms from the term set (using the column that you just created) before publishing the item. The MMS and Term Store are only available in SharePoint Server, and the MMS service application and Term Store must be created by your SharePoint server administrators. If your server administrators have not created the MMS service application and Term Store, you will be severely limited when using XSP.

In this exercise, you will activate the **Cross-Site Collection Publishing** site collection feature, and then configure a library to be available using XSP.

 SET UP **Open the top level site of a site collection where you wish to activate the Cross-Site Collection Publishing feature.**

IMPORTANT Verify that you have sufficient rights to enable a site collection feature, and amend library settings. If in doubt, see Appendix A.

1   From the **Settings** menu, click **Site settings**, and then under **Site Collection Administration**, click **Site collection features**. To the right of **Cross-Site Collection Publishing**, click **Activate**, if it is not already active.

2   Go to the library that you want to configure as a product catalog, and then on the **Library** tab, in the **Manage Views** group, click **Create Column**.

3   In the **Column Name** box, type **Department**, and under **The type of information for this column is**, select **Managed Metadata**.

4   Scroll down, and in the **Term Set Settings** section, click the arrow to the left of your Managed Metadata Service to display the term set groups.

5   Click the arrow to the left of one of the term set groups, such as **People**, and then click a term set, such as **Department**. Click **OK** to create the column.

6   On the **Library** tab, click **Library Settings**, and then under **General Settings**, click **Catalog Settings**.

7   On the **Catalog Settings** page, in the **Catalog Sharing** section, select **Enable this library as a catalog**.

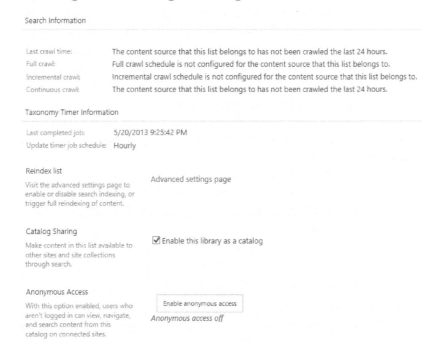

8   In the **Catalog Item URL Fields** section, under **Available Field**, click **Department**, and then click **Add**.

9   Click **OK**.

✖ CLEAN UP **Leave the browser open if you are continuing to the next exercise.**

Defining a SharePoint site policy

With SharePoint Server 2013, site policies have been improved to include retention policies for sites and site mailboxes. You can use site policies to help control site proliferation. A site policy defines the life cycle of a site by specifying when the site will be closed and when it will be deleted. When you close or delete a site, any subsites are also closed or deleted. If an Exchange mailbox is associated with a site, the mailbox is deleted from Exchange Server 2013 when the site is deleted.

The concept at the heart of this new functionality is site closure. When you close a site, applications that aggregate open sites to site members—such as Microsoft Office Outlook, Outlook Web Access, and Microsoft Office Project Server—will trim links to the site. The site can still be accessed via its URL and it can still be modified. When you select to delete a site based on its closed date, closing that site starts the countdown to its deletion. Closing a site collection, however, makes the site collection and all subsites read-only. Also, if the closed site has any subsites, when the closed site is deleted, all of its subsites are deleted, whether they are in a closed state or not. Site owners do have the option of postponing the deletion of a closed site, depending on the configuration of the site policy.

TIP A site owner can reopen a closed site. To do so, on the **Site Settings** page, click **Site Closure and Deletion**.

Site policies are created at the site-collection level, but are applied at the site level, including the top level site of a site collection. In the **New Site Policy** page, you can choose from four options:

- **Do not close or delete site automatically** Use this condition when you want the site owner to manually delete the site.

- **Delete sites automatically** Use this condition when you want to manually close the site, but the site will be deleted automatically. This option offers the same choices as the next option, in regard to deleting the site automatically, and it also requires you to specify the amount of time after its creation that the site will be closed.

- **Close and delete sites automatically** Use this condition when you want to automate site closure and deletion. You are provided with the following five configuration options:

  - **Close Event** Use this option to specify the amount of time to wait after a site is created before closing the site. You can specify the length of time in **Days**, **Months**, or **Years**.

- **Deletion Event** Use this option to specify the amount of time to wait after a site is created before deleting the site. You can specify the length of time in **Days, Months,** or **Years.**

- **Send an email notification to site owners this far in advance of deletion** Use this option to send an email to the site owner at a specified length of time before the site is scheduled for deletion.

- **Send follow-up notifications every** Use this option to send recurring follow-up notifications warnings of the site deletion and to specify the intervals at which they are to be sent.

- **Owners can postpone imminent deletion for** Use this option to allow site owners to postpone the deletion of the site for a specified length of time.

- **Run a workflow automatically to manage site closure, then delete them automatically** Use this condition when you want to add custom logic to the closure process. You can specify the name of the workflow, the amount of time after the site is created to run the workflow, and whether to rerun the workflow periodically until the site is closed.

On the **New Site Policy** page, you can optionally select the **The site collection will be read only when it is closed** check box. A notification of the read-only state is displayed in the status bar at the top of every page within the site collection, including application pages.

This site is read only at the site collection administrator's request.   ✕

You can close the notification message by clicking the **X** at the far right of the message; however, when you return to the page, the notification is redisplayed.

TIP When you define site policies in a site collection, which is a content-type hub, you can publish and share those site policies across site collections.

Once a site policy is created, you can apply it to any site within your site collection. From the **Site Settings** page, you can display the **Site Closure and Deletion** page, which allows you to complete the following tasks:

- Apply, select, or remove a site policy. You cannot change the selected site policy of a closed site. You must first open the site, and then select a different policy. To remove all site policies, select **No Site Policy.**

- View the site policy details, such as the date and time that the site was closed and when the site will be deleted.

- Manually close a site. Before you can manually close a site, however, you must apply a site policy for which the **Do not close or delete site automatically** condition has been selected.

- Open a closed site.

In this exercise, you will define a SharePoint site policy and apply it to a site.

 SET UP **Open the top level site of a site collection where you would like to create a site policy.**

IMPORTANT Verify that you have sufficient rights to manage this site collection. If in doubt, see Appendix A.

1   On the **Settings** menu, click **Site settings**, and then under **Site Collection Administration**, click **Site Collection Features**.

2   On the **Site Collection Features** page, to the right of **Site Policy**, click **Activate**, if the site collection feature is not already activated.

3   On the breadcrumb, click **Site Settings**, and then under **Site Collection Administration**, click **Site Policies**.

4   On the **Site Policies** page, click **Create**.

5   On the **New Site Policy** page, in the **Name** box, type **Wide World Importers site policy**.

6   In the **Site Closure and Deletion** section, click **Close and delete sites automatically**.

7   Under **Close Event**, in the **Site created date** box, type **1** to set the site to close automatically after one year.

8   Under **Deletion Event**, in the **Site closed date** box, type **3** to automatically delete the site three months after the site has been closed.

9   In the **Site Collection Closure** section, select **The site collection will be read only when closed**.

Name and Description

The name and description are displayed when users classify sites under the appropriate policy.

Name:

Wide World Importers site policy

Description:

Site Closure and Deletion

You can configure how sites under this policy are closed and eventually deleted automatically.

When a site is closed, it is trimmed from places that aggregate open sites to site members such as Outlook, OWA, and Project Server. Members can still access and modify site content until it is automatically or manually deleted.

○ Do not close or delete site automatically.

○ Delete sites automatically.

◉ Close and delete sites automatically.

Close Event:

Site created date + [1] [years ▾]

Deletion Event:

Site closed date + [3] [months ▾]

☑ Send an email notification to site owners this far in advance of deletion:

[3] [months ▾]

☑ Send follow-up notifications every:

[14] [days ▾]

☑ Owners can postpone imminent deletion for:

[1] [months ▾]

Site Collection Closure

When a site collection is closed, you can choose for it to become read only. Visitors will receive a notification that the site collection is closed and in read only mode.

☑ The site collection will be read only when it is closed.

15

10   Click **OK** to create the new policy.

11   Go to the site in the site collection where you would use the site policy. On the **Settings** menu, click **Site settings**, and then under **Site Administration**, click **Site Closure and Deletion**.

12   On the **Site Closure and Deletion** page, in the **Site Policy** list, select **Wide World Importers Site Policy**.

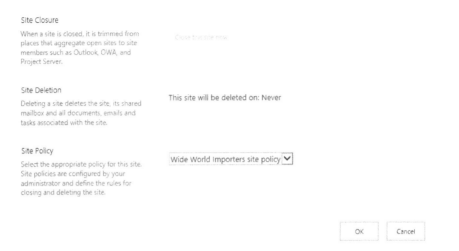

Site Settings › Site Closure and Deletion ⓘ

Site Closure

When a site is closed, it is trimmed from places that aggregate open sites to site members such as Outlook, OWA, and Project Server.

Close this site now

Site Deletion

Deleting a site deletes the site, its shared mailbox and all documents, emails and tasks associated with the site.

This site will be deleted on: Never

Site Policy

Select the appropriate policy for this site. Site policies are configured by your administrator and define the rules for closing and deleting the site.

Wide World Importers site policy ⌄

OK   Cancel

13   Click **OK**, and then under **Site Administration**, click **Site Closure and Deletion** to review the site closure and deletion dates, which are set based on the policy.

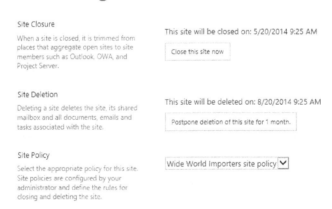

Site Settings › Site Closure and Deletion ⓘ

Site Closure

When a site is closed, it is trimmed from places that aggregate open sites to site members such as Outlook, OWA, and Project Server.

This site will be closed on: 5/20/2014 9:25 AM

Close this site now

Site Deletion

Deleting a site deletes the site, its shared mailbox and all documents, emails and tasks associated with the site.

This site will be deleted on: 8/20/2014 9:25 AM

Postpone deletion of this site for 1 month.

Site Policy

Select the appropriate policy for this site. Site policies are configured by your administrator and define the rules for closing and deleting the site.

Wide World Importers site policy ⌄

✖ CLEAN UP **Close the browser.**

Key points

- The **Document ID** feature assigns documents unique IDs, which can be used to retrieve a document, even if its location has changed during its lifetime.

- The Content Organizer allows documents to be routed to their correct location based on rules, which are configured to use the content type and columns of a document.

- The **Records Center** can be used in conjunction with the **Send To** connection in SharePoint to centralize the storage and management of documents that must be treated as a record.

- Records management in SharePoint Server supports the creation of records, either manually or by using automated processes such as workflow.

- You can declare and manage records on any site using in place records management.

- Web Content Management is one of the functions included in the SharePoint Server Enterprise Content Management capability.

- The key concept of publishing sites is page layouts. A master page controls the appearance of the branding and navigation, whereas the page layout controls the appearance of the content portion of the page.

- Page layouts are stored in the Master Page Gallery library in the top level site of a site collection. Content approval, minor versioning, and major versioning are enabled in this library; therefore, you must publish a page layout as a major version and approve it before any pages that are based on it can be viewed by visitors to your site.

- Page layouts are created from page layout content types and publishing pages are created from a page layout.

15

SharePoint 2013 user permissions and permission levels

Microsoft SharePoint 2013 includes 33 user permissions that determine the specific actions that users can perform on a SharePoint site. Permissions are grouped into permission levels. In essence, each permission level is a named collection of permissions that can be assigned to SharePoint users and groups.

There are a number of default permission levels available on a SharePoint 2013 site. For example, seven default permission levels are available on every team site: View Only, Read, Contribute, Edit, Design, Full Control, and Limited Access. When your site is based on a site template other than the Team site template, you will see additional default SharePoint permission levels available on your site. For example, three default permission levels are available on every publishing site: Restricted Read, Approve, and Manage Hierarchy. Every community site provides a Moderate permission level.

Table A-1 lists and describes the default permission levels, along with their corresponding permissions, in SharePoint 2013.

Table A-1 *Default permission levels*

Permission level	Description	Permissions included by default
Limited Access	Allows access to shared resources in the website so that users can access an item within the site. Designed to be combined with fine-grained permissions to provide users with access to a specific list, document library, item, or document without giving users access to the entire site. Cannot be customized or deleted.	View Application Pages, Browse User Information, Use Remote Interfaces, Use Client Integration Features, Open
View Only	Enables users to view application pages. The View Only permission level is used for the Excel Services Viewers group.	View Application Pages, View Items, View Versions, Create Alerts, Use Self-Service Site Creation, View Pages, Browse User Information, Use Remote Interfaces, Use Client Integration Features, Open

Permission level	Description	Permissions included by default
Read	Allows read-only access to the website.	View Application Pages, Browse User Information, Use Remote Interfaces, Use Client Integration Features, Open, View Items, Open Items, View Versions, Create Alerts, Use Self-Service Site Creation, View Pages
Contribute	Allows users to create and edit items in existing lists and document libraries.	View Application Pages, Browse User Information, Use Remote Interfaces, Use Client Integration Features, Open, View Items, Open Items, View Versions, Create Alerts, Use Self-Service Site Creation, View Pages, Add Items, Edit Items, Delete Items, Delete Versions, Browse Directories, Edit Personal User Information, Manage Personal Views, Add/Remove Personal Web Parts, Update Personal Web Parts
Edit	Enables users to manage lists.	View Application Pages, Browse User Information, Use Remote Interfaces, Use Client Integration Features, Open, View Items, Open Items, View Versions, Create Alerts, Use Self-Service Site Creation, View Pages, Add Items, Edit Items, Delete Items, Delete Versions, Browse Directories, Edit Personal User Information, Manage Personal Views, Add/Remove Personal Web Parts, Update Personal Web Parts, Manage Lists
Design	Allows users to create lists and document libraries, as well as edit pages in the website.	View Application Pages, Browse User Information, Use Remote Interfaces, Use Client Integration Features, Open, View Items, Open Items, View Versions, Create Alerts, Use Self-Service Site Creation, View Pages, Add Items, Edit Items, Delete Items, Delete Versions, Browse Directories, Edit Personal User Information, Manage Personal Views, Add/Remove Personal Web Parts, Update Personal Web Parts Manage Lists, Override Check Out, Approve Items, Add and Customize Pages, Apply Themes and Borders, Apply Style Sheets
Full Control	Allows full control. Cannot be customized or deleted.	All permissions
Restricted Read	View pages and documents. For publishing sites only.	View Items, Open Items, View Pages, Open

Permission level	Description	Permissions included by default
Manage Hierarchy	Create sites; edit pages, list items, and documents, and change site permissions. For publishing sites only.	View Application Pages, Browse User Information, Use Remote Interfaces, Use Client Integration Features, Open, View Items, Open Items, View Versions, Create Alerts, Use Self-Service Site Creation, View Pages, Add Items, Edit Items, Delete Items, Delete Versions, Browse Directories, Edit Personal User Information, Manage Personal Views, Add/Remove Personal Web Parts, Update Personal Web Parts Manage Lists, Override Check Out, Add and Customize Pages, Manage Permissions, Enumerate Permissions, View Web Analytics Data, Create Subsite, Manage Alerts, Manage Web Site
Approve	Edit and approve pages, list items, and documents. For publishing sites only.	View Application Pages, Browse User Information, Use Remote Interfaces, Use Client Integration Features, Open, View Items, Open Items, View Versions, Create Alerts, Use Self-Service Site Creation, View Pages, Add Items, Edit Items, Delete Items, Delete Versions, Override List Behaviors, Approve Items, Browse Directories, Edit Personal User Information, Manage Personal Views, Add/Remove Personal Web Parts, Update Personal Web Parts
Moderate	View, add, update, delete, and moderate list items and documents.	View Application Pages, Browse User Information, Use Remote Interfaces, Use Client Integration Features, Open, View Items, Open Items, View Versions, Override List Behaviors, Manage Lists, Create Alerts, Use Self-Service Site Creation, View Pages, Add Items, Edit Items, Delete Items, Delete Versions, Browse Directories, Edit Personal User Information, Manage Personal Views, Add/Remove Personal Web Parts, Update Personal Web Parts

In addition to using the default permission levels provided by SharePoint Server, you can create new permission levels that contain specific permissions, as well as change which permissions are included in the default permission levels, with a few exceptions. Although it is not possible to remove permissions from the Limited Access and Full Control permission

A

levels, your SharePoint administrator can make specific permission levels unavailable for the entire web application by using SharePoint Central Administration. If you are a SharePoint administrator and want to do this, do the following: in **SharePoint Central Administration**, from the **Application Management** page, select **Manage Web Applications**, choose your web application, click the **Permission Policy** button on the ribbon, and then delete the permissions levels that you would like to disable.

Depending on the scope, user permissions in SharePoint 2013 can be grouped into three categories: list permissions, site permissions, and personal user permissions. Table A-2 lists and describes user permissions in SharePoint 2013, in alphabetical order, and includes scope, permission dependencies, and the permission levels that are included by default.

Table A-2 *User permissions*

Permission	Description	Scope	Dependent permissions	Included in these permission levels by default
Add and Customize Pages	Adds, changes, or deletes Hypertext Markup Language (HTML) pages or Web Part pages; edits the website by using a SharePoint Foundation–compatible editor.	Site	View Items, Browse Directories, View Pages, Open	Design, Full Control, Manage Hierarchy
Add Items	Adds items to lists, documents to document libraries, and web discussion comments.	List	View Items, View Pages, Open	Contribute, Design, Edit, Full Control, Approve, Moderate, Manage Hierarchy
Add/Remove Personal Web Parts	Adds or removes personal Web Parts on a Web Part page.	Personal Permissions	View Items, View Pages, Open	Contribute, Design, Edit, Full Control, Approve, Moderate, Manage Hierarchy
Apply Style Sheets	Applies a style sheet (.css file) to the website.	Site	View Pages, Open	Design, Full Control
Apply Themes and Borders	Applies a theme or borders to the entire website.	Site	View Pages, Open	Design, Full Control

Permission	Description	Scope	Dependent permissions	Included in these permission levels by default
Approve Items	Approves minor versions of list items or documents.	List	Edit Items, View Items, View Pages, Open	Design, Full Control, Approve
Browse Directories	Enumerates files and folders in a website by using Microsoft SharePoint Designer and Web DAV interfaces.	Site	View Pages, Open	Contribute, Design, Edit, Full Control, Approve, Moderate, Manage Hierarchy
Browse User Information	Views information about users of the website.	Site	Open	All
Create Alerts	Creates email alerts.	List	View Items, View Pages, Open	Read, Contribute, Design, Edit, Full Control, Approve, Moderate, Manage Hierarchy, View Only
Create Groups	Creates a group of users that can be used anywhere within the site collection.	Site	View Pages, Browse User Information, Open	Full Control
Create Subsites	Creates subsites such as Team sites.	Site	View Pages, Browse User Information, Open	Full Control, Manage Hierarchy
Delete Items	Deletes items from a list, documents from a document library, and web discussion comments in documents.	List	View Items, View Pages, Open	Contribute, Design, Edit, Full Control, Approve, Moderate, Manage Hierarchy
Delete Versions	Deletes past versions of list items or documents.	List	View Items, View Versions, View Pages, Open	Contribute, Design, Edit, Full Control, Approve, Moderate, Manage Hierarchy

Permission	Description	Scope	Dependent permissions	Included in these permission levels by default
Edit Items	Edits items in lists, documents in document libraries, and web discussion comments in documents; customizes Web Part pages in document libraries.	List	View Items, View Pages, Open	Contribute, Design, Edit, Full Control, Approve, Moderate, Manage Hierarchy
Edit Personal User Information	Users can change their own user information, such as adding a picture.	Site	Browse User Information, Open	Contribute, Design, Edit, Full Control, Approve, Moderate, Manage Hierarchy
Enumerate Permissions	Enumerates permissions in the website, list, folder, document, or list item.	Site	Browse Directories, View Pages, Browse User Information, Open	Full Control
Manage Alerts	Manages alerts for all users of the website.	Site	View Items, View Pages, Open	Full Control
Manage Lists	Creates and deletes lists, adds or removes columns in a list, and adds or removes public views of a list.	List	View Items, View Pages, Open, Manage Personal Views	Design, Edit, Full Control, Moderate, Manage Hierarchy
Manage Permissions	Creates and changes permission levels on the website; assigns permissions to users and groups.	Site	View Items, Open Items, View Versions, Browse Directories, View Pages, Enumerate Permissions, Browse User Information, Open	Full Control, Manage Hierarchy
Manage Personal Views	Creates, changes, and deletes personal views of lists.	Personal Permissions	View Items, View Pages, Open	Contribute, Design, Edit, Full Control, Approve, Moderate, Manage Hierarchy

Permission	Description	Scope	Dependent permissions	Included in these permission levels by default
Manage Web Site	Performs all administration tasks and manages content for the website.	Site	View Items, Add and Customize Pages, Browse Directories, View Pages, Enumerate Permissions, Browse User Information, Open	Full Control, Manage Hierarchy
Open	Opens a website, list, or folder to access items inside that container.	Site	None	All
Open Items	Views the source of documents with server-side file handlers.	List	View Items, View Pages, Open	Read, Contribute, Design, Edit, Full Control, Approve, Moderate, Manage Hierarchy, Restricted Read
Override List Behaviors	Discards or checks in a document that is checked out to another user without saving the current changes.	List	View Items, View Pages, Open	Design, Full Control, Approve, Moderate, Manage Hierarchy
Update Personal Web Parts	Updates Web Parts to display personalized information.	Personal Permissions	View Items, View Pages, Open	Contribute, Design, Edit, Full Control, Approve, Moderate, Manage Hierarchy
Use Client Integration Features	Uses features that start client applications; without this permission, users must work on documents locally and then upload their changes.	Site	Use Remote Interfaces, Open	Read, Contribute, Design, Edit, Full Control, Approve, Moderate, Manage Hierarchy, Limited Access, View Only
Use Remote Interfaces	Use Simple Object Access Protocol (SOAP), Web DAV, or SharePoint Designer interfaces to access the website.	Site	Open	Read, Contribute, Design, Edit, Full Control, Approve, Moderate, Manage Hierarchy, Limited Access, View Only

A

Permission	Description	Scope	Dependent permissions	Included in these permission levels by default
Use Self-Service Site Creation	Creates a website by using Self-Service Site Creation.	Site	View Pages, Browse User Information, Open	Read, Contribute, Design, Edit, Full Control, Approve, Moderate, Manage Hierarchy, View Only
View Application Pages	Views forms, views, and application pages; enumerates lists.	List	Open	Read, Contribute, Design, Edit, Full Control, Approve, Moderate, Manage Hierarchy, Limited Access, View Only
View Items	Views items in lists, documents in document libraries, and web discussion comments.	List	View Pages, Open	Read, Contribute, Design, Edit, Full Control, Approve, Moderate, Manage Hierarchy, Restricted Read, View Only
View Pages	Views pages in a website.	Site	Open	Read, Contribute, Design, Edit, Full Control, Approve, Moderate, Manage Hierarchy, Restricted Read, View Only
View Versions	Views past versions of list items or documents.	List	View Items, Open Items, View Pages, Open	Read, Contribute, Design, Edit, Full Control, Approve, Moderate, Manage Hierarchy
View Web Analytics Data	Views reports on website usage.	Site	View Pages, Open	Full Control, Manage Hierarchy

SharePoint 2013 features

Microsoft SharePoint 2013 provides different sets of features and capabilities in on-premises deployments (not to be confused with Microsoft SharePoint Online, which is available in Microsoft Office 365 and as a stand-alone cloud offering). The specific feature sets that are available depend on the client access licenses (CALs) activated in your organization:

- SharePoint Server 2013 Enterprise CAL
- SharePoint Server 2013 Standard CAL
- SharePoint Foundation 2013

SharePoint Server 2013 Enterprise provides enterprise-level features and capabilities, which are not offered in SharePoint Server 2013 Standard. For an organization to determine whether it requires the SharePoint Server 2013 Enterprise or the SharePoint Server 2013 Standard feature set, it needs to assess which solution meets its needs and aligns with its goals.

Microsoft SharePoint Foundation 2013 is a collection of services for Windows Server 2012. It is available as a free download. SharePoint Server 2013 is built on top of SharePoint Foundation 2013. SharePoint Server 2013 extends SharePoint Foundation by providing many more features and capabilities. All features of SharePoint Foundation are available in SharePoint Server 2013.

TIP To download SharePoint Foundation 2013, go to *www.microsoft.com/en-us/download/details.aspx?id=35488*.

Table B-1 lists the features that are available in each SharePoint 2013 solution. The features are grouped by content features, business intelligence features, search features, sites features, and social features.

Table B-1 *Available SharePoint 2013 features*

Feature	SharePoint 2013 solution		
	Foundation	Server Standard CAL	Server Enterprise CAL
Content features			
Accessibility standards support	Yes	Yes	Yes
Asset library enhancements/video support	Yes	Yes	Yes
Auditing	No	Yes	Yes
Auditing & Reporting (e.g., doc edits, policy edits, deletes)	No	Yes	Yes
Auditing of view events	No	Yes	Yes
Content Organizer	No	Yes	Yes
Design Manager	No	Yes	Yes
Document sets	No	Yes	Yes
Document translation in Word Web App	Yes*	Yes*	Yes*
eDiscovery	No	No	Yes
Folder sync	No	Yes	Yes
Information Rights Management (IRM)	No	Yes	Yes
In-Place Hold	No	Yes	Yes
Managed Metadata Service	No	Yes	Yes
Metadata-driven navigation	No	Yes	Yes
Multistage Disposition	No	Yes	Yes
Office Web Apps (edit)	Yes*	Yes*	Yes*
Office Web Apps (view)	Yes*	Yes*	Yes*
Office Web Apps Server integration	Yes	Yes	Yes
PowerPoint Automation Services	No	Yes	Yes
Preservation hold library	No	No	Yes
Quick Edit	Yes	Yes	Yes
Records management	No	Yes	Yes
Recycle Bin (site collection)	No	No	No

Related Items	Yes	Yes	Yes
Rich Media management	Yes	Yes	Yes
Shared Content Types	No	Yes	Yes
SharePoint Translation Services	No	Yes	Yes
Site mailbox	No	Yes**	Yes**
Excel Surveys	No	Yes*	Yes*
Unique document IDs	No	Yes	Yes
Video Search	No	No	Yes
WCM: Analytics	No	Yes	Yes
WCM: Catalog	No	No	Yes
WCM: Cross-site publishing	No	No	Yes
WCM: Designer tools	No	Yes	Yes
WCM: Faceted navigation	No	No	Yes
WCM: Image renditions	No	No	Yes
WCM: Mobile and device rendering	No	Yes	Yes
WCM: Multiple domains	No	Yes	Yes
WCM: OOTB Recommendations Web Parts	No	Yes	Yes
WCM: Search Engine Optimizations (SEO)	No	Yes	Yes
WCM: Topic pages	No	No	Yes
Word Automation Services	No	Yes	Yes

Business intelligence features

Business Intelligence Center	No	No	Yes
Calculated measures and members	No	No	Yes
Data Connection library	No	No	Yes
Decoupled PivotTables and PivotCharts	No	No	Yes
Excel Services	No	No	Yes
Field list and Field support	No	No	Yes
Filter enhancements	No	No	Yes
Filter search	No	No	Yes

B

PerformancePoint Services	No	No	Yes
PerformancePoint Services (PPS) dashboard migration	No	No	Yes
Power View	No	No	Yes
PowerPivot	No	No	Yes
Quick Explore	No	No	Yes
Scorecards & Dashboards	No	No	Yes
SQL Server Reporting Services (SSRS) Integrated Mode	No	No	Yes
Timeline slicer	No	No	Yes
Visio Services	No	No	Yes
Search features			
Advanced content Processing	Yes	Yes	Yes
Content Search Web Part	No	No	Yes
Continuous crawl	Yes	Yes	Yes
Custom entity extraction	No	No	Yes
Deep links	No	Yes	Yes
Event-based relevancy	No	Yes	Yes
Expertise search	Yes	Yes	Yes
Extensible content processing	No	No	Yes
Graphical refiners	No	Yes	Yes
Hybrid search	Yes	Yes	Yes
Managed navigation	No	Yes	Yes
Phonetic name matching	Yes	Yes	Yes
Query rules—add promoted results	No	Yes	Yes
Query rules—advanced actions	No	No	Yes
Query spelling correction	Yes	Yes	Yes
Query suggestions	No	Yes	Yes
Query throttling	No	Yes	Yes
Quick preview	Yes	Yes	Yes

Recommendations	No	Yes	Yes
Refiners	Yes	Yes	Yes
Result sources	Yes	Yes	Yes
Search connector framework	No	Yes	Yes
Search results sorting	Yes	Yes	Yes
Search vertical: Conversations	No	Yes	Yes
Search vertical: People	No	Yes	Yes
Search vertical: Video	No	No	Yes
Tunable relevancy	No	No	Yes

Sites features

Change the look	Yes	Yes	Yes
Connections to Microsoft Office clients	Yes	Yes	Yes
Cross-browser support	Yes	Yes	Yes
Custom-managed paths	Yes	Yes	Yes
Governance	Yes	Yes	Yes
Large list scalability and management	Yes	Yes	Yes
Mobile connectivity	Yes	Yes	Yes
Multilingual user interface	Yes	Yes	Yes
My Tasks	Yes	Yes	Yes
OOTB Web Parts	Yes	Yes	Yes
Permissions management	Yes	Yes	Yes
Project functionality for team sites	No	Yes	Yes
Project site template	No	Yes	Yes
Project Summary Web Part	No	Yes	Yes
Project workspace	No	Yes	Yes
SharePoint lists	Yes	Yes	Yes
SharePoint ribbon	Yes	Yes	Yes
Task list	Yes	Yes	Yes
Team Site: drag & drop	Yes	Yes	Yes

B

Team Site: notebook	Yes*	Yes*	Yes*
Team Site: simplified access	Yes	Yes	Yes
Templates	Yes	Yes	Yes
Themes	Yes	Yes	Yes
Variations	No	Yes	Yes
Usage analytics	Yes	Yes	Yes
Work Management service	No	Yes	Yes
Social features			
Ask Me About	No	Yes	Yes
Blogs	Yes	Yes	Yes
Communities Reputation, Badging, and Moderation	No	Yes	Yes
Community	No	Yes	Yes
Company feed	No	Yes	Yes
Follow	No	Yes	Yes
Microblogging	No	Yes	Yes
Newsfeed	No	Yes	Yes
One-click sharing	No	Yes	Yes
People, Sites, Document recommendations	No	Yes	Yes
Personal site	No	Yes	Yes
Photos and presence	Yes	Yes	Yes
Profile	No	Yes	Yes
Ratings	No	Yes	Yes
Site feed	No	Yes	Yes
SkyDrive Pro	No	Yes	Yes
Tag profiles	No	Yes	Yes
Tasks integrated with Outlook	No	Yes	Yes
Trending tags	No	Yes	Yes
Wikis	Yes	Yes	Yes

* Requires connection to Microsoft Office Web Apps Server 2013 or Office 365.

** Requires connection to Microsoft Exchange Server or Microsoft Exchange Online.

SharePoint 2013 solutions required to complete the exercises in this book

The exercises in this book use features and capabilities that are available in Microsoft SharePoint 2013 solutions deployed on-premises. SharePoint 2013 provides specific feature sets, depending on the following client access licenses (CALs) activated in your organization:

- SharePoint Server 2013 Enterprise CAL

- SharePoint Server 2013 Standard CAL

- SharePoint Foundation 2013

In order to complete the exercises in the book, you need access to a SharePoint 2013 solution that includes the features that are used in each exercise. Table C-1 lists each exercise and the SharePoint 2013 solution that you can use to complete it. The exercises are organized by chapter.

SEE ALSO For a list of the Microsoft SharePoint 2013 features and capabilities that are available in each SharePoint 2013 solution, please refer to Appendix B, "SharePoint 2013 features."

Table C-1 *The SharePoint 2013 solutions needed to complete the exercises in this book*

Exercise	SharePoint 2013 solution		
	Foundation	Server Standard CAL	Server Enterprise CAL
Chapter 1: Introducing SharePoint 2013			
Familiarizing yourself with a SharePoint site	Yes	Yes	Yes
Chapter 2: Navigating a SharePoint site			
Navigating the home page and the SharePoint site	Partial (steps 1–8)	Yes	Yes
Understanding the site structure	Yes	Yes	Yes
Navigating the ribbon	Yes	Yes	Yes
Customizing site navigation using in-page editing	Yes	Yes	Yes

Customizing site navigation using dragging from Site Contents	Yes	Yes	Yes
Customizing site navigation using Site Settings	Yes	Yes	Yes
Displaying the tree view of the site structure	Yes	Yes	Yes
Understanding app parts and Web Part pages	Yes	Yes	Yes
Using the site Recycle Bin	Yes	Yes	Yes
Using the site collection Recycle Bin	Yes	Yes	Yes

Chapter 3: Working with documents and information in lists and libraries

Discovering lists and libraries in a site	Yes	Yes	Yes
Creating a list	Yes	Yes	Yes
Adding and editing list items	Yes	Yes	Yes
Creating a library	Yes	Yes	Yes
Creating a new document in a library	Yes	Yes	Yes
Adding and editing documents in a library	Yes	Yes	Yes
Checking documents in and out from a library	Yes	Yes	Yes
Working with version history	Yes	Yes	Yes
Creating a new folder in a list or a library	Yes	Yes	Yes
Adding, editing, and removing list and library columns	Yes	Yes	Yes
Sorting and filtering a list and library	Yes	Yes	Yes
Deleting and restoring list items and documents	Yes	Yes	Yes
Setting up alerts	Yes	Yes	Yes
Following documents	No	Yes	Yes
Synchronizing a library to your computer	No	Yes	Yes

Chapter 4: Working with webpages

Editing a page	Yes	Yes	Yes
Changing a page layout	Yes	Yes	Yes
Creating a new wiki page	Yes	Yes	Yes
Adding links	Yes	Yes	Yes
Working with page history and versions	Yes	Yes	Yes
Using alerts	Yes	Yes	Yes
Adding Web Parts and SharePoint app parts	Yes	Yes	Yes
Removing a Web Part	Yes	Yes	Yes
Customizing a Web Part and an app part	Yes	Yes	Yes
Editing a Web Part page	Yes	Yes	Yes
Moving a Web Part	Yes	Yes	Yes

Chapter 5: Creating and managing sites

Creating a site	Yes	Yes	Yes
Sharing a site	No	Yes	Yes
Managing site users and permissions	Yes	Yes	Yes
Creating a personal site	No	Yes	Yes
Changing a site theme	Yes	Yes	Yes
Saving and using a site template	Yes	Yes	Yes
Managing site features	Yes	Yes	Yes
Managing site content syndication	Yes	Yes	Yes
Deleting a site	Yes	Yes	Yes

Chapter 6: Making lists and libraries work for you

Setting the list or library name, description, and navigation	Yes	Yes	Yes
Configuring content approval and versioning for a list	Yes	Yes	Yes
Configuring versioning and required checkout for a library	Yes	Yes	Yes

Working with advanced list settings	Yes	Yes	Yes
Working with advanced library settings	Yes	Yes	Yes
Using validation settings	Yes	Yes	Yes
Setting up ratings	No	Yes	Yes
Working with content types	Yes	Yes	Yes
Creating a view	Yes	Yes	Yes
Managing users and permissions	Yes	Yes	Yes
Sharing a document or a folder	No	Yes	Yes
Granting Item Level permissions	Yes	Yes	Yes
Deleting and restoring a list or a library	Yes	Yes	Yes

Chapter 7: Getting social

Exploring your newsfeed settings	No	Yes	Yes
Starting a conversation	No	Yes	Yes
Using the Yammer Web Part	Yes	Yes	Yes
Working with tags and notes	No	Yes	Yes
Creating a Community site	No	Yes	Yes
Managing a Community site	No	Yes	Yes

Chapter 8: Working with wikis and blogs

Creating a wiki page library	Yes	Yes	Yes
Categorizing wiki pages	Yes	Yes	Yes
Creating an Enterprise Wiki site	No	Yes	Yes
Adding categories to an Enterprise Wiki page	No	Yes	Yes
Creating a blog site	Yes	Yes	Yes
Managing blog post categories	Yes	Yes	Yes
Creating and a modifying a blog post	Yes	Yes	Yes
Adding a blog comment	Yes	Yes	Yes

Chapter 9: Searching for information and people

Searching your SharePoint site	Yes	Yes	Yes
Using search query	Yes	Yes	Yes
Configuring search behavior	No	Yes	Yes
Using Advanced Search	Yes	Yes	Yes
Setting up search alert	Yes	Yes	Yes
Influencing relevance rankings	No	Yes	Yes
Customizing search results page	No	Yes	Yes
Defining your site visibility	Yes	Yes	Yes
Searching for people	No	Yes	Yes

Chapter 10: Managing work tasks

Creating a Project site		Yes	Yes
Working with the timeline	Yes	Yes	Yes
Creating and manage subtasks	Yes	Yes	Yes
Working with the Project Summary Web Part	No	Yes	Yes
Managing tasks in one place	No	Yes	Yes
Managing projects with SharePoint and Project Professional	Yes	Yes	Yes
Using Project Server	Yes	Yes	Yes

Chapter 11: Working with workflows

Adding and configuring a workflow	Yes	Yes	Yes
Working with a workflow	Yes	Yes	Yes
Managing workflows	Yes	Yes	Yes
Managing workflow tasks from within Outlook 2013	Yes	Yes	Yes
Terminating a workflow instance	Yes	Yes	Yes
Removing workflows from lists and libraries	Yes	Yes	Yes
Associating workflows with content types	Yes	Yes	Yes

Chapter 12: Using SharePoint with Excel and Access

Importing data from an Excel spreadsheet to a list in SharePoint	Yes	Yes	Yes
Exporting a SharePoint list to an Excel spreadsheet	Yes	Yes	Yes
Exporting an Excel table to a SharePoint site	Yes	Yes	Yes
Building an Access app	No	No	Yes
Creating a table in an Access app	No	No	Yes
Working with Access apps in the browser	No	No	Yes
Exporting data from an Access desktop database to a list	Yes	Yes	Yes
Importing data from a list	Yes	Yes	Yes
Linking to a list	Yes	Yes	Yes
Moving data from a desktop database to a list	Yes	Yes	Yes
Working offline	Yes	Yes	Yes

Chapter 13: Working with business intelligence

Understanding SharePoint BI capabilities and components	No	No	Yes
Using Excel Services	No	No	Yes
Working with data models	N/A*	N/A*	N/A*
Creating and publishing PowerPivot dashboards	No	No	Yes
Publishing PowerPivot dashboards using an Excel Web Part	No	No	Yes
Building visualizations with Power View	No	No	Yes
Creating and using Power View reports with multiple views	No	No	Yes
Displaying a Power View report in a Web Part	No	No	Yes

Chapter 14: Using SharePoint with Outlook and Lync

Syncing your My Tasks with Outlook	No	Yes	Yes
Connecting a SharePoint Contacts list app to Outlook	Yes	Yes	Yes
Moving an Outlook contact to a SharePoint Contacts list	Yes	Yes	Yes
Copying SharePoint contacts into Outlook	Yes	Yes	Yes
Sending an email using a SharePoint Contacts list	Yes	Yes	Yes
Viewing SharePoint Calendars and personal calendars in Outlook	Yes	Yes	Yes
Taking SharePoint content offline	Yes	Yes	Yes
Managing SharePoint alerts in Outlook	Yes	Yes	Yes
Configuring an RSS feed	Yes	Yes	Yes
Using Presence with documents in libraries	Yes	Yes	Yes
Using site mailboxes	No	Yes	Yes

Chapter 15: Working with content management

Working with Document IDs	No	Yes	Yes
Working with Document Sets	No	Yes	Yes
Organizing content	No	Yes	Yes
Creating a Records Center	No	Yes	Yes
Managing records	No	Yes	Yes
Configuring in place records management	No	Yes	Yes
Creating publishing sites	No	Yes	Yes
Creating page layouts	No	Yes	Yes
Managing page layouts	No	Yes	Yes
Using reusable content	No	Yes	Yes
Using product catalogs	No	No	Yes
Defining a SharePoint site policy	No	Yes	Yes

*Requires Microsoft Office Excel 2013

Glossary

Access app A Microsoft SharePoint app that stores data in its own SQL 2012 database. The browser is used to view and edit data, and Microsoft Office Access 2013 is used to design the Access app.

Access Services Hosts an Access database within the context of an Access app. This service is only available in Microsoft SharePoint Server 2013 Enterprise.

Access Web App See *Access app*.

Access web database SharePoint site based on an Access database. It can only be created using Access 2010 and Microsoft Access Services 2010.

App Package file SharePoint apps can be distributed as app packages and shared by deploying them to an organization's app catalog or to the Microsoft SharePoint Store.

app part A Part that can be added to a page that displays information from an app.

blogger A person who creates blog posts.

blogging To create or maintain blog posts. When the blogging mechanism only allows for short posts, it is known as *microblogging*.

blogs The word *blog* is slang for *web log*, which is a web-based personal journal.

business intelligence Business intelligence (BI) is a set of tools and capabilities that work together to turn large amounts of data into meaningful information for better decision making.

camel case The formatting used, when two or more words are concatenated. The first letter of each word is capitalized and the remaining letters are lowercase; for example, GardenFurniture.

checking out When you check out documents, you let others know what documents you are working on so that they don't work on them at the same time. When you check out a file, you lock the file for editing to prevent other users from editing the file at the same time.

column You can use a column to provide property values for list items.

community site This template provisions an environment for community members to discuss the topics of common interest.

content organizer A feature that controls the automatic filing of a file or record based on its properties (metadata).

Content Query Web Part Used to roll up content within in a site collection and includes the ability to filter the content results by the page navigation term. It uses Extensible Stylesheet Language Transformations (XSLT) to render content.

Content Search Web Part Used to show content that is the result set of a search query specified as a Web Part property.

content type A content type is made up of the site columns and other configurations, such as workflows. Each content type has a predefined specific set of columns, workflows, and metadata. This enables you to reuse a group of site columns and optionally have a workflow associated with the content type, which you would then add to an existing list or library.

CQWP See *See Content Query Web Part*.

cross-site collection publishing A feature that enables you to reuse content across multiple site collections when used together with the Content Search Web Part.

CSWP See *Content Search Web Part.*

data model A data model is a collection of data from multiple sources with relationships between different fields, which you can create and organize by using PowerPivot for Microsoft Office Excel. In Excel Services for SharePoint 2013 and Microsoft Office Excel 2013, you can bring data from a variety of sources into one cohesive data set, and then use it to create charts, tables, reports, and dashboards.

desktop database A database designed for use by one to five users, traditionally stored on a person's computer or on a file share. Desktop databases can be created using products such as Access and FileMaker Pro.

developer site A template that provides a site for developers to create and publish Office apps.

document library A document library is used to store your documents on a SharePoint site, rather than on your local computer's hard drive, so that other people can find and work with these documents more easily.

ECM See *Enterprise Content Management.*

eDiscovery set A combination of sources, queries, and possibly in-place holds.

Enterprise Content Management The strategies, methods, and tools used to capture, manage, store, preserve, and deliver content and documents related to organizational processes.

enterprise social network Focuses on the use of online social networks or social relations among people who share business interests.

Enterprise Wiki site A publishing site that should be used as a wiki for sharing and updating large volumes of information across an enterprise.

Exchange ActiveSync Support A feature built into Microsoft Office Outlook 2013 that allows you to receive emails, appointments, and contacts from Outlook.com and Hotmail in Outlook.

file plan A description of the types of content that an organization recognizes as official business records. The plan includes the location of the records and provides information that differentiates one type of record from another.

hashtag A keyword, topic, or phrase (no spaces) preceded by a hashtag symbol (#) that categorizes a microblog so that you and other users can find content.

hold A hold preserves content. Once a hold is placed on a record, items within that hold are exempt from retention and deletion policies.

home page The main page of a SharePoint site. It provides a navigational structure that links the site components together.

hover panel A hover panel displays a search result callout in a search result page when you hover over the search result. The search results page allows you to act on the search results without opening them by using the callout that appears to the right of the result so that you can preview the search result content. With the hover panel, you can also act on the result with contextual actions based on the result itself.

in-place holds Used to preserve sites and Microsoft Exchange mailboxes.

library apps A library app generates a new library with a specific functionality. Library apps are accessible from the Your Apps page.

library A SharePoint library can be thought of as a list of files. Libraries are a great place to store documents, pictures, forms, or other types of files.

list SharePoint lists represent editable, web-based tables that facilitate concurrent, multiuser interactions against a common, centralized, extensible set of columns and rows. Using lists, you can provision your own repositories of structured information, in which list items behave like rows consisting of self-labeled columns.

list apps A list app generates a new a list with a specific functionality and a set of columns. List apps are accessible from the Your Apps page too.

list item A list item is represented by a row in a list.

managed metadata A hierarchical collection of centrally managed terms that you can define, and then use as attributes for content items. Consistent use of metadata across sites in your organization helps with content discoverability.

Managed Metadata Service A shared service that publishes a Term Store and, optionally, a set of content types.

microblogging This is a form of a brief blog post, usually of a hundred words or less, often posted on a frequent basis. These brief messages are also known as *conversations*.

Minimal Download Strategy A new technology introduced in SharePoint 2013, which allows pages to load faster.

MMS See *Managed Metadata Service*.

Outlook Social Connector This works with SharePoint Server, SharePoint Workspace, Microsoft Lync client, and all Office client applications that support presence information and Contact Card support. Popular social networks such as LinkedIn, Facebook, and Windows Live are offering providers for the Outlook Social Connector, allowing information from those sites to be available in Outlook.

overlay mode A method of displaying two or more calendars where the content is merged; however, the two calendars remain color-coordinated, as do the appointments in both calendars.

permission level Specifies the permissions that users have on a SharePoint site. These permissions determine the specific actions that users can perform on the site. Each permission level is a collection of permissions.

PMO See *project management office*.

posts Entries written and published to a blog.

project management office A group or department within an organization that defines and maintains project management standards, and provides metrics on past and present projects.

Project Professional A desktop application that enables project managers to create, publish, and manage projects.

Project Server A web-based project management, work management, and portfolio management system that is deployed on SharePoint Server.

project site A site template that provisions a site for collaborating on a project, with all information and artifacts relevant to the project available in one place.

promoted result Search results that are displayed on the search results page above all ranked results based on a query rule.

publishing page A page that has a strict layout and has an approval process.

query rule A query rule provides a mechanism to influence the ranking of search results. A query rule consists of a query rule condition and a query rule action. When a query matches a query rule condition, it triggers a query rule action. For example, by using a query rule, you can show a search result above all ranked results.

Quick Launch A set of links in the left navigation panel on a team site. Typically, the Quick Launch contains the links to the parts of the site; for example, the site home page, the built-in Documents library, and the Site Contents page.

ranking model A ranking model calculates the ranking score of a particular item in the search results based on the predefined algorithms. By default, search results are sorted in descending order based on their ranking score. Items with the top score get the top position in search results.

Records Center A repository where all records are stored.

records declaration A record submitted either manually or automatically to a records repository.

Recycle Bin Provides a safety net when deleting sites, documents, document sets, list items, lists, libraries, folders, and files. The deleted items are kept in a site's Recycle Bin for 30 days so that the user can restore them, if needed, within this time.

relevance rank A relevance rank for a search result is calculated by the search engine and defines the order in which the search results appear.

reusable content An item of reusable content can consist of either HTML or plain text. You can reuse items of reusable content rather than copying and managing duplicate copies of content manually in different locations. On a publishing site, you can add items to the Reusable Content list; you can then add those items to the page content of a publishing page.

search query A search query contains one or more words that represent the content that you are trying to find. When executing a query, SharePoint returns a set of content items that form a result set.

search results A list of results that match a search query. The search results contain links to the webpages, documents, list items, lists, libraries, or sites that you want to find.

search verticals Search pages that are targeted for searching specific content, including Everything, for a search across all content; People, for specific people searches; Conversations, for searching newsfeed conversations; and Videos, for searching different types of videos.

server database A database used for multiuser applications and run on high-performance servers. Server databases include Microsoft SQL Server, Oracle, and IBM DB2.

SharePoint app A piece of code that can be added to a site. The code may not execute its logic within the SharePoint environment; however, the results from the execution of the code can be displayed on the site using pages and app parts.

site collection SharePoint sites are organized hierarchically within a site collection. There is always one top level site and there can be one or more child sites.

site column A site column can be described as a shared column. You create a site column once, and it resides in a gallery at the level of a site or a site collection. It is inherited by the all sites in the collection that are beneath the site in which it was created.

site contents tree The representation of the overall hierarchical structure of a SharePoint site that has the site's own items—such as pages, document libraries, lists, and other apps—as well as the child sites.

site SharePoint sites are containers for the web pages and the apps, such as lists and libraries, as well as features and settings that provide the site's functionality.

site templates Used in SharePoint as a blueprint to jump-start a new site's usefulness by autogenerating webpages and apps that likely will be most useful in a given situation.

Social Connector A feature built in to Outlook 2013 in which you can see updates from people in your social networks, such as LinkedIn and Facebook.

sync You can synchronize, or sync, a SharePoint library to your computer. This process creates a copy of the library on your computer in the SharePoint Libraries folder, under the name that combines the name of the source SharePoint site with the name of the source library, and includes a hyphen between them; for example, Team Site-Documents.

team site A Team Site template provisions a collaboration site with a Documents library, which is made more visible by placing a Web Part for it on the site's default home page for easier collaboration.

term set A collection of related terms; for example, a term set named *Department* could include the terms HQ, Human Resources, IT, and Sales & Marketing. Term sets are created in the Term Store by designated users from a browser or imported from a .csv file.

Term Store A database that stores managed metadata, including term sets, terms, and managed keywords. You can go to the Term Store from the Site Settings page by clicking Term Store Management under Site Administration.

top level site A site that does not have a parent site. It is an initial site created in a SharePoint site collection. Top level sites are created from within SharePoint Central Administration because they don't have a parent site. Although the top level site functionally is not different from its child sites, it includes administrative links on its Site Settings page to manage the site collection.

top link bar A navigation aid that is located in the top navigation area, above the page title in a team site and is displayed on all pages within the team site. It The top link bar typically includes the current site link, as well as links to the subsites that are optional.

variations The variations feature in SharePoint Server 2013 and SharePoint Online makes content available to specific audiences on different sites, usually multilanguage sites, by syncing content from a source variation site to each target variation site.

versioning When versioning is enabled, SharePoint 2013 creates a separate copy of the document each time it is edited, so that you can revert to an older version of the document if necessary.

view A list or library view defines how the information in a list or a library is displayed to the users.

WCM See *Web Content Management.*

Web Content Management Provides mechanisms for authoring, branding, and controlled publishing of web content.

Web Part A server-side component that can be added to wiki pages and within Web Part zones on Web Part and publishing pages. These allow users to control the appearance and behavior of content. The content may or may not reside within SharePoint.

Web Part page A page that contains one or more Web Part zones, so that users can edit the page directly from a browser.

web template When you save a website as a template, a custom web template is created by SharePoint and saved as a file with a .wsp extension in the Solutions gallery of the site collection. This is done by using the Save Site as Template link in the Site Action section of the Site Settings page of any site.

wiki page A page to which users can easily add static text and images. Users can use simple text syntax for creating new pages and creating links to pages in the Site Pages library app.

WikiWords or **WikiNames** A naming convention for wiki pages is to concatenate two or more words, where each word is composed of two or more letters with no space between the words, using camel case formatting.

workflow association form A web page that is displayed when a user associates (adds) a workflow template to a content type, site, list, or library. Only workflow authors use the association form.

workflow association An association of a workflow template to a specific list, library, site, or content type. Also known as *adding a workflow.*

workflow author A user who associates (adds) a workflow template with a content type, site, list, or library.

workflow creator A user who creates a workflow template.

workflow initiator A user who starts a workflow instance on a file or list item.

workflow instance The progress of a list item or file through a workflow.

workflow manager A new, highly scalable workflow framework installed separately from SharePoint that allows the use of SharePoint 2013 workflows with SharePoint Server 2013. Previously known as *Windows Azure Workflow.*

workflow participant A user who completes task items that support workflow instances.

workflow Task list A list that stores the sequence of actions or tasks for a business process.

workflow template A blueprint of a process that is associated with lists, libraries, sites, or content types. They can be created using Microsoft SharePoint Designer or Microsoft Visual Studio.

workflow The automation of a business process during which documents, information, or tasks are passed from one user to another according to a set of procedural rules.

XSP See *cross-site collection publishing.*

Index

inherited permissions
    breaking inheritance, 159, 164–169
    overview, 157, 158
in-place holds, 628
in-place records management, 571–575
Insert Related List option, 140
Insert tab, 133
Insert Web Part pane, 550
installing SharePoint, 2
Install Silverlight wizard page, 455, 456
Internet Explorer - Security Warning dialog
        box, 518
ISAM (Indexed Sequential Access Method), 429
Issue Tracking list app, 57
Issue Tracking template, 414, 416
Item Permissions button, 237
Items Are Deleted Only option, 102
Items tab, 43
Items To Import drop-down list, 432
Item Version History settings, 195

J
Join this community link, 266

K
Keep drafts for the following number of major
        versions check box, 201
KPI List app, 57
KPIs (key performance indicators), 451
KQL (Keyword Query Language), 310

L
Languages and Translators list app, 57
layout of webpages, 118–119
Let's get social! dialog, 248
libraries
    adding columns, 92–96
    advanced settings, 210–215
    alerts, 102–105
    checking documents in and out, 86–88
    content types, 219–226
    creating, 73–74
    creating documents, 75–78
    creating folders, 90–91
    customizing, 189–191, 241
    defined, 54, 629
    deleting, 238–240
    deleting items, 99–101
    description, 192–195
    editing documents, 78–81
    filtering, 96–99
    following documents, 105–106
    name, 192–195
    navigation, 192–195
    overview, 53–54, 108
    permissions, 230–234
    ratings, 217–219
    removing columns, 92–96
    removing workflows from, 391–392
    requiring check out, 199–205
    restoring deleted, 238–240
    restoring deleted items, 99–101
    sharing documents or folders, 234–236
    sorting, 96–99
    types, 21
    uploading documents, 81–86
    users, 230–234
    validation settings, 215–217
    versioning
        configuring, 199–205
        enabling, 88–90
    views, 226–229
    working with documents offline, 106–107
Library Based Retention Schedule page, 570
Library Settings button, Settings group, 190
Library tab, 43
Limited Access permission level, 161, 162, 601
linked object, 406
linked tables, 436
links
    adding and deleting from Quick Launch, 5
    on Quick Launch, 23–24
    to apps, adding, 36
    to lists, in Access, 435–438
    on webpages, 122–123

O

ODBC (Open Database Connectivity) data source, 428
Office 365. *See* Microsoft Office 365
Office integration, 13–15. *See also* individual applications
Office Web Apps. *See* Microsoft Office Web Apps
offline
    editing documents, 516
    viewing content in Outlook, 525–528
    working with Access, 443–445
    working with documents, 106–107
Offline Client Availability setting, 208
Old Tasks Limit option, 358
Open & Check Out group, 87
Open Database Connectivity (ODBC) data source, 428
Open Default View option, 444
Opening Documents in the Browser option, 211
Open in the client application option, 213
Open Items permission, 230, 607
Open link in new tab option, Yammer, 257
Open permission, 607
Open the list when finished check box, 430
Outdent command, Tasks tab, 352
Outlook integration
    contacts
        copying SharePoint into Outlook, 521–523
        moving to SharePoint Contacts list app, 519–521
    managing workflow tasks, 387–389
    offline SharePoint content, 525–528
    overview, 15, 509–545
    RSS feed of SharePoint content, 533–536
    SharePoint alerts, 528–533
    SharePoint calendars, 523–524
    syncing tasks, 511–513
Outlook Rules and Alerts dialog box, 529
Outlook Social Connector
    defined, 629
    features of, 244
Outlook Web App
    managing tasks, 355
    overview, 541–545

overlay mode
    defined, 629
    merging calendars, 523
Override Check Out permission, 230
Override List Behaviors permission, 607
Owners can postpone imminent deletion for option, 595
Owners group, 158, 161

P

Page Approval workflow, 577
Page content type, 579
Page History page, 123–124
Page Layout designer, 577
page layouts
    creating, 579–587
    managing, 586–588
pages, categorizing. *See also* webpages
    Enterprise Wiki site, 289–292
    in general, 279–282
Page tab, 114
Page Viewer Web Part, 497
Page View tool pane, 500
Parent Content Type section, 221
Paste Clean feature, 116
Peopleresults.aspx, 328
people, searching, 334–338
People view, 515
PerformancePoint category, Web Parts, 130
PerformancePoint Content List app, 58
PerformancePoint Services, 451
permissions
    default levels, 160–161, 601–604
    defined, 629
    inherited, 157, 159, 164–169
    for libraries, 230–234
    for lists, 236–238
    page for, 159
    setting for new site, 153–154
    for SharePoint sites, 158–169

top level sites
    defined, 31, 631
    users of, 145
top link bar
    customizing, 34–36
    defined, 6, 631
    links on, 24
    on subsites, 33
Translation Management workflow template, 373
tree view of site's structure, 40–41
Trending Hashtags area, 248
trigger events for workflows, 375–376
TVF (table-valued function), 420

U

Uniform Resource Locators. *See* URLs
unique permissions
    changing from inherited permissions to, 164–169
    subsites and, 154
Unpublished Items Report, 288
Update Personal Web Parts permission, 607
Upload a new document template option, 222
uploading documents to libraries, 81–86
URLs (Uniform Resource Locators), 4, 120, 403, 530
Use Cached Exchange Mode option, 526
Use Client Integration Features permission, 607
User Account Control message box, 455
user-centric workflows, 371
Use Remote Interfaces permission, 607
user interface macros, 421
users
    for libraries and lists, 230–234
    permissions, 7–8, 604–609
    for SharePoint sites, 158–169
Use same permissions as parent site option, 158
Use Self-Service Site Creation permission, 608
Use unique permissions option, 153, 154, 158, 159

V

validation settings for libraries and lists, 215–217
variations, 631
variations page layout, 580
VB (Visual Basic), 420
Version History button, 89
Version History dialog, 204
Version History page, 124
versioning
    defined, 88, 631
    for libraries, 88–90, 199–205
    for lists, 195–199
    settings, 89, 200
    of webpages, 123–126
Video And Audio command, 129, 133
Videoresults.aspx, 328
View Application Pages permission, 230, 608
View Item button, 529
View Items permission, 230, 608
View Only permission, 161, 162, 601
View Pages permission, 608
views
    defined, 631–632
    for libraries, 226–229
View Versions permission, 230, 608
View Web Analytics Data permission level, 608
Visio Drawing (.vsdx) diagrams, 451
Visio Process Repository site template, 151
Visio Services, 451
Visio visualizations, of SharePoint workflows, 374
Visitor role, 577
Visitors group, 158, 161
Visual Basic (VB), 420

W

WAC (Web Apps Companion) servers, 277
WCM (Web Content Management), 111, 547, 631–632
web application level features, 179
Web Application Open Platform Interface (WOPI) servers, 277
Web Apps. *See* Microsoft Office Web Apps

About the authors

Olga Londer is an Architect for Microsoft, traveling across the world to work on global projects that implement Microsoft technologies and business solutions for large enterprise customers. Her particular focus is on implementing Microsoft Dynamics and Microsoft SharePoint products and solutions. She is the author of several books on SharePoint and Microsoft Internet Information Server (IIS), a winner of the British Computer Society IT Trainer award, and a frequent speaker at numerous conferences. For a number of years, Olga was a content lead for pan-European Microsoft technical conferences, such as TechEd Europe. Before joining Microsoft in 2004, Olga was a Microsoft Most Valuable Professional (MVP) in SharePoint and IIS, and she worked for QA Ltd., UK, a leading IT training and consulting company, where she led many SharePoint projects for blue-chip clients. Olga is based in London, United Kingdom.

Penelope Coventry is a multiyear recipient of the Microsoft Most Valuable Professional (MVP) Award (in Microsoft SharePoint Server), and has obtained the following certifications: Microsoft Certified Solutions Expert (MCSE) in SharePoint 2013, Microsoft Certified IT Professional (MCITP) in SharePoint Administration 2010, and Microsoft Certified Professional Developer (MCPD) in SharePoint Developer 2010. Based in the United Kingdom, she is an author, an independent consultant, and a trainer with more than 30 years of industry experience. Penny has authored and coauthored more than 10 SharePoint-related books, including *Exploring Microsoft SharePoint 2013: New Features and Functions* (Microsoft Press, 2013), *Microsoft SharePoint 2013 Inside Out* (Microsoft Press, 2013), *Microsoft SharePoint Designer 2010 Step by Step* (Microsoft Press, 2010), and *Microsoft SharePoint 2010 Administrator's Companion* (Microsoft Press, 2010). Penny has spoken at a number of conferences, including TechEd North America; SharePoint conferences in the United States, Canada, Australia, New Zealand, Sweden, and the United Kingdom; and SharePoint Saturdays. She is a keen supporter of the UK SharePoint user group community. Penny has worked with SharePoint since 2001, and when she's not writing, she works on large SharePoint deployments.

Acknowledgments

This book is the result of the collective effort of many people. We'd like to start with thanking Kenyon Brown, our acquisitions and developmental editor, who initially approached us about updating and extending the previous version of the book and provided invaluable assistance in getting this project off the ground, overseeing it with patience, and providing thoughtful support at the key points in the project that helped us to make this book a reality.

Second, we would like to thank our technical editor, Chris Casingena, for his professionalism, dedication, and a positive attitude to resolving every challenge that this project might have presented to him, especially for doing a technical review of the last chapter of this book on his birthday.

Next, we would like to thank Kristen Borg, our production editor, and Kim Burton-Weisman, our copy editor, whose precision in orchestrating the production schedule, meticulous approach to details, patience, flexibility, and good humor ensured that the book was published on time.

Last, but by no means least, we would like to thank our respective husbands, Gregory and Peter, for bearing with our work on this book in the evenings and over the weekends, and more than anything for their boundless support for this project.

Now that you've read the book...

Tell us what you think!

Was it useful?
Did it teach you what you wanted to learn?
Was there room for improvement?

Let us know at http://aka.ms/tellpress

Your feedback goes directly to the staff at Microsoft Press,
and we read every one of your responses. Thanks in advance!

 Microsoft

 **Microsoft**

How To Download Your eBook

Thank you for purchasing this Microsoft Press® title. Your companion PDF eBook is ready to download from O'Reilly Media, official distributor of Microsoft Press titles.

To download your eBook, go to

http://aka.ms/PressEbook

and follow the instructions.

Please note: You will be asked to create a free online account and enter the access code below.

Your access code:

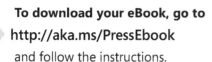

QBLMDHL

Microsoft SharePoint 2013 Step by Step

Your PDF eBook allows you to:

- Search the full text
- Print
- Copy and paste

Best yet, you will be notified about free updates to your eBook.

If you ever lose your eBook file, you can download it again just by logging in to your account.

Need help? Please contact:
mspbooksupport@oreilly.com
or call 800-889-8969.

CPSIA information can be obtained at www.ICGtesting.com
Printed in the USA
LVOW02s1722191113

361952LV00057BB/1007/P